DATABASE DEVELOPMENT ELUCIDATED

A PRAGMATICALLY APPROACH TO DATABASE
With
MICROSOFT SQL SERVER 2008

Title ID: 4926809
ISBN-13: 978-1500677213

Iwuala Chibueze

CONTENTS AS A GLANCE

Title Page	i
Preface	xii-xiv
Dedication	xv
Acknowledgement	xvi
Chapter One	
- Introduction to relational database and MS SQL Server 2008	1
Chapter Two	
- System Requirement, Installation of MS SQL Server and starting MS SQL Server Services.	12
Chapter Three	
- Dos and Don'ts in Database programming.	49
Chapter Four	
- Database Creation	87
Chapter Five	
- Microsoft SQL Server Data Types	128
Chapter Six	
- Database Tables	170
Chapter Seven	
- Data Manipulation and Maintenance.	269
Chapter Eight	
- Methods of Data Retrieval	322
Chapter Nine	
- Programming in MS SQL Server with T-SQL	365
Chapter Ten	
- Improving Data retrieval and Query Performance techniques	511
Chapter Eleven	
- Database Authentication and Authorization.	599
References	639
Index	640

Table of Contents

Preface.. xii-xiv
Dedication..xv
Acknowledgement..xvi
CHAPTER ONE...1
  1.1 INTRODUCTION..1
  1.2 RELATIONAL DATABASE 1
    1.2.1 What is a Database? 1
  1.3 MS SQL SERVER 4
  1.3.1 FEATURES OF MS SQL SERVER 2008 6
CHAPTER TWO 10
  2.1 SYSTEM REQUIREMENT 10
  2.2 INSTALLATION OF MS SQL SERVER............14
    2.2.1 Introduction to Security 15
    2.2.2 Installing SQL Server 2008.......................21
  2.3 STARTING MS SQL SERVER SERVICES AND SQL
    MANAGEMENT STUDIO.................................38
    2.3.1 Starting MS SQL Server Services 39
    2.3.2 Starting SQL Management Studio..............39
CHAPTER THREE 45
  DOs AND DON'Ts IN DATABASE PROGRAMMING 45
  3.1 Defensive Programming 46
  3.2 Advantages and Disadvantages of Defensive Programming 48
    3.2.1 Advantages..48
    3.2.2 Disadvantages 49
  3.3 Why Use a Defensive Approach to Database Development?.......53
  3.4 Dos and Don'ts in SQL Coding Technique 55
    3.4.1 Dos in SQL Coding Technique 56
CHAPTER FOUR 80
  DATABASE CREATION...80
  4.1 DATABASE OBJECTS......................................82
    4.1.1 Naming the database 84
  4.2 Starting SQL Server Management Studio 85
  4.3 CREATING DATABASE 87
    a.   Master database 91
    b.   tempdb database 92
    c.   model database 93
    d.   msdb database 94
    a.   Configuring file growth............................95
  4.4 DATABASE CREATION SYNTAX...................97
    4.4.1 Creating a database with multiple files 102
    4.4.2 Creating Using Code Template....................106
  4.5 Database Maintenance 109
    4.5.1 Deleting a Database Using SQL 111
  4.6 Database Routines.......................................113
    4.6.1 The Current Database...............................113
    4.6.2 Refreshing the List of Databases...............113
  4.7 Schemas 114
    4.7.1 Introduction to Namespaces 114
    4.7.2 Introduction to Schemas 115

4.7.3 Creating a Schema...117
4.7.4 Accessing an Object From a Schema.............................118
CHAPTER FIVE..**120**
Microsoft SQL Server Data Types...**120**
5.1 Introducing Variables Creation..**120**
5.1.1 Declaring a Variable..121
5.1.2 Variable default and scope 121
5.1.3 Incremental variables..121
5.1.4 Objects Names...122
5.1.5 Initializing a Variable 124
5.2 Data Types...**124**
5.2.1 Boolean Variables 125
5.2.2 Natural Numbers Types..126
5.2.4 Currency and Monetary Values 132
5.2.5 Characters and Strings 134
5.2.6 Date and Time Types..141
5.3 User-Defined Types..**154**
5.3.1 Creating a User-Defined Type 154
5.3.2 Application of User-Defined Type..158
5.3.3 Base Type 159
CHAPTER SIX..**160**
TABLE CREATION **160**
6.1 Tables Names **160**
6.2 Designing tables using Management Studio **161**
6.3 Column names **164**
6.4 Designing Columns using Management Studio **166**
6.4.1 Setting Columns Names 167
6.4.2 The DataTypes...168
6.4.3 The Length of Data...169
6.5 Creation of Columns with Codes **169**
6.5.1 Creating a Table..171
6.5.2 Using User-Defined Data-Types...172
Description of the Column Properties 179
Types of Indexes...198
Table Creation and Indexes 201
Table and Index Partitioning 206
A Partition Function 209
A Partition Scheme 211
Partitioning a Table 212
Tables Maintenance..229
Creating Keys..233
Database design layers 236
CHAPTER SEVEN **250**
DATA MANIPULATION AND MAINTENANCE **250**
7.1 DATA MANIPULATION..**251**
7.1.1 Table Data Navigation in the SQL Server Management Studio..251
7.1.2 Data Entry..252
7.1.3 Tables Columns and Expressions 264
7.1.4 The Nullity of a Field 266
7.1.5 The Default Value of a Column...268
7.2 DATA MAINTENANCE..**272**

Record Maintenance: 279
Deleting Records 292
CHAPTER EIGHT **296**
8.1 METHODS OF DATA RETRIEVAL **296**
8.2 WHAT SQL QUERY FLOW IS ALL ABOUT 296
8.3 FLOW OF THE QUERY STATEMENT 297
8.4 GRAPHICAL VIEW OF THE QUERY STATEMENT 298
8.5 DATA SELECTION **303**
Column Selection 310
SQL Statement Execution 313
Transact-SQL and Data Selection 314
Showing the Results of SQL Data Analysis 325
Creating a Query 328
CHAPTER NINE **336**
T-SQL PROGRAMMING IN MS SQL SERVER **336**
9.1 Creating a Stored Procedure **345**
9.1.1 Managing Procedures 346
9.1.2 Application of Stored Procedures 348
9.2 Arguments and Parameters **351**
9.2.1 Passing Arguments on Stored Procedure 352
9.2.2 Executing an Argumentative Stored Procedure ...354
9.2.3 Default Arguments 357
9.2.4 Output Parameters 360
9.3 BUILT-IN STORED PROCEDURES **363**
9.3.1 Renaming an Object 363
9.3.2 Database Email 365
9.4 FUNCTIONS **369**
9.4.1 Creating a Function 369
9.4.2 The Name of a Function 371
9.4.3 Returning a Value From a Function 371
9.4.4 Creating Functions 372
9.4.5 Calling a Function 373
9.4.6 Function Maintenance 374
9.4.7 Renaming a Function 374
9.4.8 Deleting a Function 374
9.4.9 Modifying a Function 375
9.4.10 Function Arguments 377
9.4.11 A Parameterized Function 377
9.5. ....**BUILT-IN**
   FUNCTION **381**
9.5.1 Application of Built-In Functions 382
Arithmetic Functions 391
Measure-Based Functions 398
Trigonometric Functions 400
Date and Time Based Functions 402
9.6 VIEWS **405**
Why Use Views? 406
9.6.1 The Basic View 408
9.6.2 Managing Views 411
9.6.3 Executing views 412
9.6.4 Altering and dropping a view 413

9.6.5 More on Views 414
9.7 TRIGGERS **424**
9.7.1 Trigger Basics 425
9.7.2 Transaction flow 425
9.7.3 Creating triggers 427
9.7.4 After triggers.. 427
9.7.5 Instead of triggers 429
9.7.6 Trigger limitations 430
9.7.7 Disabling triggers.. 430
9.7.8 Listing triggers... 432
9.7.9 Triggers and Security 433
9.7.10 Working with the Transaction 435
9.7.11 Determining the Updated Columns 435
9.7.12 Inserted and deleted logical tables 437
9.7.13 Developing multi-row-enabled triggers 439
9.7.14 Trigger organization 441
9.7.15 Nested triggers.. 441
9.7.16 Recursive triggers 443
9.7.17 Instead of and after triggers.. 445
9.7.18 Multiple after triggers.. 446
9.7.19 Trigger Management... 447
9.8 T-SQL EXCEPTION HANDLING.. **448**
9.8.1 Types of Errors 448
9.9 Handling an Exception.. **451**
Identifying an Error 454
Characteristics of Exception Handling.. 461
CHAPTER TEN.. **467**
IMPROVING DATA RETRIEVAL AND QUERY PERFORMANCE
      TECHNIQUES **467**
10.1 Data Selection and Expressions................................. **468**
10.2 Sorting the Records.. **472**
10.2.1 Query Window or Query Designer Records Sorting 472
10.3 Restrictions on Data Selection..................................... **475**
10.4 CREATING A TABLE VIA AN EXISTING TABLE USING *SELECT*480
10.5 Combining Records **481**
10.5.1 Selecting from Different Tables 481
10.5.2 Uniting the Records 483
10.6 Copying Records **485**
10.6.1 Copying a Table 485
10.6.2 Merging Records 486
10.6.3 Outputting the Results of a Merge 488
10.7 Common Table Expressions (CTE) **490**
10.7.1 Application of Common Table Expressions 490
10.7.2 Recursive Common Table Expressions 494
10.7.3 Data Joins 495
10.8 Logical Conjunctions and Disjunctions **512**
10.8.1 Logical Conjunctions.. 512
10.8.2 Logical Disjunction 514
10.8.3 Logical Operations on Queries 516
10.9 Data Selection using Functions.................................... **518**
10.9.1 Data Selection and Built-In Functions 518

10.9.2 User-Defined Functions and Data Selection 519
10.10 Transactions **520**
10.10.1 The ACID Properties..520
10.10.2 The Myths of Transaction Abortion 522
10.10.3 Programming Transactions.......................................523
10.10.4 Nested transactions..526
10.10.5 Implicit transactions 528
10.10.6 Save points 529
10.10.7 Default Locking and Blocking Behaviour of Transaction 529
10.10.8 Deadlocks...532
10.10.9 Transaction Isolation Levels.....................................536
10.11 Committing a Transaction **538**
10.12 Rolling Back a Transaction **541**
CHAPTER ELEVEN..**545**
DATABASE AUTHENTICATION AND AUTHORIZATION **545**
11.1 DIFFERENCE BETWEEN USER AND LOGINS **546**
11.1.1 Server-Level Security...547
11.1.2 Database-Level Security 548
11.1.3 Windows Security 549
Using Windows Security 549
11.1.4 SQL Server login 550
11.2 .... Server
Security 550
11.3 .... Windows
Authentication...551
11.3.1 Adding a new Windows login 552
11.3.2 Removing a Windows login 552
11.3.3 Denying a Windows login...553
11.4 Setting the default database **553**
11.4.1 SQL Server logins...554
11.4.2 Updating a password...555
11.5 Server roles...**555**
11.6 Database Security...**557**
11.6.1 Guest logins...557
11.6.2 Granting access to a database 558
11.7 Fixed database roles **559**
Assigning fixed database roles with Management Studio 560
11.8 Application roles **562**
11.8.1 Connecting with an Application Role...........................562
11.9 Objects **563**
11.9.1 Object Ownership 563
11.9.2 Object Security 564
11.10 Stored procedure Execute As **570**
11.11 Data Organization Using Schemas **573**
11.12 Basic Impersonation Using EXECUTE AS **576**

PREFACE

Database development is one of the areas many IT Professionals fears to trade; yet a lot of IT Professional who are into it have done very well in that they have developed good functioning database; while some are still struggling to find recognition in that area with respect to doing real development using the available DBMS. Hence, Microsoft SQL Server, it is a relational database management system developed by Microsoft. As a database, it is a software product whose primary function is to store and retrieve data as requested by other software applications, be it those on the same computer or those running on another computer across a network (including the Internet). There are almost a dozen different editions of Microsoft SQL Server aimed at different audiences and for different workloads (ranging from small applications that store and retrieve data on the same computer, to millions of users and computers that access huge amounts of data from the Internet at the same time). Its primary query languages are T-SQL and ANSI SQL.

T-SQL (Transact-SQL) is the primary means of programming and managing SQL Server if the language is used very well by a developer. It exposes keywords for the operations that can be performed on SQL Server, including creating and altering database schemas, entering and editing data in the database as well as monitoring and managing the server itself; so that is where this book comes in. Client applications that consume data or manage the server will leverage SQL Server functionality by sending T-SQL queries and statements which are then processed by the server and results (or errors) returned to the client application such as VB.NET. SQL Server allows it to be managed using T-SQL. For this, it exposes read-only tables from which server statistics can be read. Management functionality is exposed via system-defined stored procedures which can be invoked from T-SQL queries to perform the management operation.

Furthermore, as the name of this book implies "Database Development Elucidated", it will give the readers the knowledge and technique, required of them to develop databases using MS SQL Server platform. Therefore, it is an incontestable fact that those who are eager and so desirous to increase their knowledge and experience in database development but have not been able to do that as a result of lack well explained resource materials; will heave a sigh of relief because this book has what it takes to help them realized their dreams. This book, written with 100% practical examples on all topics in the chapters; is from many years of experience.

More so, probably, when you are done with this material, your mentality in terms of how data is stored and retrieved using SQL Server entails will definitely change. Any doubt about it? You will find out soon. So, read this book and in between lines, then God will help you; for those that believe in Him.

The book has eleven chapters; each chapter introduces new topics or throw more light on a topic already treated. Chapter one deals on Introduction to relational database and MS SQL Server 2008, chapter two deals on System Requirement, Installation of MS SQL Server and starting MS SQL Server Services, chapter three talks about Dos and Don'ts in Database programming, chapter four talks about Database Creation, chapter five talks about Microsoft SQL Server Data Types, chapter six is about the things you need to know about Database Tables, chapter seven is all about Data Manipulation and Maintenance, chapter eight will teach you Methods of Data Retrieval, chapter nine deals on Programming in MS SQL Server with T-SQL, chapter ten talks about Improving Data retrieval and Query performance techniques and finally chapter eleven deals on Database Authentication and Authorization.

The purpose of this of book is to ensure that you learn and know the basis of database development with MS SQL Server through teaching yourself, with the easy to go procedures, which you have to follow. It is also to skyrocket and to enhance your speed, technique and full implementation of the ACID nature of the DBMS of database development for those who are already database developers. Finally, to ameliorate some difficulties people encounter while developing database using MS SQL Server.

Lecturers, Teachers, IT Professionals, should have at the back of their minds that the effectiveness, quality and efficacy of their lecturing/teaching, rely solely on experience as well as valuable resource materials like this one. Therefore, Lecturers, Teachers, IT Professionals, and Students will undisputedly find this book invaluable, because it is mainly prepared to meet the requirements of the aforementioned persons and those who hungers to learn how to develop database but haven't the opportunity to do so, and those who wants to improve their skills, and experience, in database development.

Thanks and God bless.

IWUALA CHIBUEZE

DEDICATION
To the memory of Late Chibuisi Iwuala

ACKNOWLEDGEMENT

I humbly wish to express my profound gratitude to Prof. Chiso Okafor for writing the forward of this book despite her tight schedule as a Professor; her experienced contributions and advice made this book a wonderful one. My thanks also goes to the following people: Engr. Kenny Uchie-Okoro, Mr. Lucky Nwoha, Hon. C. C Uzoho (JP), Dr. Lazarous Okoroji the HOD of transport management technology FUTO, Prof. S. M Nzotta, for their supports; Hon. Justice Jeco Osondu, Mr B. B Olofin, Dr. Andy Chimeremeze Okebugwu; Rev. Fr. Odoemena A. Nnamdi, Rev. Fr. Joseph A. A Anuonye, Rev. Fr. Edmund Igboanusi and Rev. Sr. Marylucy Mbamara for their spiritual advice; Mrs Nwachukwu Joy for her prayers, Mr. K. C Aguwa, Mr. Charles Ikerionwu, Mr Enyeribe Onyekachi Sampson, Late Mrs Nwanyieze Iheukwumere, Mr Ifeanyi S. Ochije, Mr Okafor Christian, Mr. Amadi Emeka Christian, Mr. Udourom, Enomfon Eseme, Hon. Nneji, Mr. McDonald Oparah and all who in one way or the other contributed to the success of this book.

In a special way I thank Ezinna Goodluck I. Iwuala and Mrs. Catharine Goodluck for all their contributions and support to my growth in life; and my siblings (Onyekachi, Nneoma, Ugonna, Obinna, Ndudrim and Ikenna) for their encouragement, Chinwendu Chibueze my dear wife and finally my daughter Oluchi Chibueze.

CHAPTER ONE

1.1   INTRODUCTION

SQL (*structured query language*) is an industry-standard language specifically designed to enable people to create databases, add data to databases, maintain and manipulate the data, and retrieve selected all or parts of the data from the database as they see fit. Various kinds of databases exist, each adhering to a different conceptual model. SQL was originally developed to operate on data in databases that follow the *relational model*. Recently, the international SQL standard has incorporated part of the *object model,* resulting in hybrid structures called object-relational databases. In this chapter, little will be said about object-relational database; we will devote a section to how the relational model compares with other major models, and provide a look at the important features of relational databases.

1.2   RELATIONAL DATABASE

Before we take a look at the relationships existing in the database via tables; whence the relational database. It will be ideal to take a look at in brief what database is, because in chapter two of this book we talk about database in full.

1.2.1   What is a Database?

A database is a collection different data.

There are two types of databases: operational and analytical. Operational is used in everyday businesses, institutions and organizations. They are primarily used to store data that is collected, maintained and modified (dynamic data). Analytical is used to track historical data (static data). Track trends, view statistical data, and so on.

Insertion anomalies and redundant data are problems associated with an early database model known as a hierarchical table (parent-child table). Network database (owner-member table) models were problematic as well. These two models led to the development of the relational database model.

Dr. E. F. Codd applied mathematical theories known as first order predicate logic and set theory to design relational databases. These theories are the foundation for the Relational Database Model (RDM). They are important because they makes the RDM predictable and reliable. It is not necessary to fully understand these theories to develop a sound database design.

In a RDM, data are stored in a relation or table (those terms may be used interchangeably.) Each table contains rows or records, (also called tuples), and columns which represent attributes or fields. Each record or row is represented by a unique field known as the Primary key. The categories of relationships in a RDM are one-to-one, one-to-many, and many-to-many. A many-to-many relationship must be broken down into numerous one-to-many relationships. If a pair of tables share a relationship, data can be retrieved based on matching values of a shared field between the tables. Data is retrieved by specifying fields and tables using a standard query language known as Structured Query Language (SQL). Most DBMSs (Database Managements Systems) use SQL to build, modify, maintain and manipulate databases. Thorough knowledge of SQL is not always necessary for nonprofessional database developers since most DMBSs use a graphical interface to generate SQL statements and retrieve data. It is good, however, to have basic knowledge of SQL, so that you can debug your codes or statement when something goes run.

Large volumes of centrally located shared data have come about in recent history, creating the need for client/server software. Data security and integrity can be implemented through the database server. Relational Database Model gave birth to Relational Databases, so let take a look at relational database as it concerns MS SQL Server.

A Relational Database treats all of its data as a collection of relations.

A relational database uses relations, or two-dimensional tables, to store the information needed to support a business. Let us go over to the basic components of a traditional relational database system and look at how a relational database is designed. Once you have a solid understanding of what rows, columns, tables, and relationships are, you will be well on your way to leveraging the power of a relational database using SQL Server.

A table in a relational database, alternatively known as a relation, is a two-dimensional structure used to hold related information. A database consists of one or more related tables. Do not confuse a relation with relationships. A relation is essentially a table, and a relationship is a way to correlate, join, or associate the two or more tables.

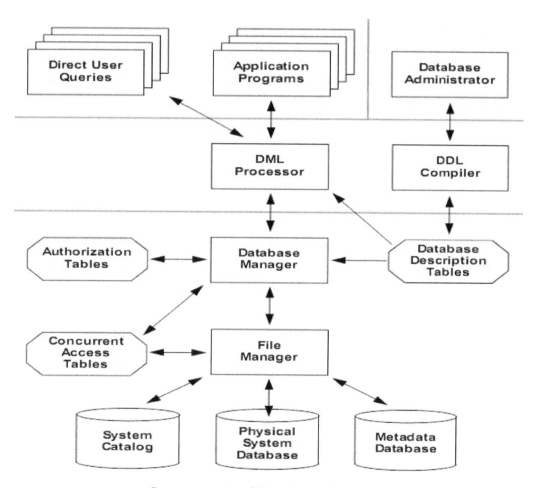

Components of Database Systems

1.3   MS SQL SERVER

SQL 2008 server is one of the latest in the line of Microsoft database servers, this chapter discusses, what MS SQL SERVER 2008 is all about, its features, challenges one may face in installing the Enterprise version of it, which was released in November 2007. On a virgin machine the software probably installs without a hitch. It will also install on a new created administrative account.

Microsoft SQL Server is an application used to create computer databases for the Microsoft Windows family of operating systems. It provides an environment used to generate databases that can be accessed from workstations, the web, standalone applications that run on PCs, or other media such as a personal digital assistant (PDA). On the hand, it can be used to manage any data, any place, and any time; store data from structured, semi-structured, and unstructured documents, such as images and rich media files, directly within the database. SQL Server 2008 delivers a rich set of integrated services that enable you to do more with your data such as query, search, synchronize, report, and analyze.

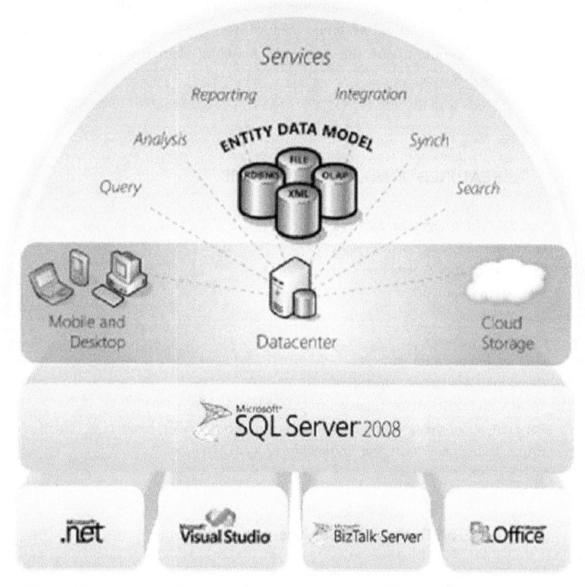

We will provide lessons and other topics on how to use Microsoft SQL Server 2008, in this book.

In order to follow the lessons on this book, you must have access to a computer in which Microsoft SQL Server 2008 is installed because this book is written with 100% percent practical examples. To start, you must have a computer that runs any appropriate operating system, Such Microsoft Windows XP Professional, Microsoft Windows Vista, or Microsoft Windows Server 2003, Microsoft Windows Server 2008 and Windows 8; we assume that the readers of this book are beginners and students.

To use Microsoft SQL Server, you must install it on a computer. You can install it on the aforementioned operating systems. Before we go to the next page for the installation, let us talk about the features, benefits, demerits and probable the importance of SQL Server.

1.3.1 FEATURES OF MS SQL SERVER 2008

i. SQL SERVER Integration Services
ii. Policy Based Management System
iii. Transparent Data Encryption
iv. Filestream Data type
v. Data Auditing
vi. Merge
vii. Declare and Initialize Variables
viii. Compound Assignment Operators
ix. Table Value Constructor Support through Values Clause
x. For more about the new features like Cast, Convert and so on visit: http://technet.microsoft.com/enus/library/cc721270.aspx

SQL SERVER Integration Services

SSIS (SQL Server Integration Services) is a built in application for developing and executing ETL (extraction, transformation, and load) packages. It replaced SQL 2000 DTS. Integration Services includes the necessary wizards, tools, and tasks for creating both simple import export packages, as well very complex data cleansing operations.

Policy Based Management System

Makes managing multiple SQL Server instances easier. It allows you to define centralized configuration policies, and SQL Server will enforce and report on those settings throughout the enterprise. Policy-Based Management, which requires no changes to your applications or databases to function, also allows you to run a T-SQL query against multiple servers from a centralized management server. This is (sort of) a part of the Policy-Based Management framework.

Transparent Data Encryption

If you deal with sensitive data, transparent data encryption improves SQL Server's encryption capabilities by transparently encrypting the entire database file rather than specific columns.

Filestream Data type

My favorite new feature is the FILESTREAM data type. It takes binary large objects (BLOBs), such as the varchar (MAX) data type, out of the database files and moves them to standalone files on the Windows file system. This helps cut down on the database size and actually provides great performance (as it turns out, Windows is pretty good at reading and writing files all by itself).

Data Auditing

Finally, if you're dealing with compliance and auditing concerns, the new data auditing features help audit events like logons, password changes, data access, data modification, schema modification and more.

MERGE

SQL 2008 includes the TSQL command MERGE. Using this statement allows a single statement to UPDATE, INSERT, or DELETE a row depending on its condition. Example is show below:

MERGE InventoryMaster AS im
USING (SELECT InventoryID, Descr FROM NewInventory) AS src
ON im.InventoryID = src.InventoryID
WHEN MATCHED THEN

```
UPDATE SET im.Descr = src.Descr
WHEN NOT MATCHED THEN
INSERT (InventoryID, Descr) VALUES (src.InventoryID, src.Descr);
```

Declare and Initialize Variables

Microsoft SQL Server® 2008 enables you to initialize variables inline as part of the variable
declaration statement instead of using separate DECLARE and SET statements. This
enhancement helps you abbreviate your code. The following code example demonstrates inline
initializations using a literal and a function:

```
DECLARE @i AS INT = 0, @d AS DATETIME = CURRENT_TIMESTAMP;
SELECT @i AS [@i], @d AS [@d];
```

Compound Assignment Operators

Compound assignment operators help abbreviate code that assigns a value to a column or a
variable. The new operators are:

+= (plus equals)

-= (minus equals)

*= (multiplication equals)

/= (division equals)

%= (modulo equals)

You can use these operators wherever assignment is normally allowed—for example, in the SET
clause of an UPDATE statement or in a SET statement that assigns values to variables. The
following code example demonstrates the use of the += operator:

```
DECLARE @price AS MONEY = 10.00;
SET @price += 2.00;
SELECT @price;
```

This code sets the variable @price to its current value, 10.00, plus 2.00, resulting in 12.00.
Isn't that great?

Table Value Constructor Support through Values Clause

SQL Server 2008 introduces support for table value constructors through the VALUES clause. You can now use a single VALUES clause to construct a set of rows. One use of this feature is to insert multiple rows based on values in a single INSERT statement, as follows:

```
CREATE TABLE dbo.Customers
(
custid INT          NOT NULL,  companyname VARCHAR(25) NOT NULL,
phone         VARCHAR(20) NOT NULL,  address       VARCHAR(50) NOT NULL,
CONSTRAINT PK_Customers PRIMARY KEY(custid)
);
GO


INSERT INTO dbo.Customers(custid, companyname, phone, address)
VALUES (1, 'cust 1', '(111) 111-1111', 'address 1'),
(2, 'cust 2', '(222) 222-2222', 'address 2'),
(3, 'cust 3', '(333) 333-3333', 'address 3');
GO
```

"It is almost always true for most of the software I have installed, not necessarily limited to Microsoft. However, most of Microsoft products need entry in the Window's registry and it is almost certain that one has to follow a certain protocol if one wishes to have a successful install. In fact the unsuccessful install flags out what went wrong while the initial steps do verify the requirements during installation. Despite this help and warnings one may face problems simply because it is not possible to foresee all possible combinations of hardware, software, user created error issues at launch time of the product. Again this article does not guarantee a successful install if one were to follow the steps delineated but gives you some guidance based on the author's experience."

Before installing Microsoft SQL Server 2008, make sure you have installed all service packs on your operating system. If you plan to use Microsoft Visual Studio 2008 to create Microsoft SQL Server 2008 databases, you should install Microsoft SQL Server 2008 first, then install Microsoft Visual Studio 2008.

CHAPTER TWO

SYSTEM REQUIREMENT, INSTALLATION OF MS SQL SERVER AND STARTING MS SQL SERVER SERVICES

2.1 SYSTEM REQUIREMENT

If you intend to transport 600 bags of Garri from Isiala-Ngwa North to Port Harcourt, it will be unreasonable to use a Hilux jeep instead of a Heavy duty trucks. Also it will be somehow to install SQL Server on slow processing computers that are made for MS Office suit.

The following requirements apply to all SQL Server 2008 installations:

Component	Requirement
Framework[2]	SQL Server Setup installs the following software components required by the product: .NET Framework 3.5[1] SQL Server Native Client SQL Server Setup support files
Software[2]	SQL Server Setup requires Microsoft Windows Installer 4.5 or a later version, and Microsoft Data Access Components (MDAC) 2.8 SP1 or a later version After installing required components, SQL Server Setup will verify that the computer where SQL Server 2008 will be installed also meets all the other requirements for a successful installation. For more information, see Check Parameters for the System Configuration Checker.
Network Software	Network software requirements for the 64-bit versions of SQL Server 2008 are the same as the requirements for the 32-bit versions. Supported operating systems have built-in network software. Stand-alone named and default instances support the following network protocols: Shared memory Named Pipes TCP/IP VIA

Virtualization	SQL Server 2008 is supported in virtual machine environments running on the Hyper-V role in Windows Server 2008 Standard, Enterprise and Data Center editions. The virtual machine must run an operating system supported for the specific SQL Server 2008 edition listed later in this topic.
	
	In addition to resources required by the parent partition, each virtual machine (child partition) must be provided with sufficient processor resources, memory, and disk resources for its SQL Server 2008 instance. Requirements are listed later in this topic.[3]
	
	Within the Hyper-V role on Windows Server 2008, a maximum of four virtual processors can be allocated to virtual machines running Windows Server 2008 32-bit or 64-bit editions. A maximum of 2 virtual processors can be allocated to virtual computers that are running Windows Server 2003 32-bit editions. For virtual computer that host other operating systems, a maximum of one virtual processor can be allocated to virtual computers.
	
	Notes:
	
	    It is recommended that SQL Server 2008 be shut down before shutting down or the virtual machine.
	
	    Guest failover clustering (configuring failover clustering in SQL Server 2008) is not supported in a Hyper-V environment.

Internet Software	Microsoft Internet Explorer 6 SP1 or a later version is required for all installations of SQL Server 2008. Internet Explorer 6 SP1 or a later version is required for Microsoft Management Console (MMC), SQL Server Management Studio, Business Intelligence Development Studio, the Report Designer component of Reporting Services, and HTML Help.
Hard Disk	See Table 2.3 below.
Drive	A CD or DVD drive, as appropriate, is required for installation from disc.
Display	SQL Server 2008 graphical tools require VGA or higher resolution: at least 1,024x768 pixel resolution.
Other Devices	Pointing device: A Microsoft mouse or compatible pointing device is required.

Table 2.1 List of components requirement of SQL Server

1. The following .NET Framework versions are required:

- SQL Server 2008 on Windows Server 2003 (64-bit) IA64 — .NET Framework 2.0 SP1
- All other editions of SQL Server 2008 — .NET Framework 3.5

Installation of .NET Framework requires a restart of the operating system. If Windows Installer installation also requires a restart, Setup will wait until .NET Framework and Windows Installer components have installed before restarting.

2. SQL Server Setup will not install the following required components for SQL Server Express and SQL Server Express with Advanced Services. You must install these components manually before you run SQL Server Setup:

- SQL Server Express —.NET Framework 2.0 SP2 and Windows installer 4.5. On Windows Vista, use .NET Framework 3.5 SP1.
- SQL Server Express with Advanced Services — .NET Framework 3.5 SP1, Windows Installer 4.5, and Windows PowerShell 1.0.

3. As with all virtualization technologies, SQL Server 2008 running in a Windows Server 2008 Hyper-V virtual computer will be slower than on a physical computer with the same physical resources.

The following table shows system requirements for SQL Server 2008 Enterprise (64-bit) x64 and this form the basis for the minimum system resources requirement:

Component	Requirement
Processor	Processor type: Minimum: AMD Opteron, AMD Athlon 64, Intel Xeon with Intel EM64T support, Intel Pentium IV with EM64T support Processor speed: Minimum: 1.4 GHz Recommended: 2.0 GHz or faster
Operating System	Windows XP Professional 2003 64-bit x64[3] Windows Server 2003 SP2 64-bit x64 Standard[1] Windows Server 2003 SP2 64-bit x64 Data Center[1] Windows Server 2003 SP2 64-bit x64 Enterprise[1] Windows Vista 64-bit x64 Ultimate[3] Windows Vista 64-bit x64 Home Premium[3] Windows Vista 64-bit x64 Home Basic[3] Windows Vista 64-bit x64 Enterprise[3] Windows Vista 64-bit x64 Business[3] Windows 7 64-bit x64 Ultimate[3] Windows 7 64-bit x64 Home Premium[3] Windows 7 64-bit x64 Home Basic[3] Windows Server 2008 64-bit x64 Standard Windows Server 2008 64-bit x64 Standard without Hyper-V[2,4] Windows Server 2008 64-bit x64 Data Center Windows Server 2008 64-bit x64 Data Center without Hyper-V[1,2] Windows Server 2008 64-bit x64 Enterprise,

	Windows Server 2008 64-bit x64 Enterprise without Hyper-V[1,2]
Memory	RAM: Minimum:512 MB Recommended: 2.048 GB or more Maximum: Operating system maximum

Table 2.2 System Requirements

1. Applications function in 32-bit mode even though the underlying operating system is running on the 64-bit operating system.
2. SQL Server 2008 is not supported on Windows Server 2008 Server Core installations.

Hard Disk Space Requirements (32-Bit and 64-Bit)

- During installation of SQL Server 2008, Windows Installer creates temporary files on the system drive. Before you run Setup to install or upgrade SQL Server, verify that you have at least 2.0 GB of available disk space on the system drive for these files. This requirement applies even if you install SQL Server components to a non-default drive.

- Actual hard disk space requirements depend on your system configuration and the features that you decide to install. The following table provides disk space requirements for SQL Server 2008 components:

Feature	Disk space requirement
Database Engine and data files, Replication, and Full-Text Search	280 MB
Analysis Services and data files	90 MB
Reporting Services and Report Manager	120 MB
Integration Services	120 MB
Client Components	850 MB
SQL Server Books Online and SQL Server Compact Books Online	240 MB

Table 2.3 Hard drive Space Requirements

2.2   INSTALLATION OF MS SQL SERVER

SQL Server 2008 has new Setup architecture for the following scenarios: installation, upgrade, maintenance, failover clustering, and command prompt installations.

Before installing Microsoft SQL Server 2008, make sure you have installed all service packs (you will need to install the .Net 3.5 or 4.0 Framework) on your operating system, especially operating system like windows XP and windows Vista, but it comes pre-installed on Windows 2008 Server and Windows 7 & 8. If you plan to use Microsoft Visual Studio 2008 on this computer where you installed Microsoft SQL Server 2008, you should install Microsoft SQL Server 2008 first, and then install Microsoft Visual Studio 2008.

Developers and system administrators will find this installation guide on this book very useful, as well as seasoned DBAs. It will teach you the basics required for a typical, problem-free installation of SQL Server 2008, allowing you to add other components later if you wish.

First off I will recommend you copy the entire directory structure from the SQL Server 2008 installation disc to the C: drive of the machine you are going to install it on. Although this means you need to grab a cup of coffee whilst it's copying, this has three advantages:

- It makes the installation process much faster.

- It allows you to easily add or remove components later, without using the installation CDs/DVD.

- If your media is damaged and a file won't copy, you will find out, rather than halfway through the installation.

- It helps you make a copy of the installation media incase the media is damage or got lost.

2.2.1 Introduction to Security

One of the main concerns of a database is security, and this is central to Microsoft SQL Server; when you tamper with windows OS password where SQL Server is installed will understand what I mean. Security is exercised at different levels: in the room where the computer(s) is(are) located (the computer(s) that hold the server application (Microsoft SQL Server), the computer(s) that will use the databases (clients)) and the people who will use all these resources.

When it comes to the room that houses the computer on which you will install Microsoft SQL Server, you should make sure the room can be locked at any time and restricted to many people, thus, only a few selected people have access to it. For maximum security, you should also put the computer in a locked closet. The computer runs OS; the server resides in the OS, while the database resides in the server. So we also talk about the OS, Server and Database Securities. We will take a look at the Windows OS security while we assume that that home is taken care off by looking the house where the computer is kept.

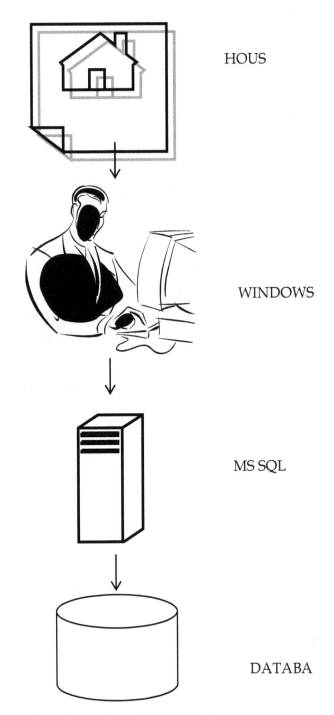

HOUS

WINDOWS

MS SQL

DATABA

Fig 2.1 Security Hierarchy of MS SQL Server

i. User's Account

To actually install Microsoft SQL Server 2008, you must use a user account that has the ability to install it, whence an administrative account. If you are using Microsoft Windows XP or Vista or Windows 7, you should use the Administrator account or create a new account that has administrative rights. The account you will use must also use/have a password. Alternatively, after logging in as Administrator, create an account that has administrative rights, because it is advisable to install the MS SQL Server on a fresh user's account. Below are the steps to follow for proper installation of MS SQL Server.

1. Click on start button, to open to start menu; then click Control Panel.

2. Click User Accounts

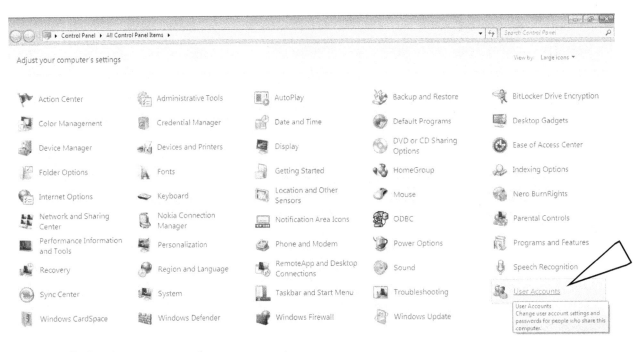

3. Click Manage another account

4. Click Create a new account

5. Type the name of the account in textbox provided for it, as SQLBOOK, select Administrator radio button to activate it and click Create Account.

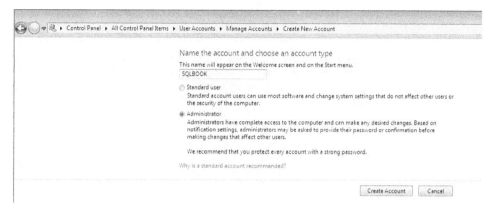

6. The preview of the created user's account with other user's account existing in the computer. The account type is display right below the account name. To assign a password to the account, click the account name to activate it.

7. Click Create a password

8. In the textboxes below, type sql+book@12 and press Tab

9. Type sql+book@12 to confirm.

10. Type anything in the last textbox that will enable you remember the password.

11. Click Create Password

2.2.2 Installing SQL Server 2008

1. I assumed that you have copied the installation files or to drive to your drive C:, if it's on DVD/CD disc, I enumerated the disadvantages and advantages of installing the software from drive C: above. Double click on the **setup.exe** file.

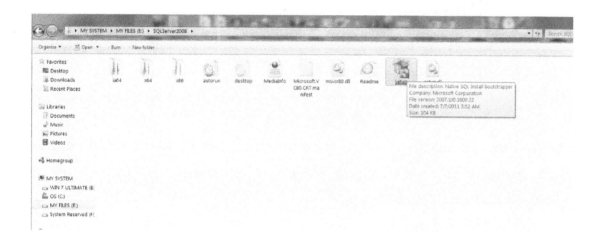

2. After a few seconds a dialog box appears, as show below. Click **Run program** button.

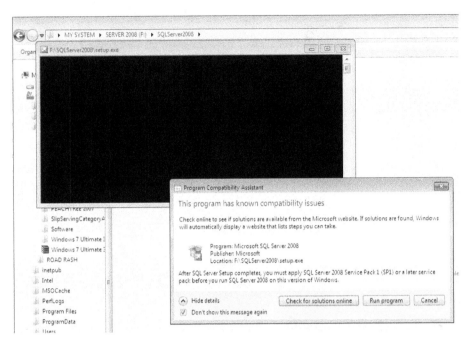

3. Click **Installation**, it is an installation hyperlink so your mouse should change to a hand when you point at the Installation on the main installation window or MS SQL Server installation home page.

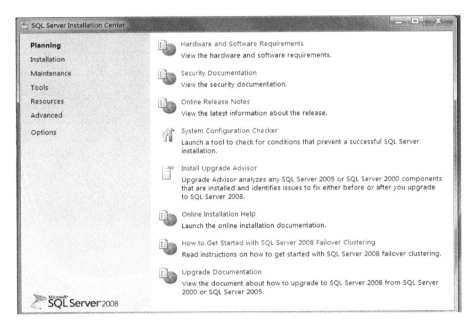

4. Click **New SQL Server stand-alone installation** link.

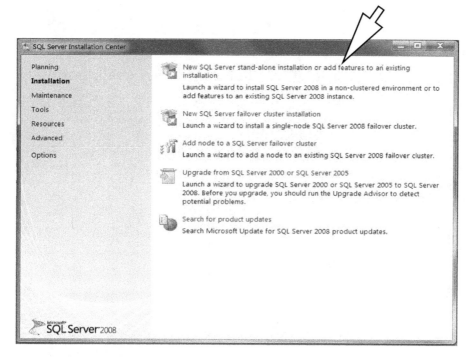

5. Click **install** button.

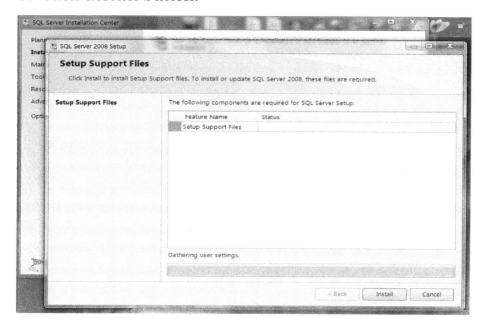

6. Click **Next** button.

Note:

A check will be carried out on your system to ensure that all is well with the system in order to support files. In case of any failure, Show details button or click the report link to view it then correct the errors and click Re-run button to repeat the check. Click **Next** when you are done.

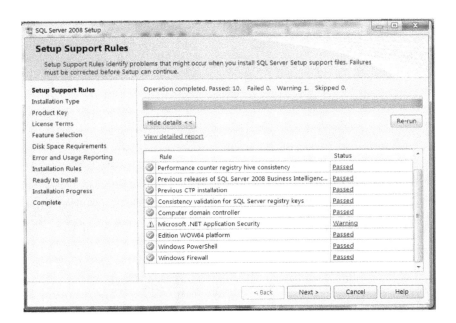

7. Click ***Enter the product key*** or ***Specify a free edition*** if you don't have the product key. Type the product key in the textbox provided for it and click **Next** button. Please note that the product key shown below is not valid for your PC.

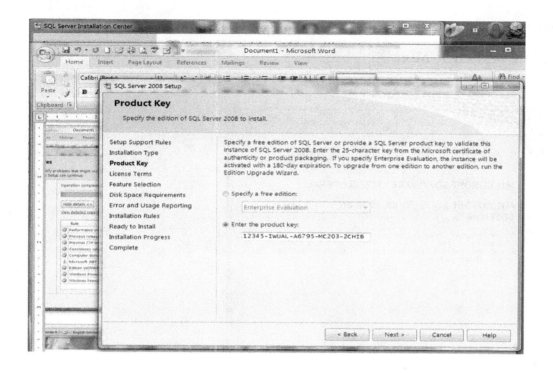

8. On the "License terms" page, click ***I accept the license terms*** checkbox to activate and click ***Next***.

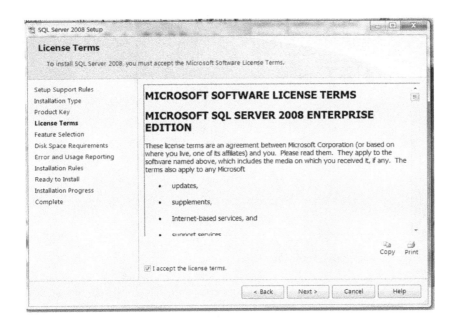

9. In the "Feature Selection" section, select any feature by clicking on it to activate it. What you need will be dependent on what you want to do with the SQL Server. But you must select at least you must select **Database Engine Services, SQL Server Books Online, Client Tools, Connectivity, Management Tools-Basic;** to install all the features click **Select All** button. Click ***Next*** button.

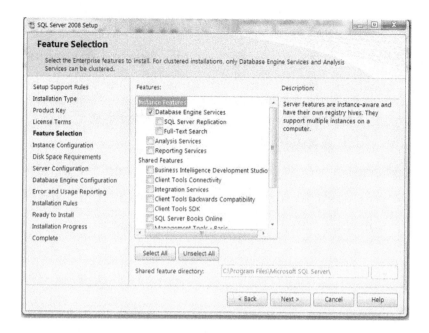

10. In "Instance Configuration" page we have to be very careful because some people makes wrong selection in choosing the instance of the SQL Server they want installed.

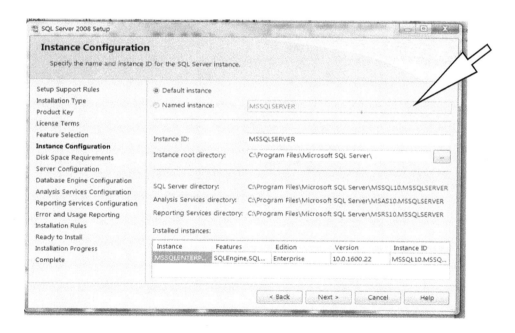

When you are installing the SQL Server for the first leave the **_default instance_**, but if you are installing an extra instance use the **_Named instance_**, then enter the name of the instance (server name) you want. Note that the **_Name instance_** textbox is deactivated and can only be activated when you select the **_Name instance_** radio. Click **Next** button.

11.   You will see an optional window which shows the capacity or size of your hard drive where you want to install the software and total space required to install the software and the available space after your installation.

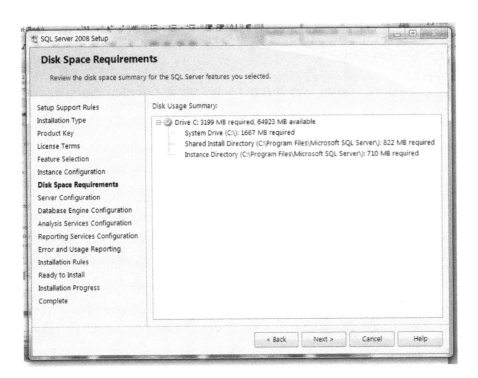

12. In "Server Configuration" page, the major services of MS SQL Server you selected above will require your configuration to enable them run on your PC. You remember the administrative account you created above, this is the time to use it; enter the *Account Name* and *Password* then choose automatic *Startup Type* for all the services, though that of *SQL Server Agent* can manual. Then click *Next* button. On the other hand, you can choose default or inbuilt Network Service Account which works perfectly well but it requires no *Password*.

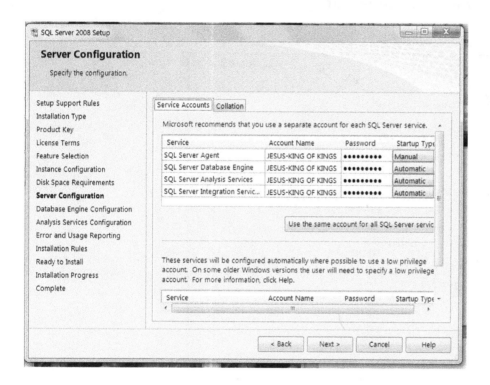

13. In "Database Engine Configuration", if you intend to be logging into the SQL Server using a password and username then select **Mixed Mode** radio button; else select **Windows authentication mode** which needs no password. Enter your password in the textboxes provided for it under **Built**-*in SQL Server system administrator account* section. Then add those who will be given full or unrestricted access to the SQL Server, under the *Specify SQL Server administrators* section. When you are done supplying the required data, click *Next* button. Or go to step number 15 below for explanation on *Data Directories* tab.

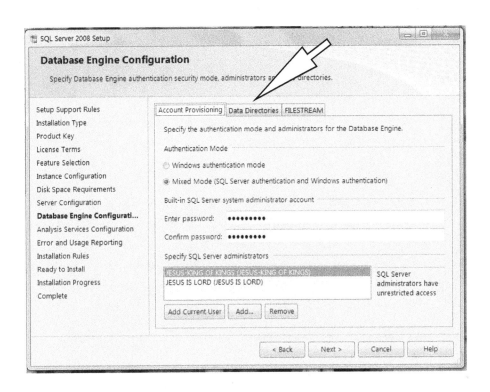

14. Under the *Data Directories* tab, though is optional, but you can still make changes to the directories where you want SQL Server to stored your database and the default database or system database. But its advice you leave the default directories to avoid confusion in the future. If you must alter the default directories, then leave that of the **Data root directory** textbox unchanged. The arrow at the diagram below points to the **Data root directory**.

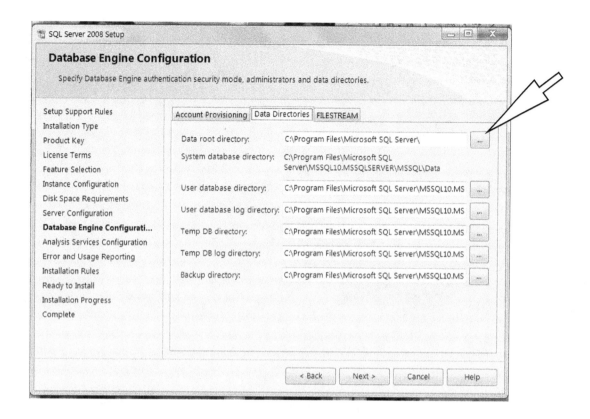

15. The *FILESTREAM* tab is optional unless you have a need for it.

16. In the "Analysis Services Configuration" page, you need to add the users that will have unrestricted access to the Analysis Services of the SQL Server. You can click *Add Current User* button to add the User that is installing the software or *Add...* button to add other administrators who will have unrestricted access to Analysis Services. Click **Next** button when you are done.

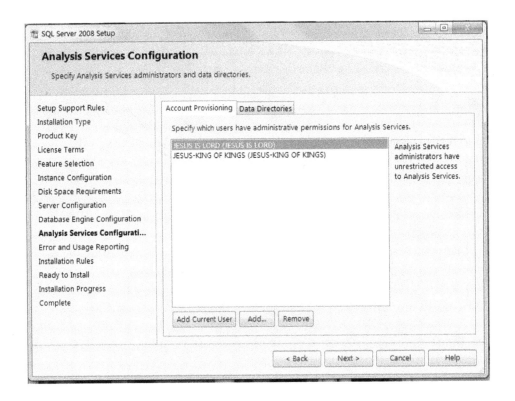

17. In the "Error and Usage Reporting page", you can click on the checkboxes to indicate that you want to send Error message should it occur during installation, then click *Next* button to continue. Though, this is optional can be skipped by click on the *Next* button.

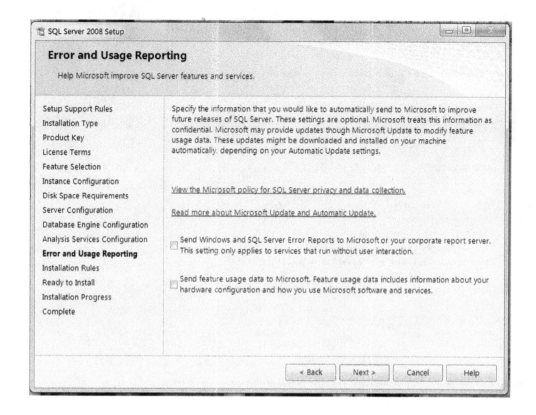

18. "Installation Rules" page will quickly check if anything will hinder SQL Server from been installed on your PC, so click **Next** button if no issue is raised.

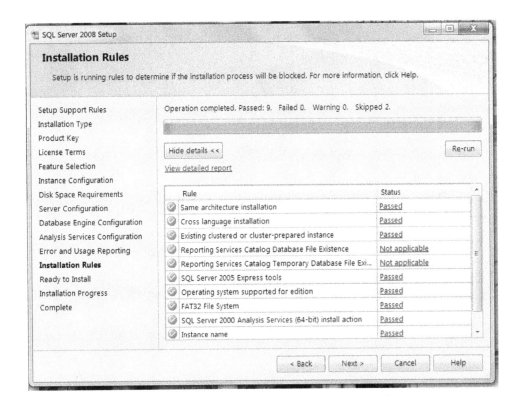

19. "Ready to install" page gives you the last opportunity to make changes from your configuration and choices of what you intend to install, or to cancel the installation. After this page, you will not be able modify anything should you change your mind midway. When you are satisfied with the summary of what is to be installed, click **Install** button.

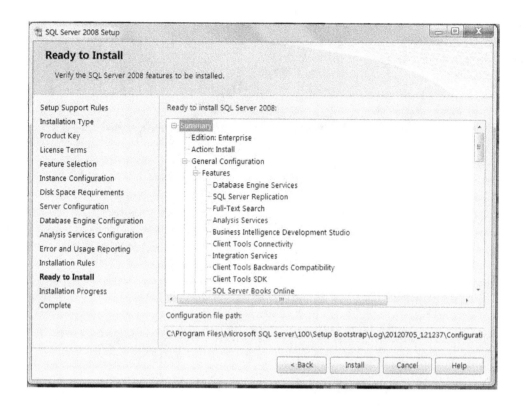

20. The "Installation Progress" shows you the installation progress on the progress bar. How long the installation takes, strictly depend on how fast is your PC and the installation media. When the installation is ongoing the Next button will be disabled.

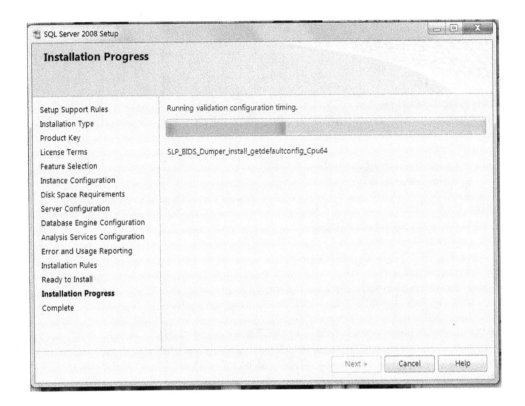

21. The **Next** button is enabled here because the installation is completed. Click **Next** button.

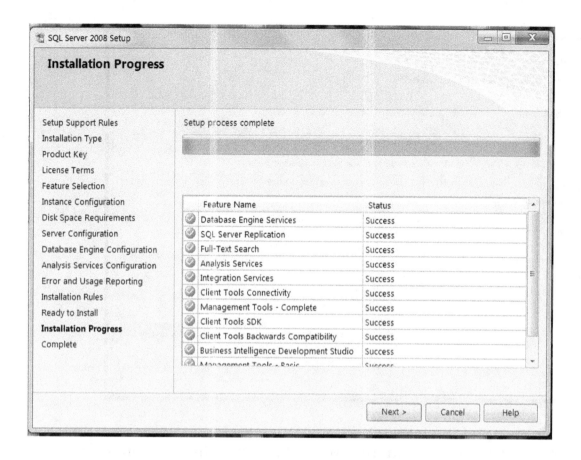

22. In the "Complete" page, you see if the SQL Server installed successfully and the link to installation log will be created. Click **Close** button marks the end of the installation, so you will return to the MS SQL Server Installation home page.

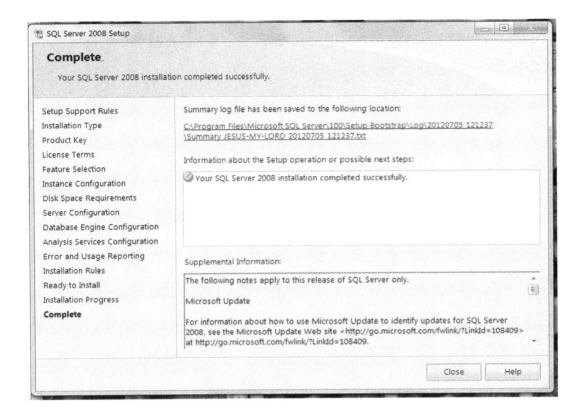

23. Finally, click close when the MS SQL Server Installation home page appears.

NOTE: A dialogue box may appear demanding that you restart your computer, you option of either to restart it continue with what you were doing.

2.3 STARTING MS SQL SERVER SERVICES AND SQL MANAGEMENT STUDIO

Below are some post-installation checks which are useful to perform after re-booting your new SQL Server. You don't have to run these, and there are other ways to check, but they are very useful for non-DBAs to be sure that the installation is basically sound and a connection can be made to the new SQL Server before handing it over to the students or whoever the installation was made for.

2.3.1 Starting MS SQL Server Services

i.   Go to control panel and click Administrative tools

ii. Click on Services, then the system services will appear as show below.

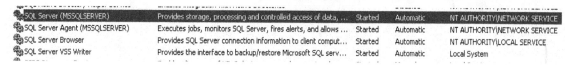

iii. You will see that SQL Server has started, else

iv. Right click on the SQL Server and click start on the pop up menu.

2.3.2 Starting SQL Management Studio

i.   Click on SQL Server Management Studio on all programs, this image is as show below

ii. A preview of a screen shot will appear temporarily, then after the image below is shown for you supply the login details and click connect.

iii. Click on New Query to display the query window or working area as the case may be, below is an image showing New Query button and the query window.

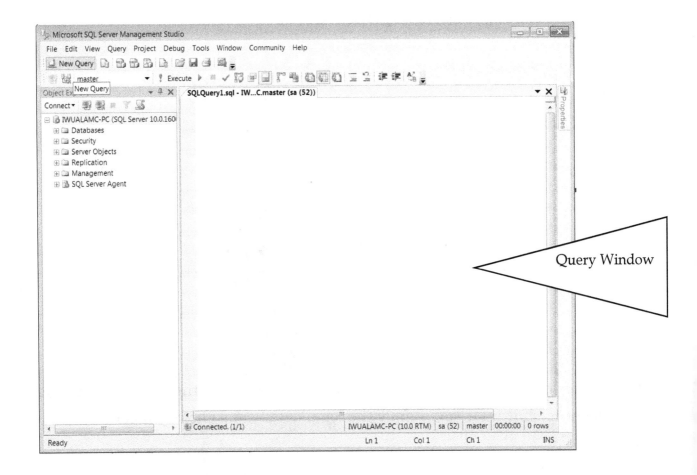

iv. type select @@Version in query and press F5 to execute it, below is an image showing the executed code and the result

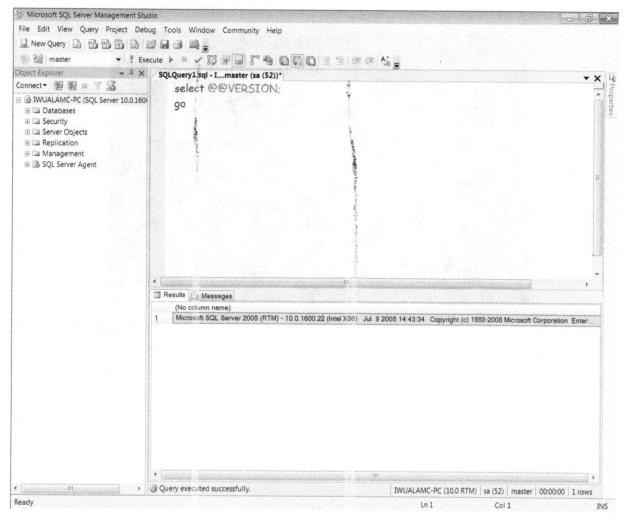

v. On the other hand, you can still check if the installation succeeded and if the server is running via command prompt. Click Run from start menu and type cmd and click OK, as shown below

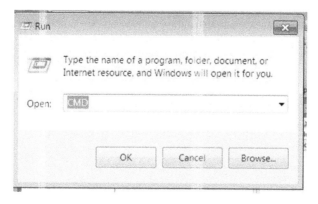

vi.   Type isql –L (or osql –L) on the command prompt window and press enter key, the image below shows the command prompt window.

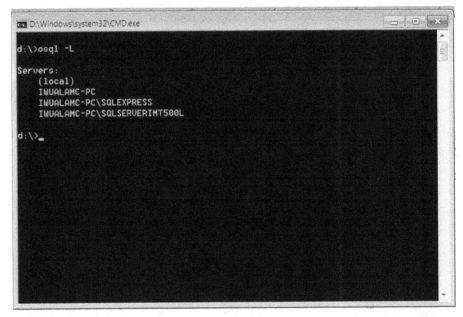

If you did not see the new SQL Server in this list, check that the SQL Server Browser service is started on the machine where you have just installed SQL Server.

vii. Enable the TCP/IP network protocol library on the Server. Click All Programs, click SQL Server 2008, and click on Configuration Tools and click SQL Server Configuration Manager. The image is shown below for easy assimilation

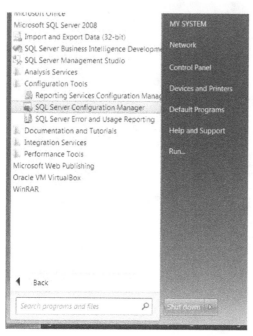

viii. Double Click on SQL Server Network configuration, then click any of the servers you want to configure its protocol.

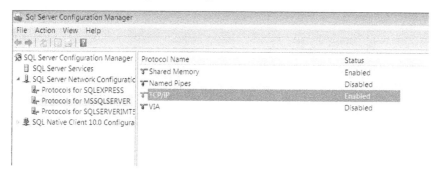

ix. On the right hand side, double click on the TCP/IP you want to enable and the dialogue below should appear.

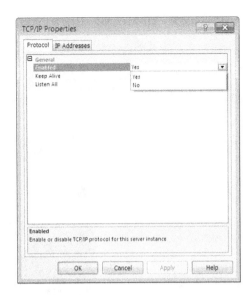

x. Enable TCP/IP by selecting Yes if No is selected on the Enabled dropdown list box.

xi. Finally, click OK and restart the Server and the remote connection would have been fixed.

CHAPTER THREE

DOs AND DON' Ts IN DATABASE PROGRAMMING

Software development is not just a practical discipline performed by coders, but also an area of academic research and theory which are done serious minded and logical reasoning developers. There is now a great body of knowledge concerning software development, and lengthy academic papers have been written to propose, dissect, and discuss different approaches to software development. Various methodologies have emerged, which includes *test-driven development* (TDD), *agile and extreme programming* (XP), and *defensive programming*, and there have been countless arguments concerning the benefits afforded by each of these schools of thought; by many scholars.

The practices described in this chapter, and the approach taken throughout the rest of this book, are most closely aligned with the philosophy of defensive programming because database is the backbone of software and should be guided against any error should in case the software fails. However, the topics discussed here can be applied just as readily in any environment. While software theorists may argue the finer differences between different methodologies (and undoubtedly, they do differ in some respects), when it comes down to it, the underlying features of good programming remains on the logical flow of the codes and mainly on the methodology you apply.

I do not intend to provide an exhaustive, objective guide as to what constitutes best practice, but rather to highlight some of the standards that I believe demonstrate the level of professionalism that database developers, students, lecturers and lovers of database development using codes, require in order to do a good job. I will present the justification of each argument with explained examples from a defensive point of view, but remember that they are generally equally valid in other programming environments; let us go.

3.1 Defensive Programming

Defensive programming is a methodology used in software development that suggests that developers should proactively anticipate and make allowances for (or "defend against") unforeseen future events (errors). The objective of defensive programming is to create applications that can remain robust, durable and effective, even when faced with unexpected situations.

Defensive programming essentially involves taking a pessimistic view of the world, thus, assuming that something can go wrong and it will; though it may not be always. We can expect network resources to become unavailable halfway through a transaction; required files can be absent or corrupt; users can input data in any number of ways different from that expected, power can fail midway to completion of transaction, and so on. Rather than leave anything to chance or to the fate of the users of the application, a defensive programmer will have predicted the possibility of these eventualities, and would have written appropriate handling code to check for and deal with these situations. This means that prospective error conditions can be detected and handled before an actual error occurs.

In many cases, it may be possible to identify and isolate a particular component responsible for a failure, allowing the rest of the application to continue functioning depending on how important the transaction may be. There is no definitive list of defensive programming practices or guides, but adopting a defensive stance to development is generally agreed to include the following principles:

- **Keep things simple (or KISS—keep it simple, stupid).** Applications are not made powerful and effective by their complexity, but by their elegant simplicity. Complexity allows bugs to be concealed, and should be avoided in both application design and in coding practice itself because it makes debugging almost impossible.

- **Be challenging, thorough, and cautious at all stages in development.** "What if?" analyses should be conducted in order to identify possible exceptional scenarios that might occur during normal (and abnormal) application usage.

- **Extensive code reviews and testing**. Should be conducted with different peer groups, including other developers or technical teams, consultants, end users, and management, whence the need for teamwork and prototype in software development. Each of these different groups may have different implicit assumptions that might not be considered by a closed development team.

- **Assumptions should be avoided wherever possible.** If an application requires a certain condition to be true in order to function correctly, there should be an explicit assertion to this effect, and relevant code paths should be inserted to check and act accordingly based on the result.

- **Applications** should be built from short, highly cohesive, loosely coupled modules. Modules that are well encapsulated in this way can be thoroughly tested in isolation, and then confidently reused throughout the application. Reusing specific code modules, rather than duplicating functionality, reduces the chances of introducing new bugs.

- **"If it isn't broke, fix it anyway."** Rather than waiting for things to break, defensive programming encourages continuous, proactive testing and future-proofing of an application against possible breaking changes in the future. Finally, patience and the versatile knowledge of the coding syntax and semantics plays, great role to successful defensive programming; because lengthy code are involved and at the same time simplicity with accuracy are maintained.

In a nutshell, defensive programming practices aim to improve the resilience and reliability of software applications when faced with unforeseen circumstances. Given the typical expected lifespan of database applications and the potential severity of the consequences should a bug occur, it makes sense to adopt a defensive approach to ensure that the applications remain robust over a long period of time, and that the need for on-going maintenance is kept to a minimum. Throughout the remainder of this chapter, I will be providing simple examples in SQL database programming what I believe to be best practices of database development; demonstrating each of these principles, and these concepts itemized below will be continually re-examined in later chapters of this book.

3.2   Advantages and Disadvantages of Defensive Programming

Irrespective of how good anything is, it must be criticized by others either constructively or destructively. Let us see what the advantages are and disadvantage.

3.2.1 Advantages

- Defensive applications are typically robust but stable, require fewer essential bug fixes, and are more resilient to situations that may otherwise lead to expensive failures or crashes. As a result, they have a long expected lifespan, and relatively cheap on-going maintenance costs.
- In many cases, defensive programming can lead to an improved user experience. By actively foreseeing and allowing for exceptional circumstances, errors can be caught *before* they occur, rather than having to be handled afterward. Exceptions can be isolated and handled with a minimum negative effect on user experience, rather than propagating an entire system failure. Even in the case of extreme unexpected conditions

being encountered, the system can still degrade gracefully and act according to documented behaviour.

3.2.2 Disadvantages

i. *Defensive code takes longer to develop.*

It is certainly true that following a defensive methodology can result in a longer up-front development time when compared to applications developed following other software practices. Defensive programming places a strong emphasis on the initial requirements-gathering and architecture design phases, which may be longer and more involved than in some methodologies. Coding itself takes longer because additional code paths may need to be added to handle checks and assertions of assumptions. Code must be subjected to an extensive review that is both challenging and thorough, and then must undergo rigorous testing. All these factors contribute to the fact that the overall development and release cycle for defensive software is longer than in other approaches.

There is a particularly stark contrast between defensive programming and so-called "agile" development practices, which focus on releasing frequent iterative changes on a much accelerated development and release cycle. However, this does not necessarily mean that defensive code takes longer to develop when considered over the full life cycle of an application. The additional care and caution invested in code at the initial stages of development are typically paid back over the life of the project, because there is less need for code fixes to be deployed once the project has gone live, it's better to be late than to be the late.

ii. *Writing code that anticipates and handles every possible scenario makes defensive applications bloated.*

Code bloat suggests that an application contains unnecessary, inefficient, or wasteful code. Defensive code protects against events that may be unlikely to happen, but that certainly doesn't mean that they can't happen. Taking actions to explicitly test for and handle exceptional circumstances up front can save lots of hours spent possibly tracing and debugging in the future. Defensive applications may contain more total lines of code than other applications, but all of that code should be well designed, with a clear purpose. Note that the label of "defensive programming" is sometimes misused: the addition of unnecessary checks at every opportunity without consideration or justification is *not* defensive programming. Such actions lead to code that is both complex and rigid. Remember that true defensive programming promotes simplicity, modularization, and code reuse, which actually reduces code bloat.

iii.   *Defensive programming hides bugs that then go unfixed, rather than making them visible.*

This is perhaps the most common misconception applied to defensive practices, which manifests from a failure to understand the fundamental attitude toward errors in defensive applications. By explicitly identifying and checking exceptional scenarios, defensive programming actually takes a very proactive approach to the identification of errors. However, having encountered a condition that could lead to an exceptional circumstance, defensive applications are designed to fail gracefully—that is, at the point of development, potential scenarios that may lead to exceptions are identified and code paths are created to handle them. To demonstrate this in practical terms, consider the following code listing, which describes a simple stored procedure to divide one number by another:

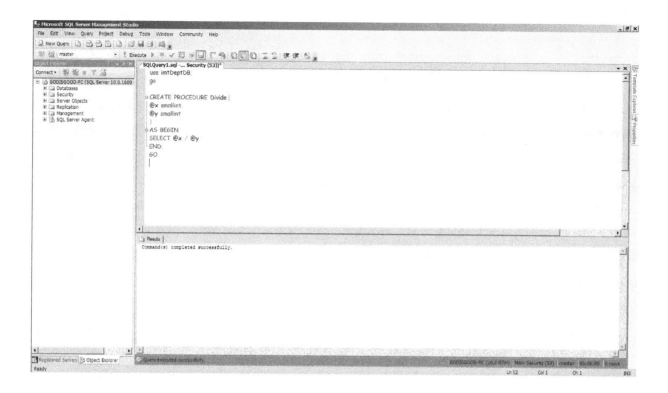

Based on the code as written previously, it would be very easy to cause an exception using this procedure if, for example, the supplied value of @y was 0. If you were simply trying to prevent the error message from occurring, it would be possible to consume (or "swallow") the exception in a catch block, as follows:

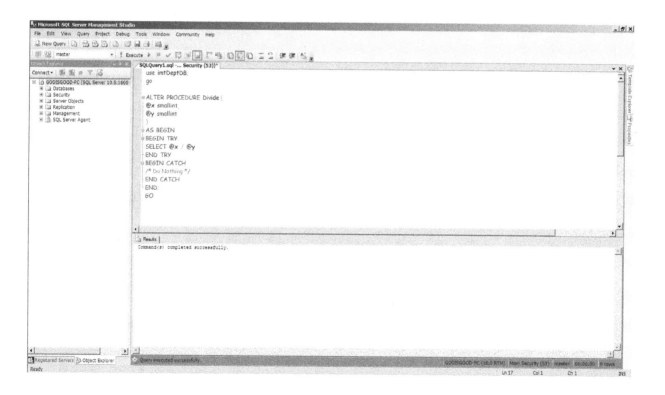

However, it is important to realize that the preceding code listing is *not* defensive—it does nothing to prevent the exceptional circumstance from occurring, and its only effect is to allow the system to continue operating, pretending that nothing bad has happened. **Exception hiding** such as this can be very dangerous, and makes it almost impossible to ensure the correct functioning of an application. The defensive approach would be, before attempting to perform the division, to explicitly check that all the requirements for that operation to be successful are met. This means asserting such things as making sure that values for @x and @y are supplied (i.e., they are not NULL), that @y is not equal to zero, that the supplied values lie within the range that can be stored within the small integer datatype, and so on.

The following code listing provides a simplified defensive approach to this same procedure:

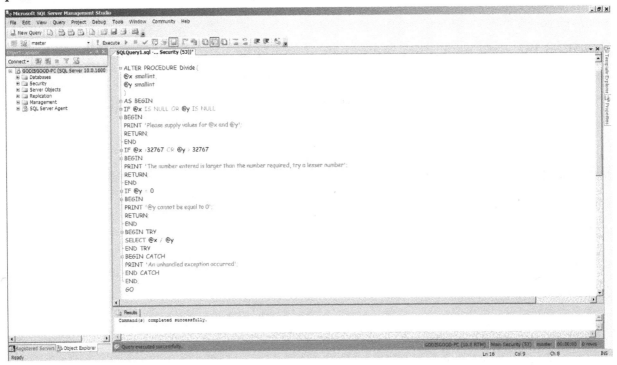

For the purposes of the preceding example, each assertion was accompanied by a simple PRINT statement to advise which of the conditions necessary for the procedure to execute failed. In real life, these code paths may handle such assertions in a number of ways—typically logging the error, reporting a message to the user, and attempting to continue system operation if it is possible to do so. In doing so, they prevent the kind of unpredictable behaviour associated with an exception that has not been expected.

Defensive programming can be contrasted to the **fail fast** methodology, which focuses on immediate recognition of any errors encountered by causing the application to halt whenever an exception occurs. Just because the defensive approach doesn't espouse ringing alarm bells and flashing lights doesn't mean that it hides errors—it just reports them more elegantly to the end user and, if possible, continues operation of the core part of the system.

3.3   Why Use a Defensive Approach to Database Development?

As stated previously, defensive programming is not the only software development methodology that can be applied to database development. Other common approaches include TDD, XP, and fail-fast development. So why have I chosen to focus on just defensive programming in this chapter, and throughout this book in general? I believe that defensive programming is the most appropriate approach for database development because of the following reasons:

i.   **Database applications tend to have a longer expected lifespan than other software applications**. Although it may be an overused stereotype to suggest that database professionals are the sensible, fastidious people of the software development world, the fact is that database development tends to be more slow-moving and cautious than other technologies. Web applications, for example, may be revised and re-launched on a nearly annual basis, in order to take advantage of whatever technology is current at the time. In contrast, database development tends to be slow and steady, and a database application may remain current for many years without any need for updating from a technological point of view. As a result, it is easier to justify the greater up-front development cost associated with defensive programming. The benefits of reliability and bug resistance will typically be enjoyed for a longer period.

ii.   **Users (and management) are less tolerant of bugs in database applications**. Most end users have come to tolerate and even expect bugs in desktop and web software. While undoubtedly a cause of frustration, many people are routinely in the habit of hitting Ctrl+Alt+Delete to reset their machine when a web browser hangs, or because some application fails to shut down correctly. However, the same tolerance that is shown to personal desktop software is not typically extended to corporate database applications. Recent highly publicized scandals in which bugs have been exploited in the systems of several governments and large organizations have further heightened the general public's ultra-sensitivity toward anything that might present a risk to database integrity.

iii. **Any bugs that do exist in database applications can have more severe consequences than in other software**. It can be argued that people are absolutely right to be more worried about database bugs than bugs in other software. An unexpected error in a desktop application may lead to a document or file becoming corrupt, which is a nuisance and might lead to unnecessary rework. But an unexpected error in a database may lead to important personal, confidential, or sensitive data being placed at risk, which can have rather more serious consequences. The nature of data typically stored in a database warrants a cautious, thorough approach to development, such as defensive programming provides. Think of the damages that an incomplete transaction that is not well handled with rollback transaction will cause to customers if a million naira transaction failed on the process of trying to dispense cash.

iv.   **Designing for longevity.** Consumer software applications have an increasingly short expected shelf life, with compressed release cycles pushing out one release barely before the predecessor has hit the shelves. However, this does not have to be the case in a well-designed, defensively programmed application because it can continue to operate for many years.

3.4   Dos and Don' ts in SQL Coding Technique

Having looked at some of the theory behind different software methodologies, and in particular the defensive approach to programming, you are now probably wondering about how to put this into practice. As I stated earlier, programming is all about the logical flow of the codes and not necessarily the methodology, defensive programming is more concerned with the mind-set with which you should approach development than prescribing a definitive set of rules to follow. As a result, this section will only provide examples that illustrate the overall concepts involved, and should not be treated as an exhaustive list. I will try to keep the actual examples as simple as possible in every case, so that you can concentrate on the reasons I consider these to be best way to do your codding, rather than the code itself.

3.4.1   Dos in SQL Coding Technique

i.   Identify Hidden Assumptions in Your Code

One of the core tenets of defensive programming is to identify all of the assumptions that lie behind the proper functioning of your code. Once these assumptions have been identified, the function can either be adjusted to remove the dependency on them, or explicitly test each condition and make provisions should it not hold true. In some cases, "hidden" assumptions exist as a result of code failing to be sufficiently explicit.

To demonstrate this concept, consider the following code listing, which creates and populates a Customers and an Orders table:

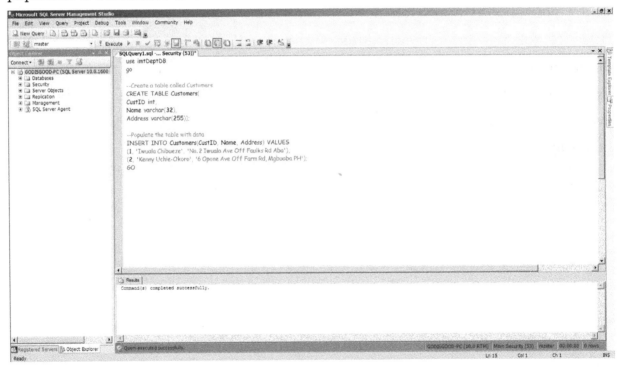

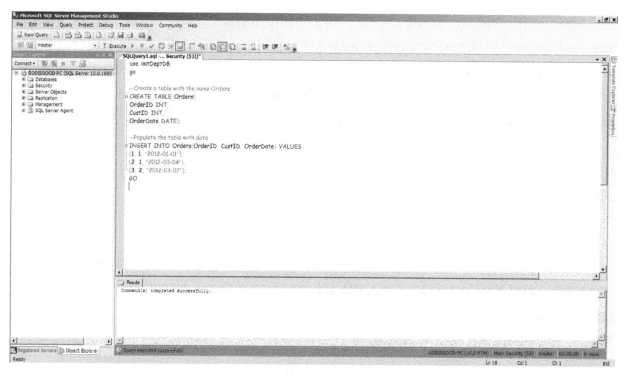

Now consider the following query to select a list of every customer order, which uses columns from both tables:

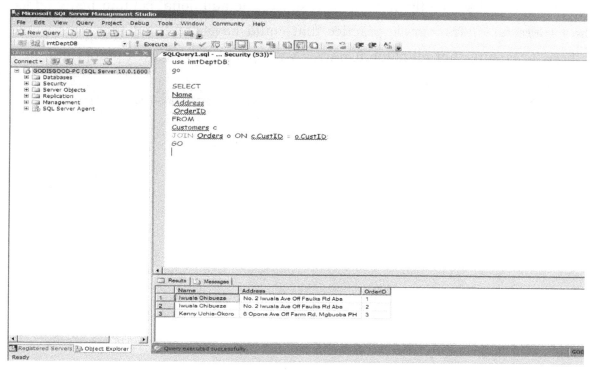

The query executes successfully and we get the results expected:

But what is the hidden assumption? The column names listed in the SELECT query were not qualified with table names, so what would happen if the table structure were to change in the future? Suppose that an Address column were added to the Orders table to enable a separate delivery address to be attached to each order, rather than relying on the address in the Customers table:

```
ALTER TABLE Orders ADD Address varchar(255);
GO
```

The unqualified column name, Address, specified in the SELECT query, is now ambiguous because the interpreter will be confused because Address appears in the two tables, and if we attempt to run the original query again we will receive an error:

Msg 209, Level 16, State 1, Line 1

Ambiguous column name 'Address'.

By not recognizing and correcting the hidden assumption contained in the original code, the query subsequently broke as a result of the additional column being added to the Orders table. The simple practice that could have prevented this error would have been to ensure that all column names were prefixed with the appropriate table name or alias:

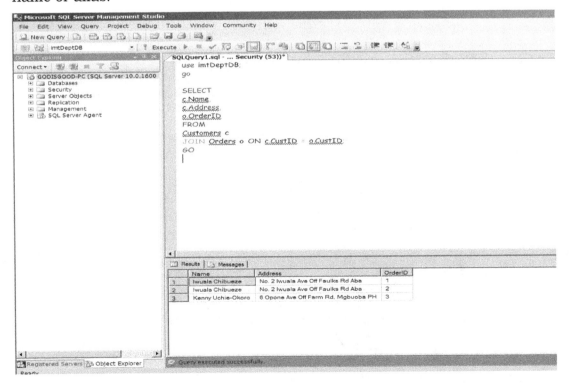

ii.   Don't Take Shortcuts is risky

It is human nature to want to take shortcuts if we believe that they will allow us to avoid work that we feel is unnecessary. In programming terms, there are often shortcuts that provide a convenient, concise way of achieving a given task in fewer lines of code than other, more standard methods. However, these shortcut methods can come with associated risks. Most commonly, shortcut methods require less code because they rely on some assumed default values rather than those explicitly stated within the procedure. As such, they can only be applied in situations where the conditions imposed by those default values holds true.

By relying on a default value, shortcut methods may increase the rigidity of your code and also introduce an external dependency—the default value may vary depending on server configuration, or change between different versions of SQL Server. Taking shortcuts therefore reduces the portability of code, and introduces assumptions that can break in the future. For instance, consider what happens when you CAST a value to a varchar datatype without explicitly declaring the appropriate data length:

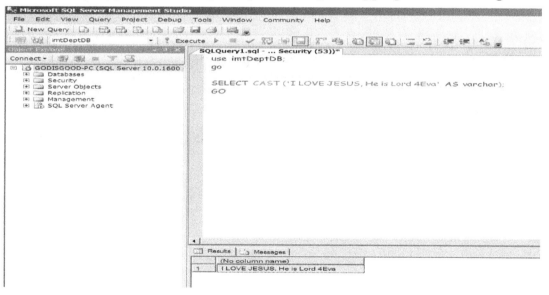

The query appears to work correctly, and output displayed.

It seems to be a common misunderstanding among some developers that omitting the length for the varchar type as the target of a CAST operation results in SQL Server dynamically assigning a length sufficient to accommodate all of the characters of the input. However, this is not the case, as demonstrated in the following code listing:

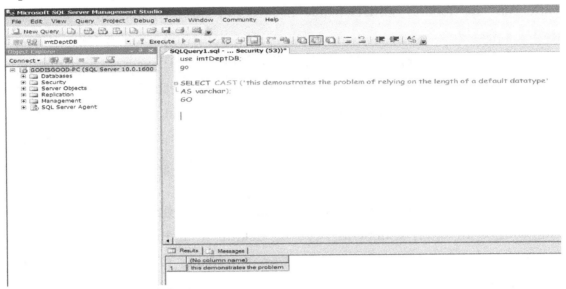

The query executed correctly and output displayed but the characters where cut.

If not explicitly specified, when CASTing to a character datatype, SQL Server defaults to a length of 30 characters. In the second example, the input string is silently truncated to 30 characters, even though there is no obvious indication in the code to this effect. If this was the intention, it would have been much clearer to explicitly state varchar(30) to draw attention to the fact that this was a planned truncation, rather than simply omitting the data length.

Another example of a shortcut sometimes made is to rely on implicit CASTs between datatypes. Consider the following code listing:

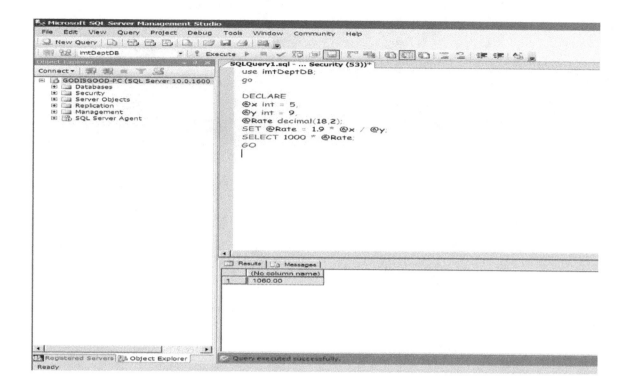

In this example, @Rate is a multiplicative factor whose value is determined by the ratio of two parameters, @x and @y, multiplied by a hard-coded scale factor of 1.9. When applied to the value 1000, as in this example, the result is as follows:

1060

Now let's suppose that management makes a decision to change the calculation used to determine @Rate, and increases the scale factor from 1.9 to 2. The obvious (but incorrect) solution would be to amend the code as follows:

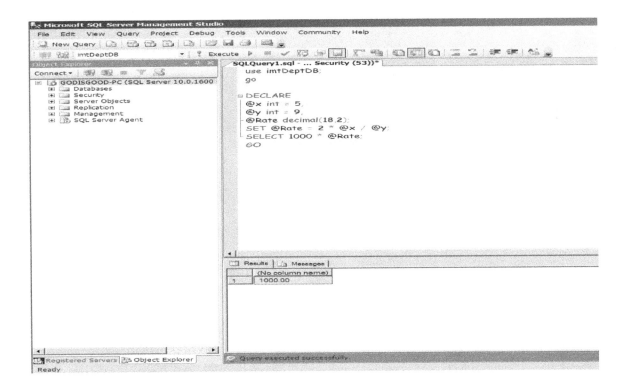

Rather than increasing the rate as intended, the change has actually negated the effect of applying any rate to the supplied value of 1000. The problem now is that the sum used to determine @Rate is a purely integer calculation, 2 * 5 / 9. In integer mathematics, this equates to 1. In the previous example, the hard-coded value of 1.9 caused an implicit cast of both @x and @y parameters to the decimal type, so the sum was calculated with decimal precision.

This example may seem trivial when considered in isolation, but can be a source of unexpected behaviour and unnecessary bug-chasing when nested deep in the belly of some complex codes. To avoid these complications, it is always best to explicitly state the type and precision of any parameters used in a calculation, and avoid implicit CASTs between them.

Another problem with using shortcuts is that they can obscure what the developer intended the purpose of the code to be. If we cannot tell what a line of code is *meant* to do, it is incredibly hard to test whether it is achieving its purpose or not. Consider the following code listing:

```
DECLARE @Date datetime = '03/05/1979';
SELECT @Date + 365;
```

At first sight, this seems fairly innocuous: take a specific date and add 365. But there are actually several shortcuts used here that add ambiguity as to what the intended purpose of this code is:

The first shortcut is in the implicit CAST from the string value '03/05/1979' to a datetime. As I'm sure you know, there are numerous ways of presenting date formats around the world, and 03/05/1979 is ambiguous. In the United Kingdom it means the 3rd of May, but to American readers it means the 5th of March. The result of the implicit cast will depend upon the locale of the server on which the function is performed.

Even if the dd/mm/yyyy or mm/dd/yyyy ordering is resolved, there is still ambiguity regarding the input value. The datatype chosen is datetime, which stores both a date and time component, but the value assigned to @Date does not specify a time, so this code relies on SQL Server's default value of midnight: 00:00:00. However, perhaps it was not the developer's intention to specify an instance in time, but rather the whole of a calendar day. If so, should the original @Date parameter be specified using the date datatype instead? And what about the result of the SELECT query—should that also be a date?

Finally, the code specifies the addition of the integer 365 with a datetime value. When applied to a date value, the + operator adds the given number of days, so this appears to be a shortcut in place of using the DATEADD method to add 365 days. But, is *this* a shortcut to adding 1 year? If so, this is another example of a shortcut that relies on an assumption—in this case, that the year in question has 365 days.

The combination of these factors has meant that it is unclear whether the true intention of this simple line of code is

```
SELECT DATEADD(DAY, 365, '1979-03-05');
```
which leads to the following result:
```
1980-03-04 00:00:00.000
```
or whether the code is a shortcut for the following:
```
SELECT CAST(DATEADD(YEAR, 1, '1979-05-03') AS date);
```
which would lead to a rather different output:

Perhaps the most well-known example of a shortcut method is the use of SELECT * in order to retrieve every column of data from a table, rather than listing the individual columns by name. As in the first example of this chapter, the risk here is that any change to the table structure in the future will lead to the structure of the result set returned by this query *silently* changing. At best, this may result in columns of data being retrieved that are then never used, leading to inefficiency. There are many other reasons why SELECT * should be avoided, such as the addition of unnecessary rows to the query precluding the use of covering indexes, which may lead to a substantial degradation in query performance.

iii.   Testing

Defensive practice places a very strong emphasis on the importance of testing and code review throughout the development process. In order to defend against situations that might occur in a live production environment, an application should be tested under the same conditions that it will experience in the real world. In fact, defensive programming suggests that you should test under extreme conditions (**stress testing**)—if you can make a robust, preformat application that can cope with severe pressure, then you can be more certain it will cope with the normal demands that will be expected of it. In addition to performance testing, there are functional tests and unit tests to consider, which ensure that every part of the application is behaving as expected according to its contract, and performing the correct function.

When testing an application, it is important to consider the sample data on which tests will be based. You should not artificially cleanse the data on which you will be testing your code, or rely on artificially generated data. If the application is expected to perform against production data, then it should be tested against a fair representation of that data, warts and all. Doing so will ensure that the application can cope with the sorts of imperfect data typically found in all applications—missing or incomplete values, incorrectly formatted strings, NULLs, and so on. Random sampling methods can be used to ensure that the test data represents a fair sample of the overall data set, but it is also important for defensive testing to ensure that applications are tested against extreme edge cases, as it is these unusual conditions that may otherwise lead to exceptions.

Even if test data is created to ensure a statistically fair representation of real-world data, and is carefully chosen to include edge cases, there are still inherent issues about how defensively guaranteed an application can be when only tested on a relatively small volume of test data. Some exceptional circumstances only arise in a full-scale environment. Performance implications are an obvious example: if you only conduct performance tests on the basis of a couple of thousand rows of data, then don't be surprised when the application fails to perform against millions of rows in the live environment (you will be amazed at the number of times With careful query design and well-tuned indexes, some applications may scale very well against large data sets. The performance of other applications, however, may degrade exponentially (such as when working with Cartesian products created from CROSS JOINs between tables). Defensive testing should be conducted with consideration not only of the volumes of data against which the application is expected to use now, but also by factoring in an allowance for expected future growth.

iv.   Code Review

Whereas testing is generally an automated process, code review is a human-led activity that involves peer groups manually reviewing the code behind an application. The two activities of automated testing and human code review are complementary and can detect different areas for code improvement. While automated test suites can very easily check whether routines are producing the correct output in a given number of test scenarios, it is very difficult for them to conclusively state that a routine is coded in the most robust or efficient way, that correct logic is being applied, or the coding standards followed best practice. In these cases, code review is a more effective approach.

Consider the following code listing, which demonstrates a T-SQL function used to test whether a given e-mail address is valid:

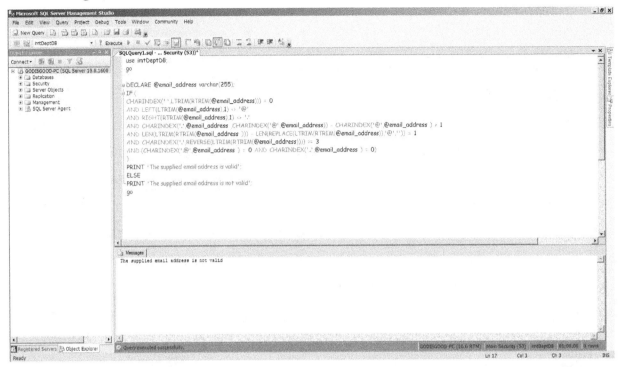

This code might well pass functional tests to suggest that, based on a set of test email addresses provided, the function correctly identifies whether the format of a supplied e-mail address is valid. However, during a code review, an experienced developer could look at this code and point out that it could be much better implemented as a user-defined function using the regular expression methods provided by the .NET Base Class Library, such as shown here:

```
SELECT dbo.RegExMatch('\b[A-Z0-9._%+-]+@[A-Z0-9.-]+\.[A-Z]{2,4}\b',
@email_address);
```

Note that this example assumes that you have registered a function called RegExMatch that implements the Match method of the .NET System.Text.RegularExpressions.Regex class. While both methods achieve the same end result, rewriting the code in this way creates a routine that is more efficient and maintainable, and also promotes reusability, since the suggested RegExMatch function could be used to match regular expression patterns in other situations, such as checking whether a phone number is valid. Challenging and open code review has a significant effect on improving the quality of software code, but it can be a costly exercise, and the effort required to conduct a thorough code review across an entire application is not warranted in all situations. One of the advantages of well-encapsulated code is that those modules that are most likely to benefit from the exercise can be isolated and reviewed separately from the rest of the application.

v.   Validate All Input

Defensive programming suggests that you should never trust any external input—don't make assumptions about its type (e.g. alphabetic or numeric), its length, its content, or even its existence! These rules apply not just to user input sent from an application UI or web page, but also to any external file or web resource on which the application relies.

A good defensive stance is to assume that all input is invalid and may lead to exceptional circumstances unless proved otherwise, whence the need for validation. There are a number of techniques that can be used to ensure that input is valid and safe to use:

• Data can be "massaged." For example, bad characters can be replaced or escaped. However, there are some difficulties associated in identifying exactly what data needs to be treated, and knowing the best way in which to handle it. Silently modifying input affects data integrity and is generally not recommended unless it cannot be avoided.

- Data can be checked against a "blacklist" of potentially dangerous input and rejected if it is found to contain known bad items. For example, input should not be allowed to contain SQL keywords such as DELETE or DROP, or contain non-alphanumeric characters, because DELETE and DROP are just phrase and makes no sense, thus, can be replace with numbers; e.g. 1 = DELETE and 2 = DROP.
- Input can be accepted only if it consists solely of content specified by a "whitelist" of allowed content. From a UI point of view, you can consider this as equivalent to allowing users to only select values from a predefined drop-down list, rather than a free-text box. This is arguably the most secure method, but is also the most rigid, and is too restrictive to be used in many practical applications, though it depends on the type of input and the users supply the data.

All of these approaches are susceptible to flaws. For example, consider that you were using the ISNUMERIC() function to test whether user input only contained numeric values. You might expect the result of the following to reject the input:

```
DECLARE @Input varchar(32) = '10E2';
SELECT ISNUMERIC(@Input);
```

Most exceptions occur as the result of unforeseen but essentially benign circumstances. However, when dealing with user input, you should always be aware of the possibility of deliberate, malicious attacks that are targeted to exploit any weaknesses exposed in a system that has not been thoroughly defended. Perhaps the most widely known defensive programming techniques concern the prevention of **SQL injection** attacks. That is, when a user deliberately tries to insert and execute malicious code as part of user input supplied to an application.

SQL injection attacks typically take advantage of poorly implemented functions that construct and execute dynamic SQL-based on invalidated user input. Consider the following example:

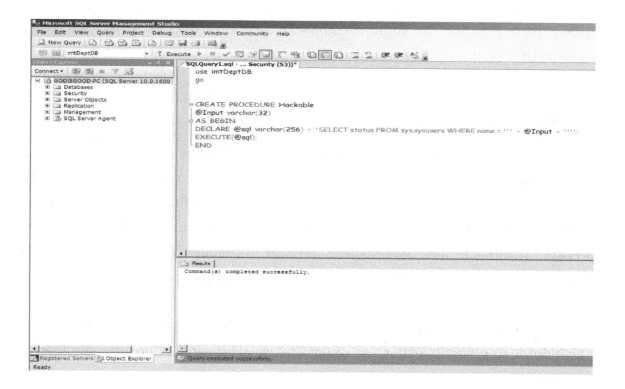

The intended purpose of this code is fairly straightforward—it returns the status of the user supplied in the parameter @Input. So, it could be used in the following way to find out the status of the user John:

EXEC **Hackable** 'chibyke';

GO

But what if, instead of entering the value John, the user entered the input 'public'' or 1=1 --', as follows?

EXEC Hackable @Input='public'' or 1=1 --';

GO

This would lead to the SQL statement generated as follows:

SELECT status FROM sys.sysusers WHERE name = 'public' OR 1 = 1;

The condition OR 1 = 1 appended to the end of the query will always evaluate to true, so the effect will be to make the query list every row in the sys.sysusers table.

Despite this being a simple and well-known weakness, it is still alarmingly common. Defending against such glaring security holes can easily be achieved, and various techniques for doing so are beyond the scope of this book; but it will be covered under the topic database encryption and security in the next edition of this book.

vi.   Future-proof Your Code

In order to prevent the risk of bugs appearing, it makes sense to ensure that any defensive code adheres to the latest standards. There are no ways to guarantee that code will remain resilient, but one habit that you should definitely adopt is to ensure that you rewrite any old code that relies on deprecated features, and do not use any deprecated features in new development in order to reduce the chances of exceptions occurring in the future. Deprecated features refer to features that, while still currently in use, have been superseded by alternative replacements. While they may still be available for use (to ensure backward compatibility), you should not develop applications using features that are known to be deprecated. Consider the following code listing:

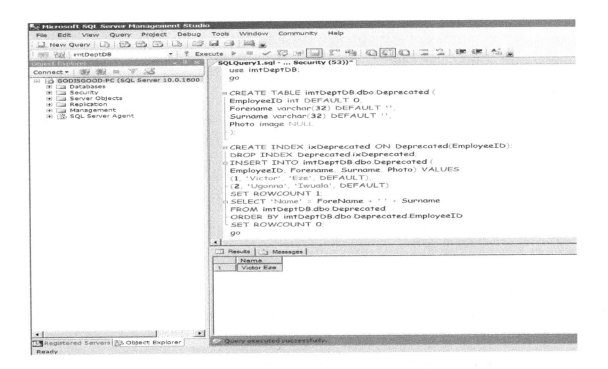

This query works as expected in SQL Server 2008, but makes use of a number of deprecated features, which should be avoided. Fortunately, spotting usage of deprecated features is easy—the sys.dm_os_performance_counters dynamic management view (DMV) maintains a count of every time a deprecated feature is used, and can be interrogated as follows:

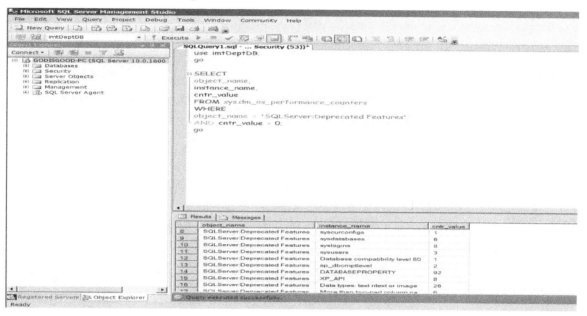

A related, although perhaps more serious, threat to defensive applications is code that relies on *undocumented* features. Many such features exist in SQL Server—the following code listing demonstrates the undocumented sp_MSForEachTable stored procedure, for example, which can be used to execute a supplied query against every table in a database.

While it is certain that deprecated features will be removed at some point in the future, that time scale is generally known, and there is usually a documented upgrade path to ensure that any functionality previously provided by features that are deprecated will be replaced by an alternative method. Undocumented features, in contrast, may break at any time without warning, and there may be no clear upgrade path. I strongly recommend that you avoid such risky practices.

vii.   Limit Your Exposure

If defensive programming is designed to ensure that an application can cope with the occurrence of exceptional events, one basic defensive technique is to limit the number of such events that can occur. It follows logically that exceptions can only occur in features that are running, so don't install more features than necessary—by reducing the application surface area, you limit your exposure to potential attacks. Don't grant EXTERNAL_ACCESS to an assembly when SAFE will do. Don't enable features such as database mail unless they add value or are strictly required by your application.

All users should be authenticated, and only authorized to access those resources that are required, for the period of time for which they are required. Unused accounts should be removed immediately, and unnecessary permissions revoked. Doing so reduces the chance of the system being compromised by an attack, and is discussed in more detail in Chapter 10.

viii.   Exercise Good Coding Etiquette

Good coding etiquette, by which I refer to practices such as clearly commented code, consistent layout, and well-named variables, should be considered as a vital part of *any* software development methodology not only in defensive programming methodology,. I have chosen to include it here, partly because I consider it so vital that it can never be restated too often, but also because the nature of defensive programming emphasizes these areas more than other approaches, for the following reasons:

As stated previously, the aim of defensive programming is to minimize the risk of errors occurring as a result of future unforeseen events (errors). Those future events may be construed to include future maintenance and enhancements made to the code. By creating clear, well-documented code now, you enhance its future understandability, reducing the chances that bugs will be accidentally introduced when it is next addressed.

Furthermore, since defensive programming aims as creating robust, resilient applications, these applications may continue running for a very long duration without any need for manual intervention. When they are next reviewed some years later, the development team responsible may be very different, or the original developers may no longer remember why a certain approach was taken. It is vitally important that this information be documented and clearly visible in the code itself, so that errors or new assumptions are not introduced that could damage the stability of the application.

Code that is well *laid* out often goes hand in hand with code that is well *thought* out. By undertaking such simple steps as indenting code blocks, for example, you can easily identify steps that lie within a loop, and those that are outside the loop, preventing careless mistakes. Most IDEs and code editors provide layout features that will automatically apply a consistent format for tabs, whitespace, capitalization, reserved-words and so on, and these settings can normally be customized to match whatever coding standards are in place in a given organization.

Well-laid-out, meaningfully commented code will make it easier for thorough code review. If the code needs to be revised, it will be much easier to quickly establish the best method to do so. Finally, if a bug is discovered in a section of code, it is much easier to track down within a well-coded function, and hence resolved with the minimum amount of disruption. For these reasons, I believe exercising good code etiquette to be a key part of defensive programming. You will find below, more specific aspects of coding etiquette.

ix.   Comments

Everybody knows that comments are an important part of any code, and yet few of us comment our code as well as we should (one reason commonly put forward is that developers prefer to *write* code rather than *writing about* code or that they don't want another person to borrow their coding techniques/logic). Almost every school of thought on best coding practice states that you should make liberal use of comments in code, and defensive programming is no different. Well-written comments make it easier to tell what a function is aiming to achieve and why it has been written a certain way, which by implication means that it is easier to spot any bugs or assumptions made that could break that code.

Good comments should give additional information to whoever is reading the code—not simply point out the obvious or restate information that could easily be found in Books Online. The following comment, for example, is not helpful:

```
-- Set x to 5
SET @x = 5;
```

In general, comments should explain why a certain approach has been taken and what the developer is aiming to achieve. Using comments to describe *expected* behaviour makes it much easier to identify cases of *unexpected* behaviour. In general it is not necessary to simply comment what a built-in function does, but there may be exceptions to this rule. For example, at a single glance, can you say what you expect the result of the following to be?

```
UPDATE yr1schema.GradetableRS SET RSGPA = (SELECT
CAST((((((dbo.gpaCal(GRS.gr1))* GRS.cu1+((dbo.gpaCal(GRS.gr2))*
GRS.cu2)+((dbo.gpaCal(GRS.gr3)) * GRS.cu3) +
+((dbo.gpaCal(GRS.gr5))* GRS.cu5)+((dbo.gpaCal(GRS.gr5))*
GRS.cu5)+((dbo.gpaCal(GRS.gr6)) * GRS.cu6)+((dbo.gpaCal(GRS.gr7))*
GRS.cu7)+((dbo.gpaCal(GRS.gr8))* GRS.cu8)))/CAST(GRS.TCU as decimal(5,3))) AS
DECIMAL(3,2))
```

```
FROM yr1schema.GradetableRS GRS where (GRS.RegNo =@RegNo)),yr1CGPA=(select
CAST(((GHS.HSGPA + GRS.RSGPA) /2) AS DECIMAL(3,2))
FROM yr1schema.GradetableRS GRS INNER JOIN yr1schema.GradetableHS GHS
ON GHS.REGNO = GRS.REGNO WHERE GRS.RegNo=@RegNo)
WHERE RegNo=@RegNo
```

Above is a procedure in an automated CGPA calculation and transcript processing application, where it was being used to determine those who have graduate and their final grade calculated. In case you haven't figured it out, the result gives you the CGPA of a student whose RegNo is supplied. The code actually fulfils its purpose, but without any comments it took me a while to recall what the purpose is.

In many cases, you can obviate the need for writing explicit comments by using *self-documenting* code—choosing well-named variables, column aliases, and table aliases.

x.   Indentations and Statement Blocks

Code indentations and liberal use of whitespace can help to identify logical blocks of code, loops, and batches, creating code that is understandable, easily maintained, and less likely to have bugs introduced in the future. However, these practices clearly have no direct effect on the execution of the code itself. It is therefore worthy to note, that the visual layout of code reinforces its logical behaviour, as poorly presented code may actually be misleading. Consider the following example:

```
IF 1 = 1
PRINT 'True';
ELSE
PRINT 'False';
PRINT 'Then Print this';
```

In this case, the indentation on the final line of code makes it appear to be part of the ELSE clause, but this is not the case, and the result Then Print this will be printed irrespective of the result of the test.

To avoid such misleading situations, I always recommend the liberal use of statement blocks marked by BEGIN and END, even if a block contains only one statement, as follows:

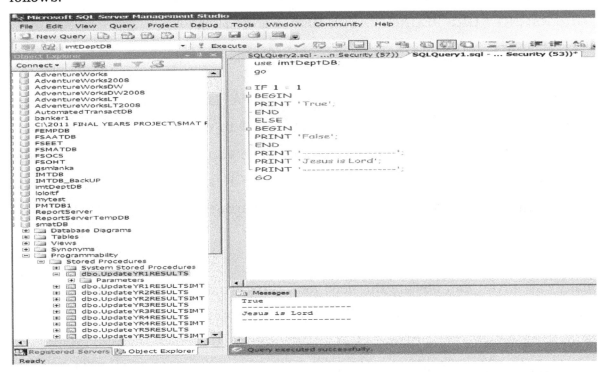

Another misleading practice that can easily be avoided is the failure to use parentheses to explicitly demonstrate the order in which the components of a query are resolved. Consider the following code listing:

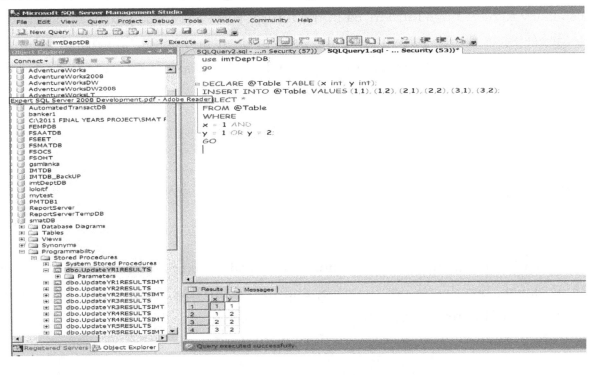

In this case, as before, the code indentation actually detracts from the true logic of the code, which is to select all rows where x=1 AND y=1, or where y=2.

xi.   If All Else Fails.

A fundamental feature of defensive programming is to make assertions to ensure that exceptional circumstances do not occur. It can be argued that, if the ideal of defensive programming were ever truly realized, it would not be necessary to implement exception-handling code, since any potential scenarios that could lead to exceptions would have been identified and handled before they were allowed to occur. Unfortunately, it is not practically possible to explicitly test all exceptional scenarios and, in the real-world, exception and error handling remain very important parts of any software application. For a detailed discussion of exception and error handling in SQL Server, please refer to Chapter 8.

xii.   Question Authority

The final strategy is the most important because it breaks you out of the defensive programming mindset and lets you transition into the creative mindset. Defensive programming is authoritarian and it can be cruel. The job of this mindset is to make you follow rules because without them you will miss something or get distracted. This authoritarian attitude has the disadvantage of disabling independent creative thought. Rules are necessary for getting things done, but being a slave to them will kill your creativity.

This final strategy means you should question the rules you follow periodically and assume that they could be wrong, just like the software you are reviewing. What I will typically do is, after a session of defensive programming, I will go take a non-programming break and let the rules go. Then I will be ready to do some creative work or do more defensive coding if need to.

xiii.   Creating a Healthy Development Environment

The best applications are not created by the individual brilliance of one or two coders, but by the coordinated, effective collaboration of a development team; though it appears to be different in less developed countries where peanut are paid to programmers. Successful defensive development is most likely to occur when coding is a shared, open activity.

The benefits of collaborative coding are that you can draw on a shared pool of technical knowledge and resources to ensure that coding is thorough and accurate. Different people will be able to critically examine code from a number of different points of view, which helps to identify any assumptions that might have gone unnoticed by a single developer.

If developers work in isolation, they may introduce dependencies that present a risk to the future maintainability of the code. If only one developer knows the intricacies of a particularly complex section of code and then that developer leaves or is unavailable, then is possible you may encounter difficulties maintaining that code in the future. In fact, individual competiveness between developers can lead to developers *deliberately* adding complexity to an application. Coders may seek to ensure that only they understand how a particular section of complex code works, either as a way of flaunting their technical knowledge, for reasons of personal pride, or as a way of creating a dependence on them—making themselves indispensable and ensuring their future job security. All of these create an unhealthy development environment and are likely to negatively affect the quality of any code produced.

Managers responsible for development teams should try to foster an environment of continued professional development, in which shared learning and best practice are the key. Software development is a constantly changing area—what is considered best practice now may well be obsolete within a few years. In order to make sure that applications remain cutting edge, individual training of developers and knowledge-sharing between peers should be promoted and encouraged. The success (or otherwise) of attempts to implement defensive development may also be influenced by wider corporate decisions, including reward systems. For example, a company may implement a reward scheme that pays individual bonuses for any developer that discovers and solves bugs in live applications. Although presumably designed to improve software quality, the effect may actually be completely the opposite—after all, what is the incentive to code defensively (preventing errors before they occur) when it removes the opportunity for a developer to allow bugs through and personally receive the reward for fixing them later? Such policies are likely to encourage competitive, individualistic behaviour where developers only look after themselves, instead of taking actions based on the best interests of the project.

Another factor affecting the success of defensive development concerns the way in which budget and project deadlines are managed. Penalties are normally incurred for delivering software projects after deadline. It is an unfortunate fact that, when deadlines are brought forward or budgets slashed, it is defensive practices (such as rigorous testing) that management regard as nonessential, and are among the first to be dropped from the scope of the project. Managers that demand quick-fix solutions based on unrealistic short-term time scales are likely to encourage piecemeal coding practices that create holes. These are unlikely to use defensive programming and will not stand up to rigorous testing. Software development must be crafted with patience and care, yet management demands often necessitate that shortcuts must be taken, and rarely can truly defensive programming projects be seen to completion. For these reasons, true defensive programming might be seen as an ideal, rather than an achievable objective.

CHAPTER FOUR

DATABASE CREATION

A database is primarily a group of computer files that each has a name and a location. Just as there are different ways to connect to a server, in the same way, there are different ways to create a database. To create a new database in Microsoft SQL Server Management Studio, in the Object Explorer, you can right-click the Databases node and click New Database. This would open the New Database dialog box.

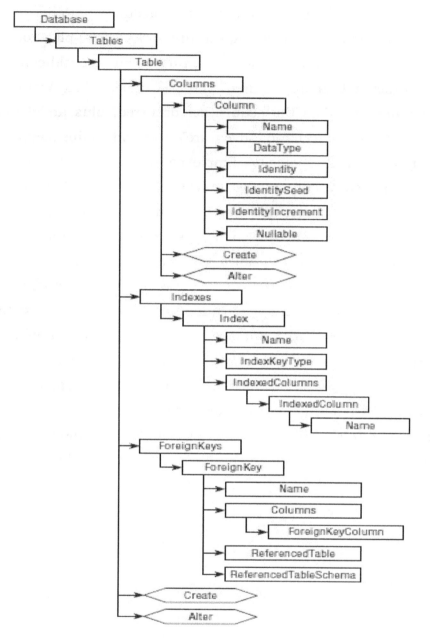

Fig 4.1 Hierarchy of database tables

After the table and columns have been defined, the next step is to define an index and set its IndexKeyType property to indicate the index is a primary key. (Without a primary key, a foreign key to the table can't be defined.) The last step is to create a clustered index on one table to improve query performance against that table. Finally, the Create method is used to create the table.

In our example scenario, AdventureWorks has acquired another company. Their employees are being merged into the AdventureWorks HR application, but key data items need to be maintained for the short term based on their old company's records. To this end, two new tables are required. The first table, called AcquisitionCompany, will hold the name and date the acquisition occurred, plus an identity-based key called CompanyID. (In this scenario, AdventureWorks will do this again.)

The second table, called AcquisitionEmployee, contains the employee's original employee ID, original start date, number of hours available for time off this year, plus a column that indicates whether this employee earned a kind of reward called a Star Employee. The AcquisitionEmployee table also needs a column to reference the AcquisitionCompany table. These tables will be created in the HumanResources schema. After creating the tables, the next step is to add foreign key references from AcquisitionEmployee to both the AcquisitionCompany and the existing Employee tables. Because AdventureWorks management likes the Star Employee idea, that column will be added to the existing Employee table but will be kept separate from the StarEmployee column in the AcquisitionEmployee table because the criteria are different. Once the tables are created, the required foreign keys to the AcquisitionEmployee table can be added by creating a ForeignKey object, defining the ForeignKey columns, and adding them to the ForeignKey object and defining the referenced table and schema.

4.1   DATABASE OBJECTS

The database is all about objects, and the arrangement of these objects brings about the SQL server. The image below has more to explain about the hierarchy and arrangement of these objects.

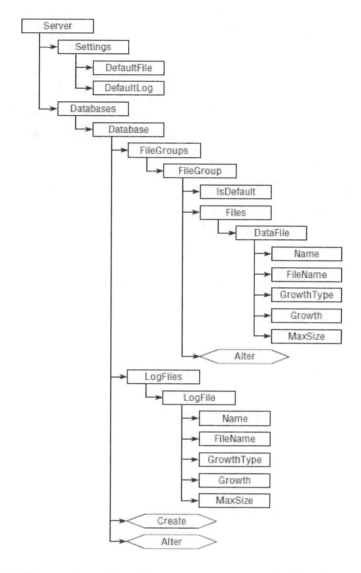

Fig 4.2 Hierarchy of database arrangement in the SQL server

SQL Server requires that a database have a PRIMARY filegroup and that the system tables (the database meta-data) reside in that filegroup. It is recommended that you keep your application data out of the PRIMARY filegroup, both from a manageability perspective and a performance perspective. When creating a database using SQL Server Management Studio (SSMS), it can be tedious to create a database with the desired size and file location and with a separate, default filegroup to hold the application data. This is a relatively simple process using SMO.

4.1.1 Naming the database

Probably the most important requirement of creating a database is to give it a name. The SQL is very flexible when it comes to names. In fact, it is very less restrictive than most other computer languages. Still, there are rules you must follow when naming the objects in your databases:

- A name can start with either a letter (a, b, c, d, e, f, g, h, i, j, k, l, m, n, o, p, q, r, s, t, u, v, w, x, y, z, A, B, C, D, E, F, G, H, I, J, K, L, M, N, O, P, Q, R, S, T, U, V, W, X, Y, or Z), a digit (0, 1, 2, 3, 4, 5, 6, 7, 8, or 9), an underscore (_) or a non-readable character. Examples are **_n**, **act**, **%783**, **Second**
- After the first character (letter, digit, underscore, or symbol), the name can have combinations of underscores, letters, digits, or symbols. Examples are **_n24** or **act_52_t**
- A name can include spaces. Example are **cOuntries st@ts**, **govmnt (records)**, or **gl0b# $urvey||**

Because of the flexibility of SQL, it can be difficult to maintain names in a database. Based on this, there are conventions we will use for our objects. In fact, we will adopt the rules used in C/C++, C#, Pascal, Java, and Visual Basic, etc. In our databases:

- Unless stated otherwise (we will mention the exceptions, for example with variables, tables, etc), a name will start with either a letter (a, b, c, d, e, f, g, h, i, j, k, l, m, n, o, p, q, r, s, t, u, v, w, x, y, z, A, B, C, D, E, F, G, H, I, J, K, L, M, N, O, P, Q, R, S, T, U, V, W, X, Y, or Z) or an underscore
- After the first character, we will use any combination of letters, digits, or underscores
- A name will not start with two underscores
- If the name is a combination of words, at least the second word will start in uppercase. Examples are **Countries Statistics**, **Global Survey**, **_RealSport**, **FullName**, or **DriversLicenseNumber**

- *database_name* can be a maximum of 128 characters, unless a logical name is not specified for the log file. If a logical log file name is not specified, SQL Server generates the *logical_file_name* and the *os_file_name* for the log by appending a suffix to *database_name*. This limits *database_name* to 123 characters so that the generated logical file name is no more than 128 characters.

- If data file name is not specified, SQL Server uses *database_name* as both the *logical_file_name* and as the *os_file_name*.

After creating an object whose name includes space, whenever you use that object, include its name between [and]. Examples are **[Countries Statistics]**, **[Global Survey]**, or **[Date of Birth]**. Even if you had created an object with a name that doesn't include space, when using that name, you can still include it in square brackets. Examples are **[UnitedStations]**, **[FullName]**, **[DriversLicenseNumber]**, and **[Country]**.

4.2 Starting SQL Server Management Studio

i.   Locate the SQL Server Management Studio on All Programs

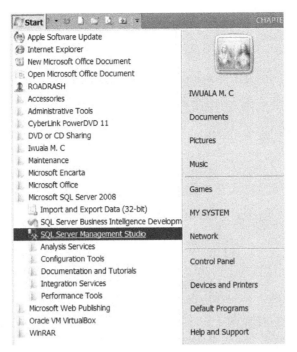

ii.   Click on SQL Server Management Studio link button to lunch it and login by entering your account details or using windows account. Then click Connect.

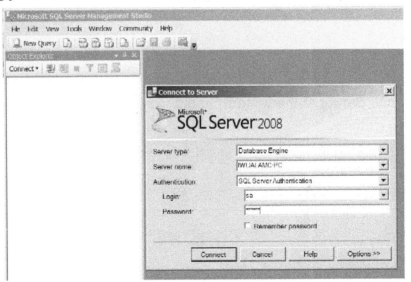

iii.   Click New Query button directly above Object Explorer to open the New Query window.

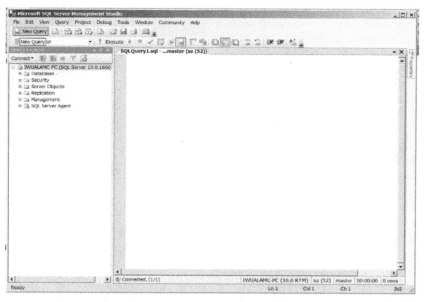

iv.   You can now create your first simple database.

4.3   CREATING DATABASE

Creating a database using the default parameters is very simple. The following data
definition language (DDL) command is used to create the database:

```
Use master;
Go


CREATE DATABASE diograndeDB;
Go
```

The CREATE command will create a data file with the name diograndeDB and .mdf file
extension, as well as a transaction log with an .ldf extension.

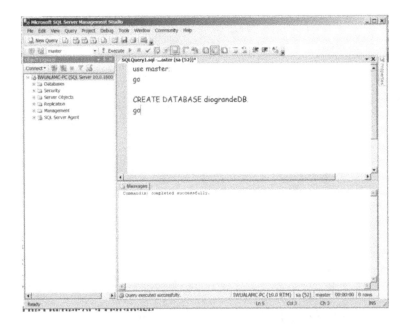

i.   The Owner of a Database

Whenever a new database is created, the server wants to keep track of who created that database; who created the database is called the database owner. By default, Microsoft SQL Server creates a special account named **dbo** (for database owner). When you create a database but do not specify the owner, this account is used. The **dbo** account is also given rights to all types of operations that can be performed on the database because it shipped with the default login or user account. This is convenient in most cases. Still, if you want, you can specify another user as the owner of the database. Of course, the account must exist, which means you should have previously created it or you can use an existing one.

The code below creates a user account called felistaDBs and gives the user the right to own databases in the server.

```
Use master;
Go


--The code below will create a user who will be the database owner
Create user [felistaDBs]
       for login [chibyke]
```

```
    with default_schema = [myDB];
go


/*The code below will create the user role to
perform all actions that assigned to db owner*/


EXEC sp_addrolemember N'db_owner', N'felistaDBs';
GO
```

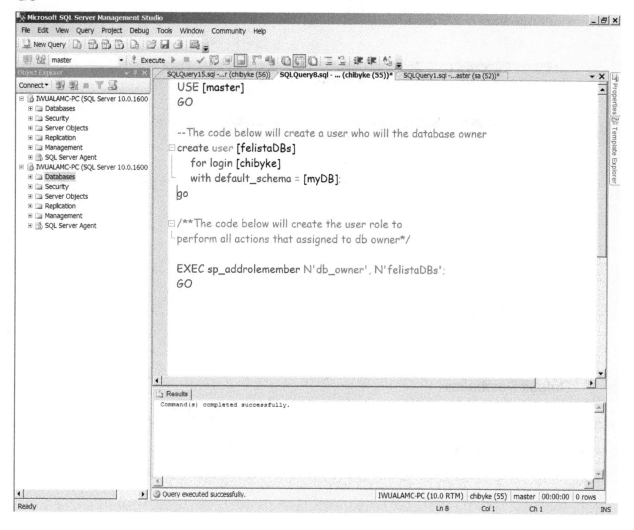

ii. Specifying the Database Owner

I will modify the database owner of the database created above for a company called DIOGRANDE GLOBAL NIGERIA LIMITED with the file name diograndeDB and assign it to the user chibyke. Below is the code:

Use diograndeDB;

go

exec sp_changedbowner chibyke;

go

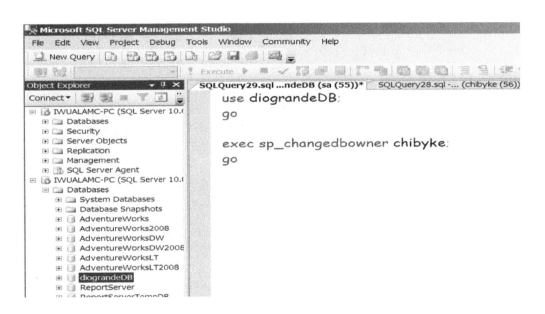

iii. Default Databases

When you install Microsoft SQL Server, it also installs 4 databases named **master**, **model**, **msdb**, and **tempdb**. These databases will be for internal use. This means that you should avoid directly using them, unless you know exactly what you are doing.

a. Master database

One of the databases installed with Microsoft SQL Server is named **master**. This database holds all the information about the machine on which your MS SQL Server is installed. For example, we saw earlier that, to perform any operation on the server, you must login. The master database identifies any person, called a user, who accesses the database, about when and how and probably the number of times a user tried logging into the MS SQL Server.

Besides identifying who accesses the system, the **master** database also keeps track of everything you do on the server, including creating and managing databases. On no account should you play with the master database; otherwise you may corrupt the system. For example, if the master database is not functioning right, the system would not work.

Restrictions

The following operations cannot be performed on the **master** database:

- Adding files or filegroups.
- Changing collation. The default collation is the server collation.
- Changing the database owner. **master** is owned by **dbo**.
- Creating a full-text catalog or full-text index.
- Creating triggers on system tables in the database.
- Dropping the database.
- Dropping the **guest** user from the database.
- Enabling change data capture.
- Participating in database mirroring.
- Removing the primary filegroup, primary data file, or log file.
- Renaming the database or primary filegroup.
- Setting the database to OFFLINE.
- Setting the database or primary filegroup to READ_ONLY.

Recommendations

When you work with the **master** database, if working with is inevitable; consider the following recommendations:

- Always have a current backup of the **master** database available.

- Back up the **master** database as soon as possible after the following operations:
  - Creating, modifying, or dropping any database
  - Changing server or database configuration values
  - Modifying or adding logon accounts
- Do not create user objects in **master**. Otherwise, **master** must be backed up more frequently.
- Do not set the TRUSTWORTHY option to ON for the **master** database.

b. tempdb database

The **tempdb** system database is a global resource that is available to all users connected to the instance of SQL Server and is used to hold the following:

- Temporary user objects that are explicitly created, such as: global or local temporary tables, temporary stored procedures, table variables, or cursors.
- Internal objects that are created by the SQL Server Database Engine, for example, work tables to store intermediate results for spools or sorting.
- Row versions that are generated by data modification transactions in a database that uses read-committed using row versioning isolation or snapshot isolation transactions.
- Row versions that are generated by data modification transactions for features, such as: online index operations, Multiple Active Result Sets (MARS), and AFTER triggers.

Operations within **tempdb** are minimally logged. This enables transactions to be rolled back. **tempdb** is re-created every time SQL Server is started so that the system always starts with a clean copy of the database. Temporary tables and stored procedures are dropped automatically on disconnect, and no connections are active when the system is shut down. Therefore, there is never anything in **tempdb** to be saved from one session of SQL Server to another. Backup and restore operations are not allowed on **tempdb**.

Restrictions

The following operations cannot be performed on the **tempdb** database:

- Adding filegroups.

- Backing up or restoring the database.
- Changing collation. The default collation is the server collation.
- Changing the database owner. **tempdb** is owned by **dbo**.
- Creating a database snapshot.
- Dropping the database.
- Dropping the **guest** user from the database.
- Enabling change data capture.
- Participating in database mirroring.
- Removing the primary filegroup, primary data file, or log file.
- Renaming the database or primary filegroup.
- Running DBCC CHECKALLOC.
- Running DBCC CHECKCATALOG.
- Setting the database to OFFLINE.
- Setting the database or primary filegroup to READ_ONLY.

c. model database

The **model** database is used as the template for all databases created on an instance of SQL Server. Because **tempdb** is created every time SQL Server is started, the **model** database must always exist on a SQL Server system. When a CREATE DATABASE statement is issued, the first part of the database is created by copying in the contents of the **model** database. The rest of the new database is then filled with empty pages. If you modify the **model** database, all databases created afterward will inherit those changes. For example, you could set permissions or database options, or add objects such as tables, functions, or stored procedures.

Restrictions

The following operations cannot be performed on the **model** database:
- Adding files or filegroups.
- Changing collation. The default collation is the server collation.
- Changing the database owner. **model** is owned by **dbo**.
- Dropping the database.
- Dropping the **guest** user from the database.
- Enabling change data capture.

- Participating in database mirroring.
- Removing the primary filegroup, primary data file, or log file.
- Renaming the database or primary filegroup.
- Setting the database to OFFLINE.
- Setting the database or primary filegroup to READ_ONLY.
- Creating procedures, views, or triggers using the WITH ENCRYPTION option. The encryption key is tied to the database in which the object is created. Encrypted objects created in the **model** database can only be used in **model**.

d. msdb database

The **msdb** database is used by SQL Server Agent for scheduling alerts and jobs and by other features such as Service Broker and Database Mail.

Restrictions

The following operations cannot be performed on the **msdb** database:
- Changing collation. The default collation is the server collation.
- Dropping the database.
- Dropping the **guest** user from the database.
- Enabling change data capture.
- Participating in database mirroring.

iv.   The Primary Size of a Database

When originally creating a database, you may or may not know how many lists, files, or objects the project would have. Still, as a user of computer memory, the database must use a certain portion at least in the beginning and not all the computer memory. The amount of space that a database is using is referred to as its size. If you use the New Database, the interpreter automatically specifies that the database would primarily use 2MB. This is enough for a starting database. Of course, you can either change this default size later on or you can increase it when necessary.

If you want to specify a size different from the default sizes then checkout 'configuring file growth'.

a. Configuring file growth

Prior to SQL Server version 7, the data files required manual size adjustment to handle additional data. Fortunately, for about a decade now, SQL Server can automatically grow thanks to the following options, below:

i. **Enable Autogrowth:** As the database begins to hold more data, the file size must grow. If autogrowth is not enabled, an observant DBA will have to manually adjust the size. If autogrowth is enabled, SQL Server automatically adjusts the size according to one of the following growth parameters:

    a. In percent: When the data file needs to grow, this option will expand it by the percent specified. Growing by percent is the best option for smaller databases. With very large files, this option may add too much space in one operation and hurt performance while the data file is being resized. For example, adding 10 percent to a 5GB data file will add 500MB; writing 500MB could take a while.
    b. In megabytes: When the data file needs to grow, this option will add the specified number of megabytes to the file. Growing by a fixed size is a good option for larger data files.

ii. **Maximum file size:** Setting a maximum size can prevent the data file or transaction log file from filling the entire disk subsystem, which would cause trouble for the operating system.

Note: The maximum size for a data file is 16 terabytes, and log files are limited to 2 terabytes. This does not limit the size of the database because a database can include multiple files.

The file sizes and growth options can be adjusted in code with the ALTER DATABASE DDL command and the MODIFY FILE option. The following code sets diogradeDB's data file to manual growth and sets the size to 20MB:

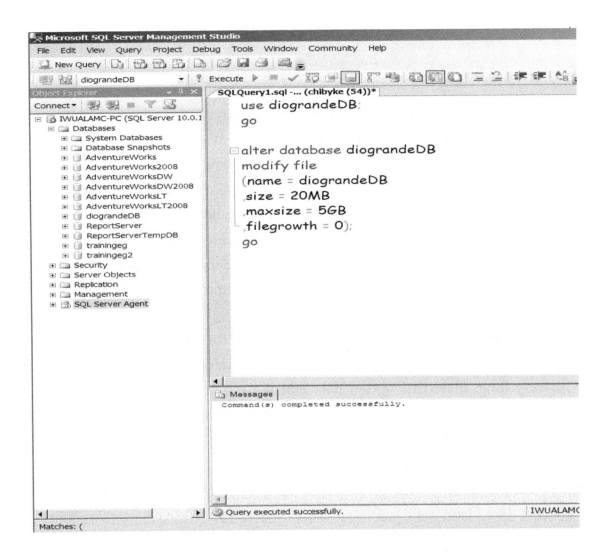

v.   The Default Location of Databases

As a computer user or programmer as the case may be, you should be aware that every computer file must have a path. The path is where the file is located in one of the drives of the computer. This allows the operating system to know where the file is stored, so that when you or another application calls it, the operating system would not be confused.

By default, when you create a new database, Microsoft SQL Server assumes that it would be located at *Drive*:\Program Files\Microsoft SQL Server\MSSQL10.MSSQLSERVER\MSSQL\DATA folder, so long as the MS SQL Server is installed on the drive. On some cases, those learning to create database newly will resort to using New Database dialog box, so if you use the New Database dialog box of the SQL Server Management Studio, if you specify the name of the database and click OK, the interpreter automatically creates a new file, and appends the .MDF extension to the file: this is the (main) primary data file of your database.

If you do not want to use the default path, you can change it. If you are using the New Database dialog box, to change the path, under the Path header, select the current string:

C:\Program Files\Microsoft SQL Server\MSSQL10.MSSQLSERVER\MSSQL\DATA
Replace it with an appropriate path of your choice. e.g.:
D:\DBs

4.4   DATABASE CREATION SYNTAX

To assist you with creating and managing databases, including their object, you use a set of language tools referred to as the Data Definition Language (DDL). This most includes commands. For example, the primary command to create a database uses the following formula:

CREATE DATABASE *DatabaseName*

To assist you with writing code, in the previous examples, we saw that you could use the query window.

The **CREATE DATABASE** (remember that SQL is not case-sensitive) expression is required. The *DatabaseName* factor is the name that the new database will have. Although SQL is not case-sensitive, you should make it a habit to be aware of the cases you use to name your objects. Every statement in SQL can be terminated with a semi-colon. Although this is a requirement in many implementations of SQL, in Microsoft SQL Server, you can omit the semi-colon. Otherwise, the above formula would be

CREATE DATABASE *DatabaseName*;

Here is an example:
CREATE DATABASE imtDB;

This formula is used if you do not want to provide any option. We saw previously that a database has one or more files and we saw where they are located by default. We also saw that you could specify the location of files if you want. To specify where the primary file of the database will be located, you can use the following formula:

CREATE DATABASE *DatabaseName*
ON PRIMARY
(NAME = *LogicalName*, FILENAME = *Path*)

The only three factors whose values need to be changed from this formula are the database name that we saw already, the logical name, and the path name. The logical name can be any one-word name but should be different from the database name. The path is the directory location of the file. This path ends with a name for the file with the extension .mdf. The path should be complete and included in single-quotes. Here is an example:

CREATE DATABASE imtDB
ON PRIMARY
(NAME = deptInfo, FILENAME = ' D:\DBs\ imtDB.mdf)
GO

Besides the primary file, you may want to create and store a log file. To specify where the log file of the database would be located, you can use the following formula:

CREATE DATABASE *DatabaseName*
ON PRIMARY
(NAME = *LogicalName*, FILENAME = *Path*.mdf)
LOG ON
(NAME = *LogicalName*, FILENAME = *Path*.ldf)

The new factor in this formula is the path of the log file. Like the primary file, the log file must be named (with a logical name). The path ends with a file name whose extension is .ldf. Here is an example:

Use master;
go

CREATE DATABASE imtDB
ON PRIMARY
(NAME = deptInfo, FILENAME = 'D:\DBs\ imtDB.mdf')
LOG ON
(NAME = deptInfoLog, FILENAME = 'D:\DBs\ imtDB.ldf');
GO

I have created a database without specifying the size of the database, though I said in previous example that it has a default or primary size which is allocated to it by the interpreter. So I will take a look at the syntax for creating the database custom sizes.

Use master;

go

CREATE DATABASE studInfoDB

ON PRIMARY

(NAME = studInfoDB,

FILENAME = 'D:\DBs\studInfoDB.mdf',

SIZE = 10MB,

MAXSIZE = 200Gb,

FILEGROWTH = 100)

LOG ON

(NAME = studInfoDBLog,

FILENAME = 'f:\DB Log\studInfoDB.ldf',

SIZE = 5MB,

MAXSIZE = 10Gb,

FILEGROWTH = 100);

Go

After typying the codes, press F5 to execute or create the database.

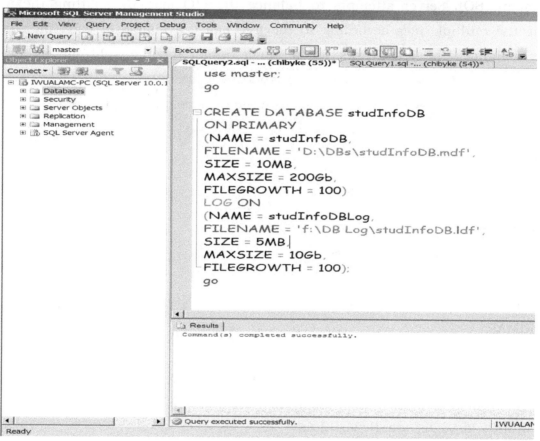

4.4.1 Creating a database with multiple files

Both the data file and the transaction log can be stored on multiple files for improved performance and to allow for growth. Any additional, or *secondary*, data files have an .ndf file extension by default. If the database uses multiple data files, then the first, or *primary*, file will contain the system tables. While it does not enable control over the location of tables or indexes, this technique does reduce the I/O load on each disk subsystem. SQL Server attempts to balance the I/O load by splitting the inserts among the multiple files according to the free space available in each file. As SQL Server balances the load, rows for a single table may be split among multiple locations; if the database is configured for such purpose.

To create a database with multiple files, type the code below and press F5:

```
use master;
go

drop database studInfoDB;
go

CREATE DATABASE studInfoDB
ON PRIMARY
(NAME = NewDB,
FILENAME = 'c:\SQLData\NewDB.mdf'),
(NAME = NewDB2,
FILENAME = 'd:\SQLData\NewDB2.ndf')
LOG ON
(NAME = NewDBLog,
FILENAME = 'd:\SQLLog\NewDBLog.ldf'),
(NAME = NewDBLog2,
FILENAME = 'c:\SQLLog\NewDBLog2.ldf');
go
```

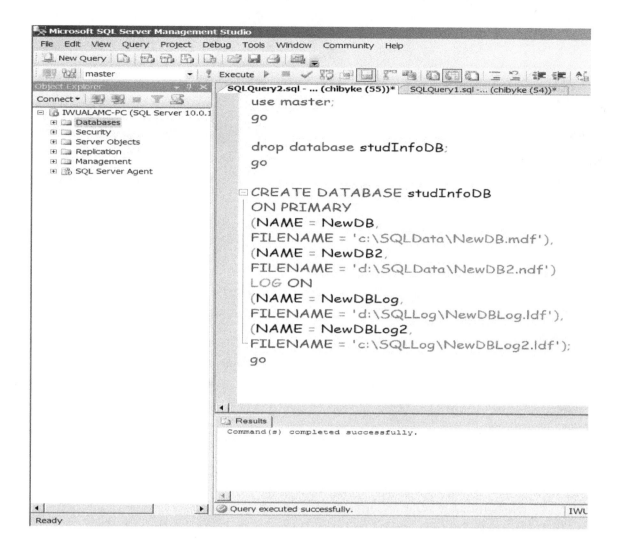

The following example creates the database Sales that has the following filegroups:

- The primary filegroup with the files zone1to3 and zone4to6. The FILEGROWTH increments for these files are specified as 15%.

- A filegroup named geoPolZones1 with the files lgaZonesOne and lgaZonesTwo.

- A filegroup named geoPolZones2 with the files lgaZonesThree and lgaZonesFour.

- A filegroup named geoPolZones3 with the files lgaZonesFive and lgaZonesSix.

```
USE master;
GO

IF DB_ID (N'Country') IS NOT NULL
DROP DATABASE Country;
```

```
GO

-- execute the CREATE DATABASE statement
CREATE DATABASE  Country
ON PRIMARY
( NAME = zone1to3,
    FILENAME = 'D:\DBs\statesInZone1.mdf',
              SIZE = 10,
              MAXSIZE = 50,
              FILEGROWTH = 15% ),
( NAME = zone4to6,
    FILENAME = 'D:\DBs\statesInZone2.ndf',
              SIZE = 10,
              MAXSIZE = 50,
              FILEGROWTH = 15% ),
FILEGROUP geoPolZones1
( NAME = lgaZonesOne,
    FILENAME = 'D:\DBs\lgaZone1.ndf',
              SIZE = 10,
              MAXSIZE = 50,
              FILEGROWTH = 5 ),
( NAME = lgaZonesTwo,
    FILENAME = 'D:\DBs\lgaZone2.ndf',
              SIZE = 10,
              MAXSIZE = 50,
              FILEGROWTH = 5 ),
FILEGROUP geoPolZones2
( NAME = lgaZoneThree,
    FILENAME = 'D:\DBs\lgaZone3.ndf',
              SIZE = 10,
              MAXSIZE = 50,
              FILEGROWTH = 5 ),
( NAME = lgaZoneFour,
    FILENAME = 'D:\DBs\lgaZone4.ndf',
              SIZE = 10,
```

```
                    MAXSIZE = 50,
                    FILEGROWTH = 5 ),
FILEGROUP geoPolZones3
( NAME = lgaZoneFive,
    FILENAME = 'D:\DBs\lgaZone5.ndf',
                    SIZE = 10,
                    MAXSIZE = 50,
                    FILEGROWTH = 5 ),
( NAME = lgaZoneSix,
    FILENAME = 'D:\DBs\lgaZone6.ndf',
                    SIZE = 10,
                    MAXSIZE = 50,
                    FILEGROWTH = 5 )
                    LOG ON
( NAME = Sales_log,
    FILENAME = 'F:\DB Log\SPri1dat.ldf',
                    SIZE = 5MB,
                    MAXSIZE = 25MB,
                    FILEGROWTH = 5MB
);
GO
```

```
Microsoft SQL Server Management Studio
File  Edit  View  Query  Project  Debug  Tools  Window  Community  Help
New Query
master                    Execute

~vs645D.sql - IW... (chibyke (51))*

USE master;
GO

IF DB_ID (N'Country') IS NOT NULL
DROP DATABASE Country;
GO

-- execute the CREATE DATABASE statement
CREATE DATABASE  Country
ON PRIMARY
( NAME = zone1to3,
    FILENAME = 'D:\DBs\statesInZone1.mdf',
        SIZE = 10,
        MAXSIZE = 50,
        FILEGROWTH = 15% ),
( NAME = zone4to6,
    FILENAME = 'D:\DBs\statesInZone2.ndf',
        SIZE = 10,
        MAXSIZE = 50,
        FILEGROWTH = 15% ),
FILEGROUP geoPolZones1
( NAME = lgaZonesOne,

Results
Command(s) completed successfully.

Query executed successfully.                          IWUAL
Ready
```

4.4.2 Creating Using Code Template

To specify more options with code, Microsoft SQL Server ships with various sample codes you can use for different assignments. For example, you can use sample code to create a database. The sample codes that Microsoft SQL Server are accessible from the Template Explorer.

To access the Template Explorer, on the main menu, you can click View -> Template Explorer. Before creating a database, open a new query window. Then:

•   To create a new database using sample code, in the Template Explorer, expand the Databases node, then drag the Create Database node and drop it in the query window. The new database would be created in the server that holds the current connection

- If you have access to more than one server, to create a database in another server or using a different connection, in the Template Explorer, expand the Databases node, right-click Create Database and click Open. In the Connect to Database Engine dialog box, select the appropriate options, and can click OK

With any of these actions, Microsoft SQL Server would generate sample code for you as shown below:

```
-- =============================================
-- Create database template
-- =============================================
USE master
GO


-- Drop the database if it already exists
IF  EXISTS (
        SELECT name
              FROM sys.databases
              WHERE name = N'<Database_Name, sysname, Database_Name>'
)
DROP DATABASE <Database_Name, sysname, Database_Name>
GO


CREATE DATABASE <Database_Name, sysname, Database_Name>
GO
```

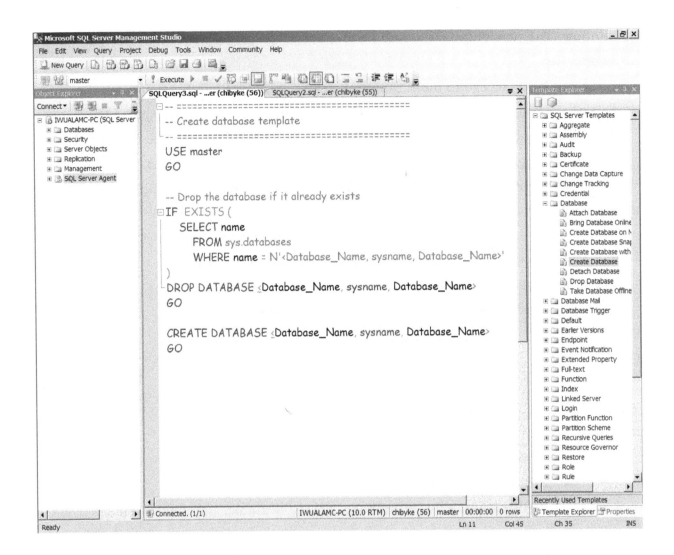

You would then need to edit the code and execute it to create the database. From the previous lessons and sections, we have reviewed some characters such as the comments -- and some words or expressions such as **GO**, **CREATE DATABASE**, and **SELECT**. We will study the other words or expressions in future lessons and sections. But with what I demonstrated in previous examples concerning database creation you will be able to edit the generated sample code.

4.5　Database Maintenance

If you have created a database but don't need it anymore, you can delete it. It is important to know, regardless of how you create a database, whether using SQL Server Management Studio, code in the query window, or the Command Prompt, every database can be accessed by any of these tools and you can delete any of the databases using any of these tools. As done with creating a database, every tool provides its own means.

SQL Server Management Studio

To delete a database in SQL Server Management Studio, in the Object Explorer, expand the Databases node, right-click the undesired database, and click Delete. A dialog box would prompt you to confirm your intention. If you still want to delete the database, you can click OK. If you change your mind, you can click Cancel.

1.　In the Object Explorer, right-click **diograndeDB** and click Delete

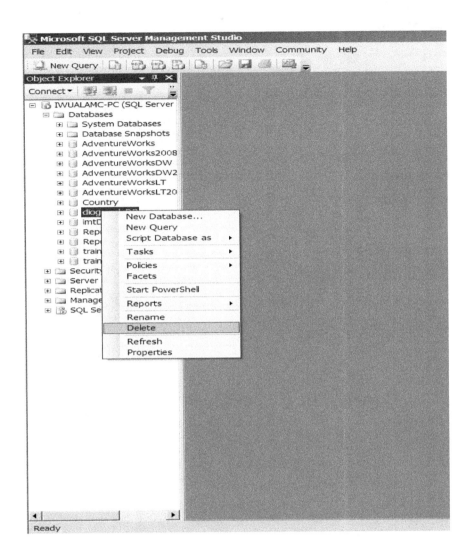

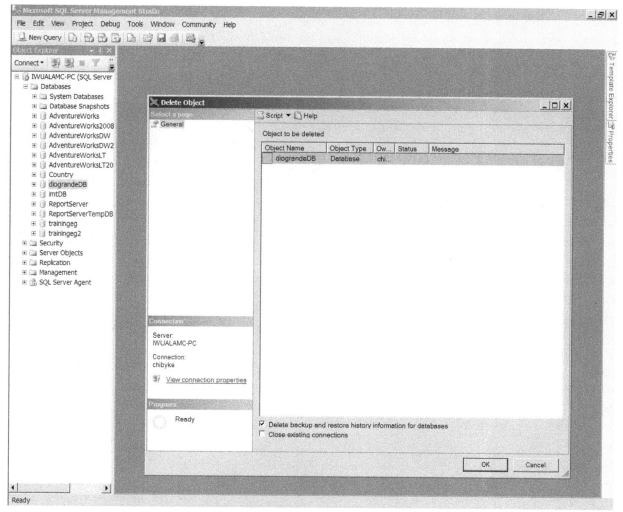

2.   In the Delete Object dialog box, click OK

4.5.1 Deleting a Database Using SQL

To delete a database in SQL Query window, you use the **DROP DATABASE** expression followed by the name of the database. The formula used is:

DROP DATABASE *DatabaseName;*

Before deleting a database in SQL Server, you must make sure the database is not being used or accessed by someone else or by another object.

1.   On the Standard toolbar, click the New Query button

2.   To delete a database, type:

DROP DATABASE diograndeDB;

GO

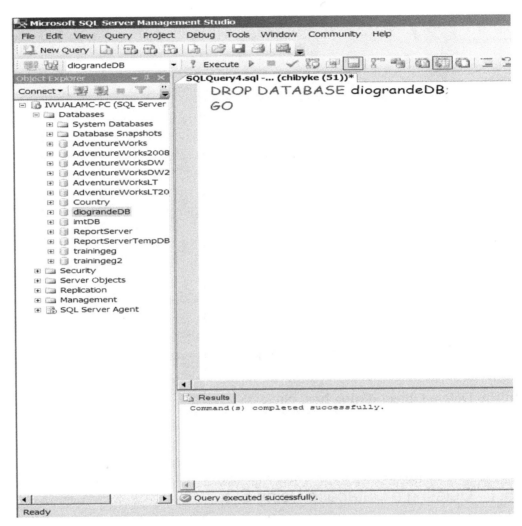

3.   Press F5 to execute the statement

4.6   Database Routines

4.6.1   The Current Database

A very observant student would have noticed the incessant use of **USE** at the begging of the Query window. While writing code in a Query Window, you should always know what database you are working on; otherwise you may add code to the wrong database. To programmatically specify the current database, type the **USE** keyword followed by the name of the database. The formula to use is:

USE *DatabaseName*;

Here is an example:

USE Master;

If you did not specify the database you are working on, then the default database which Master takes over all the objects created.

4.6.2   Refreshing the List of Databases

Some of the windows that display databases, like the SQL Server Management Studio, don't update their list immediately if an operation occurred outside their confinement. For example, if you create a database in the query windows, its name would not be updated in the Object Explorer, immediately. To view such external changes, you can refresh the window that holds the list.

In SQL Server Management Studio, to update a list, you can right-click its category in the Object Explorer and click Refresh. Only that category may be refreshed. For example, to refresh the list of databases, in the Object Explorer, you can right-click the Databases node and click Refresh.

4.7 Schemas

A schema is an object that exists purely to own database objects, most likely to segment a large database into manageable modules, or to implement a segmented security strategy, thus, one can say that schemas are containers.

In previous versions of SQL Server, objects were owned by users. Or rather, objects were owned by schema-objects that were the same as the user-owners, but no one spoke in those terms. In SQL Server 2005, the concepts of users and schema were separated. Users could no longer own objects. Typically, and by default, objects are owned by the dbo schema. The schema name is the third part of the four-part name: Server.database.**schema**.object;

When using custom schemas, other than dbo, every query has to specify the schema. That is not a bad idea, because using a two-part name improves performance, but always typing a long schema name is no fun, you know.

4.7.1 Introduction to Namespaces

A namespace is a technique of creating a series of items that each has a unique name. For example, if you start creating many databases, there is a possibility that you may risk having various databases with the same name. If using a namespace, you can isolate the databases in various namespaces. In reality, to manage many other aspects of your database server, you use namespaces and you put objects, other than databases, within those namespaces. Therefore, a namespace and its content can be illustrated as follows:

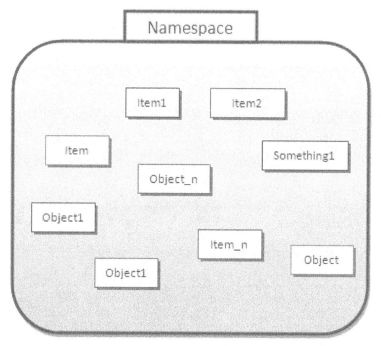

Notice that there are various types of objects within a namespace.

4.7.2 Introduction to Schemas

Within a namespace, you can create objects as you wish. To further control and manage the objects inside of a namespace, you can put them in sub-groups called schemas. Therefore, a schema is a group of objects within a namespace. This also means that, within a namespace, you can have as many schemas as you want:

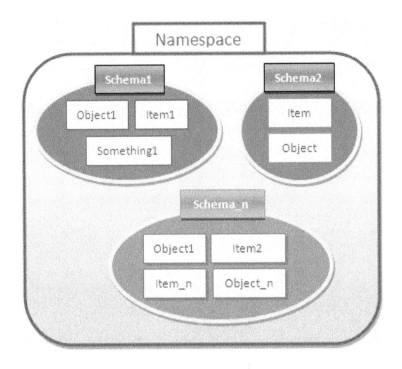

Notice that, just like a namespace can contain objects (schemas), a schema can contain objects also (the objects we will create throughout our lessons).

To manage the schemas in a namespace, you need a way to identify each schema. Based on this, each schema must have a name. In our illustration, one schema is named Schema1. Another schema is named Schema2. Yet another schema is named Schema_n.

A schema is an object that contains other objects. Before using it, you must create it or you can use an existing schema. There are two types of schemas you can use, those built-in and those you create. When Microsoft SQL Server is installed, it also creates a few schemas. One of the schemas is called **sys** which stores system objects mainly. Others are dbo, db_owner, db_ddladmin and so on.

The **sys** schema contains a list of some of the objects that exist in your system. One of these objects is called **databases**. When you create a database, its name is entered in the **databases** object using the same name you gave it. To access the schemas of a database, in the Object Explorer, expand the Databases node, expand the database that will hold or own the schema, and expand the Security node.

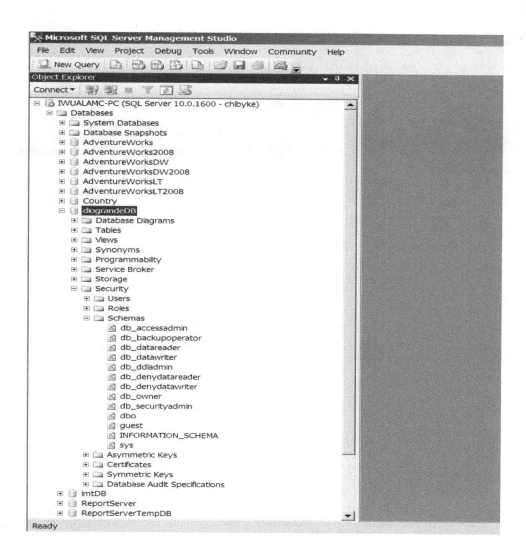

4.7.3 Creating a Schema

To create a schema, type and execute this code below:

```
USE diograndeDB ;
GO

CREATE SCHEMA Courses AUTHORIZATION Chibyke;
GO
```

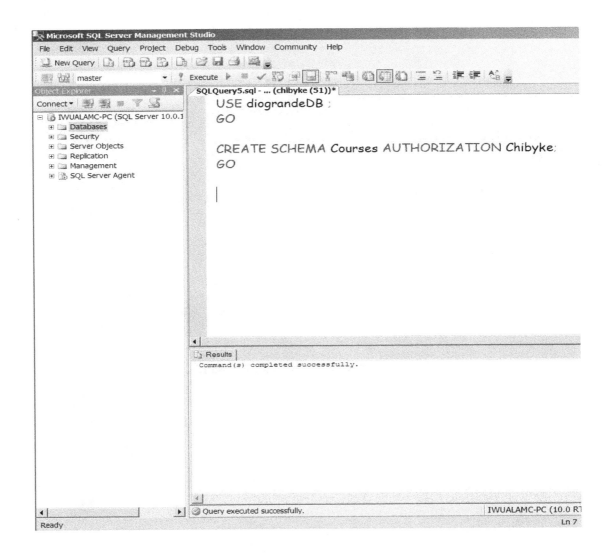

4.7.4   Accessing an Object From a Schema

Inside of a schema, two objects cannot have the same name, but an object in one schema can have the same name as an object in another schema. Based on this, if you are accessing an object within its schema, you can simply use its name, since that name would be unique. On the other hand, because of the implied possibility of dealing with objects with similar names in your server, when accessing an object outside of its schema, you must qualify it. To do this, you would type the name of the schema that contains the object you want to use, followed by the period operator, followed by the name of the object you want to use. From our illustration, to access the courseCode object that belongs to Courses, you would type:

Courses.courseCode or Server.database.Courses.courseCode;

CHAPTER FIVE

Microsoft SQL Server Data Types

Every language requires variables to temporarily or permanently store values in memory. T-SQL variables are created with the DECLARE command. The DECLARE command is followed by the variable name and data type. The available data types are similar to those used to create tables, with the addition of the table and cursor. The deprecated text, ntext, and image data types are only available for table columns, and not for variables. Multiple comma-separated variables can be declared with a single DECLARE command.

We have used some values such as 12345 or 'Eze F. Udoka'. These types of values are referred to as constant because we know them before their use and we don't change them in our statements. If you intend to use a certain category of value over and over again, you can reserve a section of memory for that value. This allows you to put the value in an area of the computer's memory, easily change the value for another, over and over.

To use the same area of memory to store and remove values as needed, the SQL interpreter needs two primary pieces of information: a name and the desired amount of space in memory capable of storing the value.

5.1   Introducing Variables Creation

1. To launch SQL Server Management Studio
2. On the Connect to Server dialog box, make the correct selections and provide the appropriate information, then click Connect

3. To open the code editor or query window, on the main menu, click File, New and Query with Current Connection to open a new Query window with the current Server connection.

5.1.1   Declaring a Variable

A variable is an area of memory used to store values that can be used in a program, as explained above. Before using a variable, you must inform the interpreter. This is also referred to as declaring a variable. To declare a variable, use the **DECLARE** keyword using the following formula:

DECLARE *Options*

The **DECLARE** keyword lets the interpreter know that you are making a declaration.

5.1.2   Variable default and scope

The scope, or application and duration, of the variable extends only to the current batch. Newly declared variables default to NULL and must be initialized if you want them to have a value in an expression. Remember that null added with a value yields null. New for SQL Server 2008 is the ability to initialize a variable to a value while declaring it, which saves. Here is an example:

DECLARE @name nvarchar(50) = N'Ikenna Goodluck';

5.1.3   Incremental variables

T-SQL finally has the increment variable feature, which saves a few keystrokes when coding and certainly looks cleaner and more modern. The basic idea is that an operation and equals sign will perform that function on the variable. For example, the code

SET @x += 5; is the logical equivalent of SET @x = @x + 5;

5.1.4 Objects Names

The **DECLARE** keyword is followed by a name for the variable. In Transact-SQL, the name of a variable starts with the @ sign. The name of a variable allows you to identify the area of memory where the value of the variable is stored. Transact-SQL is very flexible when it comes to naming variables. For example, a name can be made of digits only. Here is an example:
DECLARE @1234

Nevertheless, there are rules and suggestions that will guide you in naming variables:

- A name can start with either an underscore or a letter. Examples are **@_n**, **@act**, or **@Second**
- After the first character as an underscore or a letter, the name will have combinations of underscores, letters, and digits. Examples are **@_n24** or **@act_52_t**
- A name will not include special characters such as !, @, #, $, %, ^, &, or * and keywords that makes meaning to the interpreter.
- If the name is a combination of words, each word will start in uppercase. Examples are **@DateHired**, **@_realSport**, or **@DriversLicenseNumber**

A name cannot be one of the following words reserved for Transact-SQL internal keywords:

aggregate	alter	and	any	application
as	assembly	backup	begin	between
bigint	binary	bit	break	broker
by	case	catalog	catch	certificate
char	check	checkpoint	close	commit
compute	contains	continue	contract	create
credential	cursor	database	date	datetime

datetime2	datetimeoffset	deallocate	decimal	declare
default	delete	deny	disable	drop
else	enable	end	endpoint	event
exec	execute	false	fetch	float
foreign	from	full	fulltext	function
go	goto	grant	group	having
hierarchyid	if	image	in	index
insert	int	into	is	kill
like	login	master	merge	message
money	move	nchar	next	not
ntext	null	numeric	nvarchar	on
order	output	partition	print	proc
procedure	queue	real	receive	remote
resource	return	revert	revoke	role
rollback	rowversion	rule	save	schema
select	send	set	setuser	shutdown
smalldatetime	smallint	smallmoney	sql_variant	status
table	text	then	time	timestamp
tinyint	tran	transaction	trigger	true
try	type	union	unique	uniqueidentifier
update	use	values	varbinary	varchar
view	when	while	with	xml

To declare a variable, as we will see later, after giving a name to a variable, you must also specify the amount of memory that the variable would need. The amount of memory is also called a data type. Therefore, the declaration of a variable uses the following formula:

DECLARE @*VariableName DataType;*

You can also declare more than one variable. To do that, separate them with a comma. The formula would be:

DECLARE @*Variable1 DataType1*, @*Variable2 DataType2*, @*Variable_n DataType_n*;

Unlike many other languages like C/C++, C#, Java, or Pascal, if you declare many variables that use the same data type, the name of each variable must be followed by its own data type.

5.1.5 Initializing a Variable

After declaring a variable, the interpreter reserves a space in the computer memory for it but the space doesn't necessarily hold a recognizable value. This means that, at this time, the variable is null. One way you can change this is to give a value to the variable. This is referred to as initializing the variable.

Remember that a variable's name starts with @ and whenever you need to refer to the variable, you must make sure you include the @ sign. To initialize a variable, in the necessary section, type the **SELECT** or the **SET** keyword followed by the name of the variable, followed by the assignment operator "=", followed by an appropriate value. The formula used is:

SELECT @*VariableName* = *DesiredValue*

or

SET @*VariableName* = *DesiredValue*

Once a variable has been initialized, you can make its value available or display it. This time, you can type the name of the variable to the right side of **PRINT** or **SELECT**.

5.2   Data Types

After setting the name of a variable, you must specify the amount of memory that the variable will need to store its value. Since there are various kinds of information a database can hold or probabily deal with, SQL provides a set of data types.

5.2.1 Boolean Variables

A Boolean value is a piece of information stated as being true or false, On or Off, Yes or No, 1 or 0. To declare a variable that holds a Boolean value, you can use the **BIT** or **bit** keyword. Here is an example:

DECLARE @IsOrganDonor bit;

After declaring a Boolean variable, you can initialize it with 0 or another value. If the variable is initialized with 0, it receives the Boolean value of False. If it is initialized with any other number, it receives a True value. Here is an example of using a Boolean variable:

Using Boolean Variables

1. In the SQL CMD Query window, type the following:

DECLARE @IsMarried bit
SET @IsMarried = 100
SELECT @IsMarried AS [Is Married?];
GO

```
SQLCMD
PS SQLSERVER:\SQL\IWUALAMC-PC\DEFAULT+chibyke\> sqlcmd
1> DECLARE @IsMarried bit
2> SET @IsMarried = 100
3> SELECT @IsMarried AS [Is Married?];
4> GO
Is Married?
-----------
          1

(1 rows affected)
1> _
```

2. Execute the statement

5.2.2 Natural Numbers Types

An integer, also called a natural number, or a whole number, is a number that can start with a + or a - sign and is made of digits. Between the digits, no character other than a digit is allowed. In the real world, when a number is (very) long and becomes difficult to read, such as 79435794, you are allowed to type a symbol called the thousand separator in each thousand increment. An example is 79,435,794. In your SQL expressions, never include the thousand separator because you would receive an error. When the number starts with +, such as +44 or +8025, such a number is referred to as positive and you should omit the starting + sign. This means that the number should be written as 44 or 8025. Any number that starts with + or simply a digit is considered as greater than 0 or positive. A positive integer is also referred to as *unsigned*. On the other hand, a number that starts with a - symbol is referred to as negative.

i.   Normal Integers

If a variable would hold natural numbers in the range of -2,147,483,648 to 2,147,483,647, you can declare it with the **int** keyword as data type. Here is an example:

DECLARE @item int;

SET @ item = 1450;

PRINT @ item;

GO

This would produce 1450:

```
SQLCMD
PS SQLSERVER:\SQL\IWUALAMC-PC\DEFAULT+chibyke\> sqlcmd
1> DECLARE @item int;
2> SET @item = 1450;
3> PRINT @item;
4> GO
1450
1>
```

The length of an integer is the number of bytes its field can hold. For an **int** type, that would be 4 bytes.

ii.   Small Integers

If you want to use very small numbers such as student's ages, or the number of pages of a brochure or newspaper, use the **tinyint** data type. A variable with the **tinyint** data type can hold positive numbers that range from 0 to 255. Here is an example:

Declare @studAge tinyint;

Set @studAge = 18;

Select @studAge AS [Student's Age];

GO

```
SQLCMD
PS SQLSERVER:\SQL\IWUALAMC-PC\DEFAULT+chibyke\> sqlcmd
1> Declare @studAge tinyint;
2> Set @studAge = 18;
3> Select @studAge AS [Student's Age];
4> GO
Student's Age
-------------
           18

(1 rows affected)
1>
```

The **smallint** data type follows the same rules and principles as the **int** data type except that it is used to store smaller numbers that would range between -32,768 and 32,767. Here is an example:

DECLARE @NumOfPgs smallint;

SET @NumOfPgs = 430;

```
SELECT @NumOfPgs AS [Number of Pages];
GO
```

```
SQLCMD
PS SQLSERVER:\SQL\IWUALAMC-PC\DEFAULT+chibyke\> sqlcmd
1> DECLARE @NumOfPgs smallint;
2> SET @NumOfPgs = 430;
3> SELECT @NumOfPgs AS [Number of Pages];
4> GO
Number of Pages
---------------
            430

(1 rows affected)
1>
```

iii. Long Integers

The **bigint** data type follows the same rules and principles as the **int** data type except that it can hold very large numbers from -9,223,372,036,854,775,808 to 9,223,372,036,854,775,807. Here is an example:

DECLARE @NaijaPopulation BigInt;

SET @NaijaPopulation = 150000000;

SELECT @NaijaPopulation AS 'Nigerian Population';

GO

```
PS SQLSERVER:\SQL\IWUALAMC-PC\DEFAULT+chibyke\> sqlcmd
1> DECLARE @NaijaPopulation BigInt;
2> SET @NaijaPopulation = 150000000;
3> SELECT @NaijaPopulation AS 'Nigerian Population';
4> GO
Nigerian Population
-------------------
          150000000

(1 rows affected)
1> _
```

- **Binary Integers**

The binary data type is used for a variable that would hold hexadecimal numbers. Examples of hexadecimal numbers are 0x7238, 0xFA36, or 0xAA48D. Use the binary data type if all values of the variable would have the exact same length (or quantity). If you anticipate that some entries would be different than others, then use the alternative **varbinary** data type. The **varbinary** type also is used for hexadecimal numbers but allows dissimilar entries, as long as all entries are hexadecimals.

DECLARE @BinaryVariable2 BINARY(4);

SET @BinaryVariable2 = 123456;
SET @BinaryVariable2 = @BinaryVariable2 + 1;
SELECT @BinaryVariable2;

SELECT CAST(@BinaryVariable2 AS INT);
GO

5.2.3 Decimal Numbers Types

A decimal number is a number that can have a period (or the character used as the decimal separator as set in the Control Panel) between the digits. An example would be 12.625 or 44.80. Like an integer, a decimal number can start with a + or just a digit, which would make it a positive number. A decimal number can also start with a - symbol, which would make it a negative number. If the number represents a fraction, a period between the digits specifies what portion of 1 was cut.

i.   Decimal and Numeric Types

If you anticipate such a number for a field, specify its data type as **numeric** or **decimal** (either **decimal** or **numeric** would produce the same effect in MS SQL Server). Here is an example:

DECLARE @Distance DECIMAL(5,2);

SET @Distance = 648.16;

PRINT @Distance;

GO

```
SQLCMD                                                            _|□|x|
PS SQLSERVER:\SQL\IWUALAMC-PC\DEFAULT+chibyke\> sqlcmd
1> DECLARE @Distance DECIMAL(5,2);
2> SET @Distance = 648.16;
3> PRINT @Distance;
4> GO
648.16
1>
```

ii.   Real Numeric Types

A floating-point number is a fractional number, like the decimal type. Floating-point numbers can be used if you would allow the database engine to apply an approximation to the actual number. To declare such a variable, use the **float** or the **real** keyword. Here is an example:

DECLARE @Radius FLOAT;

SET @Radius = 48.9625;

SELECT @Radius AS Radius;

GO

```
SQLCMD                                                               _ □ ×
PS SQLSERVER:\SQL\IWUALAMC-PC\DEFAULT+chibyke\> SQLCMD
1> DECLARE @Radius FLOAT;
2> SET @Radius = 48.9625;
3> SELECT @Radius AS Radius;
4> GO
Radius
------------------------
       48.962499999999999

(1 rows affected)
1> _
```

A precision is the number of digits used to display a numeric value. For example, the number 42005 has a precision of 5, while 226 has a precision value of 3. If the data type is specified as an integer (the **int** and its variants) or a floating-point number (**float** and **real**), the precision is fixed by the database and you can just accept the value set by the Microsoft SQL Server interpreter. For a decimal number (**decimal** or **numeric** data types), Microsoft SQL Server allows you to specify the amount of precision you want. The value must be an integer between 1 and 38 (28 if you are using SQL Server 7). A decimal number is a number that has a fractional section. Examples are 12.05 or 1450.4227. The scale of a number if the number of digits on the right side of the period (or the character set as the separator for decimal numbers for your language, as specified in Control Panel). The scale is used only for numbers that have a decimal part, which includes currency (**money** and **smallmoney**) and decimals (**numeric** and **decimal**). If a variable is declared with the **decimal** or **numeric** data type, you can specify the amount of scale you want. The value must be an integer between 0 and 18.

Application of Decimal Variables

1. Change the statement as follows:

DECLARE @IsMarried bit,
    @EmplStatus int,

@WeeklyHours Decimal(4,2);

SET @IsMarried = 1;

SET @EmplStatus = 2;

SET @WeeklyHours = 36.50;

SELECT @IsMarried AS [Is Married?],

    @EmplStatus AS [Employment Status],

    @WeeklyHours AS Hours;

GO

  2. Execute the statement

5.2.4 Currency and Monetary Values

If a variable would hold monetary values, you can declare it with the **money** keyword. A variable with a **money** data type can hold positive or negative values from -922,337,203,685,477.5808 to +922,337,203,685,477.5807. Here is an example:

DECLARE @YrIncome Money;

SET @YrIncome = 48500.15;

SELECT @YrIncome AS [Yearly Income];

GO

```
PS SQLSERVER:\SQL\IWUALAMC-PC\DEFAULT+chibyke\> SQLCMD
1> DECLARE @YrIncome Money;
2> SET @YrIncome = 48500.15;
3> SELECT @YrIncome AS [Yearly Income];
4> GO
Yearly Income
--------------------
            48500.1500

(1 rows affected)
1>
```

While the **money** data type can be used for a variable that would hold large quantities of currency values, the **smallmoney** data type can be applied for a variable whose value cannot be lower than -214,748.3648 nor higher than 214,748.3647. The precision and scale of a **money** or **smallmoney** variable are fixed by Microsoft SQL Server. The scale is fixed to 4.

Application of Currency Variables

1. Change   the   statement   as   follows:

```
DECLARE @EmplStatus int,
    @IsMarried bit,
    @WeeklyHours Decimal(6,2),
    @HourlySalary SmallMoney,
    @WeeklySalary SmallMoney;
SET @IsMarried = 1;
SET @EmplStatus = 2;
SET @WeeklyHours = 36.50;
SET @HourlySalary = 15.72;
SET @WeeklySalary = @WeeklyHours * @HourlySalary;
SELECT @EmplStatus AS [Employee Status],
    @IsMarried AS [Married?],
    @WeeklyHours AS [Hours],
    @HourlySalary AS Hourly,
    @WeeklySalary AS Weekly;
GO
```

2. Execute the statement

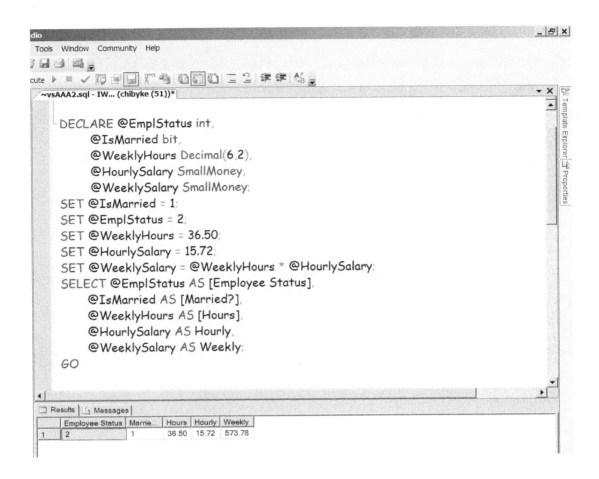

5.2.5   Characters and Strings

iii.   Character Values

A field of characters can consist of any kinds of alphabetical symbols in any combination, readable or not. If you want a variable to hold a fixed number of characters, such as the book shelf numbers of a library, declare it with the **char** data type. Here is an example:

DECLARE @Gender char;

By default, the **char** data type can be applied to a variable that would hold one character at a time. After declaring the variable, when initializing it, include its value in single-quotes. Here is an example:

```
DECLARE @Gender char;
SET @Gender = N'M';
SELECT @Gender AS Gender;
GO
```

By default, when you initialize a character variable, the interpreter reserves 8 bits of memory for the variable. This could be a problem if you want to store characters other than those used in US English. The alternative is to ask the interpreter to reserve 16 bits of space and follow Unicode rules. To do this, when initializing the variable, precede its value with N, just like in the above example.

If you include more than one character in the single-quotes, only the first (most left) character would be stored in the variable, the reason is because char without any fixed value will only accommodate one character. So other characters will be truncated. Here is an example:

```
DECLARE @Gender char;
SET @Gender = N'Male';
SELECT @Gender AS Gender;
GO
```

If you include more than one character in the single-quotes, all the characters would be stored in the variable, the reason is because char(4) is assigned with the required fixed value to be able to accommodate the number of characters provided. Here is an example:

```
DECLARE @Gender char(4);
SET @Gender = N'Male';
```

SELECT @Gender AS Gender;

GO

```
SQLCMD                                                              _ |□| x|
PS SQLSERVER:\SQL\IWUALAMC-PC\DEFAULT+chibyke\> SQLCMD
1> DECLARE @Gender char(4);
2> SET @Gender = N'Male';
3> SELECT @Gender AS Gender;
4> GO
Gender
------
Male

(1 rows affected)
1>
```

iv.   Strings

A string is a character or a combination of characters. If a variable will hold strings of different lengths, declare it with the **varchar** data type. The maximum length of text that a field of **varchar** type can hold is equivalent to 8 kilobytes. In some cases, you will need to change or specify the number of characters used in a string variable. Although a First Name and a Book Title variables should use the **varchar** type, both variables would not have the same length of entries. As it happens, people hardly have a first name that is beyond 30 characters and many book titles go beyond 40 characters. In this case, both variables would use the same data type but different lengths.

To specify the maximum number of characters that can be stored in a string variable, on the right side of **char** or **varchar**, type an opening and a closing parentheses. Inside of the parentheses, type the desired number. To initialize the variable, if you are using the Command Prompt (Powershell), include its value between double-quotes, though it's optional. Here is an example:

```
SQLCMD                                                                    _ |□| x|
PS SQLSERVER:\SQL\IWUALAMC-PC\DEFAULT+chibyke\> SQLCMD
1> DECLARE @firstName varchar(30),
2>                           @lastName varchar(30);
3> SET                 @firstName = "Philip";
4> SET                 @lastName  = "Ihueze";
5> SELECT              @firstName AS [First Name],
6>      @lastName  AS [Last Name];
7> GO
First Name                        Last Name
------------------------------    ------------------------------
Philip                            Ihueze

(1 rows affected)
1> _
```

If you are using the query window, don't include the string value in double-quotes; otherwise, you would receive an error:

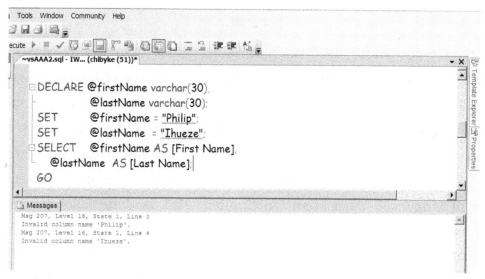

Therefore, if using the query window includes the string in single-quotes, you will get the required answer:

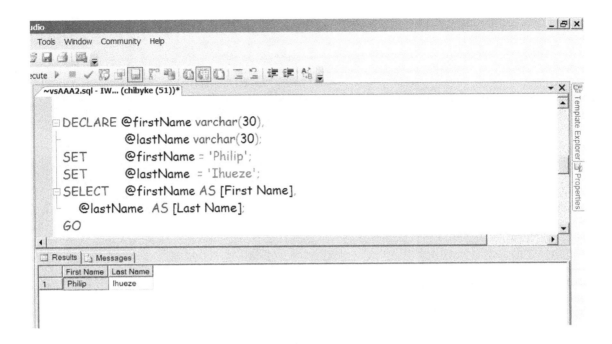

The **text** data type can be used on a variable whose data would consist of ASCII characters. As opposed to a **varchar** type of field, a text type of field can hold text that is longer than 8 kilobytes, though the text data type is outdated and may not be supported by newer version MS SQL Server edition. The **nchar**, **nvarchar**, and **ntext** types follow the same rules as the **char**, **varchar**, and **text** respectively, except that they can be applied to variables that would hold international characters, that is, characters of languages other than US English. This is done following the rules of Unicode formats.

When initializing the variable, to follow Unicode rules, precede its value with N follow by single-quotes. This rule applies to both the Query window and PowerShell as I have demonstrated in previous examples.

Notice that, in Powershell, if you are not using Unicode rules, the string must be included in double-quotes and if you are using Unicode, the string must be included in single-quotes.

Application of String Variables

1. Change   the   statement   as   follows:

```sql
DECLARE @FirstName   nvarchar(20),
        @LastName    nvarchar(20),
        @FullName    nvarchar(40),
        @EmplStatus  int,
        @IsMarried   bit,
        @WeeklyHours Decimal(6,2),
        @HourlySalary SmallMoney,
        @WeeklySalary SmallMoney;
SET @FirstName    = N'Goodluck';
SET @LastName     = N'Iwuala';
SET @FullName     = @LastName + N', ' + @FirstName;
SET @IsMarried    = 1;
SET @EmplStatus   = 2;
SET @WeeklyHours  = 8.50;
SET @HourlySalary = 100.1;
SET @WeeklySalary = @WeeklyHours * @HourlySalary;
SELECT @FullName As [Full Name],
       @EmplStatus AS [Employee Status],
       @IsMarried AS [Married?],
       @WeeklyHours AS [Hours],
       @HourlySalary AS Hourly,
       @WeeklySalary AS Weekly;
GO
```

   2. Execute the statement

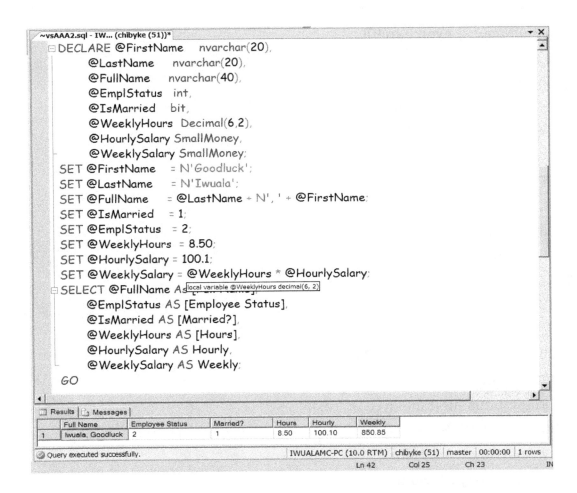

```
~vsAAA2.sql - IW... (chibyke (51))*
DECLARE @FirstName    nvarchar(20),
        @LastName     nvarchar(20),
        @FullName     nvarchar(40),
        @EmplStatus   int,
        @IsMarried    bit,
        @WeeklyHours  Decimal(6,2),
        @HourlySalary SmallMoney,
        @WeeklySalary SmallMoney;
SET @FirstName   = N'Goodluck';
SET @LastName    = N'Iwuala';
SET @FullName    = @LastName + N', ' + @FirstName;
SET @IsMarried   = 1;
SET @EmplStatus  = 2;
SET @WeeklyHours = 8.50;
SET @HourlySalary = 100.1;
SET @WeeklySalary = @WeeklyHours * @HourlySalary;
SELECT @FullName AS [local variable @WeeklyHours decimal(6, 2)]
       @EmplStatus AS [Employee Status],
       @IsMarried AS [Married?],
       @WeeklyHours AS [Hours],
       @HourlySalary AS Hourly,
       @WeeklySalary AS Weekly;
GO
```

	Full Name	Employee Status	Married?	Hours	Hourly	Weekly
1	Iwuala, Goodluck	2	1	8.50	100.10	850.85

Query executed successfully.   IWUALAMC-PC (10.0 RTM) | chibyke (51) | master | 00:00:00 | 1 rows

Ln 42   Col 25   Ch 23   IN

3. Save the file as **Variables** in your My Documents folder if you are so desirous, for future us.

5.2.6   Date and Time Types

i.   Time Values

A time is a non-spatial measure used to count a certain number of lapses that have occurred from a non-spatial starting point. The primary starting point is called midnight. The primary unit of measure of time is called the second. A second is identified by an integer. In reality, the second is divided in 1000 fractions, counted from 0 to 999 and called milliseconds. A millisecond is identified by an integer. Starting with the second, a measure of 60 seconds, counted from 0 to 59, is called a minute. A minute is identified by an integer. A group of 60 minutes, counted from 0 to 59, is called an hour. An hour is also identified by an integer.

To represent a time value, there are rules you must follow. The rules can be verified in the Time tab of the Customize Regional Options of the Regional and Language Options of the Control Panel:

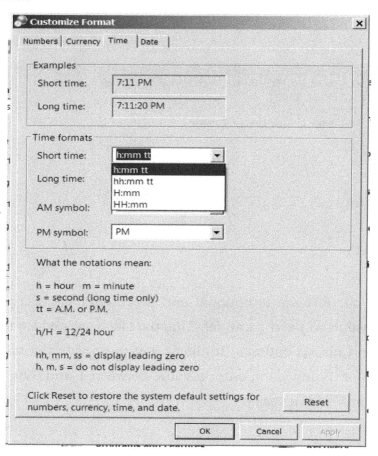

To support time values, Transact-SQL provides the **TIME** data type. To declare a variable that would hold a time value, use **TIME** as the data type. To initialize the variable, use the following formula:

hh:mm

hh:mm:ss

hh:mm:ss[.*fractional seconds*]

The first part includes the hour with a value between 1 and 23. If the value is less than 10, you can write it with a leading 0, as in 08. The second part represents the minutes and holds a value between 1 and 59. If the value is less than 10, you can type it with a leading 0, as in 04. The values are separated by : . The value is included in single-quotes. To indicate that you want to follow Unicode rules, precede the value with N. Here is an example:

DECLARE @arrivalTime time;

SET @arrivalTime = N'19:22';

SELECT @arrivalTime AS [Arrival Time];

GO

```
PS SQLSERVER:\SQL\IWUALAMC-PC\DEFAULT+chibyke\> SQLCMD
1> DECLARE @arrivalTime time;
2> SET @arrivalTime = N'19:22';
3> SELECT @arrivalTime AS [Arrival Time];
4> GO
Arrival Time
----------------
19:22:00.0000000

(1 rows affected)
1>
```

The third part of our formula is optional and represents the seconds portion of the time and holds a value between 1 and 59. This part is separated from the previous one with :. The last part also is optional. It allows you to provide the milliseconds part of the time. If you want to provide it, enter a value between 1 and 999. This is separated from the seconds part with a period .

v. Date Values

A group of 24 hours, counted from 1 to 23, is called a day. In reality, a day is made of 24 hours and a few more seconds. Those are various ways used to identify a day. We will mention them below. Above the day, the unit of measure is called a year. A year is identified by a numeric value. Normally, a year is represented with 4 digits, from 0 to 9999. To make it easy to manage years, they are grouped in some units. The years that occurred before Jesus Christ are identified as BC. Then, there is a starting point referred to as 0. A group of 1000 years is called a millennium. The years in a millennium must each be identified with 4 digits. An example is 1608. Another example is 1978. Yet another example is 2118.

A group of 100 years is called a century. The years in a century can be identified with 2 digits. An example is 08. Another example is 78. One more example is 18. Within a year, each day can be identified by a numeric value. The first day is 1, or can be referred to as Day 1. Each of the other days in a year can be identified with a natural number, such as 216; that would be Day 216 starting from the beginning of the year. The number of days in a year depends on various factors. For example, in some scenarios, such as some commercial or accounting procedures, a year would count for 360 days. In most calendars, a year can have 365 days every year except that, after 4 years, the year would have 366 days (remember, we mentioned that a day is actually made of 24 hours and a few seconds; these seconds are grouped every 4 years to count as a whole day). This is referred to as a leap year.

To help manage the days of a year, a year is divided in 12 units each called a month. Each month can be identified by a number or a name. When a month is identified with a number, it can use a value between 1 and 12. When it comes to names, a month can use a long and/or a short name. The long names are January, February, March, April, May, June, July, August, September, October, November, and December. The short names are represented with three characters: Jan, Feb, Mar, Apr, May, Jun, Jul, Aug, Sep, Oct, Nov, and Dec. Each month has a certain number of days. A day in a month can be identified with an integer. The first day of the month is 1. The 15th day would be identified as 15 or Day 15. The number of days in a month depends on various factors.

We mentioned that a day in a month can be identified with a number and a month has a name, within a year. A day can be identified by its number, its month, and the numeric value of the year. There are various rules you must follow to represent a date. The rules can be checked in the Date tab of the Customize Regional Options accessible from the Regional and Language Options of the Control Panel:

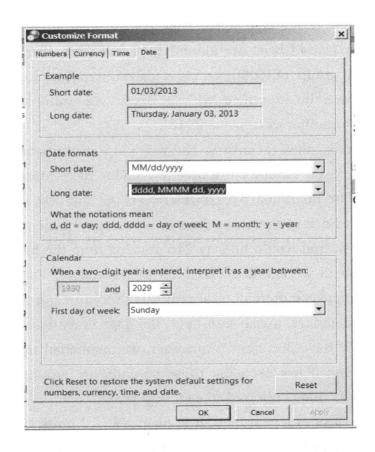

To help manage the months of a year, a year can be divided in either quarters or semesters. A year has 4 quarters that each contains 3 months. A year also has 2 semesters that each has 6 months. To help manage the days in a month, the month in divided in parts each called a week. Normally, each week has 7 days and each month is expected to have 4 weeks.

To assist you with date values, Microsoft SQL Server provides the **DATE** data type. This data type counts dates starting from January 1st, 0001 up to December 31st, 9999. Therefore, to declare a variable that would hold a date value, use the **DATE** data type. To initialize a **DATE** variable, use one of the following formulas:

YYYYMMDD

YYYY-MM-DD

MM-DD-YY

MM-DD-YYYY

MM/DD/YY

MM/DD/YYYY

You can start the value with a 4-year digit. If you use the first formula, YYYYMMDD, you must provide 4 digits for the year, immediately followed by 2 digits for the month, immediately followed by 2 digits for the day. An example would be:

DECLARE @BD DATE;

SET @BD = N'19791226';

SELECT @BD AS [Special Day];

GO

In US English, this represents December 26th, 1979:

You can provide the value in one unit with 6 digits. In this case, the left 2 digits would be considered the year. Consider the following example:

DECLARE @BD DATE;

SET @BD = N'791226';

SELECT @BD AS [Special Day];

GO

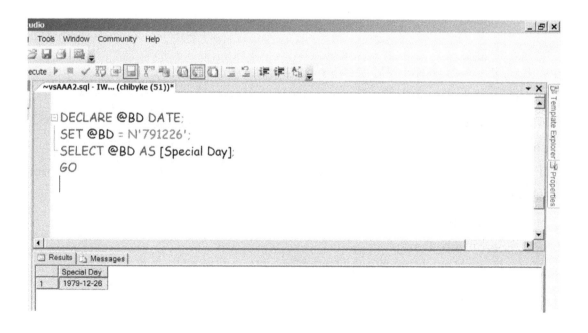

Instead of providing the whole value in one combination of digits, you can use the second formula. Once again you must provide 4 digits for the year, followed by the "-" separator, followed by 1 or 2 digits for the month, followed by the "-" separator, followed by 1 or 2 digits for the day. An example would be

DECLARE @EventDay date;

SET @EventDay = N'1960-10-1';

SELECT @EventDay AS [Independent Day];

GO

In US English, this represents October 1st, 1960

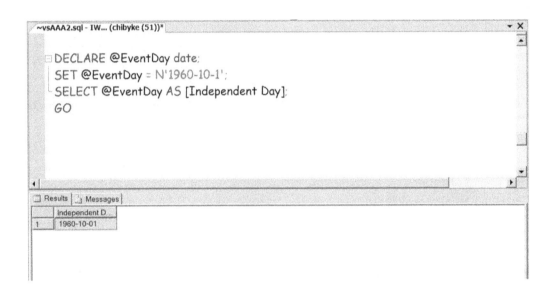

We saw that, if you use the MM-DD-YY or MM/DD/YY, you can provide a year with 2 digits. In this case:

1. If the number representing the year is less than 50, the year would be considered as belonging to the current century
2. If the number representing the year is greater than 50, the year is considered as belonging to the previous century

    Here are examples:

DECLARE @SomeDate Date;

SET   @SomeDate = N'5-7-05';

PRINT @SomeDate;

GO

PRINT N'-----------';

GO

```
DECLARE @SomeDate Date;
SET        @SomeDate = N'5/7/05';
PRINT @SomeDate;
GO
PRINT N'-----------';
GO
DECLARE @SomeDate Date;
SET        @SomeDate = N'5-7-41';
PRINT @SomeDate;
GO
PRINT N'-----------';
GO
DECLARE @SomeDate Date;
SET        @SomeDate = N'5/7/41';
PRINT @SomeDate;
GO
PRINT N'-----------';
GO
DECLARE @SomeDate Date;
SET        @SomeDate = N'5-7-81';
PRINT @SomeDate;
GO
PRINT N'-----------';
GO
DECLARE @SomeDate Date;
SET        @SomeDate = N'5/7/81';
PRINT @SomeDate;
GO
PRINT N'-----------';
GO
```
Here are examples of results

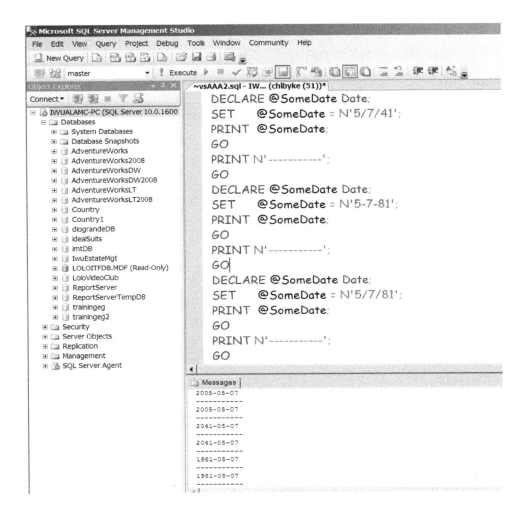

Once again, it is better to provide a year with 4 digits.

Application of Date/Time Variables

1. Type the statement in the Query window as follows:

```
DECLARE @FirstName    nvarchar(20),
    @LastName    nvarchar(20),
    @FullName    nvarchar(40),
    @DateHired    date,
    @EmplStatus    int,
    @IsMarried    bit,
    @WeeklyHours  decimal(6,2),
```

```
        @HourlySalary SmallMoney,
        @WeeklySalary SmallMoney;
SET @FirstName    = N'Cathrine';
SET @LastName     = N'Goodluck';
SET @FullName     = @LastName + N', ' + @FirstName;
SET @DateHired    = N'12/05/1998';
SET @IsMarried    = 1;
SET @EmplStatus   = 2;
SET @WeeklyHours  = 100.50;
SET @HourlySalary = 25.72;
SET @WeeklySalary = @WeeklyHours * @HourlySalary;
SELECT @FullName As [Full Name],
        @DateHired AS [Date Hired],
        @EmplStatus AS [Empl Status],
        @IsMarried AS [Married?],
        @WeeklyHours AS [Hours],
        @HourlySalary AS Hourly,
        @WeeklySalary AS Weekly;
GO
```

2. Execute the statement

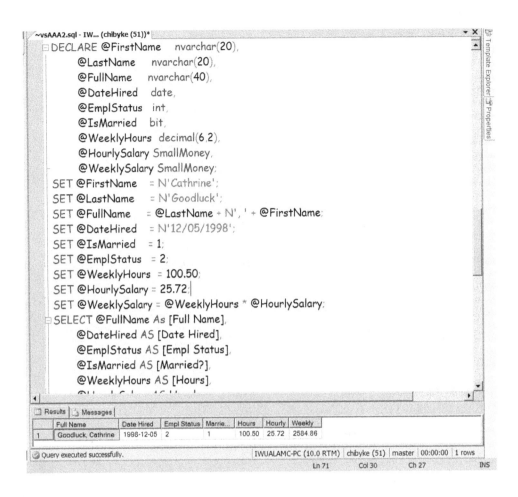

3. Close the query window
4. If asked whether you want to save the file, click No

Date and Time Values

Instead of singly declaring a date or a time value, you may want to combine both values. To support this, Transact-SQL provides the **DATETIME2** data type. This data type counts dates from January 1st, 0001 and ends on December 31st, 9999. Therefore, to declare a variable that supports a date value, a time value, or a combination of a date and time values, use the **DATETIME2** data type. To initialize the variable, use one of the following formulas:

YYYYMMDD

YYYYMMDD hh:mm:ss

YYYYMMDD hh:mm:ss[.*fractional seconds*]

YYYY-MM-DD

YYYY-MM-DD hh:mm:ss

YYYY-MM-DD hh:mm:ss[.*fractional seconds*]

MM-DD-YY

MM-DD-YY hh:mm:ss

MM-DD-YY hh:mm:ss[.*fractional seconds*]

MM-DD-YYYY

MM-DD-YYYY hh:mm:ss

MM-DD-YYYY hh:mm:ss[.*fractional seconds*]

MM/DD/YY

MM/DD/YY hh:mm:ss

MM/DD/YY hh:mm:ss[.*fractional seconds*]

MM/DD/YYYY

MM/DD/YYYY hh:mm:ss

MM/DD/YYYY hh:mm:ss[.*fractional seconds*]

Remember to include the value in single-quotes. Here are examples:

```
DECLARE @FullName nvarchar(60),
        @DateOfBirth date,
        @DateRegistered datetime2

SET @FullName      = N'Chibueze Iwuala';
SET @DateOfBirth   = N'19900426';
SET @DateRegistered = N'20090629';
SELECT @FullName AS [Full Name],
    @DateOfBirth AS [Date of Birth],
    @DateRegistered AS [Date Registered];

SET @FullName      = N'Eze Felista Udoka';
SET @DateOfBirth   = N'1969-10-25';
SET @DateRegistered = N'2009-08-02';
SELECT @FullName AS [Full Name],
    @DateOfBirth AS [Date of Birth],
    @DateRegistered AS [Date Registered];
```

```sql
SET @FullName     = N'Nwachukwu C. A. N';
SET @DateOfBirth   = N'06-16-70';
SET @DateRegistered = N'2009-12-24 12:36';
SELECT @FullName AS [Full Name],
    @DateOfBirth AS [Date of Birth],
    @DateRegistered AS [Date Registered];


SET @FullName     = N'Eze Vigor';
SET @DateOfBirth   = N'1996-10-16';
SET @DateRegistered = N'10/14/94 09:42:05.136';
SELECT @FullName AS [Full Name],
    @DateOfBirth AS [Date of Birth],
    @DateRegistered AS [Date Registered];


SET @FullName     = N'Eze Ikechukwu';
SET @DateOfBirth   = N'08/10/70';
SET @DateRegistered = N'2009-06-02 12:36';
SELECT @FullName AS [Full Name],
    @DateOfBirth AS [Date of Birth],
    @DateRegistered AS [Date Registered];


SET @FullName     = N'Esther Okunwa';
SET @DateOfBirth   = N'03-10-1983';
SET @DateRegistered = N'7/22/2009 10:24:46.248';
SELECT @FullName AS [Full Name],
    @DateOfBirth AS [Date of Birth],
    @DateRegistered AS [Date Registered];


SET @FullName     = N'Andy Okebugwu';
SET @DateOfBirth   = N'06/16/1980';
SET @DateRegistered = N'02-09-2009 12:36';
SELECT @FullName AS [Full Name],
    @DateOfBirth AS [Date of Birth],
    @DateRegistered AS [Date Registered];
```

GO

If you start the value with two digits, the first part is considered a month and not the year. Besides the **DATE**, the **TIME**, and the **DATETIME2** data types, Transact-SQL supports the **smalldatetime** and the **datetime** data types. These are old data types. Although still available, they are kept for backward compatibility and you should stop using them.

System Data Types

bigint	binary	bit	char	CLR
cursor	date	datetime	datetime2	datetimeoffset
decimal	float	hierarchyid	image	int
money	nchar	ntext	numeric	nvarchar

real	rowversion	smalldatetime	smallint	smallmoney
sql_variant	table	text	time	timestamp
int, bigint, smallint, and tinyint (Transact-SQL)	varbinary	varchar	uniqueidentifier	xml (Transact-SQL)

5.3   User-Defined Types

If you have programmed in languages like C/C++ or Pascal, you are probably familiar with the ability to give a friendly name to a known data type. Transact-SQL also gives you this option. A user-defined data type (UDT) is a technique of creating a data type based on an existing Transact-SQL data type, though I have discussed this topic in previous chapter, but in brief.

5.3.1   Creating a User-Defined Type

Before creating a user-defined data type, you must be familiar with the existing data types. If you want, you can create an alias name for one of these data types. You can do this visually or programmatically.

To visually create a UDT, in the Object Explorer, expand a database, expand its Programmability node, and expand the Types item. Under Types, right-click User-Defined Data Types and click New User-Defined Data Type...

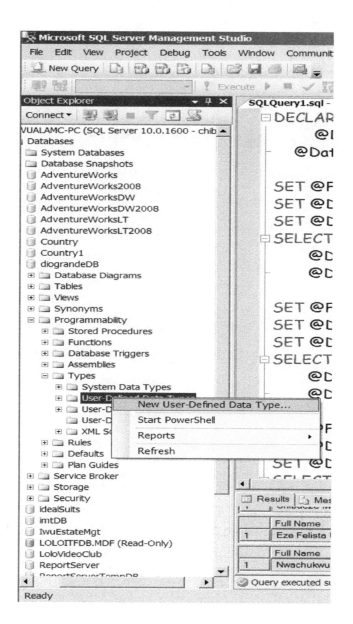

This would open:

The first piece of information you must provide is the schema that will own the new type. Normally, a default schema is provided and you can just accept it. The two most important pieces of information you must provide are a name for the new type as alias and the Transact-SQL type on which the type will be based. In the Name text box, enter a name of your choice. The name must follow the rules of naming objects in Transact-SQL. In the Data Type combo box, select the data type of your choice. Of course, you must know what type you want to use. After entering and selecting the desired information, click OK.

To create a UDT with SQL Code, the basic formula to use is:

CREATE TYPE *AliasName* FROM *BaseType*

To get assistance from template code, open a Query window. From the Templates Explorer, expand the User-Defined Data Type node. Drag Create User-Defined Data Type and drop it in the Query window. Skeleton code will be generated for you:

```
-- ================================
-- Create User-defined Data Type
-- ================================
USE <database_name,sysname,AdventureWorks>
```

```
GO


-- Create the data type
CREATE TYPE <schema_name,sysname,dbo>.<type_name,sysname,Phone>
        FROM <base_type,,nvarchar> (<precision,int,25>) <allow_null,,NULL>


-- Create table using the data type
CREATE TABLE <table_name,sysname,test_data_type>
(
        ID int NOT NULL,
        Phone <schema_name,sysname,dbo>.<type_name,sysname,Phone> NULL
)
GO
```

You start with the **CREATE TYPE** expression, followed by the desired name for the new type. After the **FROM** keyword, type an existing Transact-SQL data type. Here is an example:

```
CREATE TYPE NaturalNumber FROM int;
GO
```

In the same way, you can create as many aliases of known data types as you want. You must also be aware of rules that govern each data type. Here are examples:

```
CREATE TYPE NaturalNumber FROM int;
GO
CREATE TYPE ShortString FROM nvarchar(30);
GO
CREATE TYPE atomString FROM nchar(6);
GO
CREATE TYPE LongString FROM nvarchar(80);
GO
CREATE TYPE Salary FROM smallmoney;
GO
CREATE TYPE Boolean FROM bit;
GO
```

5.3.2 Application of User-Defined Type

After creating a UDT, you can use it as you see fit. For example, you can declare a variable for it. Then, before using it, you must initialize it with the appropriate value, just like other system data types. Here are examples:

```
DECLARE @EmployeeID NaturalNumber,
        @gender atomString,
        @EmployeeNumber atomString,
        @FirstName ShortString,
        @LastName ShortString,
        @Address LongString,
        @HourlySalary Salary,
        @IsMarried Boolean;
SET    @EmployeeID = 1;
SET    @EmployeeNumber = N'01-380';
SET    @FirstName = N'Ujunwa';
SET    @LastName = N'Iheanacho';
SET    @Address = N'Mbano Imo State';
SET    @HourlySalary = 50.75;
SET    @IsMarried = 0;
SET         @Gender =N'Female';
SELECT  @EmployeeID AS [Employee ID], @EmployeeNumber AS [Employee #],
    @FirstName AS [First Name], @LastName AS [Last Name],
    @Address, @HourlySalary AS [Hourly Salary], @Gender AS [Gender],
    @IsMarried AS [Is Married ?];
GO
```

Often times, student will ask if the UDT can be mixed with SQL Server data types. Of course, you can mix Transact-SQL data types and your own defined type in your code.

5.3.3 Base Type

The Transact-SQL data type on which the alias data type is based is called *Base Type*. *base_type* is **sysname**, with no default, and can be one of the following values:

bigint	**binary(n)**	**bit**	**char(n)**
date	**datetime**	**datetime2**	**datetimeoffset**
decimal	**float**	**image**	**int**
money	**nchar(n)**	**ntext**	**numeric**
nvarchar(n | max)	**real**	**smalldatetime**	**smallint**
smallmoney	**sql_variant**	**text**	**time**
tinyint	**uniqueidentifier**	**varbinary(n | max)**	**varchar(n | max)**

CHAPTER SIX

TABLE CREATION

Like all relational databases, SQL Server is table-oriented. Once the database is created, the next step is to create the tables. A SQL Server database may include up to 2,147,483,647 objects, including tables, so there is effectively no limit to the number of tables you can create. A table is primarily a list of items or a group of lists. To manage such a list, it should be meticulously organized in such a way that it can be retrieved with ease. To organize this information, it is divided in sections. Here is an example:

Name	Age	Gender	Relationship
Ugonna	25	Male	Brother
Obinna	23	Male	Brother
Nneoma	36	Female	Sister
Catharine	Unknown	Female	Mother
Andy	Unknown	Male	Class Mate

Based on this, a list is simply an arrangement of information and this information, also called data, is stored in a table or tables.

6.1   Tables Names

To complete the creation of a table, you must save it. If you are newly creating a table and decide to save it, you would be prompted to name it. The name of a table:

- Can be made of digits only. For example you can have a table called 12345

- Can start with a digit, a letter, or an underscore
- Can be made of letters, digits, and spaces.

  Besides these rules, you can make up yours to suit the type of table you want to create. But to be consistent and to avoid confusion, here are the rules more preferable to me for the name tables:
- A name can start with a letter. Examples are **abc** or **eze**
- After the first character or a letter, the name will have combinations of underscores, letters, and digits. Examples are **_abc123**, **eze_52_t**
- Unless stated otherwise, a name will not include special characters such as !, @, #, $, %, ^, &, or * because some of it makes meaning to the interpreter.
- If the name is a combination of words, each word will start in uppercase. Examples are **regNo** or **phoneNum or StudInfo** and so on.
- Names of tables must be meaningful and must represent its contents. Examples are: StudBiodata, Courses, personalInfo and so on.
- For the primary key, use the table name + ID. For example, the primary key for the Student table is studentID or studID.
- Give foreign keys the same name as their primary key unless the foreign key enforces a reflexive/recursive relationship, such as MotherID referring back to PersonID in the Family sample database, or the secondary table has multiple foreign keys to the same primary key, such as the many-to-many reflexive relationship in the Material sample database (BillofMaterials.MaterialID to Material.MaterialID and BillofMaterials.SourceMaterialID to Material.MaterialID).
- Avoid inconsistent abbreviations.
- Ensure that you organize a large complex database objects with schemas.

6.2   Designing tables using Management Studio

If you prefer working in a graphical environment, Management Studio provides two primary work surfaces for creating tables, both of which you can use to create new tables or modify existing ones:

i.   The Table Designer tool below lists the table columns vertically and places the column properties below the column grid.

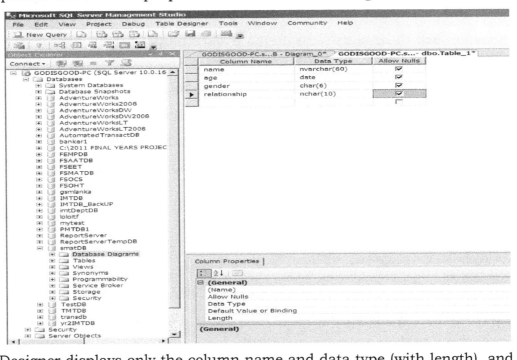

Table Designer displays only the column name and data type (with length), and allows nulls in the column grid. While these are the main properties of a column, I personally find it annoying to have to select each column in order to inspect or change the rest of the properties. Each data type is explained in detail later in this chapter. For some data types, the length property sets the data length, while other data types have fixed lengths. Nulls are discussed in the section "Creating User-Data Columns," later in this chapter. Once an edit is made to the table design, the Save Change Script toolbar button is enabled. This button displays the actual code that the Table Designer will run if the changes are saved.

ii. The Database Designer tool below is more flexible than the Table Designer form in that it can display foreign-key constraints as connections to other tables, if the table is design with a primary key.

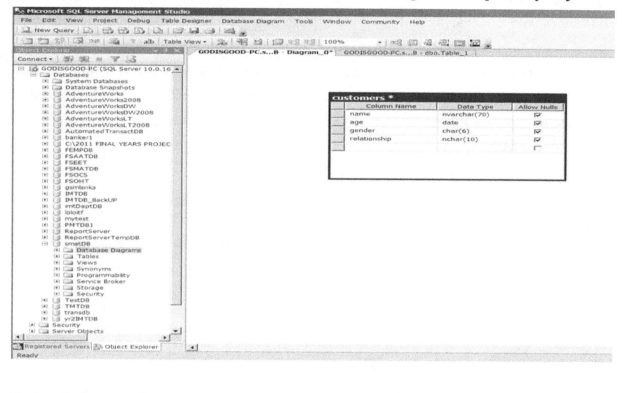

Each of these tools presents a graphical design of the table. Once the design is complete, Management Studio generates a SQL script that applies the changes to the database. When modifying an existing table, often the script must save the data in a temporary table, drop several items, create the new tables, and reinsert the data.

The information of a table is organized in categories called columns or fields and horizontal arrangements called records or rows. A column holds a category of data that is common to all records. A table must have at least one column. This means that you cannot create a table without defining at least one column.

6.3 Column names

SQL Server is very liberal with table and column names, allowing up to 128 Unicode characters and spaces, as well as both uppercase and lowercase letters. Of course, taking advantage of that freedom with wild abandon will be regretted later when typing the lengthy column names and having to place square brackets around columns with spaces. It is more dangerous to discuss naming conventions with programmers than it is to discuss politics in a mixed crowd. Nevertheless, here is an argument between two camps. There is a debate over whether table names should be singular or plural. The plural camp believes that a table is a set of rows, just like object-oriented classes, and as such should be named with a plural name. The reasoning often used by this camp is, "A table of customers is a set of customers. Sets include multiple items, so the table should be named the Customers table, unless you only have one customer, in which case you don't need a database."

From my informal polling, however, the singular-name view is held by about three-fourths of SQL Server developers. These developers hold that the customer table is the customer set, rather than the set of customers. A set of rows is not called a *rows set*, but a *row set,* and because tables are generally discussed as singular items, saying "the Customer table" sounds cleaner than "the Customers table." Most (but not all) developers would agree that consistency is more important than the naming convention itself; what do you think?

Personally, I think that developers choose their naming conventions as a way to distance themselves from sloppy designs they have had to work with in the past. Having worked on poorly designed flat-file databases with plural names, I slightly prefer singular names; anyway, you can still make your choice.

To be able to recognize the categories of information that a column holds, the column should have a customized name. In Microsoft SQL Server, the name of a column displays in the top, the header part, of the column. The name of a column allows the database as a file to identify the column. The name of a column also will help you, the database developer, to identify that column. There are rules and suggestions you must or should follow when naming the columns of a table, is just similar to the ones discussed above in naming rules of tables.

The name of a column:

- Can start with a letter, a digit, or an underscore
- Can include letters, digits, and spaces in any combination

  After respecting these rules, you can add your own rules. Throughout this book, here are the rules we will use to name our columns:

- A name will start with a letter. Examples are **n**, **Vigor**, or **Second**
- After the first character, an underscore or a letter, the name will have combinations of underscores, letters, and digits. Examples are **n24** or **col_52_t**
- Unless specified otherwise, a name will not include special characters such as !, @, #, $, %, ^, &, or *
- If the name is a combination of words, each word will start in uppercase. Examples are **Date Hired**, **LastName**, **Drivers License Number**, or **emailAddress**

In our introduction to tables, we saw that a list could be organized in categories called columns. Here is the example we saw:

Name	Age	Gender	Relationship
Chidiebere	18	Male	Friend
Vigor	24	Unknown	Friend
Vivian	10	Female	Friend
Ikechukwu	12	Male	Friend
Onyii	25	Female	Friend

As you can see from this arrangement, a column is used to particularly classify one type of data. For example, one column can be used to list some names. Another column can be used to list numbers. Yet another column can be used for a select list of items that keep repeating those items.

To organize the information that a column holds, a table needs a series of details about each column. Two aspects are particularly important: a name and the type of data that a column will hold.

6.4   Designing Columns using Management Studio

1.   Create a database called imtDeptDB

2.   In the Object Explorer, expand the imtDeptDB node (click its + button)

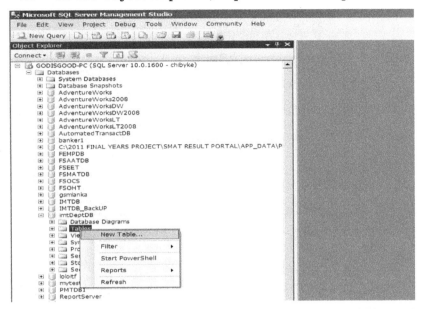

3.   Under imtDeptDB, right-click Tables and click New Table...

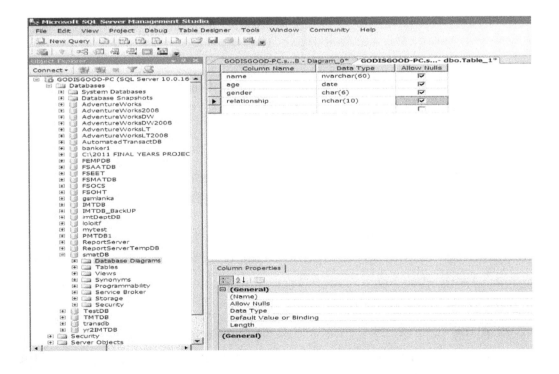

6.4.1 Setting Columns Names

i. As the caret is blinking under the Column Name column, type **name**

ii. Click the arrow of the combo box under the Data Type column

iii. Select **nvarchar(50)** from the list

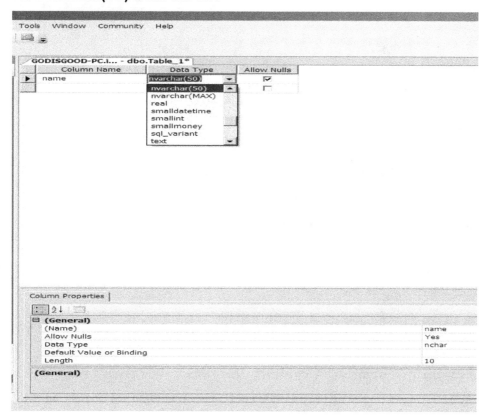

iv. Click the first empty field under name and type **age**

v. Click the arrow of the combo box under the Data Type of age column.

vi. Select **tinyint** from the list box.

vii. Repeat steps i – iii above until all the columns are created.

viii. The complete table will look as follow:

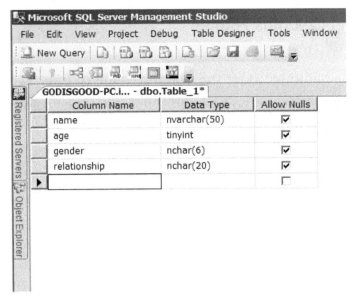

ix. To save your table, on the Standard toolbar, click the Save button 💾

x. In the Choose Name dialog box, type **directoryTbl**

xi. Click OK and close the table.

6.4.2 The DataTypes

After deciding on the name of a column, the database needs to know what kind of information the column would hold. Since there are various kinds of information a database can deal with, we saw the types of data that Microsoft SQL Server can support in chapter five. Therefore, you must specify the data type that is necessary for a particular column, while doing that, consider the computer memory and ensure that memory space are not waited due to improper allocation space to columns. It is worthy to note that datatypes in Columns serves two purposes:

i. It enforces the first level of data integrity. Character data won't be accepted into a datetime data or numeric column. Lazy and unqualified database developers design databases with every column set to nvarchar to ease data entry; this is tantamount to a wasting of system resources. The data type is a valuable data-validation tool that should not be overlooked.

ii. It determines the amount of disk storage allocated to the column.

6.4.3 The Length of Data

A database deals with various types of data, appropriate or not for certain fields. This means that you should take care of jobs behind the scenes as much as you can. One way you can do this is by controlling the amount of information that can be stored in a particular field. As various columns can hold different types of data, so can the same data type control its own mechanism of internal data entered. The length of data means different things to different fields. Columns that carry the same data type can have different lengths.

6.5 Creation of Columns with Codes

We saw that the primary formula to create a table was:
CREATE TABLE *TableName*

After specifying the name of the table, you must list the columns of the table. The list of columns starts with an opening parenthesis "(". The list ends with a closing parenthesis ")". Each column must be separated from the next with a comma, except for the last column and if the table has only one column. You can include all columns on the same line if possible as follows:

CREATE TABLE Country(*Column1, Column2, Column3*)

Alternatively, to make your statement easier to read and I recommend this arrangement, you should create each column on its own line as follows:

```
CREATE TABLE Country(
Column1
,Column2
,Column3);
```

There are two primary pieces of information you must specify for each column: its name and its type. Therefore, the syntax of creating a column is:

ColumnName DataType Options

The name of a column should follow the same rules and suggestions we reviewed for the columns above. After typing the name of the column, type the appropriate data type for the column. Remember that some of the data types need to have a length. In the case of text-based columns, when using SQL Code to create your columns, you cannot rely on the default length of strings suggested by SQL; I explained the reason in chapter three. As it happens, the SQL Server Management Studio specifies different default values for text-based columns. Therefore, when using SQL Code to create your columns, you should (strongly) specify your own default length for text-based columns.

We also saw that you could use sample code to create a table. This allows you to have more control over the various columns you want the table to have. To do this, open an empty query window and display the Templates Explorer. Expand the Table node. Under Table, you can drag Create Table, Add Column, or Drop Column, and drop it in the query window. If you use dropped Add Column or Drop Column, you can delete the undesired sections of the code and isolate only the part that handles table creation. Here is an example:

```
--=============================================================
-- Add column template
--
-- This template creates a table, then it adds a new column to the table.
--=============================================================
USE <database, sysname, imtDeptDB >
GO
```

```
CREATE     TABLE     <schema_name,     sysname,     dbo>.<table_name,     sysname,
sample_table>
(
        column1 int
        ,column2 char(10)
)
GO
```

6.5.1   Creating a Table

1.   In the Object Explorer, right-click imtDeptDB and click New Query
2.   In the code editor, type the following:

```
USE imtDeptDB;
GO


--This code will create Customers Table in imtDeptDB database.

BEGIN TRY
        CREATE TABLE Customers (
                DriverLicNum nvarchar(32)
                ,DateIssued DATE
                ,DateExpired date
                ,CustomerName nvarchar(60)
                ,CustomerAddress NVARCHAR(120)
                ,CustomerCity NvarChar(40)
                ,CustomerState NVarChar(2)
                ,CustomerPostalCode nvarchar(20)
                ,HomePhone nvarchar(20)
                ,OrganDonor BIT);
END TRY
BEGIN CATCH
        SELECT N'Report the following error: ' + ERROR_MESSAGE();
END CATCH
```

GO

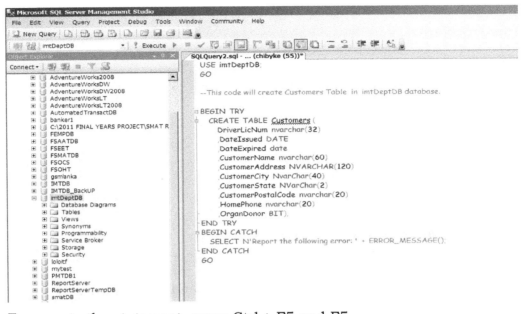

3. To execute the statement, press Ctrl + F5 and F5.

4. Close the Query window

5. When asked whether you want to save the text, click No if you don't want to save the code.

6.5.2 Using User-Defined Data-Types

A user-data column stores user data. These columns typically fall into two categories: columns users use to identify a person, place, thing, event, or action, and columns that further describe the person, place, thing, event, or action. SQL Server tables may have up to 1,024 columns, but well-designed relational-database tables seldom have more than 25, and most have only a handful.

Data columns are created during table creation by listing the columns as parameters to the CREATE TABLE command. The columns are listed within parentheses as column name, data type, and any column attributes such as constraints, nullability, or default value:

CREATE TABLE TableName (

ColumnName DATATYPE Attributes,
ColumnName DATATYPE Attributes
);
GO

Data columns can be added to existing tables using the ALTER TABLE ADD *columnname* command. Here is an example:

```
ALTER TABLE TableName
ADD ColumnName DATATYPE Attributes;
GO
```

An existing column may be modified with the ALTER TABLE ALTER COLUMN command. Here is an example:

```
ALTER TABLE TableName
ALTER COLUMN ColumnName NEWDATATYPE Attributes;
GO
```

In chapter 5, we saw that you can create *user-defined data types* for existing Transact-SQL data types. In chapter 5, we stored our types in the master database. If you are working on a database, you can create and store your new types in it. As mentioned in chapter 5, to visually create a UDT, in the Object Explorer, expand your database, expand its Programmability node, and expand its Types node. You will see the DataTypes you created.

To create the data type(s). Here are examples:
```
USE imtDeptDB;
GO
```

```
--This code will create User Define DataType (UDT) in imtDeptDB database.
CREATE TYPE naturalNumber FROM int;
GO
CREATE TYPE smallXter FROM nvarchar(20);
GO
```

```
CREATE TYPE gender FROM nchar(6);
GO
CREATE TYPE longXter FROM nvarchar(80);
GO
CREATE TYPE Salary FROM money;
GO
CREATE TYPE Boolean FROM bit;
GO
CREATE TYPE dateOfBirth FROM date;
GO
```

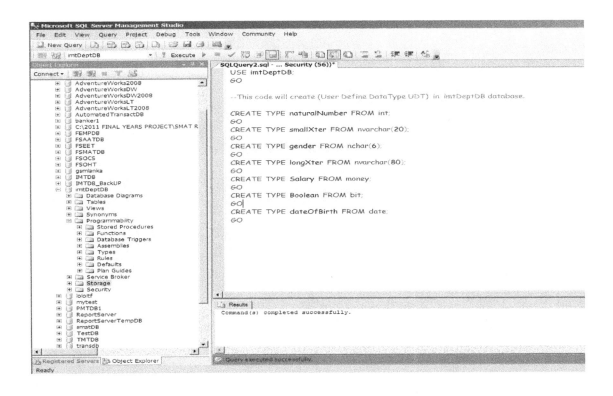

After creating the UDT(s), you can use it (them) for your column(s) when creating tables. To do this visually, after displaying the table in design view, click the column name; click the arrow of the Data Type combo box to display a mix of Transact-SQL types and your own defined types.

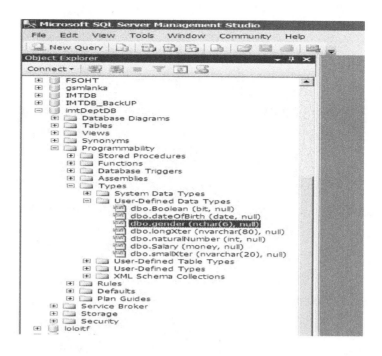

Referring to a Column

We will write many expressions that include the names of columns. In such expressions, you will need to indicate the particular column you are referring to. There are various ways you can do this. To refer to, or to indicate a table:

- You must type the name of the table to which the column belongs, followed by the period operator, followed by the name of the column. An example would be **customer.name**

- You can type extraYrschema, followed by the period operator, followed by the name of the table to which the column belongs, followed by the period operator, followed by the name of the column. An example would be **extraYrschema. customer.name**

- You can type the name of the database that owns the table's column, followed by the period operator, followed by **extraYrschema** which is the schema name, followed by the period operator, followed by the name of the table to which the column belongs, followed by the period operator, followed by the name of the column. An example would be **imtDeptDB. extraYrschema.customer.name**

Using the Alias Name of a Table

You can create an alias name of a table as show in previous lesson above, to use in an expression that involves a column. To do this, type a letter or a word that will represent the table to which the column belongs. The letter or the word is followed by a period operator, and followed by the name of the column. An example would be **C.name**. After FROM clause, you must type the name of the table in full, followed by space, and followed by the letter or the word. An example would be **customer.C**.

Columns Maintenance

Column maintenance consists of reviewing or changing any of the columns properties. This includes reviewing the structure of columns of a table, renaming a column, deleting a column, changing the data type or the nullity of a column, and so on.

Column Review

To see the structure of a table in the SQL Server Management Studio, in the Object Explorer, you can expand it, as shown below:

To view the columns of a table using SQL code, in a query window, execute **sp_columns** followed by the name of the table the columns belongs to. Here is an example:

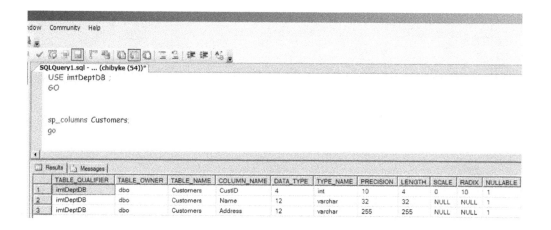

The Properties of a Column

A column property on a table controls what kind of data is appropriate for that particular column. The characteristics that identify or describe such a table are defined as its properties. As we have seen previously, three primary properties are particularly important and required for each column: the name, the data type, and the length. Besides these, some other properties can be used to further control the behaviour of a particular field (column). Besides the name, data type and length of a column, you can control the columns of a table using the **Columns** property sheet in the lower section of the table in Design View. These properties sometimes depend on the data type of the column. Therefore, to specify the properties of a column, you must first select it in the upper section of the table. This selection can be done by just clicking the name, the data type, or the length of the column. Then you can either press F6 or click the first field in the lower section, select the desired property and type the necessary value, these is not necessary if you are creating the table with SQL Script:

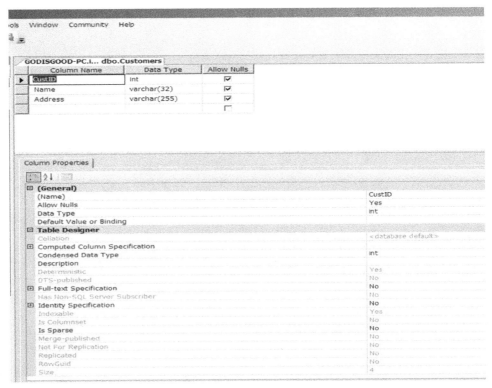

Description of the Column Properties

Description: Common and enabled for all fields, the description is used for a sentence that describes the column. You can type anything on that field.

Collation

Because different languages use different mechanisms in their alphabetic characters, this can affect the way some sort algorithms or queries are performed on data, you can ask the database to apply a certain language mechanism to the field by changing the **Collation** property. Otherwise, you should accept the default collation of the table.

To specify the collation of a column when creating using SQL Script, type **COLLATE**, followed by the desired collation code. Below is an example:
CREATE TABLE Customers(
name varchar(50) COLLATE SQL_Latin1_General_CP1_CI_AS
);

Modifying a Column

When making a change to a column, you are altering the table. Therefore, you must notify the table about your intention to alter it; to support this operation SQL starts with the following formula:
ALTER TABLE *TableName*

When using this statement, the **ALTER TABLE** expression is required and it is followed by the name of the table.

Adding a New Column

After a table has already been created, you can still add a new column to it.
To add a new column in SQL Server Management Studio, first right-click the table and click Design Table. To add a new column to the end of the table, click the first empty field under Column Name, type a name, and specify the other options.

To insert a new column between two existing one, right-click the column that will succeed it and click Insert Column:

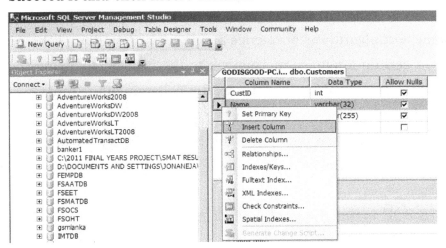

This would create a new empty field. Type the desired name and specify the other options.

In SQL Code, the basic formula to add a new column to an existing table is:
ALTER TABLE *TableName*
ADD *ColumnName Properties*

The *ColumnName* factor is required. In fact, on the right side of the ADD keyword, define the column by its name and using all the options we reviewed for columns.

Here is an example:
use **imtDeptDB**;

-- This code will Alter the Customers Table and a Column to it

alter table **customers**

```
       add phoneNum char(11) null;
GO
```

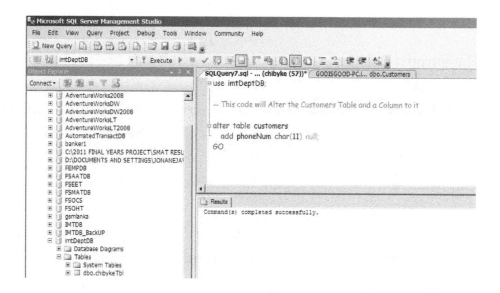

When this code is executed, a new column name phoneNum, of type **char**, with a limit of 11 characters, it will allow empty entry if a customer does not have a Phone Number; will be added to a table named Customers in the current database.

You can also use sample code to add a new column to a table. First display an empty query window and display the Templates Explorer. Expand the Table node. Under Table, drag Add Column and drop it in the query window. Delete the undesired sections of code and keep only the part that deals with adding a column. Here is an example:

```
--=================================================================
-- Add column template
--
-- This template creates a table, then it adds a new column to the table.
--=================================================================
USE <database, sysname, AdventureWorks>
GO

-- Add a new column to the table
ALTER TABLE <schema_name, sysname, dbo>.<table_name, sysname, sample_table>
     ADD <new_column_name, sysname, column3>
       <new_column_datatype,, datetime>
       <new_column_nullability,, NULL>
```

GO

Renaming a Column

If you find out that the name of a column is not appropriate, you can change it. To rename a column in the Object Explorer, right-click the table that the column belongs to and click Design. In the design view, highlight the name of the desired column to put it into edit mode and edit it, by typing the desired new column name.

In SQL Script, to change the name of a column, first open an empty query window or you can type the query in an existing query window, then highlight the code and execute it. In a query window, execute **sp_rename** using the following format:

sp_rename 'TableName.ColumnName', 'NewColumnName', N'COLUMN'

The **sp_rename** factor and the **'COLUMN'** string are required. The TableName factor is the name of the table that the column belongs to. The ColumnName is the current name of the column. The NewColumnName is the desired name you want to give to the column.
Here is an example:
use **imtDeptDB**;

-- This code will Alter the Customers Table and rename the name of a Column in the column

exec sp_rename N'customers.name', N'firstName', N'column';
GO

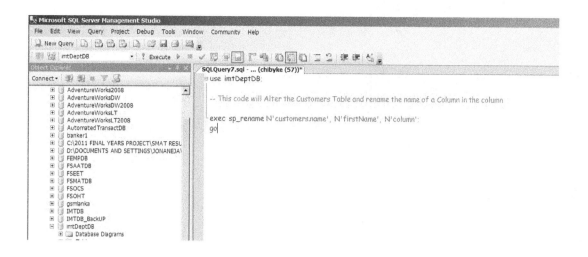

When this code is executed, the interpreter will look for a column named name in the Customers table of the current or selected database. If it finds that column in the table, then it renames it to firstName.

Deleting a Column

If you have an undesired column that you don't want any more in a table, you can get rid of it. To visually delete a column, in the Object Explorer, expand the database, the Tables, and the Columns nodes. Right-click the unwanted column and click Delete. The Delete Object dialog box would display. If you still want to delete the column, click OK. If you have changed your mind, click Cancel.

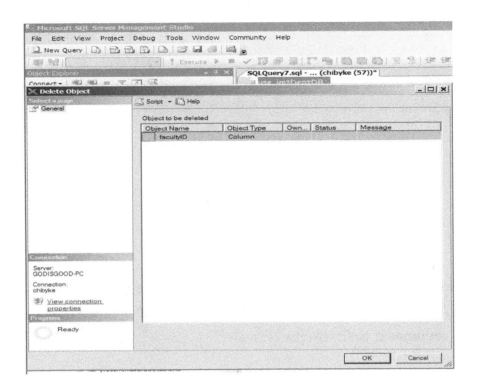

To delete a column using code, first open or access an empty query window though not necessary, and use the following formula:

ALTER TABLE *TableName*
DROP COLUMN *ColumnName*

On the right side of the **ALTER TABLE** expression, type the name of the table. On the right side of the **DROP COLUMN** expression, enter the name of the undesired column. Here is an example:

use **smatDB**;

-- This code will Alter the Customers Table and a Column to it

alter table **dept**
    drop column **facultyID**;
GO

When this code is executed, the interpreter will look for a column named **facultyID** in a **dept** table of the current or selected database. If it finds that column, it will remove it from the table.

Microsoft SQL Server can also assist you when you forgot how to delete column from a table by generating sample code. Before doing this, first display an empty query window and display the Templates Explorer. Expand the Table node. In the Table section, drag Drop Column and drop it in the query window. Delete the unwanted sections of code and keep only the part that deals with adding a column. Here is an example:

```
--===============================================
-- Drop column template
--
-- This template creates a table, then it
-- drops one of the columns of the table.
--===============================================
USE <database, sysname, AdventureWorks>
GO


IF     OBJECT_ID('<schema_name,     sysname,     dbo>.<table_name,     sysname,
sample_table>', 'U') IS NOT NULL
  DROP    TABLE    <schema_name,    sysname,    dbo>.<table_name,    sysname,
sample_table>
GO


CREATE    TABLE    <schema_name,    sysname,    dbo>.<table_name,    sysname,
sample_table>
(
      column1 int     NOT NULL,
      column2 char(10) NULL,
      <new_column_name, sysname, column3> datetime NULL
)
GO
```

-- Drop a column from the table

ALTER TABLE <schema_name, sysname, **dbo**>.<table_name, sysname, **sample_table**>

DROP COLUMN <new_column_name, sysname, **column3**>

GO

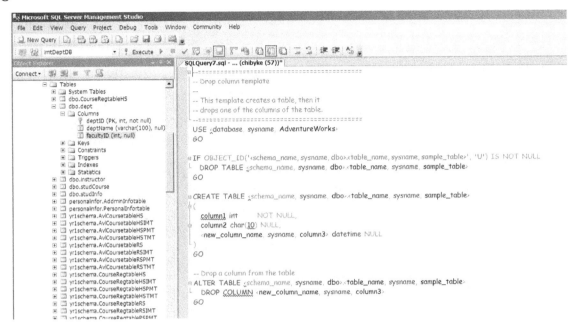

Calculated columns

A calculated column is powerful in that it presents the results of a predefined expression the way a view does, but without the overhead of a view. Calculated columns also improve data integrity by performing the calculation at the table level, rather than trusting that each query developer will get the calculation correct, thus, with calculated columns more codes to perform calculation is eliminated. By default, a calculated column does not actually store any data; instead, the data is calculated when queried. However, since SQL Server 2005, calculated columns may be optionally persisted; in which case they are calculated when entered and then sorted as regular, but read-only, row data. They may even be indexed. Personally, I have replaced several old triggers with persisted, indexed, calculated columns with great success. They are easy, and fast. The syntax simply defines the formula for the calculation in lieu of designating a data type:

ColumnName as Expression

Here is an example that will create a table:

```
USE imtDeptDB;
GO


CREATE TABLE yr1schema.studGPA (
regNo    bigint    constraint    FK_StudRegNo    foreign    key    references
personalInfoTable(RegNo)
,FirstSemester decimal(3,2) NOT NULL
,SecondSemester decimal(3,2) NOT NULL
,GPA AS FirstSemester * SecondSemester Persisted
)
ON [Primary];
GO
```

Sparse columns

New for SQL Server 2008, sparse columns use a completely different method for storing data within the page. Normal columns have a predetermined designated location for the data. If there is no data, then some space is wasted. Even nullable columns use a bit to indicate the presence or absence of a null for the column. Sparse columns, however, store nothing on the page if no data is present for the column for that row. To accomplish this, SQL Server essentially writes the list of sparse columns that have data into a list for the row (5 bytes + 2–4 bytes for every sparse column with data); is that not great? If the columns usually hold data, then sparse columns actually require more space than normal columns. However, if the majority of rows are null (I have heard a figure of 50%, but I would rather say is much higher), then the sparse column will save space.

Because sparse columns are intended for columns that infrequently hold data, they can be used for tables that hold up to 30,000 columns. To create a sparse column, add the SPARSE keyword to the column definition. The sparse column must be nullable.

Here is an example of a student's detail table with home phone number as SPARSE column:

USE **[smatDB]**
GO

/* Create a table to store student's data, with home phone number column as SPARSE column*/

CREATE TABLE **[personalinfor]**.[PersonalInfortable](
    [RegNo] [bigint] NOT NULL
    ,[FNAME] [nvarchar](25) NOT NULL
    ,[MNAME] [nvarchar](25) NULL
    ,[LNAME] [nvarchar](25) NOT NULL
    ,[GENDER] [char](6) NOT NULL
    ,[DoB] [date] NULL
    ,[phoneNum] [char](11) NOT NULL
    ,[homePhoneNum] [char](10) **SPARSE** NULL
    ,[pw] [varchar](30) NULL
    ,[confirmpw] [varchar](30) NULL
    ,[dept] [varchar](30) NULL
    ,[level] [tinyint] NULL
) ON **[PRIMARY]**;
GO

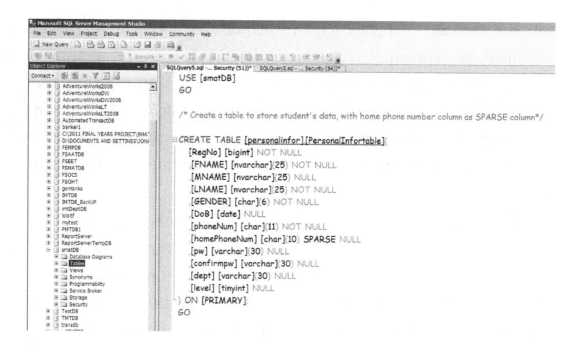

Column constraints and defaults

The database is only as good as the quality of the data in it. A constraint is an on-real time data-validation check or business-logic check performed at the database-engine level. Besides the data type itself, SQL Server includes five types of constraints, you learn more about the column constraints later in this chapter:

i. Primary key constraint: Ensures a unique non-null key

ii. Foreign key constraint: Ensures that the value points to a valid key

iii. Nullability: Indicates whether the column can accept a null value

iv. Check constraint: Custom Boolean constraint

v. Unique constraint: Ensures a unique value

SQL Server also includes the following column option:

i.   **Column Default:** Supplies a value if none is specified in the INSERT statement. The column default is referred to as a type of constraint on one page of SQL Server Books Online, but is not listed in the constraints on another page. I call it a column option because it does not constrain user-data entry, nor does it enforce a data-integrity rule. However, it serves the column as a useful option, because there are columns that don't need to be empty.

ii.   **Column nullability:** A null value is an unknown value; typically, it means that the column has not yet receive a data entry. Whether or not a column will even accept a null value is referred to as the nullability of the column and is configured by the null or not null column attribute. New columns in SQL Server default to not null, meaning that they do not accept nulls. However, this option is normally overridden by the connection property ansi_null_dflt_on. The ANSI standard is to default to null, which accepts nulls, in table columns that are not explicitly created with a not null option.

The following code demonstrates the ANSI default nullability versus SQL Server's nullability. The first test uses the SQL Server default by setting the database ANSI NULL option to false, and the ANSI_NULL_DFLT_OFF connection setting to ON:

Here is an example of nullability configuration:

```
USE TempDB;
EXEC sp_dboption 'TempDB', ANSI_NULL_DEFAULT, 'false';
SET ANSI_NULL_DFLT_OFF ON
GO
```

The NullTest table is created without specifying the nullability:

```
USE mytest;
GO
```

```
CREATE TABLE NullTest(
PK INT IDENTITY,
One VARCHAR(50)
);
GO
```

The following code attempts to insert a null into the table:

```
INSERT NullTest(One)
VALUES (NULL);
GO
```

Result:

Msg 515, Level 16, State 2, Line 1

Cannot insert the value NULL into column 'One', table 'mytest.dbo.NullTest'; column does not allow nulls. INSERT fails.

The statement has been terminated.

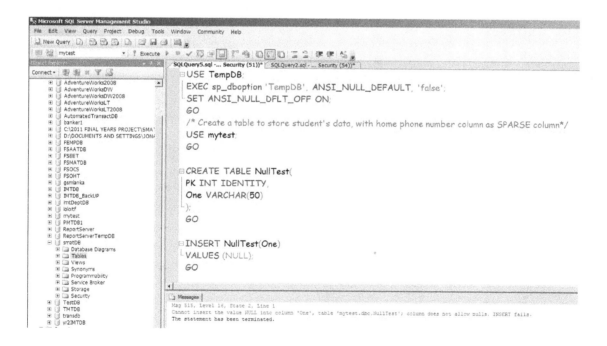

Because the nullability was set to the SQL Server default when the table was created, the column does not accept null values. The second example will rebuild the table with the ANSI SQL nullability default:

```
USE TempDB;
EXEC sp_dboption 'TempDB', ANSI_NULL_DEFAULT, 'True';
SET ANSI_NULL_DFLT_ON ON;
GO


USE mytest;
GO


DROP TABLE NullTest;
GO


CREATE TABLE NullTest(
PK INT IDENTITY,
One VARCHAR(50)
);
GO


INSERT NullTest(One)
VALUES (NULL);
GO
```

Result:

(1 row(s) affected)

Creating Indexes

Indexes are the bridge from a query to the data. Without indexes, SQL Server must scan and filter to select specific rows which can take almost a decade. With the right indexes, SQL Server screams. SQL Server uses two types of indexes: *clustered indexes*, which reflect the logical sort order of the table, and *non-clustered indexes*, which are additional b-trees typically used to perform rapid searches of non-key columns. The columns by which the index is sorted are referred to as the *key columns*. Within the SQL Server Management Studio's Object Explorer, existing indexes for each table are listed under the *DatabaseName,* Tables, *TableName,* Indexes node. Every index property for new or existing indexes may be managed using the Index Properties page, below. The page is opened for existing indexes by right-clicking on the index and choosing Properties. New indexes are created from the context menu of the Indexes node under the selected table.

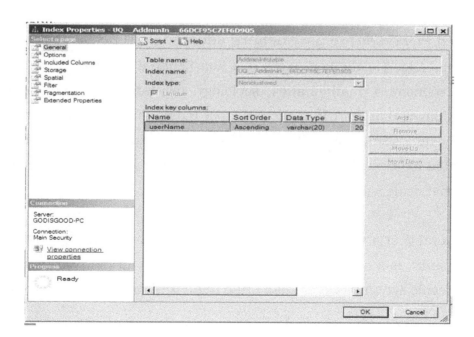

So using Management Studio, indexes are visible as nodes under the table in Object Explorer. Use the Indexes context menu and select New Index to open the New Index form, is about six pages:

i.   *General* index information includes the index name, type, uniqueness, and key columns.

ii. Index *Options* control the behavior of the index. In addition, an index may be disabled or re-enabled.

iii. *Included Columns* are non-key columns used for covering indexes.

iv. The *Storage* page places the index on a selected filegroup.

v.   The *Spatial* page has configuration options specific to indexes for the spatial data type.

vi. The *Filter* page is for SQL Server 2008's new WHERE clause option for indexes.

When opening the properties of an existing index, the Index Properties form also includes two additional pages:

i.   The *Fragmentation* page displays detailed information about the health of the index.

ii. *Extended Properties* are user-defined additional properties.

     If you take a look at the last pages of a non-fictional book (such as a book about history, economics, mathematics, sociology, or statistics, etc), you may find a series of pages that start in a section label Index. The words in that series allow you to locate a section of the book that mentions, explains, or describes the word and related topics. An index in a book makes it easy and fast to get to a section of a book that deals with a particular topic.

Like a book, a table or a view can use the mechanism provided by an index. In a table or a view, an index is a column (or many columns) that can be used to locate records and take a specific action based on some rule reinforced on that (those) column(s).

Creating an Index with SQL

To create an index in SQL, the basic syntax formula to follow is:

CREATE INDEX *IndexName* ON *Table/View(Column(s))*

On an index starts with the **CREATE INDEX** expression, followed by a name for the index, followed by the **ON** keyword. In the *Table/View* placeholder, enter the name of the table or view for which you want to create the index, followed by parentheses in which you enter at least one column. Here is an example:

```
-- ===============================================
-- Database: employeeDB
-- Name: Iwuala Chibueze
-- Table: staffMembers
-- Index: indxStaffMemb
-- ===============================================
USE master
GO


-- Drop the database if it already exists
IF  EXISTS (
      SELECT name
            FROM sys.databases
            WHERE name = N'employeeDB'
)
DROP DATABASE employeeDB
GO


-- Create the new database
CREATE DATABASE employeeDB
GO
```

```sql
USE employeeDB;
GO


CREATE TABLE staffMembers
(
        empID int identity (10000,1) NOT NULL,
        LastName nvarchar(30) NOT NULL,
        FirstName nvarchar(30),
        Username nchar(8) NOT NULL,
        DateHired date NULL,
        HourlySalary money
);
GO


INSERT INTO staffMembers
VALUES(N'Goodluck', N'Nneoma', N'talk2nne', N'1998-10-25', 750),
    (N'Eze', N'Ikechukwu', N'ikeze', N'2006-06-22', 500.20),
```

(N'Ubochi', N'Onyinyechi', N'onyiiJ', N'2001-10-16', **250.05**),

(N'Iwuala', N'Ugonna', N'ugoPaul', N'08/10/2009', **100.22**),

(N'Nwachukwu', N'C.A.N', N'canN', N'03-10-1995', **680.48**),

(N'Okebugwu', N'Andy', N'andyO', N'06/16/2007', **720**);

GO

CREATE INDEX **indxStaffMemb**

ON **staffMembers**(empID);

GO

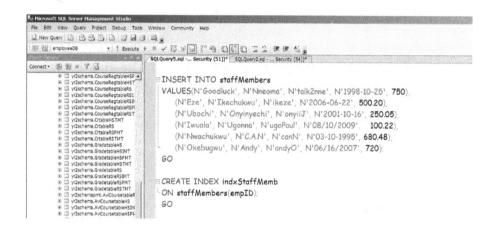

Composite indexes

A *composite index* is a clustered or non-clustered index that includes multiple key columns. Most nonclustered indexes are composite indexes. If you use SQL Server Management Studio's Index Properties form, composite indexes are created by adding multiple columns to the index in the General page. When creating a composite index with code, it must be declared in a CREATE INDEX DDL statement after the table is created.

Here is an example of a composite clustered index, created on staffMembers table:

Since the index is composite, list the columns separated by commas.

CREATE CLUSTERED INDEX **indxStaffMemb**

ON **staffMembers**(LastName, **Username**);

GO

The order of the columns in a composite index is important. In order for a search to take advantage of a composite index it must include the index columns from left to right. If the composite index is lastname, username, a search for Username will not use the index, but a search for lastname, or lastname and Username, will. This has to be taken into consideration during your design and development.

Types of Indexes

Microsoft SQL Server supports various types of indexes. The two broadest categories are clustered and non-clustered. An observation would have asked, why the *CLUSTERED* before index in previous examples.

Clustered Indexes

In our introduction, we saw that an index is primarily created using one or more columns from a designated table. This means that, when it comes to using the index, we would use the values stored in the column(s) that was (were) selected for the index. Such an index is referred to as clustered. The columns that were made part of an index are referred to as keys as I explained above.

To visually create a clustered index, display the Indexes/Keys dialog box. In the dialog box, when creating a new indexed or after clicking the name of an existing index, in the right list, click Create As Clustered and select Yes:

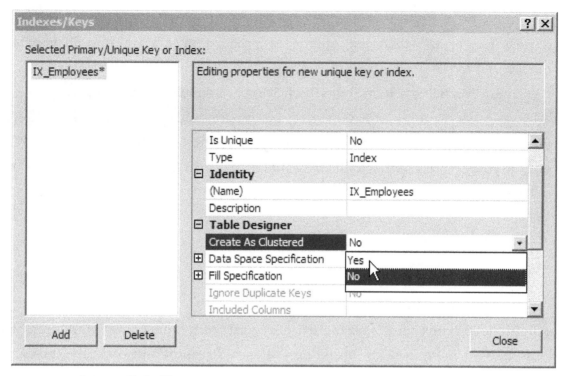

Once you are done, click Close.

To create a clustered index in SQL Code, use the following formula:

CREATE CLUSTERED INDEX *IndexName* ON *Table/ View(Column(s))*

From the description we gave previously, the only new keyword here is **CLUSTERED**.

Based on this, here is an example:

USE **employeeDB**;

GO

IF EXISTS (SELECT **NAME** FROM sys.indexes WHERE **name**=N'indxStaffMemb')

DROP INDEX **indxStaffMemb**

ON **staffMembers**;

CREATE CLUSTERED INDEX **indxStaffMemb**

ON **staffMembers**(empID);

GO

A table that contains a clustered index is called a clustered table.

There are various aspects to a clustered index:

i.   To make it easy to search the records, they (the records) are sorted. This makes it possible for the database engine to proceed in a top-down approach and quickly get to the desired record

ii.   Without this being a requirement, each record should be unique.

iii.   There must be only one clustered index per table. This means that, if you (decide to) create a clustered index on a table, the table becomes equipped with one. If you create another clustered index, the previous one (clustered index) is deleted

Non-clustered Index

While a clustered index uses a sorted list of records of a table or view, another type of index can use a mechanism not based on the sorted records but on a bookmark. This is called a non-clustered index. As opposed to a clustered table that can contain only one clustered index, you can create not only one, but as many as 249 non-clustered indexes on a table. Thus, when you talk of composite index you talk of nonclustered index

To visually create a nonclustered index, display the Indexes/Keys dialog box. To create a new index, click the Add button. If an index was always created or set as clustered and you want to change it, you can change its Create As Clustered property from Yes to No.

To create a nonclustered index in SQL code, use the following formula:

CREATE NONCLUSTERED INDEX *IndexName* ON *Table/View(Column(s))*

The new keyword in this formula is **NONCLUSTERED**. Everything is the same as previously described. Based on this, here is an example:

USE **employeeDB**;

GO

IF EXISTS (SELECT **NAME** FROM sys.indexes WHERE **name**=N'indxStaffMemb')

DROP INDEX **indxStaffMemb**

ON **staffMembers**;

```
CREATE NONCLUSTERED INDEX indxStaffMemb
ON staffMembers(LastName, Username);
```

```
GO
```

If you create an index without specifying **CLUSTERED** or **NONCLUSTERED**, the database engine automatically makes it nonclustered.

Table Creation and Indexes

A table with primary key is invariably indexed; so you can specify if you want the index to be clustered or nonclustered.

Here is an example of an indexed table without the keyword create index.

```
USE employeeDB;
GO
```

```
CREATE TABLE Students
(
        StudID int PRIMARY KEY,
        FirstName nvarchar(50) NOT NULL,
        LastName nvarchar(50));
GO
```

The database engine will automatically create an index on the table and chooses the primary key column as its key. You have the option of indicating the type of index you want created. To do this, on the right side of the name of the column, enter **CLUSTERED** or **NONCLUSTERED**. If you don't specify the type of index, the **CLUSTERED** option is chosen by default.

Creating a Clustered Tables

1. Type the following:

USE **[employeeDB]**
GO

CREATE TABLE **[dbo]**.[staffInfo](
[empID] [int] IDENTITY(10000,1) PRIMARY KEY CLUSTERED NOT NULL
    ,[LastName] [nvarchar](30) NOT NULL
    ,[FirstName] [nvarchar](30) NOT NULL
    ,[Username] [nchar](10) UNIQUE NOT NULL
    ,[DateHired] [date] NULL
    ,[HourlySalary] [money] NULL
    ,[emailAdd] [nvarchar](50)
    ,[phoneNum] [nchar](11)
    ,CONSTRAINT **CK_staffContacts** CHECK ((phoneNum IS NOT NULL) OR (emailAdd IS NOT NULL))
) ON **[PRIMARY]**;

GO

2. Press F5 to execute

Data Entry and Analysis with Indexes

In our introduction, we saw that an index can make it possible to take some action during data entry, such as making sure that a column have unique values for each record or making sure that the combination of values of a group of columns on the same record produces a unique value. Besides this characteristic of indexes, they are actually very valuable when it comes to data analysis. You remember the example I gave above about a book, in the case of a database the primary goal of an index is to make it easy to locate the records of a table or view on the database.

Index Uniqueness

An index is made valuable in two ways. On one hand, the records should be sorted. A clustered index itself takes care of this aspect because it automatically and internally sorts its records. What if the records are not unique? For example, in a bad data entry on a list of employees, you may have two or more employees with the same employee's records. If you create an index for such a table, the database engine would create duplicate records on the index. This is usually not good because when it's time to select records, you may have too many records and you may have wrong result.

When creating a table, you can create index for it and let the index apply a rule that states that each record would be unique. To take care of this, you can apply a uniqueness rule on the index. If you are visually creating an index, in the Indexes/Keys dialog box, select the index on the left side. On the right list, set the Is Unique field to Yes. On the other hand, if you want to remove this rule, set the Is Unique field to No.

To create a uniqueness index in SQL code, apply the **UNIQUE** keyword in the formula:

CREATE [UNIQUE] [CLUSTERED | NONCLUSTERED] INDEX index_name ON *Table/View(Column(s))*

Start with the **CREATE UNIQUE** expression, then specify whether it would be clustered or not. The rest follows the descriptions we saw previously. Here is an example:

USE master;
GO

IF EXISTS(SELECT **name** FROM sys.databases WHERE **name**= N'staffInfo')
DROP DATABASE **staffInfo**;
GO

CREATE DATABASE **staffInfoDB**;
GO

```
USE staffInfoDB;
GO


CREATE TABLE [dbo].[staffInfo](
        [empID] [int] IDENTITY(10000,1) NOT NULL
        ,[LastName] [nvarchar](30) NOT NULL
        ,[FirstName] [nvarchar](30) NOT NULL
        ,[Username] [nchar](10) NOT NULL
        ,[DateHired] [date] NULL
        ,[HourlySalary] [money] NULL
) ON [PRIMARY];
GO


CREATE UNIQUE CLUSTERED INDEX indxStaffInfo
ON dbo.staffInfo(Username);
GO
```

Application of Index Uniqueness

Once you have specified the uniqueness of an index on a table, during data entry, if the user enters a value that exists in the table already, an error would be produced. Here is an example:

```
USE staffInfoDB;
GO


INSERT INTO staffInfo(FirstName, LastName, HourlySalary, Username )
                        VALUES(N'Chidiebere', N'Eze', 100.50, N'ezechidi')
GO


INSERT INTO staffInfo(FirstName, LastName, HourlySalary,Username )
VALUES(N'Chibuisi', N'Goodluck', 150.25, N'chibii')
GO


INSERT INTO staffInfo(FirstName, LastName,
                HourlySalary,DateHired,Username )
```

VALUES(27495, N'Onyekachi', N'Iwuala', **300.05**, '2009/09/20', N'kachi')
GO

INSERT INTO **staffInfo**(FirstName,LastName, HourlySalary, DateHired,
Username)
VALUES(22940, N'Gertrude', N'Monday', 99.55, '05/09/2000', N'Jetu')
GO

INSERT INTO **staffInfo**(FirstName,LastName, HourlySalary, DateHired,
Username)
VALUES(22940, N'Gertrude', N'Monday', **99.55**, '05/09/2000', N'Jetu')
GO

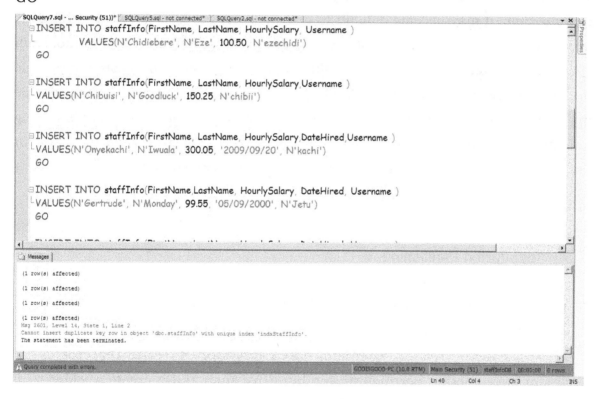

This would produce:

(1 row(s) affected)

(1 row(s) affected)

(1 row(s) affected)

(1 row(s) affected)

Msg 2601, Level 14, State 1, Line 2

Cannot insert duplicate key row in object 'dbo.staffInfo' with unique index 'indxStaffInfo'.

The statement has been terminated.

Table and Index Partitioning

Data in your database may involve many records, in thousands or millions, so much that at one time, it may become difficult to manage. One way you can deal with this is to store the records of a table in different file groups, just like we did to database in our previous chapter. This makes it possible to store one section of records in one file group, another section in another file group, possibly another section in another file group, and so on. As a result, when it's time to look for one or a few records among thousands or millions of records, it would be easier to locate it or to locate them. Of course, the data still belongs to one database and to the same table.

Introducing Partitioning

1. Open a file utility, such as Windows Explorer
2. Display the contents of the drives
3. On the C: drive, create a folder named **FCT Ministry Of Health Director**
4. If you have another partition or another drive such as D:, create a folder on it and name it **Zone1 Ministry Of Health Director**. If you don't have another drive, create another folder on the C: drive and name it **Zone1 Ministry Of Health Director**
5. If you have one more partition or another drive such as E:, create a folder on it and name it **Zone2 Ministry Of Health Director**. If you don't have another drive, on the C: drive, create another folder **Zone3 Ministry Of Health Director.**

6. You can create more folders for the remaining 3 zones, following the example I have given.
7. Check each of those folders to ensure that they are empty
8. Return to Microsoft SQL Server Management Studio
9. To create a database and the accompanying file groups, type the following:

```
USE master;
GO


CREATE DATABASE FedMinOfHealth
ON PRIMARY
  ( NAME = N'FedMinOfHealthFCT',
    FILENAME = N'C:\MoHDirectory\FCTFedMinHealth.mdf',
    SIZE = 4MB,
    MAXSIZE = 10MB,
    FILEGROWTH = 1MB),
FILEGROUP FedMinOfHealthZone1Records
  ( NAME = N'FedMinOfHealthZone1',
    FILENAME = N'C:\MoHDirectory\FedMinHealth1st.ndf',
    SIZE = 1MB,
    MAXSIZE = 10MB,
    FILEGROWTH = 1MB),
FILEGROUP FedMinOfHealthZone2Records
  ( NAME = N'FedMinOfHealthZone2',
    FILENAME = N'C:\MoHDirectory\FedMinHealth2nd.ndf',
    SIZE = 1MB,
    MAXSIZE = 10MB,
    FILEGROWTH = 1MB),
FILEGROUP FedMinOfHealthZone3Records
  ( NAME = N'FedMinOfHealthZone3',
    FILENAME = N'C:\MoHDirectory\FedMinHealth3rd.ndf',
    SIZE = 1MB,
    MAXSIZE = 10MB,
    FILEGROWTH = 1MB),
```

```
FILEGROUP FedMinOfHealthZone4Records
  ( NAME = N'FedMinOfHealthZone4',
    FILENAME = N'C:\MoHDirectory\FedMinHealth4th.ndf',
    SIZE = 1MB,
    MAXSIZE = 10MB,
    FILEGROWTH = 1MB),
FILEGROUP FedMinOfHealthZone5Records
  ( NAME = N'FedMinOfHealthZone5',
    FILENAME = N'C:\MoHDirectory\FedMinHealth5th.ndf',
    SIZE = 1MB,
    MAXSIZE = 10MB,
    FILEGROWTH = 1MB),
FILEGROUP FedMinOfHealthZone6Records
  ( NAME = N'FedMinOfHealthZone6',
    FILENAME = N'C:\MoHDirectory\FedMinHealth6th.ndf',
    SIZE = 1MB,
    MAXSIZE = 10MB,
    FILEGROWTH = 1MB)
LOG ON
  ( NAME = N'FedMinHealthLogFiles',
    FILENAME = N'C:\MoHDirectory\FedMinHealthLogger.ldf',
    SIZE = 1MB,
    MAXSIZE = 10MB,
    FILEGROWTH = 1MB);
GO
```

10.   Press F5 to execute

11. Return to the file utilities such as Windows Explorer and check the content of each of the previously created folders. Also check their sizes.

Partitioning a Table

Before partitioning a table, you must create the necessary file groups. This can be done when creating the database since it is at that time that you specify how the database will be stored; that is, what files will hold the information of the database. After creating the database and creating its file groups. Before partitioning a table, you must create a partition function and a partition scheme.

A Partition Function

A partition function is used to define the ranges of records that will be stored in what file group. The SQL formula to create a partition function is:

CREATE PARTITION FUNCTION *PartitionFunctionName* (*ParameterType*)
AS RANGE [LEFT | RIGHT]
FOR VALUES (*StartRange1*, *StartRange2*, *StartRange_n*)

The creation of a partition function starts with the **CREATE PARTITION FUNCTION** expression followed by a name. The name follows the rules for names in Microsoft SQL Server. Because you are creating a function, the name is followed by parentheses. In the parentheses of the function, you must specify the data type of the column that will be used to create a range of records. The values of that column will be used to distinguish ranges of records. This means that the values of this column must allow the database engine to predict a range of records. This is called the partitioning column. For example, you can use a column that has an incremental count of values. This is the case for an identity primary key column. As another example, you can use a column that holds a category of values, such as female customers vs male and child customers. As one more example, you can use a column that holds dates so that you can isolate ranges of records from one date to another.

After closing the parenthesis, type **AS RANGE**, which indicates that you are going to specify the ranges of values. This is followed by either **LEFT** or **RIGHT**. When the partition function will have been created and when the table itself will have been created, when the database engine is asked to look for a record or a range of records, it may have to sort the records. If you want it to sort the records from left to right, use the LEFT keyword. If you want the records sorted from right to left, use the RIGHT keyword.

The **AS RANGE LEFT** or **AS RANGE RIGHT** expression is followed by **FOR VALUES** that is followed by parentheses. When creating a partition function, you must provide a way for the database engine to get a range of records. For example, you can use records from number 1 to number 1000, then another range from 1001 to 5000, and so on. Or you can specify that a range of records would go from February 11th, 2000 to June 26th, 2005. Then another range would go from June 26th 2005 to December 14th, 2006, and so on.

You specify the range in the parentheses that follow the **FOR VALUES** expression. Type the first value of the first range, followed by a comma, followed by the first value of the second range, and so on.

Creating a Partition Function

1. Select the whole contents of the Query window and type the following:

USE **fedminofhealth**;
GO

CREATE PARTITION FUNCTION **FMHpartFunc**(int)
AS RANGE LEFT FOR VALUES(1, **100**, 1000);
GO

2. Press F5 to execute

A Partition Scheme

A partition scheme specifies the names of the file groups, in their order that will store the ranges of records that were created in the partition function. The formula to create a partition scheme is:

CREATE PARTITION SCHEME *PartitionSchemeName*
AS PARTITION *PartitionFunctionName*
[ALL] TO ({ file_group_name | [PRIMARY] } [,...n])

You start with the **CREATION PARTITION SCHEME** expression; this makes your indication know to the interpreter. This is followed by a name. The name follows the rules of objects. After the name of the partition scheme, type **AS PARTITION** followed by the name of the partition function you should have previously created.

If you are planning to use only one file group, after the name of the partition function, enter **ALL**, followed by parentheses, in which you will type PRIMARY. But if you are planning to use different file groups, after the name of the partition function, enter **TO**, followed by parentheses. We saw that, in the parentheses of the **FOR VALUES** of the partition function, you entered the starting value of the first range. In the parentheses of the TO keyword, type the name of the file group that will hold the records of the first range of the partition function. We also saw how to specify the second range in the partition function. In the parentheses of the TO clause, after the name of the first file group, type a comma followed by the name of the file group that will hold the records of the second range.

Creating a Partition Function Scheme

1. Select the whole contents of the Query window and type the following:

USE **fedminofhealth**;
GO

```
CREATE PARTITION SCHEME FMHpartSchema
        AS PARTITION FMHpartFunc
TO
(FedMinOfHealthZone1Records,FedMinOfHealthZone2Records,FedMinOfHealthZone3R
ecords,FedMinOfHealthZone4Records,FedMinOfHealthZone5Records,FedMinOfHealth
Zone6Records);
GO
```

2. On the SQL Editor toolbar, click the Execute button

Partitioning a Table

After creating the partition scheme, you can create the table. The formula to specify a partition scheme when creating a table is:

```
CREATE TABLE Name
(
    What We Have Learned So Far
) ON PartitionSchemeName(ColumnName)
```

You start with the **CREATE TABLE** expression, followed by things we have learned so far. After the name of the table, you open and close the parentheses, in which you include other things we have seen so far: the columns, the constraints, and their options. Outside the parentheses, type the ON keyword, followed by the name of the partition scheme you have created, followed by an opening and closing parentheses. Inside the parentheses of the schema name enter the name of the table's column that is the partitioning column.

After creating the table, you can use it, like any normal table, and SQL Server will take care of its record placement.

Creating a Partitioned Table

1. Create   a   New   Query   window   and   type   the   following:

```
-- ================================================
-- Author:        FunctionX
-- Modified:      Iwuala Chibueze
-- Database:      propAgentDB
-- Date Created: Monday December 31th, 2012
-- ================================================
USE master;
GO


IF EXISTS (SELECT name FROM sys.databases
      WHERE name = N'propAgentDB')
DROP DATABASE propAgentDB;
GO


CREATE DATABASE propAgentDB
ON PRIMARY
  ( NAME = N'propertyAgentMain',
    FILENAME = N'C:\garb\propertyAgentMain.mdf',
    SIZE = 4MB,
    FILEGROWTH = 1MB),
  FILEGROUP propertyAgentGr
  ( NAME = N'propertyAgent',
    FILENAME = N'C:\garb\propertyAgentGr.ndf',
    SIZE = 1MB,
    MAXSIZE = 100MB,
    FILEGROWTH = 1MB)
LOG ON
  ( NAME = N'propertyAgentMainLog',
    FILENAME = N'C:\garb\propertyAgentMainLog.ldf',
    SIZE = 1MB,
```

```
        MAXSIZE = 10MB,
        FILEGROWTH = 1MB);
GO



-- ================================================
-- Author:      FunctionX
-- Database:    propAgentDB
-- Modified:    Iwuala Chibueze
-- Table:       PropertyTypes
-- Date Created: Monday December 31th, 2012
-- ================================================
USE propAgentDB;
GO


CREATE PARTITION FUNCTION properAgentFunc(int)
AS RANGE LEFT FOR VALUES(1, 100);
GO


CREATE PARTITION SCHEME properAgentSch
        AS PARTITION properAgentFunc
            ALL TO ( propertyAgentGr);
GO


CREATE TABLE PropertyTypes
(
  PropertyTypeID int identity(1,1) NOT NULL,
  PropertyType varchar(20),
  CONSTRAINT PK_PropertyTypes PRIMARY KEY(PropertyTypeID)
) ON properAgentSch(PropertyTypeID);
GO
```

```
-- Modified:  Iwuala Chibueze
-- Table:      PropertyTypes
-- Date Created: Monday December 31th, 2012
-- ==============================================
USE propAgentDB;
GO

CREATE PARTITION FUNCTION properAgentFunc(int)
AS RANGE LEFT FOR VALUES(1, 100);
GO

CREATE PARTITION SCHEME properAgentSch
    AS PARTITION properAgentFunc
        ALL TO ( propertyAgentGr);
GO

CREATE TABLE PropertyTypes
(
    PropertyTypeID int identity(1,1) NOT NULL,
    PropertyType varchar(20),
    CONSTRAINT PK_PropertyTypes PRIMARY KEY(PropertyTypeID)
) ON properAgentSch(PropertyTypeID);
GO
```

INSERT INTO **PropertyTypes**(PropertyType)

VALUES(N'Condominium');

GO

INSERT INTO **PropertyTypes**(PropertyType)

VALUES(N'Single Family');

GO

INSERT INTO **PropertyTypes**(PropertyType)

VALUES(N'Townhouse');

GO

INSERT INTO **PropertyTypes**(PropertyType)

VALUES(N'Unknown');

GO

-- Author: FunctionX

-- Database: propertyAgentDB

-- Modified: Iwuala Chibueze

-- Table: Conditions

-- Date Created: Monday December 31th, 2012

USE **propAgentDB**;

```sql
GO

CREATE TABLE Conditions
(
  ConditionID int identity(1,1) NOT NULL,
  Condition varchar(20),
  CONSTRAINT PK_Conditions PRIMARY KEY(ConditionID)
) ON properAgentSch(ConditionID);
GO
INSERT INTO Conditions(Condition)
VALUES(N'Excellent');
GO
INSERT INTO Conditions(Condition)
VALUES(N'Good');
GO
INSERT INTO Conditions(Condition)
VALUES(N'Bad Shape');
GO
INSERT INTO Conditions(Condition)
VALUES(N'Mostly Damaged');
GO


-- Author:    FunctionX
-- Database:  propertyAgentDB
--Modified:   Iwuala Chibueze
-- Table:     Properties
-- Date Created: Monday December 31th, 2012


CREATE TABLE Properties
(
  PropertyID int identity(1,1) NOT NULL,
  PropertyNumber char(6),
  Address varchar(100),
  City varchar(50),
```

```
    State char(2),
    ZIPCode varchar(12),
    PropertyTypeID int
        CONSTRAINT FK_PropertyTypes
        FOREIGN KEY REFERENCES PropertyTypes(PropertyTypeID),
    ConditionID int
        CONSTRAINT FK_Conditions
        FOREIGN KEY REFERENCES Conditions(ConditionID),
    Bedrooms smallint,
    Bathrooms float,
    FinishedBasement bit,
    IndoorGarage bit,
    Stories smallint,
    YearBuilt smallint,
    MarketValue money,
    CONSTRAINT PK_Properties PRIMARY KEY(PropertyID)
) ON properAgentSch(PropertyID);
GO


USE propAgentDB;
GO


INSERT INTO Properties(PropertyNumber, Address, City, State,
    ZIPCode, PropertyTypeID, ConditionID, Bedrooms, Bathrooms,
    FinishedBasement, IndoorGarage, Stories, YearBuilt, MarketValue)
VALUES(N'524880', N'1640 Lombardo Ave', N'Silver Spring', N'MD',
    N'20904', 2, 2, 4, 2.5, 3, 1, 3, 1995, 495880.00);
GO


INSERT INTO Properties(PropertyNumber, Address, City, State,
    ZIPCode, PropertyTypeID, ConditionID, Bedrooms, Bathrooms,
    FinishedBasement, IndoorGarage, Stories, YearBuilt, MarketValue)
VALUES(N'688364', N'10315 North Hacht Rd', N'College Park', N'MD',
        N'20747', 2, 1, 4, 3.5, 3,
        1, 2, 2000, 620724.00);
```

```sql
GO

INSERT INTO Properties(PropertyNumber, Address, City, State,
 ZIPCode, PropertyTypeID, ConditionID, FinishedBasement,
 Stories, MarketValue)
VALUES(N'611464', N'6366 Lolita Drive', N'Laurel', N'MD',
    N'20707', 2, 2, 1, 2, 422625.00);
GO


INSERT INTO Properties(Address, City, PropertyTypeID,
 Bedrooms, MarketValue)
VALUES(N'9002 Palasko Hwy', N'Tysons Corner',
    1, 2, 422895.00);
GO


INSERT INTO Properties(PropertyNumber, State,
 ZIPCode, Bedrooms, YearBuilt, MarketValue)
VALUES(N'420115', N'DC',
    N'20011', 2, 1982, 312555);
GO


INSERT INTO Properties(PropertyNumber, City, ZIPCode,
 PropertyTypeID, Bedrooms, YearBuilt, MarketValue)
VALUES(N'917203', N'Alexandria', N'22024',
    2, 3, 1965, 345660.00);
GO


INSERT INTO Properties(PropertyNumber, Address, City, State,
 PropertyTypeID, ConditionID, Bedrooms, Bathrooms, MarketValue)
VALUES(N'200417', N'4140 Holisto Crt', N'Germantown', N'MD',
    1, 1, 2, 1, 215495.00);
GO


INSERT INTO Properties(City, State, PropertyTypeID, ConditionID,
 Bedrooms, Bathrooms,  YearBuilt, MarketValue)
```

```
VALUES(N'Rockville', N'MD', 1, 2, 2, 2, 1996, 436885.00);
GO


INSERT INTO Properties(PropertyNumber, Address, City, State,
  ZIPCode, PropertyTypeID, ConditionID, Bedrooms, Bathrooms,
  FinishedBasement, IndoorGarage, Stories, YearBuilt, MarketValue)
VALUES(N'927474', N'9522 Lockwood Rd', N'Chevy Chase', N'MD',
    N'20852', 3, 3, 3, 2.5, 3, 0, 3,
    1992, 415665.00);
GO


INSERT INTO Properties(PropertyNumber, Address, City, State,
  ZIPCode, PropertyTypeID, ConditionID, Bedrooms, Bathrooms,
  FinishedBasement, IndoorGarage, Stories, YearBuilt, MarketValue)
VALUES(N'207850', N'14250 Parkdoll Rd', N'Rockville', N'MD',
    N'20854', 3, 2, 3, 2.5, 2, 1, 2,
    1988, 325995.00);
GO


INSERT INTO Properties(City, PropertyTypeID, Bedrooms,
  YearBuilt, MarketValue)
VALUES(N'Washington', 3, 4, 1975, 366775.00);
GO


INSERT INTO Properties(PropertyNumber, Address, City, State,
  ZIPCode, PropertyTypeID, ConditionID, Bedrooms, Bathrooms,
  YearBuilt, MarketValue)
VALUES(N'288540', N'10340 Helmes Street #408', N'Silver Spring', N'MD',
    N'20906', 1, 2, 1, 1, 2000, 242775.00);
GO


INSERT INTO Properties(PropertyNumber, Address, City, State,
  ZIPCode, PropertyTypeID, ConditionID, Bedrooms, Bathrooms,
  FinishedBasement, IndoorGarage, Stories, YearBuilt, MarketValue)
VALUES(N'247472', N'1008 Coppen Street', N'Silver Spring', N'MD',
```

```
                N'20906', 2, 1,
                3, 3, 3, 1, 3, 1996, 625450.00);
        GO


        INSERT INTO Properties(City, ZIPCode, PropertyTypeID,
            Stories, YearBuilt, MarketValue)
        VALUES(N'Chevy Chase', N'20956', 2,
                3, 2001, 525450.00);
        GO


        INSERT INTO Properties(Address, City, State,
            PropertyTypeID, ConditionID, Bedrooms, MarketValue)
        VALUES(N'686 Herod Ave #D04', N'Takoma Park', N'MD',
                1, 1, 2, 360885.00);
        GO


        INSERT INTO Properties(PropertyNumber, Address, City, State,
            ZIPCode, PropertyTypeID, ConditionID, Bedrooms, Bathrooms,
            FinishedBasement, IndoorGarage, Stories, YearBuilt, MarketValue)
        VALUES(N'297446', N'14005 Sniders Blvd', N'Laurel', N'MD',
                N'20707', 3, 4,
                4, 1.5, 3, 1, 2, 2002, 412885.00);
        GO


        INSERT INTO Properties(City, ZIPCode, ConditionID, Bedrooms,
            Stories, YearBuilt)
        VALUES(N'Silver Spring', N'20905', 2,
                4, 2, 1965);
        GO


        INSERT INTO Properties(PropertyNumber, Address, City, State,
            ZIPCode, PropertyTypeID, ConditionID, Bedrooms, Bathrooms,
            FinishedBasement, IndoorGarage, Stories, YearBuilt, MarketValue)
        VALUES(N'924792', N'680 Prushia Rd', N'Washington', N'DC',
                N'20008', 2, 2,
```

```
        5, 3.5, 3, 0, 3, 2000, 555885.00);
GO


INSERT INTO Properties(PropertyNumber, Address, City, State,
  ZIPCode, PropertyTypeID, ConditionID, Bedrooms, Bathrooms,
  FinishedBasement, IndoorGarage, Stories, YearBuilt, MarketValue)
VALUES(N'294796', N'14688 Parrison Street', N'College Park', N'MD',
    N'20742', 2, 1,
      5, 2.5, 2, 1, 2, 1995, 485995.00);
GO


INSERT INTO Properties(City, State, PropertyTypeID, ConditionID,
  Bedrooms, Bathrooms,  YearBuilt, MarketValue)
VALUES(N'Rockville', N'MD', 1, 2, 1, 1, 1996, 418885.00);
GO


INSERT INTO Properties(PropertyNumber, Address, City, State,
  ZIPCode, PropertyTypeID, ConditionID, Bedrooms, Bathrooms,
  YearBuilt, MarketValue)
VALUES(N'811155', N'10340 Helmes Street #1012', N'Silver Spring',
    'MD', N'20906', 1, 2,
      1, 1, 2000, 252775.00);
GO


INSERT INTO Properties(PropertyNumber, Address, City, State,
  ZIPCode, PropertyTypeID, ConditionID, Bedrooms, Bathrooms,
  FinishedBasement, IndoorGarage, Stories, YearBuilt, MarketValue)
VALUES(N'447597', N'4201 Vilamar Ave', N'Hyattsville', N'MD',
    N'20782', 3, 1,
      3, 2, 2, 1, 3, 1992, 365880.00);
GO


INSERT INTO Properties(Address, ZIPCode, Bathrooms)
VALUES(N'1622 Rombard Str', 20904, 2.5);
GO
```

```
INSERT INTO Properties(City, State, PropertyTypeID, ConditionID,
    Bedrooms, Bathrooms, YearBuilt, MarketValue)
VALUES(N'Rockville', N'MD', 1, 2, 1, 1, 1996, 420555.00);
GO


INSERT INTO Properties(PropertyNumber, Address, City, State,
    ZIPCode, PropertyTypeID, ConditionID, Bedrooms, Bathrooms,
    FinishedBasement, IndoorGarage, Stories, YearBuilt, MarketValue)
VALUES(N'297415', N'980 Phorwick Street', N'Washington', N'DC',
        N'20004', 2, 2,
        4, 3.5, 3, 3, 1, 2004, 735475.00);
GO


INSERT INTO Properties(PropertyNumber, Address, City, State,
    ZIPCode, PropertyTypeID, ConditionID, Bedrooms, Bathrooms,
    FinishedBasement, IndoorGarage, Stories, YearBuilt, MarketValue)
VALUES(N'475974', N'9015 Marvin Crow Ave', N'Gaithersburg', N'MD',
        N'20872', 2, 4,
        4, 2.5, 3, 1, 1, 1965, 615775.00);
GO


INSERT INTO Properties(PropertyNumber, Address, City, State,
    ZIPCode, PropertyTypeID, ConditionID, Bedrooms, Bathrooms,
    FinishedBasement, IndoorGarage, Stories, YearBuilt, MarketValue)
VALUES(N'836642', N'3016 Feldman Court', N'Rockville', N'MD',
        N'20954', 2, 3,
        5, 3, 3, 1, 3, 1960, 528555.00);
GO


INSERT INTO Properties(Address, City, ZIPCode, PropertyTypeID,
    Bedrooms, Bathrooms, YearBuilt, MarketValue)
VALUES(N'2444 Arielson Rd', N'Rockville', N'20854',
        1, 2, 1, 1996, 475555.00);
GO
```

```sql
INSERT INTO Properties(City, State, PropertyTypeID, Stories)
VALUES(N'Rockville', N'MD',
      3, 1);
GO


INSERT INTO Properties(PropertyNumber, Address, City, State,
  ZIPCode, PropertyTypeID, ConditionID, Bedrooms, Bathrooms,
  FinishedBasement, IndoorGarage, Stories, YearBuilt, MarketValue)
VALUES(N'208304', N'7307 Everett Hwy', N'Washington', N'DC',
      N'20012', 3, 1,
      2, 2.5, 2, 0, 4, 2006, 420550.00);
GO


INSERT INTO Properties(PropertyNumber, Address, City, State,
  ZIPCode, PropertyTypeID, ConditionID, Bedrooms,
  Bathrooms, YearBuilt, MarketValue)
VALUES(N'644114', N'10340 Helmes Street#1006', N'Silver Spring',
      'MD', N'20906', 1, 2,
      2, 2, 2000, 258445.00);
GO


INSERT INTO Properties(PropertyNumber, Address, City, State,
  ZIPCode, PropertyTypeID, ConditionID, Bedrooms, Bathrooms,
  FinishedBasement, IndoorGarage, Stories, YearBuilt, MarketValue)
VALUES(N'937966', N'7303 Warfield Court', N'Tysons Corner', N'VA',
      '22131', 2, 2,
      3, 2.5, 3, 1, 4, 2006, 825775.00);
GO


INSERT INTO Properties(City, ZIPCode, ConditionID, Bedrooms,
  Stories, YearBuilt)
VALUES(N'Fairfax', N'22232', 2, 3, 3, 1985);
GO
```

```sql
INSERT INTO Properties(PropertyNumber, Address, City, State,
  ZIPCode, PropertyTypeID, ConditionID, Bedrooms, Bathrooms,
  FinishedBasement, IndoorGarage, Stories, YearBuilt, MarketValue)
VALUES(N'297497', N'12401 Conniard Ave', N'Takoma Park', N'MD',
    N'20910', 3, 2,
    3, 2.5, 3, 1, 3, 2004, 280775.00);
GO


INSERT INTO Properties(PropertyNumber, City, ZIPCode,
  PropertyTypeID, ConditionID, Bedrooms, Bathrooms,
  YearBuilt, Stories, MarketValue)
VALUES(N'855255', N'Laurel', N'20707', 2,
    4, 3, 2, 1962, 2, 342805.00);
GO


INSERT INTO Properties(PropertyNumber, Address, City, State,
  ZIPCode, PropertyTypeID, ConditionID, Bedrooms, Bathrooms,
  FinishedBasement, IndoorGarage, Stories, YearBuilt, MarketValue)
VALUES(N'469750', N'6124 Falk Rd', N'Arlington', N'VA',
    '22031', 2, 4,
    4, 3.5, 3, 1, 1, 1982, 635995.00);
GO


INSERT INTO Properties(PropertyNumber, Address, City, State,
  ZIPCode, PropertyTypeID, ConditionID, Bedrooms, Bathrooms,
  FinishedBasement, IndoorGarage, Stories, YearBuilt, MarketValue)
VALUES(N'826927', N'5121 Riehl Ace', N'Fairfax', N'VA',
    '22232', 3, 1,
    3, 1.5, 2, 0, 1, 2002, 325620.00);
GO


INSERT INTO Properties(City, ZIPCode, PropertyTypeID, Bedrooms,
  Bathrooms, MarketValue)
VALUES(N'Silver Spring', N'20906', 1, 2, 2, 335655.00);
GO
```

```sql
INSERT INTO Properties(PropertyNumber, Address, City, State,
  ZIPCode, PropertyTypeID, ConditionID, Bedrooms, Bathrooms,
  FinishedBasement, IndoorGarage, Stories, YearBuilt, MarketValue)
VALUES(N'287064 ', N'9533 Pensulian Rd', N'Silver Spring', N'MD',
    N'20904', 2, 3,
      3, 1.5, 3, 1, 2, 1992, 485775.00);
GO


INSERT INTO Properties(PropertyNumber, City, ZIPCode,
  PropertyTypeID, ConditionID, Bedrooms, YearBuilt, Stories)
VALUES(N'724001 ', N'705 Helios Ave', N'20004',
    3, 3, 3, 1974, 4);
GO


INSERT INTO Properties(PropertyNumber, Address, City, State,
  ZIPCode, PropertyTypeID, ConditionID, Bedrooms, Bathrooms,
  FinishedBasement, IndoorGarage, Stories, YearBuilt, MarketValue)
VALUES(N'209275 ', N'944 Fryer Ave', N'Chevy Chase', N'MD',
    N'20852', 2, 1,
      5, 2.5, 3, 0, 2, 2002, 625665.00);
GO


INSERT INTO Properties(PropertyNumber, Address, City, State,
  ZIPCode, PropertyTypeID, ConditionID, Bedrooms, Bathrooms,
  FinishedBasement, IndoorGarage, Stories, YearBuilt, MarketValue)
VALUES(N'204759', N'1950 Galego Street', N'Germantown', N'MD',
    N'20874', 2, 1,
      4, 3.5, 2, 1, 4, 2007, 428665.00);
GO


INSERT INTO Properties(PropertyNumber, Address, City, State,
  ZIPCode, PropertyTypeID, ConditionID, Bedrooms, Bathrooms,
  FinishedBasement, IndoorGarage, Stories, YearBuilt, MarketValue)
VALUES(N'937259', N'12366 Fowler Ave', N'Alexandria', N'VA',
```

```
'22031', 3, 2,
     3, 1.5, 3, 1, 3, 2007, 402815.00);
GO
```

2.   On the SQL Editor toolbar, click the Execute button

Index in tempdb

The SORT_IN_TEMPDB = ON option modifies the index-creation method by forcing it to use tempdb as opposed to memory. If the index is routinely dropped and recreated, this option may shorten the index creation time. For most indexes, this option is neither required nor important.

Disabling an index

An index may be temporarily disabled, or taken offline, using the Use Index check box in the Index Properties, then Options page. Using T-SQL, to disable an index use the ALTER INDEX DDL command with the DISABLE option.

Here is an example:
ALTER INDEX [IxContact] ON [dbo].[Contact] **DISABLE**

During some intensive data import operations, it is faster to drop the index and recreate it than to update the index with every newly inserted row. The benefit of disabling an index is that the metadata for the index is maintained within the database, rather than depending on the code to recreate the correct index.

To re-enable an index, use the ALTER INDEX... REBUILD WITH command.

Here is an example:

```
USE [imtDeptDB]
GO
ALTER INDEX [PK__personal__2C6EFDC04CD638E3] ON [dbo].[personalInfoTable]
REBUILD PARTITION = ALL
WITH ( PAD_INDEX = OFF,
STATISTICS_NORECOMPUTE = OFF,
ALLOW_ROW_LOCKS = ON,
ALLOW_PAGE_LOCKS = ON,
ONLINE = OFF,
SORT_IN_TEMPDB = OFF );
GO
```

Index Maintenance

In Microsoft SQL Server (and most database systems), an index is treated as an object. That is, an index can be checked or deleted at will.

Deleting an Index

If you don't need an index anymore, you can get rid of it, if you so desire. You can do this visually or programmatically.

To visually delete an index, open its table in Design view. Right-click somewhere in the table window and click Indexes/Views. In the left frame, click the name of the index to select it, and click the Delete button. You will not receive a warning. Then click Close. If you want to change your mind and keep the index, don't save the table.

The basic syntax to delete an index in Transact-SQL is:

DROP INDEX *IndexName* ON *TableName*;

In this formula, replace the *TableName* with the name of the table that contains the index. Replace the *IndexName* with the name of the index you want to get rid of. Here is an example:

USE **employeeDB**;

```
GO

DROP INDEX indxStaffMemb
ON staffMembers;
GO
```

Checking the Existence of an Indexes

Before performing an operation on an index, you may want to check first that it exists.
For example, if you try creating an index and giving it a name that exists already, you
would receive an error.

To visually check the existence of an index, open the table or view in design view,
right-click the middle of the window and click Indexes/Keys. The list of indexes should
appear on the left side. Here is an example:

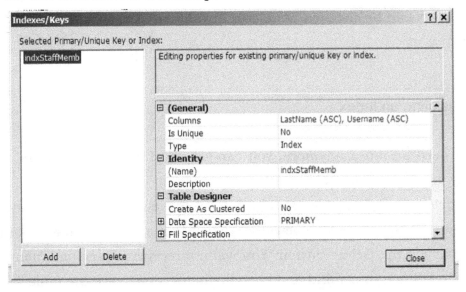

To assist you with checking the existence of an index, Transact-SQL provides the
following formula:

```
IF EXISTS (SELECT name FROM sys.indexes
WHERE name = IndexName)
```

The primary thing you need to provide in this formula is the name of the index. Once you have checked, you can take the necessary action. Here is an example:

```
USE employeeDB;
GO

IF EXISTS (SELECT NAME FROM sys.indexes WHERE name=N'indxStaffMemb')

DROP INDEX indxStaffMemb
ON staffMembers;

CREATE INDEX indxStaffMemb
ON staffMembers(empID);

GO
```

Tables Maintenance

Table maintenance consists of reviewing or changing its aspects. This includes reviewing the list of tables of a database, renaming a table, deleting it and so on.

Like every other object of a database or of the computer, a table possesses some characteristics that are proper to it. To view these characteristics, in the Object Explorer, right-click the table and click Properties.

Opening a Table

Almost all the operations require that you open a table before it can be carried out. There are various ways to open a table, depending on how you want it.

Here is an example of many ways of opening a table:

i.   To view the structure of a table, perhaps to change its columns, in the Object Explorer, expand your database and its Tables node. Right-click the table and click Design or right click the column name and click modify. The table will open in design view, the same view you used to visually create a table, in our previous examples above.

ii.   If you want to view the SQL code of a table, in the Object Explorer, right-click the table, position the mouse on Script Table AS, CREATE To, and click New Query Editor Window

iii.   To open a table to view its data, perhaps to perform data entry, in the Object Explorer, right-click the table and click Edit Top 200 Rows.

Tables Review

To see the list of tables of a database, do this: in the Object Explorer, you can click the Tables node as shown below:

To see the list of database tables via SQL Code, open a Query window, and type the codes below.

Here is an example:

USE **imtDeptDB**;

GO

```
exec sp_help;
go
```

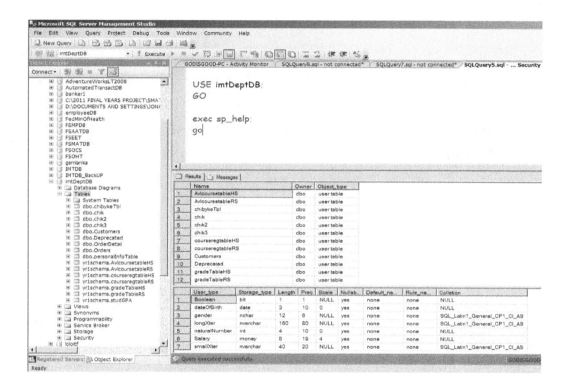

Renaming a Table

If you find out that the name of a table is not appropriate, you can change it. To change the name of a table in the SQL Server Management Studio, in the Object Explorer, right-click the table and click Rename. Type the desired name and press Enter.

To change the name of a table with SQL code, execute **sp_rename**, followed by the current name of the table, a comma, and the new desired name of the table. The formula to use is:

sp_rename *ExistingTableName, TableNewName*;

The names of tables should be included in single-quotes.

Here is an example to change *'chibykeTbl'* table name to *'adminTbl'* table name:

USE **imtDeptDB**;

```
GO
```

```
EXEC sp_rename N'chibykeTbl', N'adminTbl';
GO
```

In this case, the interpreter would look for a table named chibykeTbl in the current or selected database. If it finds it, it would rename it adminTbl and this message would appear: Caution: Changing any part of an object name could break scripts and stored procedures. If the table doesn't exist, you would receive an error.

Deleting a Table

If you have an undesired table in a database, you can get rid of it. To delete a table in the SQL Server Management Studio, in the Object Explorer, right-click the table under its database node and click Delete. You will receive a warning giving you a chance to confirm your intentions. If you still want to remove the table, click OK.

To delete a table using SQL Code, use the following formula:
DROP TABLE *TableName*

The **DROP TABLE** expression is required and it is followed by the name of the undesired table. When you execute the statement, you will not receive a warning before the table is deleted. You can also use sample code that Microsoft SQL Server can generate for you. First display an empty query window. Also display the Templates Explorer and expand the Table node. Under Table, drag Drop Table and drop it in the empty query window. Sample code would be generated for you. You can then simply modify it and execute the statement.

Here is an example of deleting a table:
USE **imtDeptDB**;
GO

```
DROP TABLE dbo.adminTbl;
GO
```

Referring to a Table

Very soon, that is in other following chapters, we will write various expressions that involve the names of tables. In those expressions, you will need to specify a particular table you want to use. There are three main ways you can do this. To refer to, or to indicate, a table:

i.   You can simply type its name. An example would be **studInfo**

ii.   You can type **dbo**, followed by the period operator, followed by the name of the table. An example would be **dbo. studInfo**

iii.   You can type the name of the database to which the table belongs, followed by the period operator, followed by **dbo**, followed by the period operator, and followed by the name of the table. An example would be **smatDB.dbo.studInfo**

Note: dbo is just a schema name as explained in previous chapter on database creation. So you can change it with the name of your schema.

Creating Keys

The primary and foreign keys are the links that bind the tables into a working relational database. I treat these columns as a domain separate from the user's data column. The design of these keys has a critical effect on the performance and usability of the physical database. The database schema must transform from a theoretical logical design into a practical physical design, and the structure of the primary and foreign keys is often the crux of the redesign. Keys are very difficult to modify once the database is in production. Getting the primary keys right during the development phase is the most important thing to do.

Primary keys

The relational database depends on the primary key, the cornerstone of the physical database schema. The debate over natural (understood by users) versus surrogate (auto-generated) primary keys is perhaps the biggest debate in the database industry.

A physical-layer primary key has two purposes:

i. To uniquely identify the row

ii. To serve as a useful object to communicate with other tables through the foreign key

SQL Server implements primary keys and foreign keys as constraints. The purpose of a constraint is to ensure that new data meets certain criteria, business rules, or to block the data-modification operation. A primary-key constraint is effectively a combination of a unique constraint (not a null constraint) and either a clustered or non-clustered unique index.

The surrogate debate: pros and cons

There is considerable debate over natural vs. surrogate keys. Natural keys are based on values found in reality and are preferred by data modellers who identify rows based on what makes them unique in reality. I know SQL Server MVPs who hold strongly to that position. But I know other, just as intelligent, MVPs who argue that the computer-generated surrogate key outperforms the natural key, and who use int identity for every primary key. The fact is that there are pros and cons to each position.

A *natural key* reflects how reality the object can be identified. People's names, automobile VIN numbers, passport numbers, and street addresses are all examples of natural keys.

There are pros and cons to natural keys:

i.   Natural keys are easily identified by humans. On the plus side, humans can easily recognize the data. The disadvantage is that humans want to assign meaning into the primary key, often creating "intelligent keys," assigning meaning to certain characters within the key.

ii. Humans also tend to modify what they understand. Modifying primary key values is troublesome. If you use a natural primary key, be sure to enable cascading updates on every foreign key that refers to the natural primary key so that primary key modifications will not break referential integrity.

iii. Natural keys propagate the primary key values in every generation of the foreign keys, creating composite foreign keys, which create wide indexes and hurt performance.

iv. Natural keys are commonly not in any organized order. This will hurt performance, as new data inserted in the middle of sorted data creates page splits.

A *surrogate key* is assigned by SQL Server and typically has no meaning to humans. Within SQL Server, surrogate keys are identity columns or globally unique identifiers. By far, the most popular method for building primary keys involves using an identity column. Like an auto-number column or sequence column in other databases, the identity column generates consecutive integers as new rows are inserted into the database. Optionally, you can specify the initial seed number and interval.

Identity columns offer three advantages:

i.   Integers are easier to manually recognize and edit than GUIDs.

ii. Integers are obviously just a logical value used to number items. There is little chance humans will become emotionally attached to any integer values. This makes it easy to keep the primary keys hidden, thus making it easier to refactor if needed.

iii. Integers are small and fast. Since SQL Server 2005, it is been possible to generate GUIDs sequentially using the newsequentialid() function as the table default. This solves the page split problem, which was the primary source of the belief that GUIDs were slow.

Here are the disadvantages to identity columns:

i.   Because the scope of their uniqueness is only tablewide, the same integer values are in many tables. GUIDs, on the other hand, are globally unique. Thus, there will be no chance of joining the wrong tables and still getting a result.

ii. Designs with identity columns tend to add surrogate primary keys to every table in lieu of composite primary keys created by multiple foreign keys. While this creates small, fast primary keys, it also creates more joins to navigate the schema structure.

Database design layers

The business entity (visible) layer, the domain integrity (lookup) layer, and the supporting entities (associative tables) layer are the database design layers. The layered database concept becomes practical when designing primary keys. To best take advantage of the pros and cons of natural and surrogate primary keys, use these rules:

i.   Domain Integrity (lookup) layer: Use natural keys — short abbreviations work well. The advantage is that the abbreviation, when used as a foreign key, can avoid a join. For example, a state table with surrogate keys might refer to Abia as StateID = 1. If 1 is stored in every state foreign key, it would always require a join. Who is going to remember that 1 is Abia?

ii. But if the primary key for the state lookup table stored "AB" for Abia, most queries would not need to add the join. The data is in the lookup table for domain integrity (ensuring that only valid data is entered), and perhaps other descriptive data.

iii. Business Entity (visible) layer: For any table that stores operational data, use a surrogate key, probably an identity. If there is a potential natural key (also called a *candidate key*), it should be given a unique constraint/index.

iv. Supporting (associative tables) layer: If the associative table will never serve as the primary table for another table, then it is a good idea to use the multiple foreign keys as a composite primary key. It will perform very well. But if the associative table is ever used as a primary table for another table, then apply a surrogate primary key to avoid a composite foreign key.

Creating primary keys

In code, you set a column as the primary key in one of two ways:

i.   Declare the primary-key constraint in the CREATE TABLE statement. The following code from the Cape Hatteras Adventures sample database uses this technique to create the Guide table and set GuideID as the primary key with a clustered index:

```
CREATE TABLE dbo.Guide (
GuideID INT IDENTITY NOT NULL PRIMARY KEY,
LastName VARCHAR(50) NOT NULL,
FirstName VARCHAR(50) NOT NULL,
```

```
Qualifications VARCHAR(2048) NULL,
DateOfBirth DATETIME NULL,
DateHire DATETIME NULL
);
GO
```

A problem with the previous example is that the primary key constraint will be created with a randomized constraint name. If you ever need to alter the key with code, it will be much easier with an explicitly named constraint:

```
CREATE TABLE dbo.Guide (
GuideID INT IDENTITY NOT NULL
CONSTRAINT PK_Guide PRIMARY KEY (GuideID),
LastName VARCHAR(50) NOT NULL,
FirstName VARCHAR(50) NOT NULL,
Qualifications VARCHAR(2048) NULL,
DateOfBirth DATETIME NULL,
DateHire DATETIME NULL
);
GO
```

ii.   Declare the primary-key constraint after the table is created using an ALTER TABLE command. Assuming the primary key was not already set for the Guide table, the following DDL command would apply a primary-key constraint to the GuideID column:

```
ALTER TABLE dbo.Guide ADD CONSTRAINT
PK_Guide PRIMARY KEY(GuideID)
ON [PRIMARY];
GO
```

Identity column surrogate primary keys

Identity-column values are generated at the database engine level as the row is being inserted. Attempting to insert a value into an identity column or update an identity column will generate an error unless set insert_identity is set to true. The following DDL code from the Cape Hatteras Adventures sample database creates a table that uses an identity column for its primary key (the code listing is abbreviated):

```
CREATE TABLE dbo.Event (
EventID INT IDENTITY NOT NULL
CONSTRAINT PK_Event PRIMARY KEY (EventID),
TourID INT NOT NULL FOREIGN KEY REFERENCES dbo.Tour,
EventCode VARCHAR(10) NOT NULL,
DateBegin DATETIME NULL,
Comment NVARCHAR(255)
)
ON [Primary];
GO
```

Setting a column, or columns, as the primary key in Management Studio is as simple as selecting the column and clicking the primary-key toolbar button. To build a composite primary key, select all the participating columns and press the primary-key button.

Using uniqueidentifier surrogate primary keys

The uniqueidentifier data type is SQL Server's counterpart to .NET's globally unique identifier (GUID, pronounced GOO-id or gwid). It is a 16-byte hexadecimal number that is essentially unique among all tables, all databases, all servers, and all planets. While both identity columns and GUIDs are unique, the scope of the uniqueness is greater with GUIDs than identity columns, so while they are grammatically incorrect, GUIDs are more unique than identity columns. GUIDs offer several advantages:

i. A database using GUID primary keys can be replicated without a major overhaul. Replication will add a unique identifier to every table without a uniqueidentifier column. While this makes the column globally unique for replication purposes, the application code will still be identifying rows by the integer primary key only; therefore, merging replicated rows from other servers causes an error because there will be duplicate primary key values.

ii. GUIDs discourage users from working with or assigning meaning to the primary keys.

iii. GUIDs are more unique than integers. The scope of an integer's uniqueness is limited to the local table. A GUID is unique in the universe. Therefore, GUIDs eliminate join errors caused by joining the wrong tables but returning data regardless, because rows that should not match share the same integer values in key columns.

iv. GUIDs are forever. The table based on a typical integer-based identity column will hold only 2,147,483,648 rows. Of course, the data type could be set to bigint or numeric, but that lessens the size benefit of using the identity column.

v. Because the GUID can be generated by either the column default, the SELECT statement expression, or code prior to the SELECT statement, it's significantly easier to program with GUIDs than with identity columns. Using GUIDs circumvents the data-modification problems of using identity columns.

The drawbacks of unique identifiers are largely performance based:

i. Unique identifiers are large compared to integers, so fewer of them fit on a page. As a result, more page reads are required to read the same number of rows.

ii. Unique identifiers generated by NewID(), like natural keys, are essentially random, so data inserts will eventually cause page splits, hurting performance. However, natural keys will have a natural distribution so the page split problem is worse with natural keys.

The Product table in the Outer Banks Kite Store sample database uses a uniqueidentifier as its primary key. In the following script, the ProductID column's data type is set to uniqueidentifier. Its nullability is set to false. The column's rowguidcol property is set to true, enabling replication to detect and use this column. The default is a newly generated uniqueidentifier. It is the primary key, and it is indexed with a non-clustered unique index:

```
CREATE TABLE dbo.Product (
ProductID UNIQUEIDENTIFIER NOT NULL
ROWGUIDCOL DEFAULT (NEWSEQUNTIALID())
PRIMARY KEY CLUSTERED,
ProductCategoryID UNIQUEIDENTIFIER NOT NULL
FOREIGN KEY REFERENCES dbo.ProductCategory,
ProductCode CHAR(15) NOT NULL,
ProductName NVARCHAR(50) NOT NULL,
ProductDescription NVARCHAR(100) NULL,
ActiveDate DATETIME NOT NULL DEFAULT GETDATE(),
DiscountinueDate DATETIME NULL
)
ON [Static];
GO
```

There are two primary methods of generating Uniqueidentifiers (both actually generated by Windows), and multiple locations where one can be generated:

i.   The NewID() function generates a Uniqueidentifier using several factors, including the computer NIC code, the MAC address, the CPU internal ID, and the current tick of the CPU clock. The last six bytes are from the node number of the NIC card.

ii. The versatile NewID() function may be used as a column default, passed to an insert statement, or executed as a function within any expression.

iii. NewsequentialID() is similar to NewID(), but it guarantees that every new uniqueidentifier is greater than any other uniqueidentifier for that table. The NewsequntialID() function can be used only as a column default. This makes sense because the value generated is dependent on the greatest Uniqueidentifier in a specific table.

Creating foreign keys

A secondary table that relates to a primary table uses a foreign key to point to the primary table's primary key. *Referential integrity (RI)* refers to the fact that the references have integrity, meaning that every foreign key points to a valid primary key. Referential integrity is vital to the consistency of the database.

The database must begin and end every transaction in a consistent state. This consistency must extend to the foreign-key references.

SQL Server tables may have up to 253 foreign key constraints. The foreign key can reference primary keys, unique constraints, or unique indexes of any table except a temporary table. It is a common misconception that referential integrity is an aspect of the primary key. It is the foreign key that is constrained to a valid primary-key value, so the constraint is an aspect of the foreign key, not the primary key.

Declarative referential integrity

SQL Server's *declarative referential integrity (DRI)* can enforce referential integrity without writing custom triggers or code. DRI is handled inside the SQL Server engine, which executes significantly faster than custom RI code executing within a trigger.

SQL Server implements DRI with foreign key constraints. Establishing or modifying a foreign key constraint in Management Studio can be done in three ways:

i. Using the Database Designer, select the primary-key column and drag it to the foreign-key column. That action will open the Foreign Key Relationships dialog.

ii. In the Object Explorer, right-click to open the context menu in the *DatabaseName* , Tables, *TableName,* Keys node and select New Foreign Key.

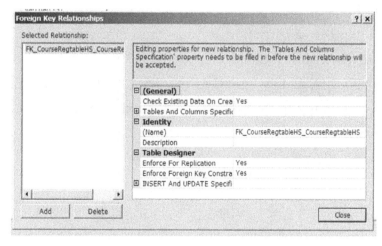

iii. Using the Table Designer, click on the Relationships toolbar button, or select Table Designer, Relationships. Alternately, from the Database Designer, select the secondary table (the one with the foreign key), and choose the Relationships toolbar button, or Relationship from the table's context menu.

Several options in the Foreign Key Relationships form define the behaviour of the foreign key:

    i.   Enforce for Replication

    ii.   Enforce Foreign Key Constraint

Enforce Foreign Key Constraint

    i.   Delete Rule and Update Rule (Cascading delete options are described later in this chapter)

Within a T-SQL script, you can declare foreign key constraints by either including the foreign key constraint in the table-creation code or applying the constraint after the table is created. After the column definition, the phrase FOREIGN KEY REFERENCES, followed by the primary table, and optionally the column(s), creates the foreign key, as follows:

ForeignKeyColumn FOREIGN KEY REFERENCES PrimaryTable(PKID)
The following code from the sample database, it creates the tour_mm_guide many-to-many junction table. As a junction table, tour_mm_guide has two foreign key constraints: one to the Tour table and one to the Guide table. For demonstration purposes, the TourID foreign key specifies the primary-key column, but the GuideID foreign key simply points to the table and uses the primary key by default:

```
CREATE TABLE dbo.Tour_mm_Guide (
TourGuideID INT
IDENTITY
NOT NULL
PRIMARY KEY NONCLUSTERED,
TourID INT NOT NULL
FOREIGN KEY REFERENCES dbo.Tour(TourID)
ON DELETE CASCADE,
GuideID INT NOT NULL
FOREIGN KEY REFERENCES dbo.Guide
ON DELETE CASCADE,
QualDate DATETIME NOT NULL,
RevokeDate DATETIME NULL
)
```

ON [Primary];
GO

Some database developers prefer to include foreign key constraints in the table definition, while others prefer to add them after the table is created, the two ways are ok. If the table already exists, you can add the foreign key constraint to the table using the ALTER TABLE ADD CONSTRAINT DDL command, as shown here:

```
ALTER TABLE SecondaryTableName
ADD CONSTRAINT ConstraintName
FOREIGN KEY (ForeignKeyColumns)
REFERENCES dbo.PrimaryTable (PrimaryKeyColumnName);
GO
```

The Person table in the Family database must use this method because it uses a reflexive relationship, also called a *unary* or *self-join* relationship. A foreign key can't be created before the primary key exists. Because a reflexive foreign key refers to the same table, that table must be created prior to the foreign key. This code, is a sample of database created already, it creates the Person table and then establishes the MotherID and FatherID foreign keys.

Here is an example:

```
CREATE TABLE dbo.Person (
PersonID INT NOT NULL PRIMARY KEY NONCLUSTERED,
LastName VARCHAR(15) NOT NULL,
FirstName VARCHAR(15) NOT NULL,
SrJr VARCHAR(3) NULL,
MaidenName VARCHAR(15) NULL,
Gender CHAR(1) NOT NULL,
FatherID INT NULL,
MotherID INT NULL,
DateOfBirth DATETIME NULL,
DateOfDeath DATETIME NULL
);
GO
```

```
ALTER TABLE dbo.Person
ADD CONSTRAINT FK_Person_Father
FOREIGN KEY(FatherID) REFERENCES dbo.Person (PersonID);
GO

ALTER TABLE dbo.Person
ADD CONSTRAINT FK_Person_Mother
FOREIGN KEY(MotherID) REFERENCES dbo.Person (PersonID);
GO
```

Optional foreign keys

An important distinction exists between optional foreign keys and mandatory foreign keys. Some relationships require a foreign key, as with an OrderDetail row that requires a valid order row, but other relationships don't require a value — the data is valid with or without a foreign key, as determined in the logical design. In the physical layer, the difference is the nullability of the foreign-key column. If the foreign key is mandatory, the column should not allow nulls. An optional foreign key allows nulls. A relationship with complex optionality requires either a check constraint or a trigger to fully implement the relationship. The common description of referential integrity is "no orphan rows" — referring to the days when primary tables were called *parent files* and secondary tables were called *child files*. Optional foreign keys are the exception to this description. You can think of an optional foreign key as "orphans are allowed, but if there is a parent it must be the legal parent."

Cascading deletes and updates

A complication created by referential integrity is that it prevents you from deleting or modifying a primary row being referred to by secondary rows until those secondary rows have been deleted. If the primary row is deleted and the secondary rows' foreign keys are still pointing to the now deleted primary keys, referential integrity is violated. The solution to this problem is to modify the secondary rows as part of the primary table transaction. DRI can do this automatically for you. Four outcomes are possible for the affected secondary rows selected in the Delete Rule or Update Rule properties of the Foreign Key Relationships form. Update Rule is meaningful for natural primary keys only:

i. **No Action:** The secondary rows won't be modified in any way. Their presence will block the primary rows from being deleted or modified. Use No Action when the secondary rows provide value to the primary rows. You don't want the primary rows to be deleted or modified if secondary rows exist. For instance, if there are invoices for the account, don't delete the account.

ii. **Cascade:** The delete or modification action being performed on the primary rows will also be performed on the secondary rows. Use Cascade when the secondary data is useless without the primary data. For example, if Order 123 is being deleted, all the order details rows for Order 123 will be deleted as well. If Order 123 is being updated to become Order 456, then the order details rows must also be changed to Order 456 (assuming a natural primary key).

iii. **Set Null:** This option leaves the secondary rows intact but sets the foreign key column's value to null. This option requires that the foreign key is nullable. Use Set Null when you want to permit the primary row to be deleted without affecting the existence of the secondary. For example, if a class is deleted, you don't want a student's rows to be deleted because the student's data is valid independent of the class data.

iv. **Set Default:** The primary rows may be deleted or modified and the foreign key values in the affected secondary rows are set to their column default values. This option is similar to the Set Null option except that you can set a specific value. For schemas that use surrogate nulls (e.g., empty strings), setting the column default to '' and the Delete Rule to Set Default would set the foreign key to an empty string if the primary table rows were deleted.

Within T-SQL code, adding the ON DELETE CASCADE option to the foreign key constraint enables the cascade operation. The following code will create a table for the details of Orders and add the necessary constraints.

use smatDB;

```sql
GO
CREATE TABLE dbo.OrderDetail (
OrderDetailID UNIQUEIDENTIFIER
NOT NULL ROWGUIDCOL DEFAULT (NEWID())
PRIMARY KEY NONCLUSTERED,

OrderID UNIQUEIDENTIFIER NOT NULL
FOREIGN KEY REFERENCES dbo.[Order]
ON DELETE CASCADE,
ProductID UNIQUEIDENTIFIER NULL
FOREIGN KEY REFERENCES dbo.Product);
GO
```

CHAPTER SEVEN

DATA MANIPULATION AND MAINTENANCE

SQL is the romance language of data, but wooing the single correct answer from gigabytes of relational data can seem overwhelming until the logical flow of the query is mastered. One of the first points to understand is that SQL is a *declarative* language. This means that the SQL query logically describes the question to the SQL Query Optimizer, which then determines the best method to physically execute the query. There are often many ways of stating the query, but each method could be optimized to the same query execution plan. This means you are free to express the SQL query in the way that makes the most sense to you and will be the easiest to maintain. In some cases, one method is considered cleaner or faster than another: I will point those instances out as well. SQL queries are not limited to SELECT, though it plays the most important role in terms of data selection. The four Data Manipulation Language (DML) commands which are, SELECT, INSERT, UPDATE, and DELETE, are sometimes taught as four separate and distinct commands. However, I see queries as a single structural method of manipulating data; in other words, it is better to think of the four commands as four verbs that may each be used with the full power and flexibility of the SQL. I will limit the discussion of data manipulation to *INSERT, UPDATE* and *DELETE*. I will talk about the data manipulation using *SELECT* in the next chapter of this book

7.1   DATA MANIPULATION

A table is an object that holds the information of a database. Because a table is the central part of a database, the information it holds must be meticulously organized. To better manage its information, data of a table is arranged in a series of fields called cells. Once a table contains information, you can review it using either SQL Server Management Studio or an external application.

The tables of a database display in the Object Explorer under their database node. To open a table for data entry, right-click it and click Edit Top 200 Rows.

7.1.1   Table Data Navigation in the SQL Server Management Studio

Data Navigation consists of displaying and viewing data. Because information of a database is stored in tables, your primary means of viewing data consists of opening a table in a way that displays its information. When a table displays its records, you navigate through its fields using the mouse or the keyboard. With the mouse, to get to any cell, you can just click it or scroll down and up then click it. To navigate through records using the keyboard, you can press:

- The right arrow key to move to the right cell; if the caret is already in the most right cell, it would be moved to the first cell of the next record, up to the last empty cell of the first empty record

- The left arrow key to move to the previous cell; if the caret is in, or reaches, the most left cell of the first record, nothing would happen when you press the left arrow key

- The down arrow key to move to the cell under the current one; if the caret is already in the last cell of the current column, nothing would happen

- The up arrow key to move to the cell just above the current one; if the caret is already in the first cell of the current column, nothing would happen

- The Page Down to move to the next group of cell that would correspond to the next page; if the number of records is less than a complete page, the caret would move to the last cell of the current column

- The Page Up to move to the next group of cell that would correspond to the next page; if the number of records is less than a complete page, the caret would move to the first cell of the current column

7.1.2   Data Entry

As you are probably aware already, columns are used to organize data by categories. Each column has a series of fields under the column header. One of the actual purposes of a table is to display data that is available for each field under a particular column. Data entry consists of providing the necessary values of the fields of a table. Data is entered into a field and every time this is done, the database creates row of data. This row is called a record. This means that entering data also self-creates rows. There are four main ways you can perform data entry for a Microsoft SQL Server table:

i.   You can use a table from the Object Explorer
ii.   You can enter data by typing code in a query window
iii. You can import data from another object or another database
iv.   You can use an external application such as Microsoft Access, Microsoft Visual Basic, Borland C++ Builder, Microsoft Visual C++, Borland Delphi, Microsoft Visual Basic, C#, Visual C#, J#, etc.

i.   Data Entry Using the Object Explorer

Probably the easiest and fastest way to enter small amount of data into a table is by using SQL Server Management Studio. Of course, you must first open the desired table from an available database. In the Object Explorer, after expanding the Databases and the Tables nodes, open a table for data entry. If the table contain data, it would appear with one empty row expecting a new record.

Here is an example:

	IWUALAMC-PC.tr... - dbo.Transact	IWUALAMC-PC.Co...y1 - dbo.admin	IWUALAMC-PC.id...ts - dbo.Rooms				
	fname	witdrawal	balance	deposit	TransID	transKey	ktrans
	Carol	50000.0000	4500.0000	10000.0000	5	001	56780
▸*	NULL	NULL	NULL	NULL	NULL	NULL	NULL

To perform data entry on a table, you can click in a field. Each column has a title, called a caption, on top. This gray section on top is called a column header. In SQL Server, it displays the actual name of the column. You refer to the column header to know what kind of data should/must go in a field under a particular column. This is why you should design your columns meticulously. After identifying a column, you can type a value. Except for text-based columns, a field can accept or reject a value if the value does not conform to the data type that was set for the column. This means that in some circumstances, you may have to provide some or more explicit information to the user, if the user will have direct access to enter data into the database. But if the data is to be entered via application or web application then there won't be any need to inform the user about the data to be supplied because the developer of the application will take care of that.

ii.   Data Entry Using SQL Server Code

1. Right-click the server name and click New Query
2. To create a new database, in the empty window, type the following:

```
USE master;
GO


CREATE DATABASE WorldPopulation;
GO


USE WorldPopulation;
GO


CREATE TABLE Countries
(
    [Country Name] NVARCHAR(50),
    Area INT
    ,[Population] BIGINT
    ,Capital NVARCHAR(50)
    ,[Internet Code] nchar(2)
```

);
GO

3. In the Object Explorer, right-click the Databases node and click Refresh. Expand the Databases node. Under Databases, expand WorldPopulation and expand Tables

4. If you do not see a table named Countries, right-click the Tables node and click Refresh.

   Right-click Countries and click Edit Top 200 Rows

5. Click the first empty cell under CountryName, type Cote d'Ivoire and press Enter

6. Type 322460 for the area and press Tab

7. Type 16,393,221 and press Enter

8. Notice that you receive an error because the commas are not allowed:

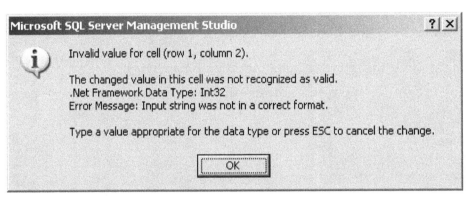

9. Click OK on the error message box.

10. Change the value to 16393221 People and press Tab

11. Notice that you receive another error because the column is configured for a natural number and not a string

12. Click OK on the error message box and delete People

13. Under Internet Code, type ci and press Enter

14. Click the field under Capital, type Yamoussoukro and press Enter twice

15. Close the table

To programmatically perform data entry after creating table, you use a Data Definition Language (DDL) command known as **INSERT;** we have been using INSERT from previous chapters. To start, if you are working in Microsoft SQL Server:

The DDL command to perform data entry is **INSERT** combined with **VALUES**. The primary statement uses the following syntax:

INSERT *TableName* VALUES(*Column1, Column2, Column_n*);

Alternatively, or to be more precise, you can use the **INTO** keyword between the **INSERT** keyword and the *TableName* factor to specify that you are entering data into the table. This is done with the following syntax:

INSERT INTO *TableName* VALUES(*Column1, Column2, Column_n*)

The *TableName* factor must be a valid name of an existing table in the database you are using. If the name is wrong, the SQL interpreter would simply consider that the table you are referring to does not exist. Consequently, you would receive an error.

The **VALUES** keyword indicates that you are ready to list the values of the columns. The values of the columns must be included in parentheses. If the column is a **BIT** data type, you must specify one of its values as 0 or 1. If the column is a numeric type, you should pay attention to the number you type. If the column was configured to receive an integer (**int**, **bigint**, **smallint**), you should provide a valid natural number without the decimal separator.
If the column is for a decimal number (**float**, **real**, **decimal**, **numeric**), you can type the value with its character separator (the period for US English).
If the column was created for a date data type, make sure you provide a valid date.

If the data type of a column is a string type, you should include its entry between single quotes. For example, a shelf number can be specified as 'HHR-604' and middle initial can be given as 'C'.

In the previous paragraphs, we were stating "you" as if you will be the one performing data entry. In reality, the user will be performing data entry on your products. Therefore, it is your responsibility to reduce, as much as possible, the likelihood of mistakes. Of course, there are various ways, through a "visual" application such as Borland C++ Builder, Microsoft Visual Basic, C#, or MS Visual C++, etc, that you can take care of this.
Here is an example of data entry:

```
USE WorldPopulation;
GO
INSERT INTO Countries ([Country Name], Area, [Population], Capital,[Internet Code] )
VALUES(N'Ghana',322460,16393221,N'Accra',N'gh');
GO
```

iii.   Adjacent Data Entry

The most common technique of performing data entry requires that you know the sequence of fields of the table in which you want to enter data. With this subsequent list in mind, enter the value of each field in its correct position.

During data entry on adjacent fields, if you don't have a value for a numeric field, you should type 0 as its value. For a string field whose data you don't have and cannot provide, type two single-quotes ' ' to specify an empty field.

1. To open a new query window, press Ctrl + N
2. In   the   query   window,   to   create   one   record,   type:

```
USE WorldPopulation;
GO

INSERT INTO Countries
VALUES(N'Cote d''Ivoire',322460,16393221,N'Yamoussoukro',N'ci'),
        (N'Panama',78200,3191319,N'Panama',N'pa'),
        (N'Nigeria',16590,160000000,N'Abuja',N'ni'),
        (N'Australia',7686850,20264082,N'Canberra',N'au'),
        (N'Canada',9984670,33098932,N'Ottawa',N'ca'),
        (N'Iran',1648000,68688433,N'Tehran',N'ir');
    GO
```

```
SQLQuery1.sql -... (chibyke (54))*    IWUALAMC-PC.tr... - dbo.Transact                          ▾ ✕
    USE WorldPopulation;
    GO
  ⊟INSERT INTO Countries
    VALUES(N'Cote d''Ivoire',322460,16393221,N'Yamoussoukro',N'ci'),
          (N'Panama',78200,3191319,N'Panama',N'pa'),
          (N'Nigeria',16590,160000000,N'Abuja',N'ni'),
          (N'Australia',7686850,20264082,N'Canberra',N'au'),
          (N'Canada',9984670,33098932,N'Ottawa',N'ca'),
          (N'Iran',1648000,68688433,N'Tehran',N'ir');
    GO|


◾ Messages
  (6 row(s) affected)
```

3. Press F5 to execute
4. Press F5 to execute the statement

iv.   Random (Customized) Data Entry

The adjacent data entry we have performed requires that you know the position of each field. The SQL Server provides an alternative that allows you to perform data entry using the name of a column instead of its position. This allows you to provide the values of columns in an order of your choice. We have just seen a few examples where the values of some of the fields were not available during data entry. Instead of remembering to type 0 or NULL for such fields or leaving empty quotes for a field, you can use the fields' names to specify the fields whose data you want to provide.

To perform data entry in an order of your choice, you must provide your list of the fields of the table, whence the name *customized*. You can either use all columns or provide a list of the same columns but in your own order. In the same way, you don't have to provide data for all fields, just those you want and in the order you want it. Here is an example:

1. To perform customized data entry, type and execute the following statement:

```
USE WorldPopulation;
GO


INSERT Countries([Country Name],Capital,[Internet Code],[Population],Area)
VALUES(N'China', N'Beijing', N'cn', 1313973713, 9596960);
GO
```
2. Press F5 to execute the statement
3. More customized data entries, type the following statement:
```
USE WorldPopulation;
GO


    INSERT Countries(Capital, [Internet Code], [Country Name])
    VALUES(N'Nouakchott', N'mr', N'Mauritania')
    GO


    INSERT Countries([Internet Code], [Population], [Country Name])
    VALUES(N'ro', 22303552, N'Romania')
    GO


INSERT Countries(Area, [Country Name], [Population])
VALUES(21040, N'El Salvador', 6822378)
GO


INSERT Countries(Capital, [Country Name])
VALUES(N'Phnom Penh', N'Cambodia')
GO
```
4. To execute the statement, press F5.
5. Close the query window.
6. When asked whether you want to save it, click No if you actually do not want to save it for future use.

v.   Creating Multiple Records

In previous sections, we added a single record to each record using the INSERT formula. You can add various records with one call of INSERT. If you are adding a value to each column of the table, after the name of the table, type VALUES, open and close the first parentheses. Inside the parentheses include the desired values. To add another record, type a comma after the closing parenthesis, open a new parenthesis, list the new values, and close the parenthesis; I have already demonstrated how to do that under Adjacent Data Entry section above. Do this as many times as you need to add records. Here is an example:

USE LoloVideoClub;

GO

INSERT INTO dbo.VideosInfo

VALUES(N'Passion of Christ', N'Rev. Fr. Odoemena A. N.', N'180min','',N'Foreign', 1998),

(N'Memoirs of a Geisha', N'Rob Marshall', N'180min','', N'Foreign', 2006),

(N'Two for the Money', N'D.J. Caruso', N'150min','',N'Foreign', 2008);

GO

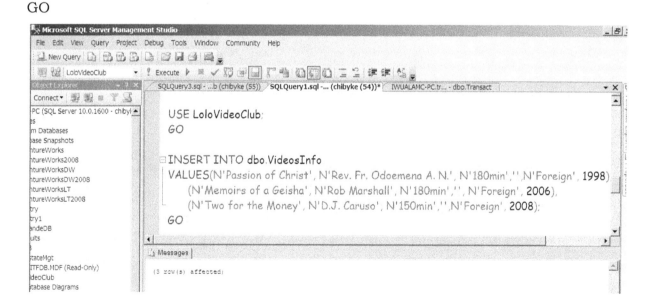

This is valid for adjacent data entry. If you want to follow your own order of columns, on the right side of the name of the table, include a list of columns in parentheses. Then, when giving the values, for each record, follow the order in which you listed the columns. Here is an example:

```
USE LoloVideoClub;
GO


INSERT INTO dbo.VideosInfo (VideoTitle, Director,yearReleased)
VALUES( N'Wall Street', N'Oliver Stone',2011),
      (N'Michael Jackson Live in Bucharest', N'Andy Morahan',2009),
      (N'Sneakers', N'Paul Alden Robinson',2012),
      ( N'Soldier', N'Paul Anderson',2012);
GO
```

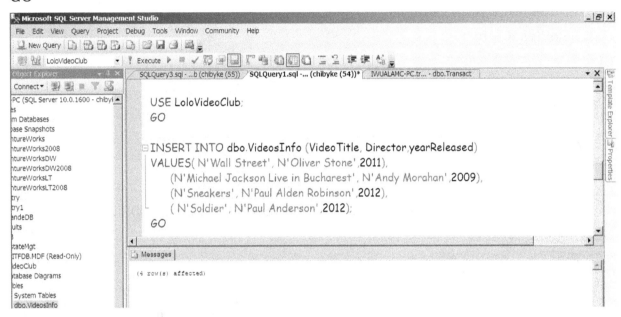

vi.   Outputting the Inserted Result

In the techniques we have used so far, when or if the records have been added to a table, whether the operation was successful or not, we had no way of finding out, though the interpreter assures me that all went well via a message. One way you can get this information is to store the inserted records in another table or display it. To support this, Transact-SQL provides the **OUTPUT** operator. The formula to use it is:

INSERT INTO *TableName*
OUTPUT INSERTED.*Columns*
VALUES(*Value_1*, *Value_2*, *Value_X*)

You start with the normal record insertion with the **INSERT INTO** *TableName* expression. This is followed by the **OUTPUT** operator followed by the **INSERTED** operator and a period. If you are adding a value for each record, follow the period with *. The statement continues with the **VALUES** operator that is followed by parentheses in which you list the values to be added to the table. Here is an example:

USE LoloVideoClub;
GO

INSERT INTO dbo.VideosInfo
OUTPUT inserted.*
VALUES(N'War of the Roses (The)', N'Dany de Vito',N'360mins', 0, N'Foreign', 2001),
    (N'What A World', N'PETE Edochie',N'180mins', 1, N'Naija', 2012),
    (N'The Nativity', N'Rev. Fr. Joseph Ahuonye',N'120mins', 1, N'Naija', 2010),
    (N'Sneakers', N'Phil Alden Robinson',N'360mins', 1, N'Foreign', 2003);
GO

When this statement executes, if you are working in the Microsoft SQL Server Management Studio, the lower part would display a list of the records that were added to specified table.

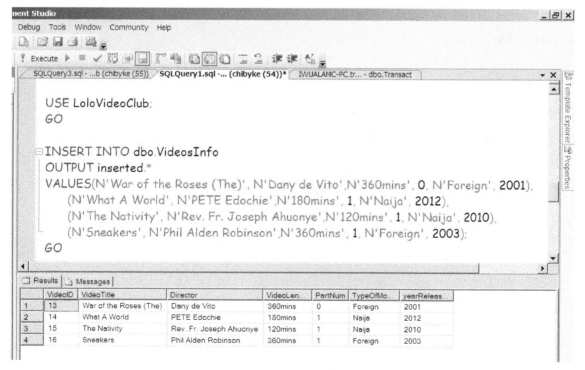

If you use the above formula, when you close the database, the reference is lost. If you want to store the list of newly created records in a table, on the right side of the **INSERTED** operator and its period, type **INTO** followed by the name of the table that will receive the values. The table must have been created; that is, it must exist at the time this inserted operation is taking place and must have the same fields with the table that the records originate. Here is an example:

```
USE [LoloVideoClub];
GO


CREATE TABLE [dbo].[VideosInfoArchives](
        [VideoID] [int] IDENTITY(1,1) NOT NULL,
        [VideoTitle] [nvarchar](120) NOT NULL,
        [Director] [nvarchar](100) NULL,
        [VideoLength] [nvarchar](30) NULL,
        [PartNum] [tinyint] NULL,
        [TypeOfMovie] [nchar](10) NULL,
        [yearReleased] [int] NULL
) ON [PRIMARY]
GO


USE LoloVideoClub;
GO


INSERT INTO dbo.VideosInfo
OUTPUT inserted. * INTO VideosInfoArchives
VALUES (N'Out Law', N'Raty Edochie',N'180mins', 1, N'Naija', 2010),
        (N'Tears of Joy', N'Patience Iwuala',N'120mins', 2, N'Naija', 2012);
GO
```

In this case, a copy of the newly created records would be stored in the specified table. The above techniques assume that you are adding a complete record; that is, you are providing a value for each column of the table. We already saw that if you want to provide values for only some columns, after the name of the table, provide the list of columns in parentheses. To get the list of newly inserted records, after the **OUTPUT** keyword, type **INSERTED** followed by a period and followed by the name of the first column. Do this for each column. The formula to use is:

INSERT INTO *TableName*(*Column_1, Column_2, Column_X*)

OUTPUT INSERTED.*Column_1*, INSERTED.*Column_2*, INSERTED.*Column_X*

VALUES(*Value_1, Value_2, Value_X*)

Of course, you can list the columns in an order of your choice, as long as both the *TableName* and the **OUTPUT** section use the exact same order. Here is an example:

USE LoloVideoClub;

GO

INSERT INTO dbo.VideosInfo (Director, VideoTitle, VideoLength)

OUTPUT inserted.Director, inserted.VideoLength, inserted.VideoTitle

VALUES(N'Jonathan Lynn', N'R', N'Distinguished Gentleman (The)', N'120mins'),

    (N'Paul Anderson', N'R', N'Soldier', N'60mins');

GO

In this case, when the statement has executed, the result would display in the lower portion of the Microsoft SQL Server Management Studio. If you want to store the result in a table, use the following formula

INSERT INTO *TableName*(*Column_1, Column_2, Column_X*)

OUTPUT INSERTED.*Column_1*, INSERTED.*Column_2*, INSERTED.*Column_X* INTO *TargetTable*

VALUES(*Value_1, Value_2, Value_X*)

Here is an example:

USE LoloVideoClub;

GO

CREATE TABLE Entertainment

(

        entertainID int identity(1,1) NOT NULL

```
        ,Title nvarchar(50)
        , Director nvarchar(50)
        ,NumOfHrs varchar(10)
);
GO


USE LoloVideoClub;
GO


INSERT INTO dbo.VideosInfo (VideoTitle,Director,VideoLength)
OUTPUT inserted.VideoTitle , inserted.Director, inserted.VideoLength
INTO Entertainment
VALUES(N'Wise Men',N'Jonathan Nwachuckwu',  N'120mins'),
    (N'The Crown',N'Paul Ugonna',  N'60mins');
GO
```

7.1.3   Tables Columns and Expressions

There are various ways you can assist the user with data entry. Besides using a function, you can create an expression using operators such as those we reviewed in lessons 3 and 5. You can create an expression when creating a table, whether in the Table window or using SQL in a query window.

i.   Visually Creating an Expression

To create an expression when visually creating a table, in the top section, specify the column's name (only the column name is important). In the bottom section, expand the Computed Column Specification field and, in its (Formula) field, enter the desired expression; you can select Is Persisted to Yes. Here is an example:

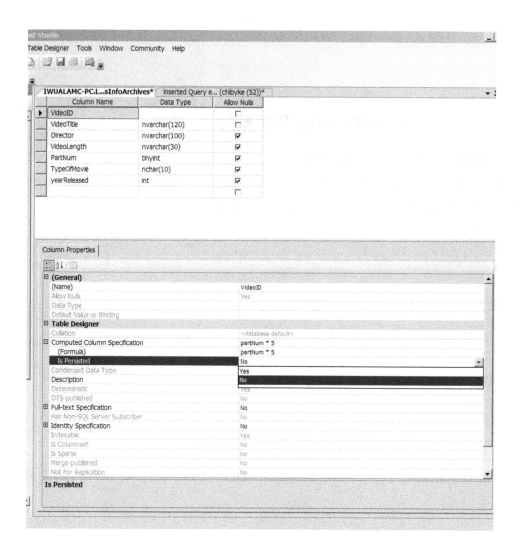

ii.　Programmatically Creating an Expression

You can also create an expression in SQL expression you are using to create a table. To do this, in the placeholder of the column, enter the name of the column, followed by AS, and followed by the desired expression. Here is an example:

```
USE diograndeDB;
GO

CREATE TABLE Circle
(
    CircleID int identity(1,1) NOT NULL,
    Radius decimal(8, 3) NOT NULL,
    Area AS Radius * Radius * PI()
```

```
);
GO
```

iii.   Application of Expression During Data Entry

When performing data entry, you must not provide a value for a column that has an expression; the SQL interpreter would provide the value automatically. Here is an example of entering data for the above Circle table:

```
USE diograndeDB;
GO


INSERT INTO Circle(Radius) VALUES(46.82);
GO


INSERT INTO Circle(Radius) VALUES(8.15);
GO


INSERT INTO Circle(Radius) VALUES(122.57);
GO
```

7.1.4   The Nullity of a Field

During data entry, users of your database will face fields that expect data. Sometimes, for one reason or another, data will not be available for a particular field. An example would be an MI (middle initial) field: some people have a middle initial, some others either don't have it or would not (or cannot) provide it. This aspect can occur for any field of your table. Therefore, you should think of a way to deal with it.

A field is referred to as null when no data entry has been made to it:

- Saying that a field is null doesn't mean that it contains 0 because 0 is a value
- Saying that a field is null doesn't mean that it is empty. A field being empty could mean that the user had deleted its content or that the field itself would

not accept what the user was trying to enter into that field, but an empty field can have a value

A field is referred to as null if there is no way of determining the value of its content (in reality, the computer, that is, the operating system, has its own internal mechanism of verifying the value of a field) or its value is simply unknown. As you can imagine, it is not a good idea to have a null field in your table. As a database developer, it is your responsibility to always know with certainty the value held by each field of your table.

A field is referred to as required if the user must provide a value for it before moving to another record. In other words, the field cannot be left empty during data entry. To solve the problem of null and required fields, Microsoft SQL Server proposes one of two options: allow or not allow null values on a field. For a typical table, there are pieces of information that the user should make sure to enter; otherwise, the data entry would not be validated. To make sure the user always fills out a certain field before moving to the next field, that is, to require the value, if you are visually creating the table, clear the Allow Nulls check box for the field. On the other hand, if the value of a field is not particularly important, for example if you don't intend to involve that value in an algebraic operation, check its Allow Nulls check box.

i. NULL or NOT NULL?

If you intend to assign NULL when creating a table using SQL Server Code, type **NULL** on the right side of the column. To specify that the values of the column are required, on the right side, type **NOT NULL**. If you don't specify **NULL** or **NOT NULL**, the column will be created as **NULL** by default. Here is an examples:

```
CREATE TABLE Persons
(
    FirstName varchar(20) NOT NULL
    ,MiddleName varchar(20)  NULL
    ,LastName varchar(20) NOT NULL
    ,Gender char(6)
);
GO
```

If the table was already created and it holds some values already, you cannot set the Allow Nulls option on such columns. After specify that a column would **NOT** allow **NULL** values, if the user tries creating a record but omits to enter a value for the column, an error would display. Here is an example:

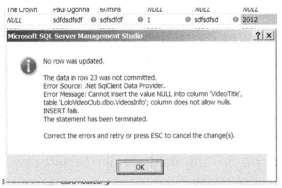

This error message box indicates that the user attempted to submit a null value for a column that required a data. To cancel the action, you can press Esc.

7.1.5   The Default Value of a Column

Sometimes most records under a certain column may hold the same value although just a few would be different. For example, if a school is using a database to register its students, all of them are more likely to be from the same state. In such a case, you can assist the user by automatically providing a value for that column. The user would then simply accept the value and change it only in the rare cases where the value happens to be different. To assist the user with this common value, you create what is referred to as a default value.

i.   Visually Creating a Default Value

You can create a default value of a column when creating a table. To specify the default value of a column, in the top section, click the column. In the bottom section, click Default Value or Binding, type the desired value following the rules of the column's data type:

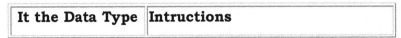

It the Data Type	Intructions

is	
Text-based (**char**, **varchar**, **text**, and their variants)	Enter the value in single-quotes
Numeric-based	Enter the value as a number but following the rules of the data type. For example, if you enter a value higher than 255 for a **tinyint**, you would receive an error
Date or Time	Enter the date as either MM/DD/YYYY or YYYY/MM/DD. You can optionally include the date in single-quotes. Enter the time following the rules set in the Control Panel (Regional Settings).
Bit	Enter True or False

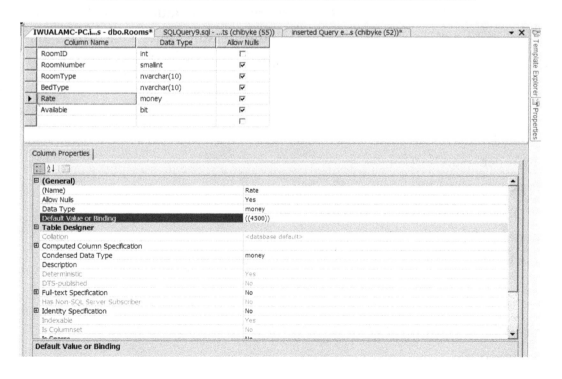

ii.   Programmatically Creating a Default Value

To specify the default value in a SQL statement, when creating the column, after specifying the other pieces of information of the column, type **DEFAULT** followed by an empty space and followed by the desired value. Here are examples of Abia State workers table:

```
CREATE TABLE Employees
(
    FullName VARCHAR(70)
   ,[Address] VARCHAR(80)
    ,City VARCHAR(20)
    ,[State] VARCHAR(2) DEFAULT 'AB'
    ,PostalCode VARCHAR(6) DEFAULT '452001'
    ,Country VARCHAR(20) DEFAULT 'Nigeria'
);
GO
```

When performing data entry on the table, the user does not have to provide a value for a column that has a default. If the user does not provide the value, the default would be used when the record is saved. If the user provides a value for a column that has a default value and then deletes the value, the default value rule would not apply anymore. The field would simply become empty

Here is another example:

```
CREATE TABLE Rooms (
RoomID int IDENTITY(1000,1) NOT NULL
,RoomNumber nvarchar(10),
RoomType nvarchar(20) default N'Single',
BedType nvarchar(40) default N'Double',
Rate money default 4500.85,
Available bit default 0);
GO
```

Populate the table with record:

```
USE idealSuits;
```

```
GO

INSERT INTO Rooms(RoomNumber, Available) VALUES(107, 1)
GO

INSERT INTO Rooms(RoomNumber, BedType, Rate) VALUES(108, N'Family',
15000.75)
GO

INSERT INTO Rooms(RoomNumber, Available) VALUES(109, 1)
GO

INSERT INTO Rooms(RoomNumber, RoomType, BedType, Rate, Available)
        VALUES(110, N'Conference', N'', 20000.00, 1)
GO
```

7.2 DATA MAINTENANCE

One of the techniques used to get data into one or more tables consists of importing already existing data from another database or from any other recognizable data file. Microsoft SQL Server provides various techniques and means of importing data. The easiest type of data that can be imported into SQL Server, and which is available on almost all database environments is the text file. Almost every database environment allows you to import a text file but data from that file must be formatted appropriately. For example, the information stored in the file must define the columns as distinguishable by a character that serves as a separator. This separator can be the single-quote, the double-quote, or any valid character. Data between the quotes is considered as belonging to a distinct field. Besides this information, the database would need to separate information from two different columns. Again, a valid character must be used. Most databases, including Microsoft SQL Server, recognize the comma as such a character. The last piece of information the file must provide is to distinguish each record from another. This is easily taken care of by the end of the line of a record or carriage return. If you are conversant with sending a lot of mails, you would have noticed that comma is used to separate a more than one email address; that is a typical example of file format.

These directives can help you manually create a text file that can be imported into Microsoft SQL Server. In practicality, if you want to import data that resides on another database, you can ask that application to create the source of data. Most applications can do that and format the data. For the data we will use in the next exercise, we have design a database on Microsoft Access database: it is data that resided on a Microsoft Access database and was designed to be imported in Microsoft SQL Server.

After importing data, you should verify and possibly format it to customize its fields.

Importing Data from an External Source

1. We will use a database called countryStateLgaDB, which located on the hard drive C:

2. In the SQL Server Management Studio, right-click the Databases node and click New Database..., you can also use already created database.

3. Type **Country** and press Enter

4. In the Object Explorer, right-click **Country**, position the mouse on **Tasks** and click **Import Data**

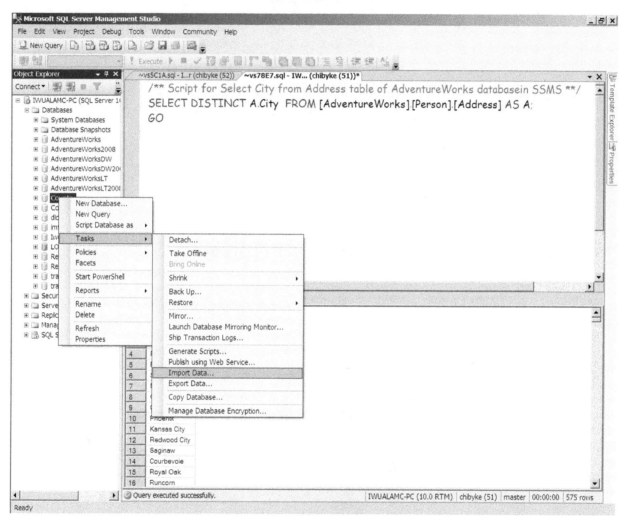

5. On the first page of the wizard, as shown below, click Next. If the wizard window does not look like the one below, then the steps was not followed properly.

6. On the second page, click the arrow of the Data Source combo box and select Microsoft Access

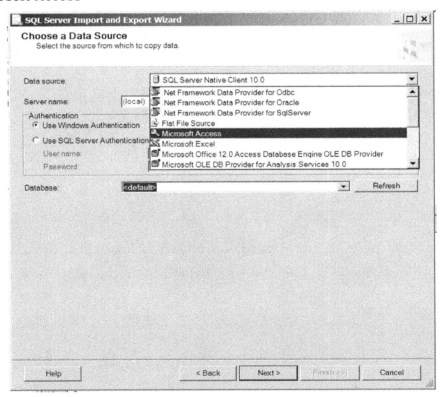

7. On the right side of File Name, click the Browse button
8. Locate and select the countryStateLgaDB file you had saved

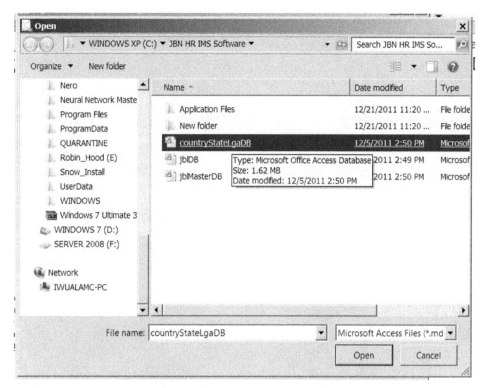

9. Enter the User name and password if any or click Next.

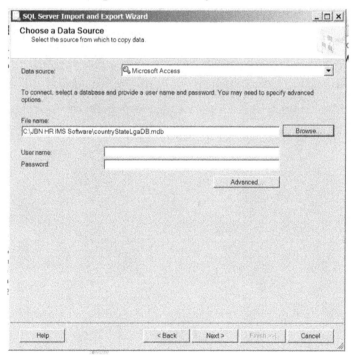

10. On the right side, click Advanced, if you want make some changes with the access permission and other database information settings. Click Next.

11. On the destination page, selection SQL Server Native Client 10.0, choose the authentication type of the Destination SQL Server

12. Choose the database you are importing the data into. Click Next.

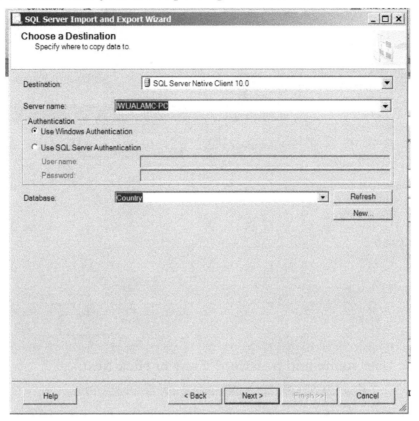

13. At this point, you can choose to write a SQL Script to manage and/or manipulate the data importation or choose to copy all the tables into the destination database. Click Copy data from one or more tables or views, and Click Next.

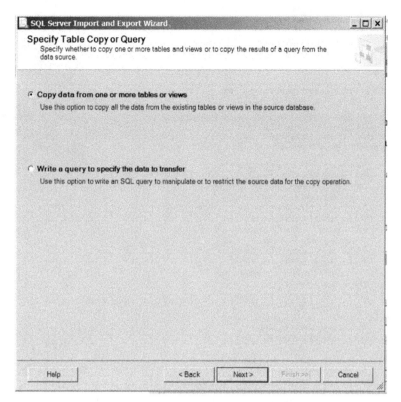

14. Select the tables you want to add to add to the database under Source Section. You can also modify the schema and table name of the table under the Destination Section. Click Next to continue.

15. Click Next twice

SQL Server Import and Export Wizard

Complete the Wizard
Verify the choices made in the wizard and click Finish.

Click Finish to perform the following actions:

Source Location : C:\JBN HR IMS Software\countryStateLgaDB.mdb
Source Provider : Microsoft.Jet.OLEDB.4.0
Destination Location : IWUALAMC-PC
Destination Provider : SQLNCLI10

- Copy rows from `admin` to [estatemgt].[admin]
  The new target table will be created.
- Copy rows from `blacklisted` to [dbo].[disengaged]
  The new target table will be created.
- Copy rows from `caste` to [dbo].[caste]
  The new target table will be created.
- Copy rows from `citytable` to [dbo].[citytable]
  The new target table will be created.
- Copy rows from `Country` to [dbo].[Country]
  The new target table will be created.
- Copy rows from `favorities` to [dbo].[favorities]
  The new target table will be created.
- Copy rows from `groups` to [dbo].[groups]
  The new target table will be created.
- Copy rows from `ignore` to [dbo].[ignore]
  The new target table will be created.
- Copy rows from `lgaAB` to [dbo].[lgaAB]
  The new target table will be created.
- Copy rows from `lgaAD` to [dbo].[lgaAD]
  The new target table will be created.

| Help | | < Back | Next > | Finish | Cancel |

16. Click Finish

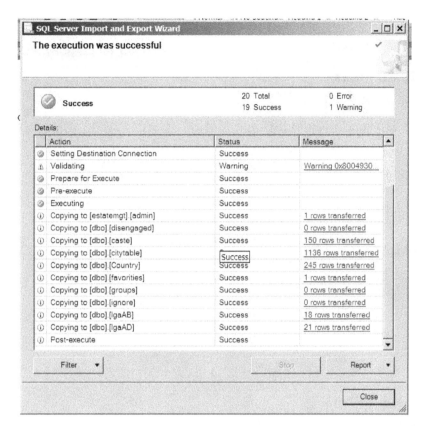

17. Click Close.

Record Maintenance:

Updating Records

Record maintenance includes viewing records, looking for one or more records, modifying one or more records, or deleting one or more records. These operations can be performed visually or programmatically using a Data Definition Languages (DDL) Here is an example:

1. On the Standard toolbar, click the New Query button
2. To create a database, type the following:

```
USE master;
GO


-- Create a databse with name idealSuits for Ideal Suits Hostels and Casino
IF  EXISTS(SELECT name
        FROM sys.databases
        WHERE name = N'idealSuits'
)
DROP DATABASE idealSuits
GO


CREATE DATABASE idealSuits
GO


USE idealSuits;
GO


CREATE TABLE Rooms (
    RoomID int identity(1000, 1) NOT NULL,
    RoomNumber smallint,
    RoomType nvarchar(10) default N'Single',
    BedType nvarchar(10) default N'Double',
    Rate money default 75.85,
    Available bit default 0
);
GO


INSERT INTO Rooms(RoomNumber) VALUES(104);
GO


INSERT INTO Rooms(RoomNumber, BedType, Rate, Available)
        VALUES(105, default, 6000, 1),
                (106, N'Family', 9000, 1);
    GO
```

INSERT INTO Rooms(RoomNumber, Available) VALUES(107, 1);
GO

INSERT INTO Rooms(RoomNumber, BedType, Rate)
        VALUES(108, N'Family', 9000);
GO

INSERT INTO Rooms(RoomNumber, Available) VALUES(109, 1);
GO

INSERT INTO Rooms(RoomNumber, RoomType, Rate, BedType, Available)
        VALUES(110, N'Large', 12000, N'', 1);
GO

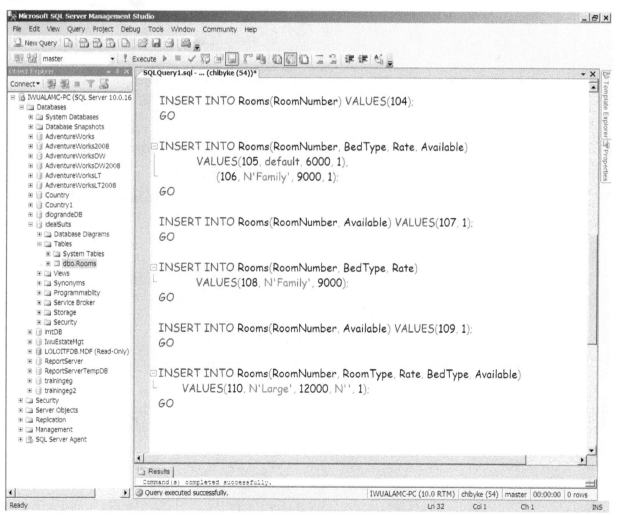

3. Press F5 to execute

Visually Selecting Records

Before you can perform visual operations on a table, you must first select one or more records. In the Table window, to select one record, position the mouse on the left button of the record and click:

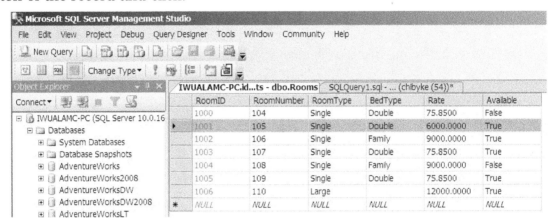

To select a range of records, click the gray button of one of the records, press and hold Shift, then click the gray button of the record at the other extreme.

To select the records in a random fashion, select one record, press and hold Ctrl, then click the gray button of each desired record:

	RoomID	RoomNumber	RoomType	BedType	Rate	Available
	1000	104	Single	Double	75.8500	False
	1001	105	Single	Double	6000.0000	True
	1002	106	Single	Family	9000.0000	True
	1003	107	Single	Double	75.8500	True
	1004	108	Single	Family	9000.0000	False
►	1005	109	Single	Double	75.8500	True
	1006	110	Large		12000.0000	True
*	NULL	NULL	NULL	NULL	NULL	NULL

To select all records of a table, click the gray button on the left of the first column:

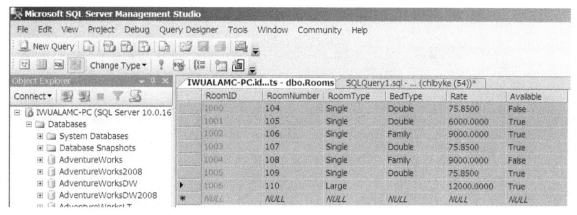

To visually modify one or more records on a table, first open it (you right-click the table in the Object Explorer and click Open Table) to view its records. Locate the record and the field you want to work on and perform the desired operation.

Updating Records

Updating a record consists of changing its value for a particular column. To visually update a record, in the Object Explorer, right-click its table (or view, in some cases) and click Edit Top 200 Rows. This would open the table as a spreadsheet, as seen above. Locate the value under the desired column header, and modify the value as you see fit.

To update a record using SQL Script, you use a Data Definition Language (DDL) command. If you are working in Microsoft SQL Server:

- In the Object Explorer, you can right click on the table, position the mouse on Script Table As, then on UPDATE To and click New Query Editor Window. or

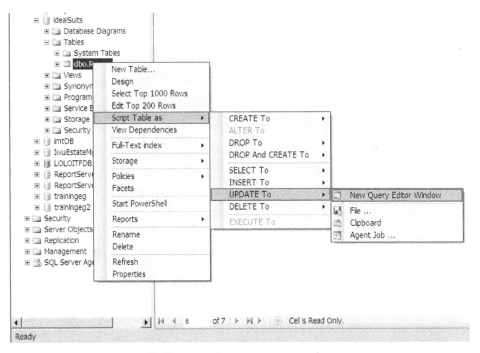

- Open an empty query window and type your code.

The DML command to update a record is **UPDATE**. The basic formula to use is:

UPDATE *TableName* SET *ColumnName* = *Expression*

With this formula, you must specify the name of the involved table as the *TableName* factor of our formula. The **SET** statement allows you to specify a new value, *Expression*, for the field under the *ColumnName* column.

Consider the following code to create a new database named VideoClub and to add a table named VideoInfo to it:

USE master;
GO

/*Create a databse with name LoloVideoClub owned by
    Mrs Nwachukwu C. A. N Video Club.*/

IF EXISTS(SELECT name
        FROM sys.databases
        WHERE name = N'LoloVideoClub'
)
DROP DATABASE LoloVideoClub

GO

CREATE DATABASE LoloVideoClub;

GO

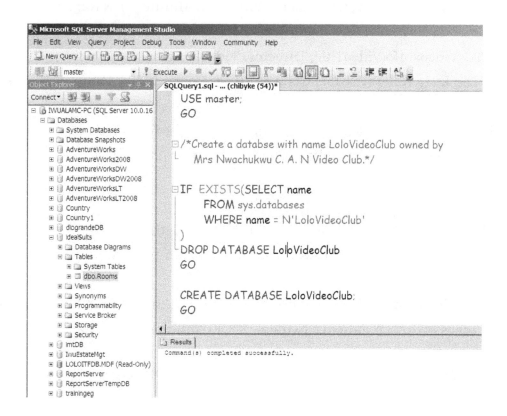

USE LoloVideoClub;

GO

--Create a table to store Details about Video Renting.

CREATE TABLE VideosInfo (

  VideoID INT NOT NULL IDENTITY(1,1)

  ,VideoTitle nvarchar(120) NOT NULL

  ,Director nvarchar(100) NULL

  ,YearReleased date

  ,VideoLength nvarchar(30) NULL

  ,PartNum tinyint

  ,TypeOfMovie nchar(10)

);

GO

```
INSERT INTO VideosInfo(VideoTitle, Director, YearReleased,
VideoLength,PartNum,TypeOfMovie)
VALUES(N'Blackberry Babes','Onyekachi',2009,'138 Minutes',1,N'Naija');

INSERT INTO VideosInfo(VideoTitle, Director, VideoLength,TypeOfMovie)
VALUES(N'The Lady Killers', N'Joel Coen & Ethan Coen', N'104 Minutes',N'Foreign');

INSERT INTO VideosInfo(VideoTitle, Director, YearReleased, VideoLength,TypeOfMovie)
VALUES(N'The Silence of the Lambs','Jonathan Demme',2006,'118
Minutes',N'Foreign');

INSERT INTO VideosInfo(VideoTitle, Director, VideoLength,TypeOfMovie)
VALUES(N'The Storm is Over', N'Nkem Owoh', N'112 Minutes',N'Naija');

INSERT INTO VideosInfo(VideoTitle, Director, VideoLength,PartNum,TypeOfMovie)
VALUES(N'Tears of Joy', N'Patience Iwuala', N'130 Minutes',2,N'Naija');
GO
```

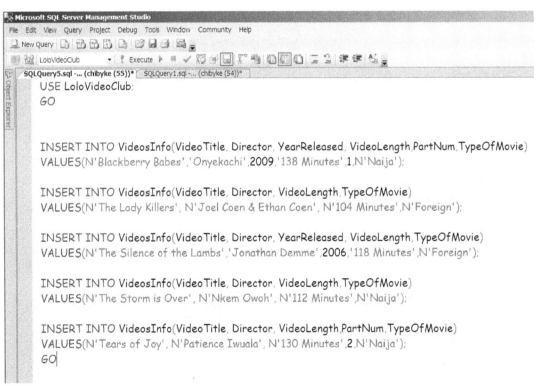

Imagine you want to indicate that all these videos are Foreign. To do this, in our formula, specify the table name. In the **SET** expression, specify the column name as TypeOfMovie and assign it Foreign as a string. This would be done as follows:

USE LoloVideoClub;

GO

UPDATE VideosInfo

SET TypeOfMovie = N'Foreign';

GO

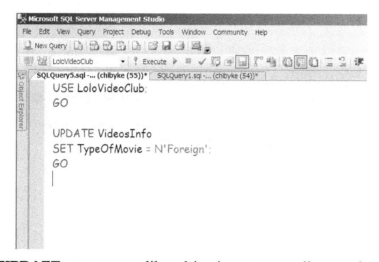

If you use the **UPDATE** statement like this, it acts on all records. The above code would produce:

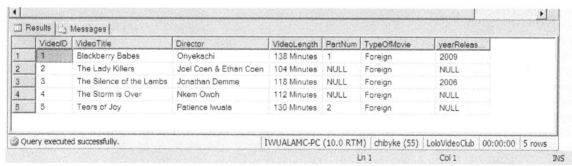

Editing Records

Editing a record consists of changing a value in a field. It could be that the field is empty, or you have the intention of changing it because of mistake:

Here is an example:

To edit a record, first open the table to view its records. Locate the record, the column on which you want to work, and locate the value you want to change, and then change it.

To edit a record, you must provide a way for the interpreter to locate the record. To do this, you would associate the **WHERE** operator in an **UPDATE** statement using the following formula:

UPDATE *TableName*

SET *ColumnName* = *Expression*

WHERE *Condition(s)*

The **WHERE** operator allows you to specify how the particular record involved would be identified. It is very important, in most cases, that the criterion used should be able to uniquely identify the record. In the above table, imagine that you ask the interpreter to change the typeofmovie to Naija where the director of the video is Onyekachi. The UPDATE statement would be written as follows:

USE LoloVideoClub;

GO

UPDATE VideosInfo

SET TypeOfMovie = N'Naija'

WHERE Director = N'Onyekachi';

GO

```
SQLQuery5.sql -... (chibyke (55))*    SQLQuery1.sql -... (chibyke (54))*

    USE LoloVideoClub;
    GO

    UPDATE VideosInfo
    SET TypeOfMovie = N'Naija'
    WHERE Director = N'Onyekachi';
    GO
```

In the above table, if the director of the videos directed more than one video; then when this statement is executed, all video records whose director is Onyekachi would be changed, which would compromise existing records that didn't need this change. This is where the identity column becomes valuable. We saw earlier that, when using it with the **IDENTITY** feature, the interpreter appends a unique value to each record. You can then use that value to identify a particular record because you are certain the value is unique.

Here is an example used to specify the missing copyright year of a particular record:

```
UPDATE [LoloVideoClub].[dbo].[VideosInfo]
SET YearReleased = 2010
WHERE VideoID = 5;
GO
```

Here is an example used to change the name of the director of a particular video:

```
UPDATE  [LoloVideoClub].[dbo].[VideosInfo]
SET Director = N'Onyekachi Goodluck'
WHERE VideoTitle = N'Blackberry Babes';
GO
```

Here is an example that will change the bedtype from single to double. I hope you remember the database we created above for Ideal Suits and Casino? I will update of the   records,   type   the   following:

```
UPDATE idealSuits.dbo.Rooms
SET BedType = N'Double'
WHERE RoomNumber = 108;
GO
```

Press F5 to execute

Here is another example that will change a room from being available to occupied.

```
USE idealSuits;
GO
```

```
UPDATE Rooms
```

```
SET Available = 0
WHERE RoomNumber = 109;
GO
```

Press F5 to execute

Outputting the Update Result

After making changes to a table using SQL Script, you don't get a visual display of what happened. With Transact-SQL, you can temporarily display the result of this operation or you can store it in a table because it will help you know what the outcome of your executed code is. We already saw how to do this when creating records. You follow the same formula when updating records, but have to add a line of code in the previous formula. The complete formula for outputting result is:

UPDATE *TableName*

SET *ColumnName* = *Expression*

OUTPUT INSERTED.*Columns*

VALUES(*Value_1*, *Value_2*, *Value_X*)

Besides the formula we have used so far, after the SET expression, start with an **OUTPUT INSERTED** expression, followed by a period. If you are to show all columns of the table, then add the * operator. Otherwise, type INSERTED followed by a period, followed by the name of the column you want to show.

Here is an example that will change a bedtype from single to double:

```
UPDATE idealSuits.dbo.Rooms
SET BedType = N'Double'
Output inserted.*
WHERE RoomNumber = 110;
GO
```

Press F5 to execute

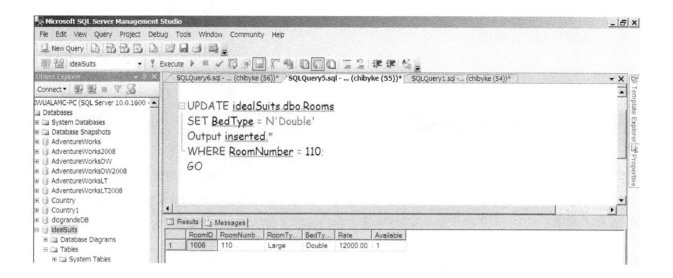

Here is an example that will change all the rooms to available:

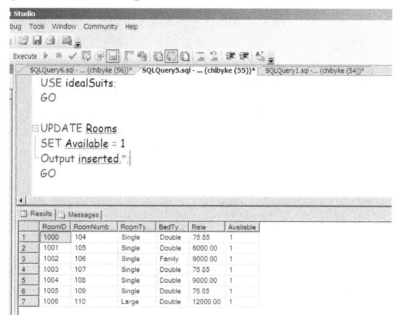

Deleting Records

Removing all Records

If you think all records of a particular table are, or have become useless, you can clear the whole table, which would still keep its structure. To delete all records from a table, first select all of them, and press Delete. You would receive a warning:

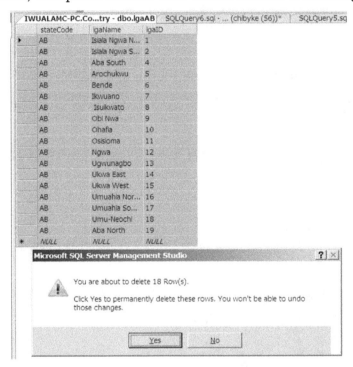

If you still want to delete the records, click Yes. If you change your mind, click No.

The DDL command to clear a table off all records is **DELETE**. It uses the following formula:

DELETE *TableName*;

When this statement is executed, all records from the *TableName* factor would be removed from the table. Be careful when doing this because once the records have been deleted, you cannot get them back.

Removing a Record

If you find out that a record is not necessary anymore, or is misplaced, you can remove it from a table. To remove a record from a table, you can right-click its gray box and click Delete. You can also first select the record and press Delete. You would receive a warning to confirm your intention.

In SQL Script, to delete a record use the **DELETE FROM** statement and includ the **WHERE** operator. The formula to follow is:

DELETE FROM *TableName*
WHERE *Condition(s)*

The *TableName* factor is used to identify a table whose record(s) would be removed.

The *Condition(s)* factor allows you to identify a record or a group of records that carries a criterion. Once again, make sure you are precise in your criteria so you would not delete the wrong record(s).

Here is an example used to remove a particular record from the table:

delete from lgaAB
where lgaID = 10;
GO

Here is an example used to clear the table of all videos:

DELETE from lgaAB;
GO

Outputting the Deleting Results

When some record(s) has(have) been deleted, the operation is performed behind the scenes and you don't see the result, though you know what happened. If you want to see a list of the records that were deleted, you can use the OUTPUT operator to display the result. To show the list of the records from a table that was completely emptied, you can use the following formula:

DELETE FROM *TableName*

OUTPUT DELETED.*Columns*

The **OUTPUT INSERTED** expression follows the description we have seen for the record update. Here is an example:

USE Country ;

GO

delete lgaAB

Output deleted.*;

GO

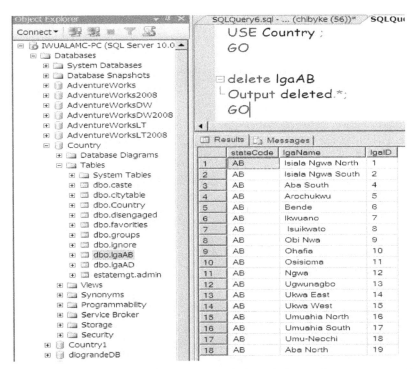

To show the list of the records that were deleted based on a condition, use the following formula:

DELETE FROM *TableName*

OUTPUT DELETED. *Columns*

WHERE *Condition(s)*

Here is an example that will delete that have state as NULL:

USE IwuEstateMgt ;

GO

DELETE from estateMgt.PropertyInfo

OUTPUT deleted. *

where [state] IS NULL;

GO

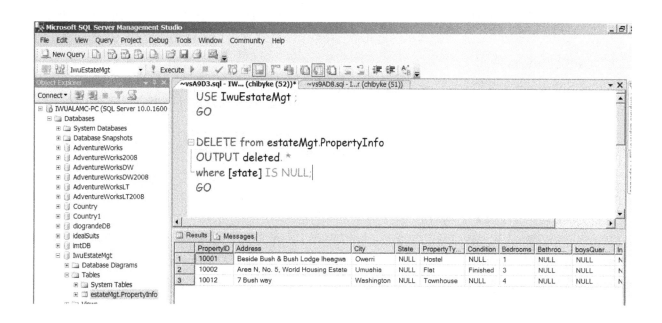

CHAPTER EIGHT

8.1   METHODS OF DATA RETRIEVAL

Neither are SQL queries limited to graphical interfaces. Many SQL developers who came up through the ranks from Access and who have built queries using only the Access query interface are amazed when they understand the enormous power of the full SQL query in MS SQL Server. This chapter builds a basic single table query and establishes the logical query execution order, critical for developing basic or advanced queries. With this foundation in place, the rest of the chapters develops the basic SELECT into what I believe is the most elegant, flexible, and powerful command in data manipulation.

8.2   WHAT SQL QUERY FLOW IS ALL ABOUT

One can think about query flow in four different ways. Personally, when I develop SQL code, I imagine the query using the logical flow method. Some developers think through a query visually using the layout of SQL Server Management Studio's Query Designer. The syntax of the query is in a specific fixed order: *SELECT – FROM – WHERE – GROUP BY – HAVING – ORDER BY*, else you will get it wrong when the result of the query displays, you remember BODMAS in mathematics; its similar thing in SQL code. To illustrate the declarative nature of SQL, the fourth way of thinking about the query flow — the actual physical execution of the query — is optimized to execute in the most efficient order depending on the data mix or the relationship of the objects and the available indexes.

8.3 FLOW OF THE QUERY STATEMENT

In its basic form, the SELECT statement tells SQL Server what data to retrieve, including which columns, rows, and tables to pull from, and how to sort the data. Here is an abbreviated syntax for the SELECT command:

SELECT [DISTINCT][TOP (n)] *, *columns*, or *expressions*

[FROM *data source(s)*]

[JOIN *data source*

ON *condition*](may include multiple joins)

[WHERE *conditions*]

[GROUP BY *columns*]

[HAVING *conditions*]

[ORDER BY *Columns*];

The SELECT statement begins with a list of columns or expressions. At least one   is required — everything else is optional. The simplest possible valid SELECT statement is as follows:

SELECT 1;

GO

The FROM portion of the SELECT statement assembles all the data sources into a result set, which is then acted upon by the rest of the SELECT statement. Within the FROM clause, multiple tables may be referenced by using one of several types of joins. When no FROM clause is supplied, SQL Server returns a single row with values. (Oracle requires a FROM DUAL to accomplish the same thing.) The WHERE clause acts upon the record set assembled by the FROM clause to filter certain rows based upon conditions, this can also be called data selection restriction. Aggregate functions perform summation-type operations across the data set. The GROUP BY clause can group the larger data set into smaller data sets based on the columns specified in the GROUP BY clause. The aggregate functions are then performed on the new smaller groups of data. The results of the aggregation can be restricted using the HAVING clause. Finally, the ORDER BY clause determines the sort order of the result set.

8.4   GRAPHICAL VIEW OF THE QUERY STATEMENT

When we talk about the graphical view of SQL Server query we are simply talking about the SQL Server Management Studio. There are two basic methods for constructing and submitting queries in SQL Server Management Studio:

Query Designer and Query Editor. Query Designer offers a graphical method of building a query, whereas Query Editor is an excellent tool for writing SQL code or ad hoc data retrieval because there are no graphics to get in the way and the developer can work as close to the SQL code as possible. From SQL Server's point of view, it does not matter where the query originates; each statement is evaluated and processed as a SQL statement. When selecting data using Query Designer, the SQL statements can be entered as raw code in the third pane. The bottom pane displays the results in Grid mode or Text mode and displays any messages. The Object Browser presents a tree of all the objects in SQL Server, as well as templates for creating new objects with code.

Logical flow of the query statement

The best way to think through a SQL DML statement is to walk through the query's logical flow shown below. The logical flow may or may not be the actual physical flow that SQL Server's query processor uses to execute the query. Nor is the logical flow the same as the query syntax. Regardless, I recommend thinking through a query in the following order.

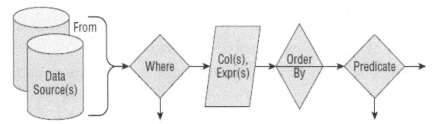

A simplified view of the logical flow of the query showing how data moves through the major clauses of the SQL select command

Here is a more detailed explanation of the logical flow of the query. Note that *every* step except step 4 is optional:

1. [From]: The query begins by assembling the initial set of data, as specified in the FROM portion of the SELECT statement.

2. [Where]: The filter process is actually the WHERE clause selecting only those rows that meet the criteria or restricting the unwanted data.

3. [Aggregations]: SQL can optionally perform aggregations on the data set, such as finding the average, grouping the data by values in a column, and filtering the groups as the case may be.

4. Column Expressions: The SELECT list is processed, and any expressions are calculated.

5. [Order By]: The resulting rows are sorted according to the ORDER BY clause.

6. [Over]: Windowing and ranking functions can provide a separately ordered view of the results with additional aggregate functions.

7. [Distinct]: Any duplicate rows are eliminated from the result set. [Top]: After the rows are selected, the calculations are performed, and the data is sorted into the desired order, SQL can restrict the output to the top few rows.

8. [Insert, Update, Delete]: The final logical step of the query is to apply the data modification action to the results of the query. I will explain these three verbs under *data manipulation* in this chapter.

9. [Output]: The inserted and deleted virtual tables (normally only used with a trigger) can be selected and returned to the client, inserted into a table, or serve as a data source to an outer query.

10. [Union]: The results of multiple queries can be stacked using a union command.

As more complexity has been added to the SQL SELECT command over the years, how to think through the logical flow has also become more complex. In various sources, you'll find minor differences in how SQL MVPs view the logical flow. That's OK — it's just a way to think through a query, and this is the way I think through writing a query. As you begin to think in terms of the SQL SELECT statement, rather than in terms of the graphical user interface, understanding the flow of SELECT and how to read the query execution plan will help you think through and develop difficult queries.

Physical flow of the query statement

SQL Server will take the SELECT statement and develop an optimized query execution plan, which may not be in the execution order you would guess (see Figure 8-3). The indexes available to the SQL Server
Query Optimizer also affect the query execution plan, as explained in Chapter 64, "Indexing Strategies." The rest of this chapter walks through the logical order of the basic query.

Table Name

USE imtDB ;

--Use of square brackets as good practice in naming Tables
SELECT S.lastName, S.FirstName
FROM studInfoTbl S;
GO

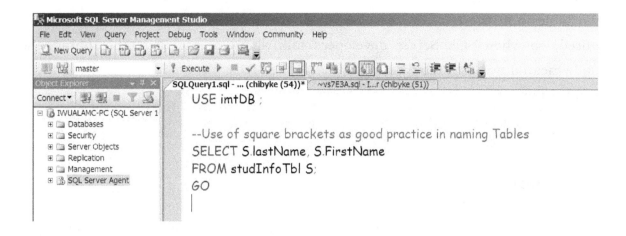

Although it is an incredibly poor practice to include spaces within the names of database objects, it is possible, nevertheless. If this is the case, square brackets are required when specifying the database object. The Order Details table in the Northwind sample database illustrates this:

USE Northwind;

GO

--Spaced table name example, though not ideal.

SELECT OrderID, ProductID, Quantity

FROM [Order Details];

GO

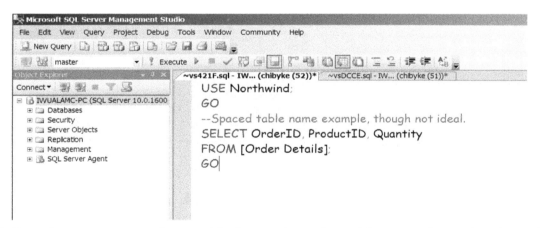

The full and proper name for a table is not just the table name but what is called a *fully qualified name*, sometimes informally referred to as the *four-part name*:

Server.Database.Schema.Table

If the table is in the current database, then the server and database name are not required, so when SQL Server developers talk about a qualified table name, they usually mean a two-part table name:

Schema.Table

Table aliases

A data source may be assigned a *table alias* within the *FROM* clause. Once the data source has an alias, it must be referred to by this new name. In some cases the data source must have an alias, because of the long name of the table and for flexibility. The following code accesses the Student table, but refers to it within the query as table S:

```
USE imtDB ;
-- From Table [AS] Table Alias example
SELECT S.lastName, S.FirstName
FROM chibykeSmatDB.studInfoTbl AS S;
GO
```

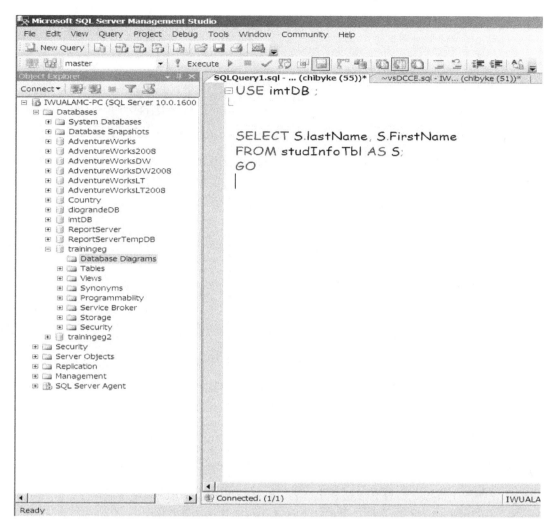

The AS that appeared before S (the alias name of the table), after the table name is optional and the code will execute and display the required result but is advised you put it; the interpreter can be confused, and wrong data would be returned when AS is not added.

8.5   DATA SELECTION

After creating a table and populated it with records, the question is what do I do with the record or how do I make the records available when needed, probably for decision making. One of the most commonly performed operations by the users of a database is to look for data or to isolate records that respond to a particular criterion. Looking for data conforms to a criterion that is referred to as querying. The result of retrieving data based on a criterion is called a query.

As a database developer, you perform queries by passing instructions to the database engine via the interpreter. This is done using some special reserved words. In Microsoft SQL Server, data analysis can be performed using a query window in Microsoft SQL Server Management Studio, at the Command Prompt, or in PowerSheel.

The Data in the Table Window

To prepare a window that assists you with data selection, in the Object Explorer, you can right-click a table and click Select Edit Top 200 rows. When you do this, the interface becomes equipped with the Query Designer toolbar.

The Query Designer window can be made of four sections:

- **Diagram**: The top section is referred to as the Diagram window. To get it:
    - On the main menu, click Query Designer -> Pane -> Diagram or
    - Right-click an area of the window -> Pane -> Diagram or
    - On the Query Designer toolbar, click the Show Diagram Pane button

    The Diagram section displays the table(s) that contain(s) the columns you want to query. Each column displays a check box on its left and the name of the column on the right. The first item of the list has a name made of an asterisk, meaning all the All Columns.
    If the list of items is too long for the allocated rectangle to display, the table would be equipped with a vertical scroll bar to enable you scroll down or up.

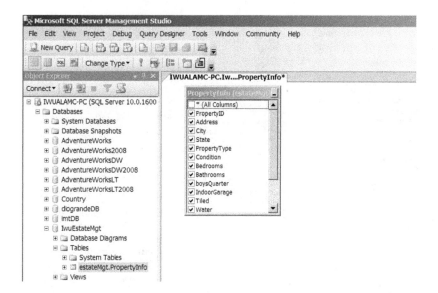

- **Criteria**: Under the Diagram section, you can use the Criteria section. To get it:

  - On the main menu, click Query Designer -> Pane -> Criteria or

  - Right-click an area of the window -> Pane -> Criteria or

  - On the Query Designer toolbar, click the Show Criteria Pane button

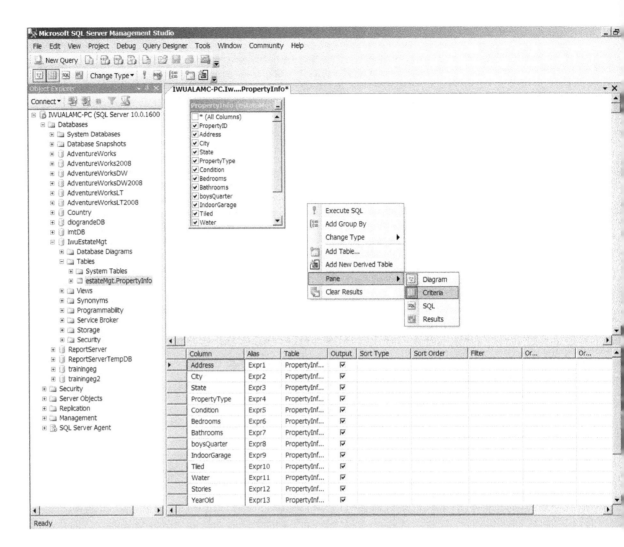

The Criteria section displays a list of columns used to visually build the SQL statement.

- **SQL**: Under the Criteria section, you can get the SQL. To get it:
    - On the main menu, click Query Designer -> Pane -> SQL or
    - Right-click an area of the window -> Pane -> SQL or
    - On the Query Designer toolbar, click the Show SQL Pane button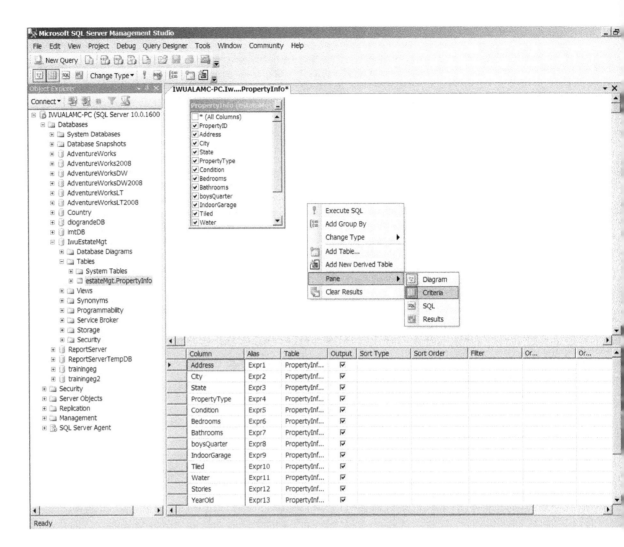

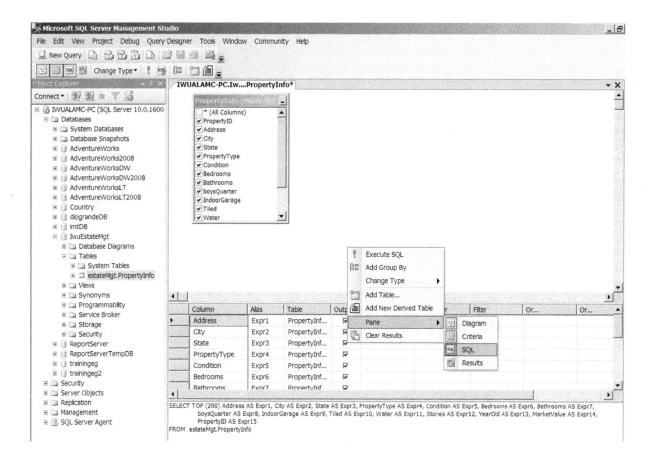

The SQL section displays the SQL statement that results from selections in the Diagram or the Criteria sections

- The bottom section of the window can display the Results section. To get it:
  - On the main menu, click Query Designer -> Pane -> Results or
  - Right-click an area of the window -> Pane -> Results
  - On the Query Designer toolbar, click the Show Results Pane button ⊞

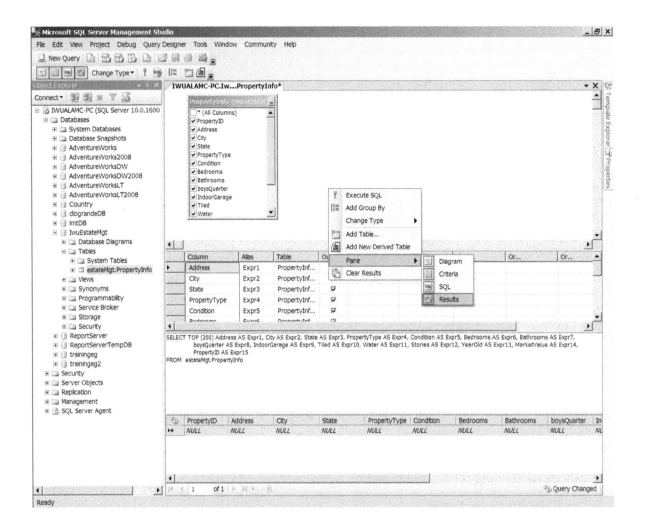

If you don't want a particular section or you want to hide some sections, you can right-click anywhere in the table, position the mouse on Pane and click the name of the section:

Below is an example that shows how to remove the *Results* section.

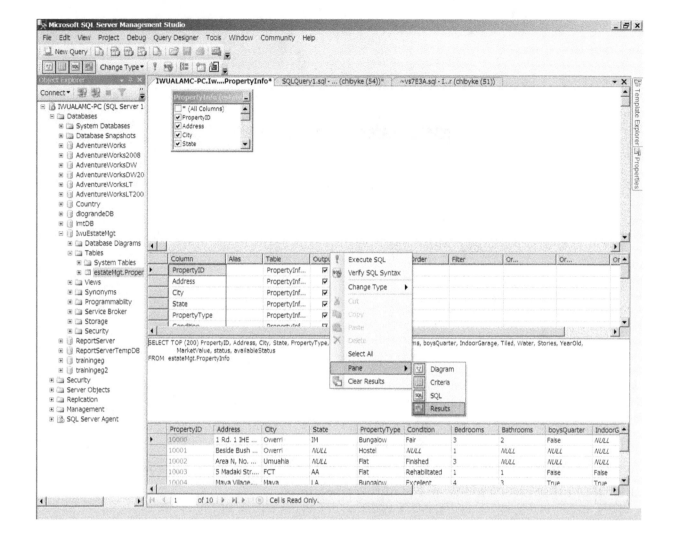

As an alternative to these techniques, to prepare a window for data selection:

- In the Object Explorer, you can right-click a table and click Select Top 1000 rows; or
- In the Object Explorer, position the mouse on Script Table As, SELECT To, New Query Editor Window; or
- Open a Query window. Right-click inside the Query window and click Design Query in Editor...

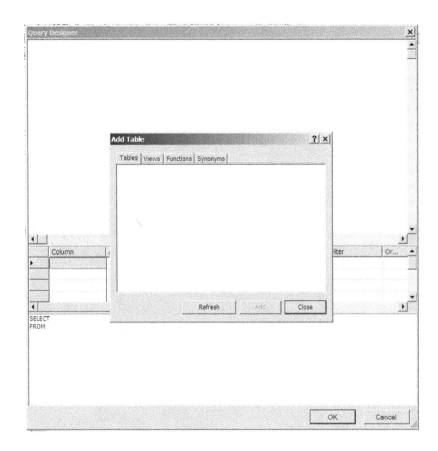

In the Add Table dialog box, click the name of the table, click Add, and click Close; this would display a window made of three sections:

Column Selection

A SQL statement is primarily built by selecting one or more columns whose data you want to view. To select a column, if you are working in the Query Designer, in the Diagram section, you can click the check box on the name:

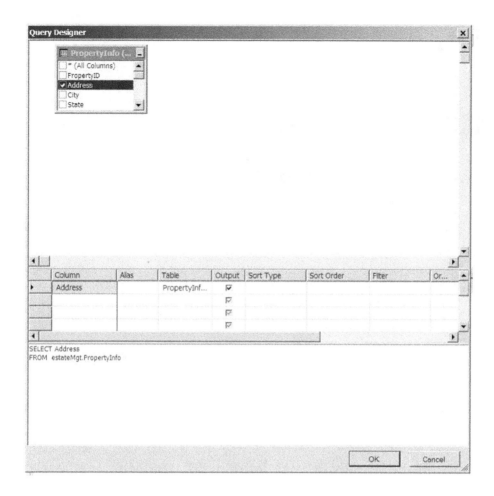

After clicking the check box of a column, it becomes selected in the Criteria section also and its name appears in the SQL section.

Another technique used to select a column consists of clicking a box under the Column header of the Criteria section. This would reveal that it is a combo box:

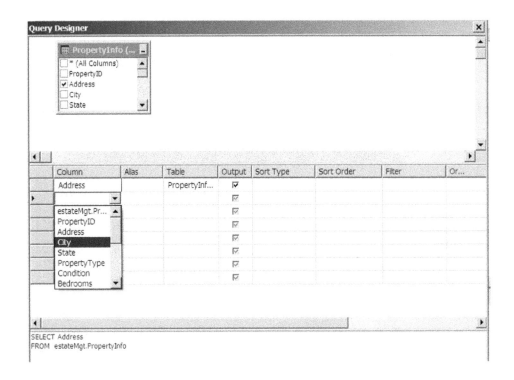

You can then click the item desired in the list to select it. In the Criteria section, if you click a combo box that already contains a column but select another, the previous one would be replaced by the new one. Also, after selecting a column in the Criteria section, its check box becomes selected in the Diagram section and its name gets added to the SQL Script section. If you know the name of a column that you want to add, which you cannot see in the Diagram section, you can enter it directly in the SQL statement.

Any of the above three techniques allows you to select one or more columns to build the desired SQL statement. After making your selections in the Query Designer, click OK. The code generated by the Query Designer is not ideal and complete, though it will still execute and produce, but as a developer you do not need to be using the Query Designer. This would display a Query with a SQL statement. Also, the SQL Editor Toolbar would be added under the Standard toolbar.

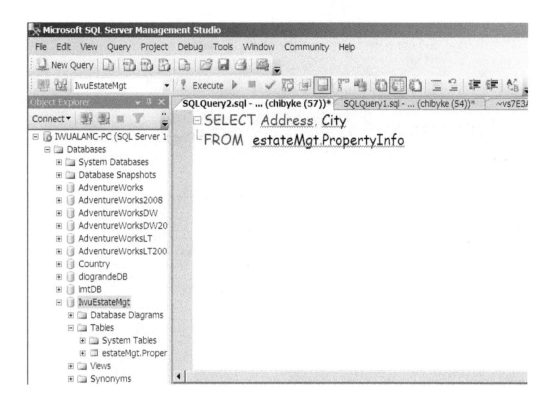

You can request for the SQL Editor Toolbar:

- On the main menu, you can click View, Toolbars, SQL Editor
- You can right-click any Toolbar and click SQL Editor

SQL Statement Execution

After creating a SQL statement, you can view its result, which you can get by executing the statement. To do this:

- Right-click anywhere in the Query window and click Execute SQL; or
- On the SQL Editor toolbar, click the Execute button ❗ Execute ; or
- On the main menu, click Query or Query Designer and click Execute or press F5.

After executing the statement, the bottom section gets filled with data from only the selected column(s) of the table. Here is an example:

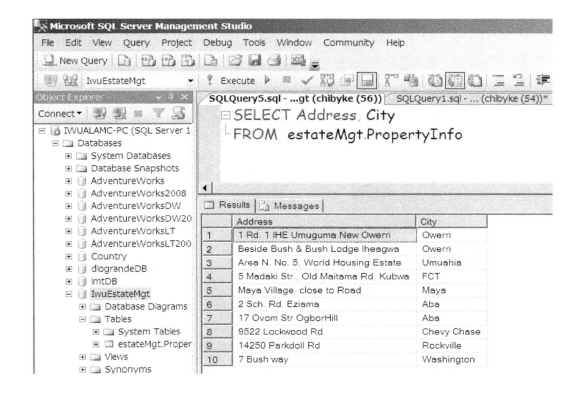

Transact-SQL and Data Selection

Data selection is actually performed using SQL code that contains one or more columns, and is the recommend method for record retrieval for database developers who knows their onion. To start, proceed as we saw previously to display a Query window.

1. Start Microsoft SQL Server with the SQL Server Management Studio and connect to the server
2. On the main menu, click File, New, Query With Current Connection

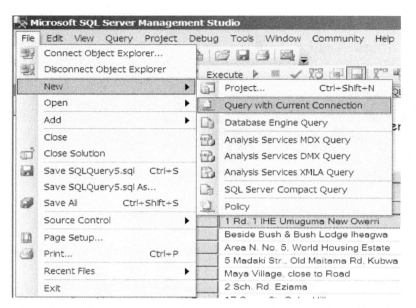

3. To prepare a database for our exercises, copy and paste the following code in the Query window:

```
USE master;
GO


/* ==============================================
Database: IwuEstateMgt
Author:   Iwuala Chibueze
Date:     Thursday 20 December 2012, 20:58
==============================================*/
IF EXISTS (
  SELECT *
   FROM sys.databases
   WHERE name = N'IwuEstateMgt'
)
  DROP DATABASE IwuEstateMgt;
GO


CREATE DATABASE IwuEstateMgt;
GO
```

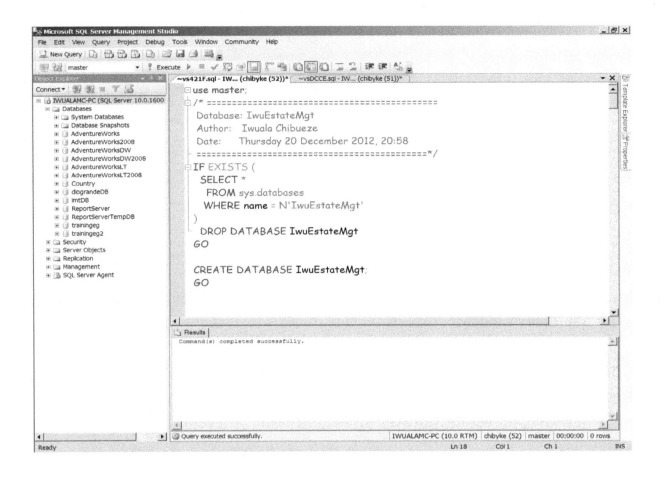

```
/* ===============================================
   Author:      Iwuala Chibueze
   Database:    IwuEstateMgt
   Table:       PropertiesInfo
   =============================================*/

USE IwuEstateMgt;
GO

CREATE TABLE estateMgt.PropertyInfo
(  [PropertyID] nchar(6)
   ,[Address] nvarchar(50)
   ,[City] nvarchar(50)
   ,[State] nchar(2)
   ,[PropertyType] nvarchar(40)
```

,[Condition] nvarchar(32)

,[Bedrooms] smallint

,[Bathrooms] float

,[boysQuarter] bit

,[IndoorGarage] bit

,[Tiled] bit

,[Water] bit

,[Stories] smallint

,[YearOld] smallint

,[MarketValue] money);

GO

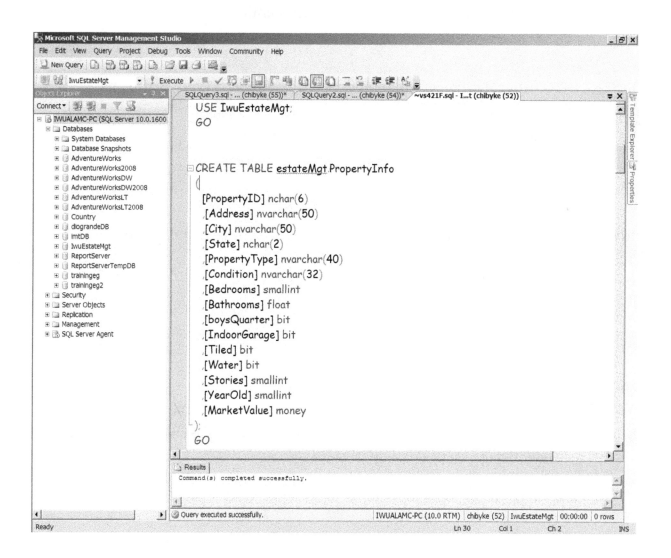

```sql
INSERT INTO estateMgt.PropertyInfo
VALUES( N'2 Sch. Rd. Eziama', N'Aba', N'AB',
    N'Duplex', N'Finished', 4, 4, 1, 1, 1,1,1,2, 15000000.00,N'To Buy', N'Available'),
        (N'17 Ovom Str OgborHill', N'Aba', N'AB',
        N'Bungalow', N'Excellent',4,3,1,1,1,1,1,1,10000000.00,N'To Buy', N'Available');
GO


INSERT INTO estateMgt.PropertyInfo (Address, City, State,
  PropertyType, Condition, Bedrooms ,Bathrooms,boysQuarter,Tiled, Water,
  Stories, MarketValue, [status])
VALUES(N'1 Rd. 1 IHE Umuguma New Owerri', N'Owerri', N'IM',
    N'Bungalow', N'Fair',3,2,0,1,0,0,1500000.00,N'Renting');
GO


INSERT INTO estateMgt.PropertyInfo (Address, City, PropertyType, Bedrooms,
Tiled, Water, MarketValue, [status])
VALUES(N'Beside Bush & Bush Lodge Iheagwa', N'Owerri',
    N'Hostel',1,1, 1,65000.00,N'Renting');
GO


INSERT INTO estateMgt.PropertyInfo ([Address], City, PropertyType, Bedrooms,
Tiled, Water, MarketValue, [status],Condition,availableStatus)
VALUES(N'Area N, No. 5, World Housing Estate', N'Umuahia',
    N'Flat',3,0, 0,1500000.00,N'To Buy',N'Finished',N'Sold');
 GO


INSERT INTO estateMgt.PropertyInfo
VALUES( N'5 Madaki Str., Old Maitama Rd, Kubwa', N'FCT', N'AA',
    N'Flat', N'Rehabilitated', 1, 1, 0, 0, 1,1,0,5, 17000.00,N'To Rent',N'Available'),
        (N'Maya Village, close to Road', N'Maya', N'LA',
        N'Bungalow', N'Excellent',4,3,1,1,1,1,1,1,180000.00,N'To Rent',N'Available');
GO


INSERT INTO estateMgt.PropertyInfo
VALUES(N'9522 Lockwood Rd', N'Chevy Chase', N'MD',
```

```sql
    N'Townhouse', N'Bad Shape', 3, 3, 1, 1, 1,1,1,8,
    415665.00,N'To Buy', N'Available'),
  ( N'14250 Parkdoll Rd', N'Rockville', N'MD',
    N'Townhouse', N'Good', 3, 2.5, 2, 1, 2,1,2,5,
    325995.00,N'To Buy', N'Available');
GO


INSERT INTO estateMgt.PropertyInfo ([Address],City, PropertyType, Bedrooms,
 MarketValue,[status],availableStatus )
VALUES(N'7 Bush way', N'Washington', N'Townhouse', 4, 366775.00,N'To
Rent',N'Available');
GO


INSERT INTO EstateMgt.PropertyInfo (PropertyNumber, State,
 ZIPCode, Bedrooms, YearBuilt, MarketValue)
VALUES(N'420115', N'DC',
    N'20011', 2, 1982, 312555);
GO


INSERT INTO EstateMgt.PropertyInfo (PropertyNumber, City, ZIPCode,
 PropertyType, Bedrooms, YearBuilt, MarketValue)
VALUES(N'917203', N'Alexandria', N'22024',
    N'Single Family', 3, 1965, 345660.00);
GO


INSERT INTO EstateMgt.PropertyInfo (PropertyNumber, Address, City, State,
 PropertyType, Condition, Bedrooms, Bathrooms, MarketValue)
VALUES(N'200417', N'4140 Holisto Crt', N'Germantown', N'MD',
    N'Condominium', N'Excellent', 2, 1, 215495.00);
GO


INSERT INTO EstateMgt.PropertyInfo
VALUES(N'927474', N'9522 Lockwood Rd', N'Chevy Chase', N'MD',
```

```
          N'20852', N'Townhouse', N'Bad Shape', 3, 2.5, 3, 0, 3,
          1992, 415665.00),
       (N'207850', N'14250 Parkdoll Rd', N'Rockville', N'MD',
          N'20854', N'Townhouse', N'Good', 3, 2.5, 2, 1, 2,
          1988, 325995.00);
   GO


   INSERT INTO EstateMgt.PropertyInfo (City, PropertyType, Bedrooms,
      YearBuilt, MarketValue)
   VALUES(N'Washington', N'Townhouse', 4, 1975, 366775.00);
   GO
   INSERT INTO EstateMgt.PropertyInfo (PropertyNumber, Address, City, State,
      ZIPCode, PropertyType, Condition, Bedrooms, Bathrooms,
      YearBuilt, MarketValue)
   VALUES(N'288540', N'10340 Helmes Street #408', N'Silver Spring', N'MD',
          N'20906', N'Condominium', N'Good', 1, 1, 2000, 242775.00);
   GO


   INSERT INTO EstateMgt.PropertyInfo
   VALUES(N'247472', N'1008 Coppen Street', N'Silver Spring', N'MD',
          N'20906', N'Single Family', N'Excellent',
          3, 3, 3, 1, 3, 1996, 625450.00);
   GO


   INSERT INTO EstateMgt.PropertyInfo (City, ZIPCode, PropertyType,
      Stories, YearBuilt, MarketValue)
   VALUES(N'Chevy Chase', N'20956', N'Single Family',
          3, 2001, 525450.00);
   GO


   INSERT INTO EstateMgt.PropertyInfo (Address, City, State,
      PropertyType, Condition, Bedrooms, MarketValue)
```

```
VALUES(N'686 Herod Ave #D04', N'Takoma Park', N'MD',
    N'Condominium', N'Excellent', 2, 360885.00);
GO


INSERT INTO EstateMgt.PropertyInfo
VALUES(N'297446', N'14005 Sniders Blvd', N'Laurel', N'MD',
    N'20707', N'Townhouse', N'Needs Repair',
    4, 1.5, 3, 1, 2, 2002, 412885.00);
GO


INSERT INTO EstateMgt.PropertyInfo (City, ZIPCode, Condition, Bedrooms,
  Stories, YearBuilt)
VALUES(N'Silver Spring', N'20905', N'Good',
    4, 2, 1965);
GO


INSERT INTO EstateMgt.PropertyInfo
VALUES(N'924792', N'680 Prushia Rd', N'Washington', N'DC',
    N'20008', N'Single Family', N'Good',
    5, 3.5, 3, 0, 3, 2000, 555885.00),
   (N'294796', N'14688 Parrison Street', N'College Park', N'MD',
    N'20742', N'Single Family', N'Excellent',
    5, 2.5, 2, 1, 2, 1995, 485995.00);
GO


INSERT INTO EstateMgt.PropertyInfo (PropertyNumber, Address, City, State,
  ZIPCode, PropertyType, Condition, Bedrooms, Bathrooms,
  YearBuilt, MarketValue)
VALUES(N'811155', N'10340 Helmes Street #1012', N'Silver Spring',
    N'MD', N'20906', N'Condominium', N'Good',
    1, 1, 2000, 252775.00);
GO
```

```sql
INSERT INTO EstateMgt.PropertyInfo
VALUES(N'447597', N'4201 Vilamar Ave', N'Hyattsville', N'MD',
    N'20782', N'Townhouse', N'Excellent',
    3, 2, 2, 1, 3, 1992, 365880.00);
GO


INSERT INTO EstateMgt.PropertyInfo (Address, ZIPCode, Bathrooms)
VALUES(N'1622 Rombard Str', 20904, 2.5);
GO


INSERT INTO EstateMgt.PropertyInfo
VALUES(N'297415', N'980 Phorwick Street', N'Washington', N'DC',
    N'20004', N'Single Family', N'Good',
    4, 3.5, 3, 3, 1, 2004, 735475.00),
    (N'475974', N'9015 Marvin Crow Ave', N'Gaithersburg', N'MD',
    '20872', N'Single Family', N'Needs Repair',
    4, 2.5, 3, 1, 1, 1965, 615775.00),
    (N'836642', N'3016 Feldman Court', N'Rockville', N'MD',
    N'20954', N'Single Family', N'Bad Shape',
    5, 3, 3, 1, 3, 1960, 528555.00);
GO


INSERT INTO EstateMgt.PropertyInfo (City, State, PropertyType, Stories)
VALUES(N'Rockville', N'MD',
    N'Townhouse', 1);
GO


INSERT INTO EstateMgt.PropertyInfo
VALUES(N'208304', N'7307 Everett Hwy', N'Washington', N'DC',
    N'20012', N'Townhouse', N'Excellent',
    2, 2.5, 2, 0, 4, 2006, 420550.00);
```

```
GO


INSERT INTO EstateMgt.PropertyInfo (PropertyNumber, Address, City, State,
  ZIPCode, PropertyType, Condition, Bedrooms,
  Bathrooms, YearBuilt, MarketValue)
VALUES(N'644114', N'10340 Helmes Street#1006', N'Silver Spring',
    N'MD', N'20906', N'Condominium', N'Good',
    2, 2, 2000, 258445.00);
GO


INSERT INTO EstateMgt.PropertyInfo
VALUES(N'937966', N'7303 Warfield Court', N'Tysons Corner', N'VA',
    N'22131', N'Single Family', N'Good',
    3, 2.5, 3, 1, 4, 2006, 825775.00);
GO


INSERT INTO EstateMgt.PropertyInfo (City, ZIPCode, Condition, Bedrooms,
  Stories, YearBuilt)
VALUES(N'Fairfax', N'22232', N'Good', 3, 3, 1985);
GO


INSERT INTO EstateMgt.PropertyInfo
VALUES(N'297497', N'12401 Conniard Ave', N'Takoma Park', N'MD',
    N'20910', N'Townhouse', N'Good',
    3, 2.5, 3, 1, 3, 2004, 280775.00);
GO


INSERT INTO EstateMgt.PropertyInfo (City, ZIPCode, PropertyType,
        Bedrooms, Bathrooms, MarketValue)
VALUES(N'Alexandria', N'22035', N'Condominium',
    2, 2, 425775.00);
GO
```

```sql
INSERT INTO EstateMgt.PropertyInfo (PropertyNumber, City, ZIPCode,
  PropertyType, Condition, Bedrooms, Bathrooms,
  YearBuilt, Stories, MarketValue)
VALUES(N'855255', N'Laurel', N'20707', N'Single Family',
    N'Needs Repair', 3, 2, 1962, 2, 342805.00);
GO


INSERT INTO EstateMgt.PropertyInfo (PropertyNumber, City, ZIPCode,
PropertyType,
  Condition, Bedrooms, Bathrooms, MarketValue)
VALUES(N'225227', N'Rockville', N'20857', N'Condominium', N'Good',
    1, 1, 525885.00);
GO


INSERT INTO EstateMgt.PropertyInfo
VALUES(N'469750', N'6124 Falk Rd', N'Arlington', N'VA',
    N'22031', N'Single Family', N'Needs Repair',
    4, 3.5, 3, 1, 1, 1982, 635995.00),
    (N'826927', N'5121 Riehl Ace', N'Fairfax', N'VA',
    N'22232', N'Townhouse', N'Excellent',
    3, 1.5, 2, 0, 1, 2002, 325620.00),
    (N'287064 ', N'9533 Pensulian Rd', N'Silver Spring', N'MD',
    N'20904', N'Single Family', N'Bad Shape',
    3, 1.5, 3, 1, 2, 1992, 485775.00);
GO


INSERT INTO EstateMgt.PropertyInfo (PropertyNumber, City, ZIPCode,
  PropertyType, Condition, Bedrooms, YearBuilt, Stories)
VALUES(N'724001 ', N'Washington', N'20004',
    N'Townhouse', N'Bad Shape', 3, 1974, 4);
GO
```

```
INSERT INTO EstateMgt.PropertyInfo
VALUES(N'209275', N'944 Fryer Ave', N'Chevy Chase', N'MD',
    N'20852', N'Single Family', N'Excellent',
    5, 2.5, 3, 0, 2, 2002, 625665.00),
    (N'204759', N'1950 Galego Street', N'Germantown', N'MD',
    N'20874', N'Single Family', N'Excellent',
    4, 3.5, 2, 1, 4, 2007, 428665.00);
GO


INSERT INTO EstateMgt.PropertyInfo (City, State, PropertyType,
  Bedrooms, Bathrooms, YearBuilt, MarketValue)
VALUES(N'Takoma PArk', N'MD',
    N'Conbominium', 2, 2, 2000, 225885.00);
GO


INSERT INTO EstateMgt.PropertyInfo
VALUES(N'937259', N'12366 Fowler Ave', N'Alexandria', N'VA',
    N'22031', N'Townhouse', N'Good',
    3, 1.5, 3, 1, 3, 2007, 402815.00);
GO
```

4. Press Ctrl + F5 and then press F5 to execute.
5. Save the file as IwuEstateMgt, if you intend to reuse the code and close the query window

Showing the Results of SQL Data Analysis

After entering the SQL statement in a Query window, you can execute it to see the result. The result would be displayed in the bottom section of the Query window. There are two ways you can display the result. To have access to these options, you can first display the SQL Editor Toolbar.

To specify how you want to show the results of your SQL statement, if you are using the Query window, the two options are:

- To show the result as text:

    o On the SQL Editor toolbar, click the Results To Text button 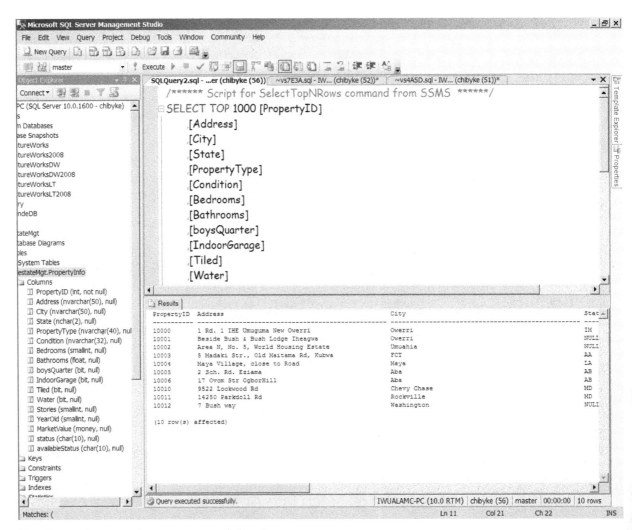 or

    o Right-click somewhere in the Query window, position the mouse on Results To, and click Results To Text.

The results would appear in columns of text. Below is an example:

- To show the result as a spreadsheet:

    o On the SQL Editor toolbar, click the Result To Grid button ⊞ or o Right-click anywhere in the Query window, position the mouse on Results To, and click Results To Grid

The results would appear as a spreadsheet of one or various columns. Below is an example:

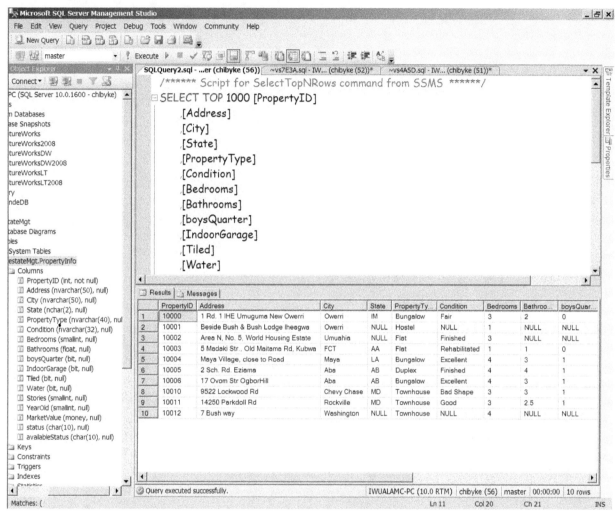

Creating a Query

Field Selection

The most fundamental keyword used by SQL Server for Record retrieval is SELECT. In order to process a request, you must specify what to select. To perform data analysis, the SELECT keyword uses the following syntax:
SELECT *What* FROM *WhatObject*;

As stated already, MS SQL Server is not case-sensitive. That means SELECT, Select, and select are just same word.

To select everything from a table, you can use the asterisk as the range of values. For example, to display all records from a table called Students, you can type:

```
/****** Script for Select ALL Rows from a table in SSMS ******/
   SELECT * FROM [AdventureWorks].[Person].[Address];
   GO
```

After writing the expression in a Query window, press F5 to execute. Here is an example:

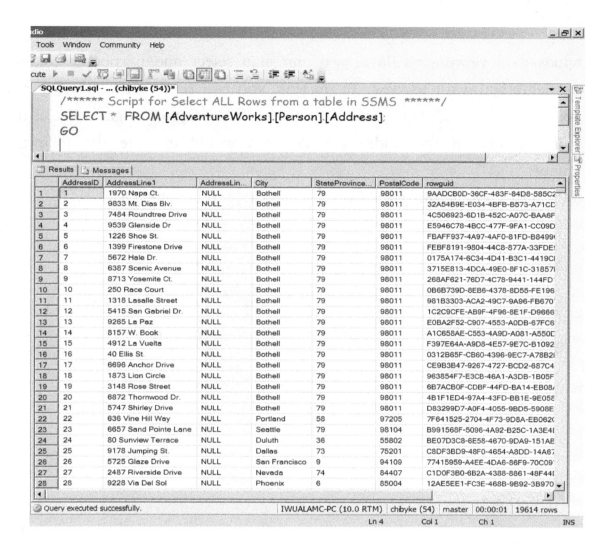

You can also qualify the * selector by preceding it with the name of the table followed by the period operator. The above statement is equivalent to:

SELECT Address.* FROM [AdventureWorks].[Person].[Address];
GO

In chapter five, we saw that you could create an alias for a table by preceding a column with a letter or a word and a period operator, and then entering the name of the table followed by that letter or word. Using this feature, the above statement can be written as:

SELECT A.* FROM [AdventureWorks].[Person].[Address] AS A;
GO

As opposed to viewing all data, you can also select one particular column whose fields you want to view. To do this, you can replace the *What* in our syntax with the name of the desired column. For example, to get a list of the *City* of Persons on the Address table, you would execute the following statement:

SELECT A.City FROM [AdventureWorks].[Person].[Address] AS A;

GO

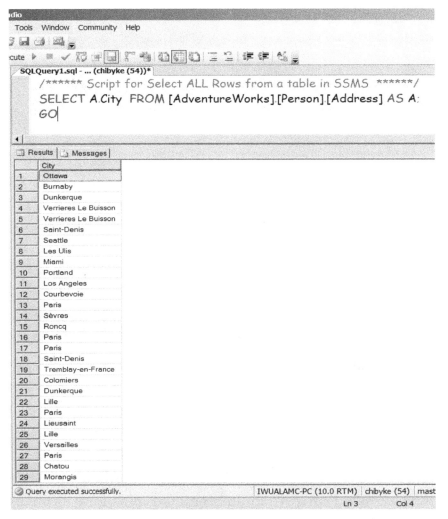

When you execute the statement, it would display only the column that contains the City. To consider more than one column in a statement, you can list them in the *What* factor of our syntax, separating them with a comma except for the last column.

The syntax you would use is:

SELECT *Column1, Column2, Column_n* FROM *WhatObject*;

For example, to display a list that includes only the stateName, stateCode, of records from a table called States, you would type:

USE country;

GO

SELECT S.stateName, S.stateID AS stateCode

  FROM [Country].[dbo].[states] AS S

  ORDER BY S.stateID ASC;

GO

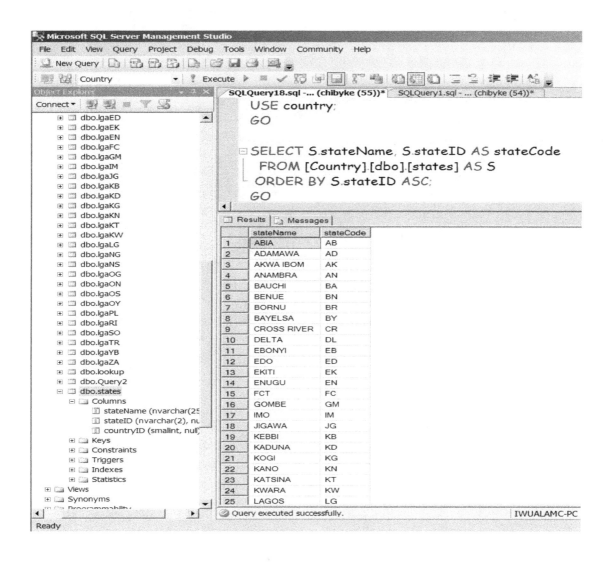

You don't have to qualify all columns; you can qualify some and forget some because there are some columns that will never be imagined to exist in other tables in the same database. The above statement is equivalent to:

USE country;
GO

SELECT S.stateName, stateID AS stateCode
  FROM [Country].[dbo].[states] AS S
  ORDER BY S.stateID ASC;
GO

When executed in a Query window, this expression would produce the same result:

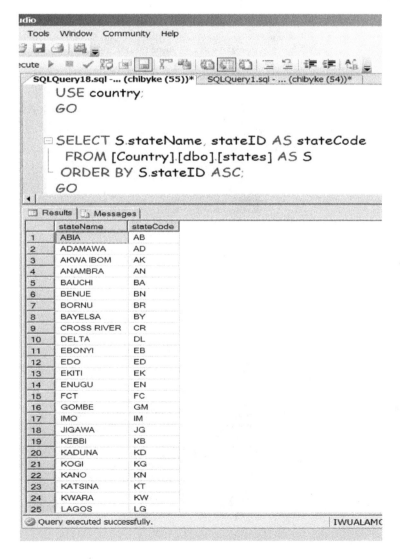

Distinct Field Selection

If you specify a column to select from a table, every record would come up. This can bring about the repetition of the same value. Sometimes you want to show each value only once. To get such a result, you can use the **DISTINCT** keyword before the name of the column in the **SELECT** statement.

In most cases, you would get a better result if you select only one column. Still, you can use as many columns as you want.

Producing Distinct Values

1. In the Diagram section, click the check box of City
2. In the SQL section, on the right side of *SELECT*, type the codes below:

    /** Script for Select City from Address table of AdventureWorks databasein SSMS **/

    SELECT A.City FROM [AdventureWorks].[Person].[Address] AS A;

    GO

3. On the Query Designer toolbar, click the Execute SQL button [!] to see the result:

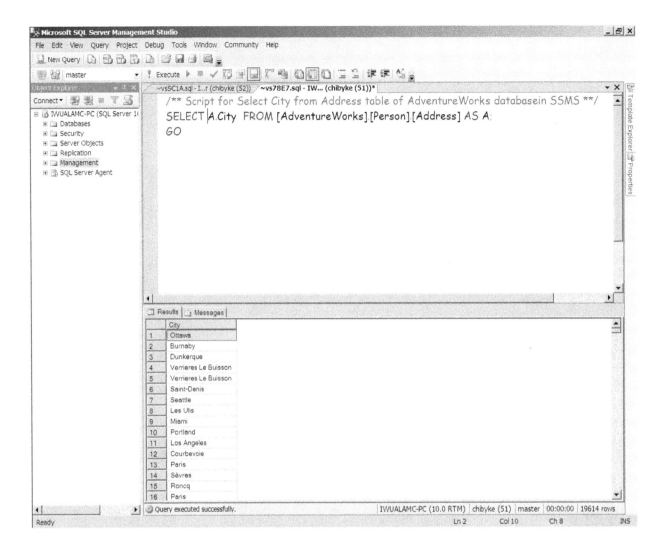

4. You will notice that 19614 rows were displayed.

5. In the SQL section, add DISTINCT to the previous codes as below:

    /** Script for Select City from Address table of AdventureWorks databasein SSMS **/

    SELECT DISTINCT A.City FROM [AdventureWorks].[Person].[Address] AS A;

    GO

6. Notice that, this time, the name of each city appears only once and recodes displayed is 575 rows.

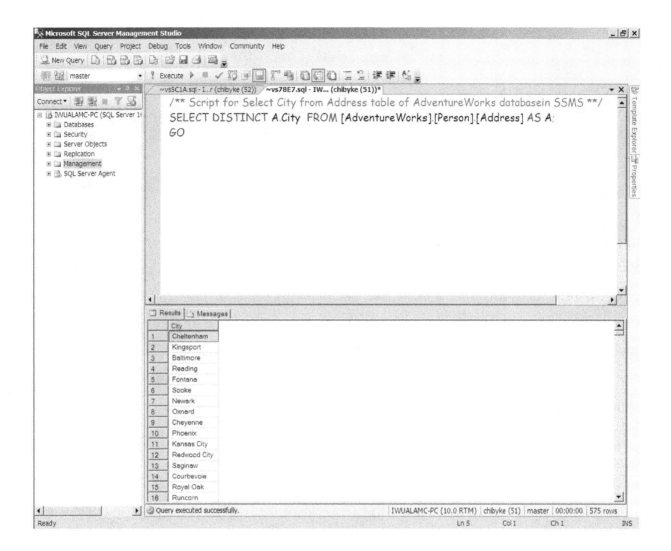

Collation

Because different languages use different mechanisms in their alphabetic characters, this can affect the way some sort algorithms or queries are performed on data, you can ask the database to apply a certain language mechanism to the field by changing the Collation property, Collation is . Otherwise, you should accept the default specified by the table. To find out what language your server is currently using, in a Query window or from PowerShell, you can type:

SELECT @@LANGUAGE;

GO

CHAPTER NINE

T-SQL PROGRAMMING IN MS SQL SERVER

While your primary job as a database developer consists of creating database objects, probably your second most important job is to assist your users with the various assignments they must perform on your application. One way you can assist is to use functions that perform otherwise complex tasks. We had in one way or the other used these functions in the previous chapters. To assist your development with the different tasks of a database, Transact-SQL ships with various already created and tested functions. You just need to be aware of these functions, their syntax, and the results they produce.

We had an introduction to some types of actions that could be performed on a database. These actions were called functions. The SQL provides another type of action called a stored procedure. If you have developed applications in some other languages such as Pascal or Visual Basic, you are probably familiar with the idea of a procedure. Like a function, a stored procedure is used to perform an action on a database. I create a database that will be used for examples in Stored Procedures.

1.   To create a new database, copy and paste the following code in the Query window:

```
-- ==============================================
-- Database: gtBankLoan
-- ==============================================
USE master
GO
-- Drop the database if it already exists
```

```sql
IF  EXISTS (
        SELECT name
                FROM sys.databases
                WHERE name = N'gtBankLoan'
)
DROP DATABASE gtBankLoan
GO


CREATE DATABASE gtBankLoan
GO
-- ==========================================
-- Table: staffMebs
-- ==========================================
USE gtBankLoan
GO


IF OBJECT_ID(N'dbo.staffMebs', N'U') IS NOT NULL
  DROP TABLE dbo.staffMebs
GO


CREATE TABLE dbo.staffMebs
(
    EmployeeID int identity(1,1) NOT NULL,
    EmployeeNumber nchar(10) NULL,
    FirstName nvarchar(20) NULL,
    LastName nvarchar(10),
    FullName AS ((LastName+ ', N') + FirstName),
    Title nvarchar(100),
    HourlySalary money,
    Username nvarchar(20),
    [Password] nvarchar(20),
    CONSTRAINT PK_staffMebs PRIMARY KEY(EmployeeID)
)
GO
```

```sql
INSERT    INTO    dbo.staffMebs(EmployeeNumber,    FirstName,    LastName,    Title,
HourlySalary)
VALUES(N'293747', N'Jane', N'Iwuala', N'Accounts Manager', 22.24);
GO


INSERT    INTO    dbo.staffMebs(EmployeeNumber,    FirstName,    LastName,    Title,
HourlySalary)
VALUES(N'492947', N'Helen', N'Eze', N'Accounts Representative', 14.55);
GO


INSERT    INTO    dbo.staffMebs(EmployeeNumber,    FirstName,    LastName,    Title,
HourlySalary)
VALUES(N'804685', N'Ugwunna', N'Nwaobasi', N'Accounts Representative', 12.75);
GO


-- =========================================
-- Table: LoanTypes
-- =========================================
USE gtBankLoan
GO


IF OBJECT_ID(N'dbo.LoanTypes', N'U') IS NOT NULL
  DROP TABLE dbo.LoanTypes
GO


CREATE TABLE dbo.LoanTypes
(
    LoanTypeID int identity(1,1) NOT NULL,
    LoanType nvarchar(50) NOT NULL,
    CONSTRAINT PK_LoanTypes PRIMARY KEY(LoanTypeID)
);
GO


INSERT INTO LoanTypes(LoanType) VALUES(N'Personal Loan');
  GO
```

```sql
INSERT INTO LoanTypes(LoanType) VALUES(N'Car Financing');
GO


INSERT INTO LoanTypes(LoanType) VALUES(N'Accomodotion Loan');
GO


INSERT INTO LoanTypes(LoanType) VALUES(N'Furniture Loan');
GO


-- =========================================
-- Table: Customers
-- =========================================
USE gtBankLoan;
GO


IF OBJECT_ID(N'dbo.Customers', N'U') IS NOT NULL
  DROP TABLE dbo.Customers
GO


CREATE TABLE dbo.Customers
(
    CustomerID int identity(1,1) NOT NULL,
    DateCreated datetime2 NULL,
    FullName nvarchar(50) NOT NULL,
    BillingAddress nvarchar(100),
    BillingCity nvarchar(50),
    BillingState nvarchar(50),
    BillingZIPCide nvarchar(10),
    EmailAddress nvarchar(100),
    CONSTRAINT PK_Customers PRIMARY KEY(CustomerID)
)
GO


INSERT INTO Customers(DateCreated, FullName,
```

```sql
    BillingAddress, BillingCity, BillingState,
    BillingZIPCide, EmailAddress)
VALUES(N'1/07/2013', N'Iwuala Chibueze',
    '2 Sch. Rd. Eziama Aba', N'Aba',
    'AB', N'45200', N'miwuala@yahoo.com');
GO


INSERT INTO Customers(DateCreated, FullName,
    BillingAddress, BillingCity, BillingState,
        BillingZIPCide)
VALUES(N'01/10/2013', N'Chinwendu Uja',
    '177 Ikot-Ekpene Rd. Ogbor-Hill', N'Aba',
    'AB', N'45200');
GO


INSERT INTO Customers(DateCreated, FullName,
    BillingAddress,   BillingCity, BillingState,
        BillingZIPCide, EmailAddress)
VALUES(N'12/3/2009', N'James Okeogu',
    '420 Faulks Road', N'Aba',
    'AB', N'20906', N'barrouchj@hotmail.com');
GO


INSERT INTO Customers(DateCreated, FullName,
    BillingAddress,   BillingCity, BillingState,
        BillingZIPCide)
VALUES(N'08/02/2009', N'Christina Chukwu',
    '825 Maitama Rd', N'Kubwa',
    'AA', N'00231');
GO


INSERT INTO Customers(DateCreated, FullName,
    BillingAddress,   BillingCity, BillingState,
        BillingZIPCide, EmailAddress)
VALUES(N'10/08/2006', N'Patrick Ugonna',
```

```
        '248 Douglas Rd.', N'Owerri',
        'IM', N'20006', N'hellerp@yahooo.com');
GO


-- ==========================================
-- Table: LoanAllocation
-- ==========================================
USE gtBankLoan;
GO

IF OBJECT_ID(N'dbo.LoanAllocations', N'U') IS NOT NULL
  DROP TABLE dbo.LoanAllocations
GO

CREATE TABLE dbo.LoanAllocations
(
    LoanAllocationID int identity(1,1) NOT NULL,
    DatePrepared datetime2 NOT NULL,
    EmployeeID int NULL
            CONSTRAINT FK_LoanPreparer
            FOREIGN KEY REFERENCES staffMebs(EmployeeID),
    CustomerID int NOT NULL
            CONSTRAINT FK_LoanReceiver
            FOREIGN KEY REFERENCES Customers(CustomerID),
    AccountNumber nchar(10),
    LoanTypeID int NOT NULL
            CONSTRAINT FK_LoanTypes
            FOREIGN KEY REFERENCES LoanTypes(LoanTypeID),
    LoanAmount money NOT NULL,
    InterestRate decimal(6,2) NOT NULL,
    Periods decimal(6,2) NOT NULL,
    InterestAmount AS ((LoanAmount*(InterestRate/(100)))*(Periods/(12))),
    FutureValue AS (LoanAmount+(LoanAmount*(InterestRate/(100)))*(Periods/(12))),
    MonthlyPayment AS
((LoanAmount+(LoanAmount*(InterestRate/(100)))*(Periods/(12)))/Periods),
```

```sql
    Notes varchar(max),
    CONSTRAINT PK_LoanAllocations PRIMARY KEY(LoanAllocationID)
)
GO


INSERT INTO LoanAllocations(DatePrepared, EmployeeID,
        CustomerID, AccountNumber, LoanTypeID, LoanAmount,
    InterestRate, Periods, Notes)
VALUES(N'2/26/2011', 2, 1, N'9171394', 4, 650000.00, 12.65, 36,
        'The loan will be delivered by our furniture business partner Ugochi Edward');
GO


INSERT INTO LoanAllocations(DatePrepared, EmployeeID,
        CustomerID, AccountNumber, LoanTypeID, LoanAmount,
    InterestRate, Periods, Notes)
VALUES(N'06/22/2012', 2, 2, N'8628064', 2, 1650000.00, 10.20, 60,
        'For this car loan, our partner Ikenna Goodluck will process and deliver the car.');
GO


INSERT INTO LoanAllocations(DatePrepared, EmployeeID,
        CustomerID, AccountNumber, LoanTypeID, LoanAmount,
    InterestRate, Periods, Notes)
VALUES(N'01/07/2013', 1, 3, N'8468364', 3, 5000000.00, 18.65, 48,
        'This is a building loan granted to Iwuala M. C.');
GO


INSERT INTO LoanAllocations(DatePrepared, EmployeeID,
        CustomerID, AccountNumber, LoanTypeID, LoanAmount,
    InterestRate, Periods, Notes)
VALUES(N'08/02/2010', 3, 4, N'2483047', 1, 350000.00, 12.74, 36,
        'This is personal/cash loan allocated to a customer who walked in the store and
requested it.');
GO


INSERT INTO LoanAllocations(DatePrepared, EmployeeID,
```

```
        CustomerID, AccountNumber, LoanTypeID, LoanAmount,
    InterestRate, Periods, Notes)
VALUES(N'10/08/2006', 2, 5, N'1311804', 4, 2270000.36, 12.28, 60,
    'This is a regular car financing loan');
GO


-- ==========================================
-- Table: PaidCusInfo
-- ==========================================
USE gtBankLoan;
GO


IF OBJECT_ID(N'dbo.PaidCusInfo', N'U') IS NOT NULL
  DROP TABLE dbo.PaidCusInfo
GO


CREATE TABLE dbo.PaidCusInfo
(
    PaymentID int identity(1, 1) NOT NULL,
    PaymentDate datetime2 NOT NULL,
    EmployeeID int NULL
            CONSTRAINT FK_staffMebs
            FOREIGN KEY REFERENCES staffMebs(EmployeeID),
    LoanAllocationID int NOT NULL
            CONSTRAINT FK_LoanAllocations
            FOREIGN KEY REFERENCES LoanAllocations(LoanAllocationID),
    PaymentAmount money NOT NULL,
    Balance money,
    Notes varchar(max),
    CONSTRAINT PK_Payments PRIMARY KEY(PaymentID)
)
GO
```

2. To execute the code, press F5

3. In the Object Explorer, expand the Databases node if necessary and expand GtBankLoan

4.   Click Database Diagram

5. When the message box comes up, read it and click Yes.

6. In the dialog box, double-click each table and, when all tables have been added, click Close

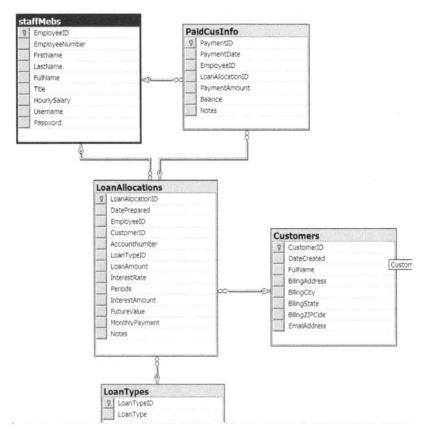

This database diagram is not necessary, it is an avenue to teach how to create database diagram to enable have a look of the relationships existing among your tables.

7. Save the diagram as **dgmGtBankLoan** and close it

9.1 Creating a Stored Procedure

To create a procedure:

i. In the Object Explorer, expand the database for which you want to create the procedure, expand its Programmability node, right-click Stored Procedures, and click New Stored Procedure... A query window with a skeleton syntax would be displayed. You can then modify that code using the techniques we will learn in this lesson.

ii. Open an empty query window associated with the database for which you want to create the stored procedure and display the Templates Explorer. In the Templates Explorer, expand the Store Procedure node. Drag Create Stored Procedure and drop it in the query window

iii. Using SQL code, to create a procedure, you start with the CREATE PROCEDURE expression. You can also use CREATE PROC. Both expressions produce the same result. Like everything in your database, you must name your procedure:

The name of a procedure can be any string that follows the rules we reviewed below:

a. A name will start with either an underscore or a letter. Examples are _n, act, or Second

b. After the first character as an underscore or a letter, the name will have combinations of underscores, letters, and digits. Examples are _n24, act_52_t

c. A name will not include special characters such as !, @, #, $, %, ^, &, or *

d. We will avoid using spaces in a name.

e. If the name is a combination of words, each word will start in uppercase. Examples are DateHired, _RealSport, or driversLicenseNumber

Refrain from starting the name of a procedure with **sp_** because it could conflict with some of the stored procedures that already ship with Microsoft SQL Server.

After the name of the procedure, type the keyword **AS**. The section, group of words, or group of lines after the **AS** keyword is called the body of the procedure. It states what you want the procedure to do or what you want it to produce. Based on this, the simplest syntax of creating a procedure is:

CREATE PROCEDURE *ProcedureName*

AS

Body of the Procedure

It is important to keep in mind that there are many other issues related to creating a procedure but for now, we will consider that syntax. After creating the procedure, you must store it as an object in your database. To do this, on the SQL Editor toolbar, you can click the Execute button. If the code of the procedure is right, it would be created and a new node for its name would be added to the Stored Procedures section of the database.

9.1.1 Managing Procedures

i. Modifying a Procedure

As a regular SQL Server database object, you can modify a stored procedure without recreating it. To do this:

  a. In the Object Explorer, you can right-click the procedure and click Modify

  b. In the Object Explorer, you can right-click the procedure, position the mouse on Script Stored Procedure As, ALTER To, click New Query Editor Window

  c. Open an empty query window associated with the database that contains the stored procedure. From the Templates Explorer, expand Stored Procedure. Drag the Drop Stored Procedure node and drop it in the empty query window

In each case, a skeleton code would be generated for you. You can then edit it to create a new version of your stored procedure. After editing the code, you can execute the SQL statement to update the stored procedure. In MS SQL Server, the basic formula to modify a stored procedure is:

ALTER PROCEDURE *ProcedureName*

AS

Body of Procedure

ii.   Deleting a Procedure

One of the biggest characteristics of a stored procedure is that it is treated like an object in its own way. Therefore, after creating it, if you don't need it anymore, you can get rid of it.

There are various types of stored procedures, some of which are considered temporary. Those types of procedures delete themselves when not needed anymore, such as when the person who created the stored procedure disconnects from the database or shuts down the computer. Otherwise, to delete a procedure, you can use either the Object Explorer or SQL code. As mentioned with tables, even if you create a procedure using the Object Explorer, you can delete it using SQL code and vice-versa. To remove a procedure in the Object Explorer, after expanding its database, its Programmability, and its Stored Procedure nodes, you can right-click the stored procedure and click Delete on the fly-out menu. You can also click it in the Object Explorer to select it and then press Delete. The Delete Object dialog box would come up to let you make a decision.

To delete a procedure in SQL Script, the syntax to use is:

DROP PROCEDURE *ProcedureName*

Of course, you should make sure you are in the right database and also that the *ProcedureName* exists.

9.1.2   Application of Stored Procedures

Probably the simplest procedure you can write would consist of selecting columns from a table. This is done with the **SELECT** clause and applying the techniques we reviewed for data analysis. For example, to create a stored procedure that would hold a list of students from a table named Students, you would create the procedure as follows:

```
CREATE PROCEDURE getStudInfo
AS
BEGIN
    SELECT FirstName, LastName, DateOfBirth, Gender
    FROM Students
END
GO
```

Besides **SELECT** operations, in a stored procedure, you can perform any of the database operations we have applied so far. These include creating and maintaining records, etc. Here is an example of creating a stored procedure:

```
USE gtBankLoan;
GO


CREATE PROC updateStaffInfo
AS
    BEGIN
        UPDATE staffMebs
        SET [Password] = N'passwordStaff
    END;
GO
```

i.   Executing a Procedure

To get the results of creating a stored procedure, you must execute it (in other words, to use a stored procedure, you must call it). To execute a procedure, you use the **EXECUTE** keyword followed by the name of the procedure. Although there are some other issues related to executing a procedure, for now, we will consider that the simplest syntax to call a procedure is:

EXECUTE *ProcedureName*

Alternatively, instead of **EXECUTE**, you can use the **EXEC** keyword:

EXEC *ProcedureName*

For example, if you have a procedure named UpdateStaffInfo, to execute it, you would type:

EXECUTE UpdateStaffInfo

You can also precede the name of the procedure with its schema, such as **dbo**. Here is an example:

EXECUTE dbo.UpdateStaffInfo;

You can also precede the name of the schema with the name of the database. Here is an example:

EXECUTE gtBankLoan.dbo.UpdateStaffInfo;

ii.   Expressions and Functions in Stored Procedures

One of the advantages of using a stored procedure is that not only can it produce the same expression as we saw during analysis of data but also it can store such an expression to be recalled any time without having to re-write it (the expression). Based on this, you can create an expression that combines a first and a last name to produce and store a full name. Here is an example:

USE AdventureWorks;

GO

CREATE PROCEDURE personInfo

AS

```
BEGIN
    SELECT FullName = FirstName + ' N' + LastName,
        phone, emailaddress
    FROM Person.Contact
END;
GO
```

A stored procedure can also call a function in its body. To do this, follow the same rules we reviewed for calling functions during data analysis. Here is an example of a stored procedure that calls an in-built function:

```
USE AdventureWorks2008 ;
GO

CREATE PROC staffNoOfYrs
AS
BEGIN
    SELECT loginID, JobTitle, gender,DATEDIFF(Year, hireDate,GETDATE ()) as N'No Of
Years'
    FROM HumanResources.Employee
END;
GO
```

Here are more examples of expressions and function in stored procedure:

```
USE gtBankLoan;
GO

/*
  Author:          IWUALA C
  Create date:     Monday, January 07, 2013
  Description:     This stored procedure creates a username for each employee. It
                   also assigns an email to the employee using the employee data.
*/
CREATE PROCEDURE userAccount
AS
    BEGIN
```

```
          UPDATE dbo.staffmebs
          SET Username = LOWER(LEFT(FirstName, 1) + LEFT(LastName, 5))


          UPDATE dbo.staffmebs
          SET emailAdd = LOWER(LEFT(FirstName, 1) + LEFT(LastName, 5))
           +  N'@gtloan.com'
          UPDATE dbo.staffmebs
          SET [password] = employeeID + LOWER(LEFT(FirstName, 3) +
          RIGHT(LastName, 3)) + N'@gtloan.com'
     END;
GO


EXECUTE userAccount;
GO
```

9.2   Arguments and Parameters

All of the stored procedures we have created and used so far assumed that the values they needed were already in a table of the database. In some cases, you may need to create a stored procedure that involves values that are not part of the database. On such a scenario, for the procedure to carry its assignment, you would supply it with one or more values. I designed a database for IMT department that will be used for checking of result, the database uses view to supply records to the application and the view uses stored procedure to retrieve records from different tables. The students are not known to me though their records may be on the database, so I must supply the procedure with the student's registration number to fetch their records.

So that registration number which is an external value that is provided to the stored procedure is called a parameter. When you create a stored procedure, you must also create the parameter if you judge it necessary. When a procedure's creation is equipped with a parameter, it is said that the stored procedure takes an argument. A stored procedure can also take more than one argument. When you execute a stored procedure that takes one or more arguments, you must provide a value for each argument. In this case, you are said to pass a value for the argument. There are cases when you don't have to provide an argument.

9.2.1 Passing Arguments on Stored Procedure

To create a stored procedure that takes an argument, type the formula **CREATE PROCEDURE** or **CREATE PROC** followed by the name of the procedure, then type the name of the argument starting with @. The parameter is created like a column of a variable. That is, a parameter must have a name, a data type and an optional length. Here is the syntax you would use:

CREATE PROCEDURE *ProcedureName*

@ParameterName DataType

AS

Body of the Procedure

When implementing the stored procedure, you can define what you want to do with the parameter(s), in the body of the procedure. One way you can use a parameter is to run a query whose factor the user would provide. For example, imagine you want to create a procedure that, whenever executed, it will display the cities in a state. Since you want the user to specify the stateid to display the cities, you can create a stored procedure that receives the stateid. Here is an example:

use Country;

GO

CREATE PROC LGAsInState

    @state NVARCHAR(2)

 AS

```sql
SELECT cityname, stateid
FROM  citytable
WHERE  stateid = @state;
GO
```

More examples:

```sql
USE GtBankLoan;
GO


CREATE PROCEDURE SpecifyCurrentBalance
    @PmtDate datetime2,
    @EmplID int,
    @LaID int,
    @PmtAmt money
AS
BEGIN
    -- Get the amount that was lent to the customer
    DECLARE @AmountOfLoan money;
    SET       @AmountOfLoan = (SELECT las.FutureValue
                FROM LoanAllocations las
                WHERE (las.LoanAllocationID = @LaID));


    -- If the customer had already made at least one payment,
    -- get the current balance of the customer's account
    DECLARE @CurrentBalance money;
    SET    @CurrentBalance = (SELECT MIN(pay.Balance)
                    FROM PaidCusInfo pay
                    WHERE (pay.LoanAllocationID = @LaID));


    -- If the customer has never made a payment (yet),
    -- to specify the balance, subtract the current payment
    -- from the original amount of the loan
    IF    @CurrentBalance IS NULL
        BEGIN
```

```
            INSERT INTO PaidCusInfo(PaymentDate, EmployeeID,
                        LoanAllocationID, PaymentAmount, Balance)
            VALUES(@PmtDate, @EmplID, @LaID, @PmtAmt,
                        @AmountOfLoan - @PmtAmt);
        END
    -- If the customer had already made at least one payment,
    -- subtract the current payment from the previous balance
    ELSE
        BEGIN
            INSERT INTO PaidCusInfo(PaymentDate, EmployeeID,
                            LoanAllocationID, PaymentAmount, Balance)
            VALUES(@PmtDate, @EmplID, @LaID,
                        @PmtAmt, @CurrentBalance - @PmtAmt);
        END
END
GO
```

9.2.2 Executing an Argumentative Stored Procedure

As mentioned already, when executing a stored procedure that takes a parameter, make sure you provide a value for the parameter. The syntax used is:

EXEC *ProcedureName ParameterValue*

If the parameter is Boolean or numeric, make sure you provide the value as 0 or for a Boolean value or another number for the numeric type. If the parameter is a character or a string, type its value in single-quotes. Here is an example:

EXEC country. LGAsInState N'AB';

Another type of stored procedure can be made to take more than one parameter. In this case, create the parameters in the section before the **AS** keyword, separated by a comma. The syntax you would use is:

CREATE PROCEDURE *ProcedureName*

@ParameterName1 DataType, @ParameterName2 DataType, @ParameterName_n DataType

AS

Body of the Procedure

Here is an example:

USE LoloVideoClub;

GO

CREATE PROCEDURE videoInfo

      @typeOfMovie nvarchar(20),

      @releasedYr smallint

AS

BEGIN

  SELECT director, VideoTitle,

  DATEDIFF(MONTH , yearReleased , GETDATE()) AS N'Year Released'

  FROM dbo.VideosInfo

  WHERE (TypeOfMovie = @typeOfMovie) AND (yearReleased >= DATEDIFF(year, @releasedYr , GETDATE()))

END

GO

When calling a stored procedure that takes more than one parameter, you must still provide a value for each parameter but you have two alternatives. The simplest technique consists of providing a value for each parameter in the exact order they appear in the stored procedure. Here is an example:

exec dbo.videoInfo N'Naija', 1095;

GO

This would produce:

Alternatively, you can provide the value for each parameter in the order of your choice, and the same result will be produced. Consider the following procedure that takes 3 arguments:

USE LoloVideoClub;

GO

EXEC dbo.videoInfo @releasedYr = 1095, @typeOfMovie= N'Naija' ;

GO

9.2.3 Default Arguments

Imagine you create a database for a department store and a table that holds the list of items sold in the store:

ItemNumber	ItemCategoryID	ItemName	ItemSize	UnitPrice
264850	2	Long-Sleeve T-Shirt	Large	2900.95
930405	4	Singlet	Medium	350.95
293004	1	Cotton Comfort Open Bottom Pant	XLarge	320.85
924515	1	Trouser Material	Yard	300.95
405945	3	Plaid Pinpoint Dress Shirt	22 35-36	500.85
294936	2	Cool-Dry Soft	36	260.55

		Cup Bra		
294545	2	Ladies Hooded Sweatshirt	Medium	1500.75
820465	2	Gold Wrist Watch	each	18000.95
294694	2	Round Neck Polo	Large	560.85
924094	3	Boxers	M	380.85
359405	3	Iron-Free Pleated Khaki Pants	32x32	250.95
192004	3	Sunglasses		1500.85

Imagine you want a way of calculating the price of an item after a discount has been applied to it. Such a procedure can be created as follows:

```
CREATE PROC ItemNetPrice
@discount Decimal
AS
SELECT ItemName, UnitPrice - (UnitPrice * @discount / 100)
FROM StoreItems;
GO
```

If you are planning to create a stored procedure that takes an argument and know that the argument will likely have the same value most of the time, you can provide that value as parameter but leave a room for other values of that argument. A value given to an argument is referred to as default. What this implies is that, when the user calls that stored procedure, if the user doesn't provide a value for the argument, the default value would be used.

To create a stored procedure that takes an argument that carries a default value, after declaring the value, on its right side, type = followed by the desired value. Here is an example applied to the above database:

```
CREATE PROC ItemNetPrice
```

```
@discount Decimal = 15.0
AS
SELECT ItemName, UnitPrice - (UnitPrice * @discount / 100)
FROM StoreItems;
GO
```

Using this same approach, you can create a stored procedure that takes more than one argument with default values. To provide a default value for each argument, after declaring it, type the desired value to its right side, you remember how you initialized variables with default values. Here is an example of a stored procedure that takes two arguments, each with a default value:

```
CREATE PROC ItemSalesPrice
@Discount decimal = 20.00,
@TaxRate  decimal = 7.75
AS
SELECT ItemName As [Item Description],
    UnitPrice As [Marked Price],
    UnitPrice * @Discount / 100 As [Discount Amt],
    UnitPrice - (UnitPrice * @Discount / 100) As [After Discount],
    UnitPrice * @TaxRate / 100 As [Tax Amount],
    (UnitPrice * @TaxRate / 100) + UnitPrice -
    (UnitPrice * @Discount / 100) + (@TaxRate / 100) As [Net Price]
FROM StoreItems;
GO
```

When calling a stored procedure that takes more than one argument and all arguments having default values, you don't need to provide a value for each argument, you can provide a value for only one or some of the arguments. The above procedure can be called with one argument as follows:

```
EXEC ItemSalesPrice 55.00
```

In this case, the other argument(s) would use their default value. Guess you are not confused? We saw that, when calling a stored procedure that takes more than one argument, you didn't have to provide the values of the arguments in the exact order they appeared in the procedure, you just had to type the name of each argument and assign it the desired value. In the same way, if a stored procedure takes more than one argument and some of the arguments have default values, when calling it, you can provide the values in the order of your choice, by typing the name of each argument and assigning it the desired value. Based on this, the above stored procedure can be called with only the value of the second argument as follows:

EXEC ItemSalesPrice @TaxRate = 8.55

In this case, the first argument would use its default value.

9.2.4 Output Parameters

Transact-SQL uses the notion of passing an argument by reference. This type of argument is passed to a procedure but it is meant to return a value. In other words, you can create a stored procedure that takes a parameter but the purpose of the parameter is to carry a new value when the procedure ends so you can use that value as you see fit.

To create a parameter that will return a value from the stored procedure, after the name of the procedure, if you want the stored procedure to take arguments, type them. Otherwise, omit them. On the other hand, you must pass at least one argument, name it starting with the @ symbol, specify its data type, and enter the **OUTPUT** keyword on its right. Based on this, the basic syntax you can use is:

CREATE PROCEDURE *ProcedureName*

@ParameterName DataType OUTPUT

AS

Body of the Procedure

In the body of the procedure, you can perform the assignment as you see fit. The primary rule you must follow is that, before the end of the procedure, you must have to specify a value for the **OUTPUT** argument. That's the value that the argument will hold when the stored procedure exits. Here is an example:

```
CREATE PROCEDURE dbo.CreateFullName
    @FName nvarchar(20),
    @LName nvarchar(20),
    @FullName nvarchar(42) OUTPUT
AS
    SELECT @FullName = @LName + ', N' + @FName
GO
```

When calling the stored procedure, you must pass an argument for the **OUTPUT** parameter and, once again, you must type **OUTPUT** to the right side of the argument. Remember that the stored procedure would return the argument. This means that, after calling the procedure, you can get back the **OUTPUT** argument and use it as you see fit. Here is an example:

```
DECLARE @FirstName nvarchar(20),
        @LastName nvarchar(20),
      @Full nvarchar(42)
SET @FirstName = N'Melanie';
SET @LastName = N'Johanssen';

EXECUTE dbo.CreateFullName @FirstName, @LastName, @Full OUTPUT

SELECT @Full;
GO
```

One of the advantages of using a function or a stored procedure is that it has access to the tables and records of its database. This means that you can access the columns and records as long as you specify the table or the view, which is done with a FROM clause associated with a SELECT statement. Consider the following stored procedure created in a database that contains a table named Students:

```
USE [LOLOITFDB.MDF];
```

```
GO

CREATE PROC showStudInfo
@FullName nvarchar(70) OUTPUT
AS
        BEGIN
        SELECT @FullName = fName + ', N' + mName + ', N' + lName
        FROM studTable
        END;
GO

DECLARE @Name varchar (70);

exec showStudInfo @Name OUTPUT;
select @Name ;
GO
```

When you execute this stored procedure, it would work on the records of the table. One of the particularities of a stored procedure that takes an OUTPUT argument is that it can return only one value. When calling such a procedure, if you don't specify a condition to produce one particular result, the SQL interpreter in this case would select the last record. This means that you should always make sure that your stored procedure that takes an OUTPUT parameter would have a way to isolate a result. If the stored procedure processes a SELECT statement, you can use a WHERE condition. Here is an example of such a procedure:

```
USE [LOLOITFDB.MDF];
GO

CREATE PROC showStudInfo
@regNo varchar(13),
@FullName nvarchar(70) OUTPUT
AS
        BEGIN
        SELECT @FullName = fName + ', N' + mName + ', N' + lName
        FROM studTable
```

```
        WHERE regNo = @regNo
        END;
GO


DECLARE @Name varchar (70);


exec showStudInfo @Name OUTPUT;
select @Name ;
GO
```

When this procedure is executed, it would produce only the record stored in the regNo supplied.

9.3   BUILT-IN STORED PROCEDURES

To assist you with managing Microsoft SQL Server databases, Transact-SQL provides many built-in stored procedures, to assist you in performing your calculation, manipulation of data, and so on.

9.3.1 Renaming an Object

To rename an object that was created in the current database, you can call the sp_rename stored procedure. Its syntax is:

sp_rename [@objname =] 'object_name' , [@newname =] 'new_name'

   [, [@objtype =] 'object_type']

The object_name is the name of the object you want to replace.

The new_name is the new name the object will have.

The object_type is optional because on some occasions you don't have to specify the object. It allows you to specify the type of object you are trying to rename.

Here is an example of how to rename a table using sp_rename:

```
USE idealSuits;
GO


EXEC sp_rename N'rooms', N'room';
GO
```

When this code runs, a table named rooms will have its name changed to room, in the idealSuits database. Here is an example of how to rename a column in a table using sp_rename:

```
USE gtBankLoan;
GO


EXEC sp_rename N'PaidCusInfo.balance', N'accBalance', 'COLUMN';
GO
```

Here is an example of how to rename an index in a table using sp_rename:

```
EXEC sp_rename N'TableName.IndexName', N'NewIndexName, N'INDEX';
GO
```

The sp_rename stored procedure can also be used to rename an alias datatype. In this case, the name of the object must be qualified. Here is an example:

```
EXEC sp_rename N'ObejctName', N'ObjectNewName', N'USERDATATYPE';
GO
```

9.3.2 Database Email

Starting with SQL Server 2005, Database Mail was introduced as an enterprise solution to send e-mails from SQL Server. Database Mail features many improvements over SQL Mail, the most important of which is that it is no longer dependent on Messaging Application Program Interface (MAPI). It uses Simple Mail Transfer Protocol (SMTP), and you do not need to install an extended MAPI client (for example, Microsoft Outlook) on your production SQL Server to use Database Mail. To give you the ability to send an email from a database, Transact-SQL provides the **sp_send_dbmail** stored procedure. This store procedure is resident in the **msdb** database. This means that you must reference it when executing this procedure. Its syntax is:

```
sp_send_dbmail [ [ @profile_name = ] 'profile_name' ]
    [ , [ @recipients = ] 'recipients [ ; ...n ]' ]
    [ , [ @copy_recipients = ] 'copy_recipient [ ; ...n ]' ]
    [ , [ @blind_copy_recipients = ] 'blind_copy_recipient [ ; ...n ]' ]
    [ , [ @subject = ] 'subject' ]
    [ , [ @body = ] 'body' ]
    [ , [ @body_format = ] 'body_format' ]
    [ , [ @importance = ] 'importance' ]
    [ , [ @sensitivity = ] 'sensitivity' ]
    [ , [ @file_attachments = ] 'attachment [ ; ...n ]' ]
    [ , [ @query = ] 'query' ]
    [ , [ @execute_query_database = ] 'execute_query_database' ]
    [ , [ @attach_query_result_as_file = ] attach_query_result_as_file ]
    [ , [ @query_attachment_filename = ] query_attachment_filename ]
    [ , [ @query_result_header = ] query_result_header ]
    [ , [ @query_result_width = ] query_result_width ]
    [ , [ @query_result_separator = ] 'query_result_separator' ]
    [ , [ @exclude_query_output = ] exclude_query_output ]
    [ , [ @append_query_error = ] append_query_error ]
    [ , [ @query_no_truncate = ] query_no_truncate ]
    [ , [ @mailitem_id = ] mailitem_id ] [ OUTPUT ]
```

i.   Configuration of database mail

Database configuration involves the following steps:

1. Enable Database Mail.

2. Create a Database Mail profile.

3.   Create a Database Mail account.

4.

dd the account to the profile. Grant permission for a user or a role to use the Database Mail profile.

The following T-SQL script can be used to perform the exact same steps that could be achieved with the Database Mail Configuration Wizard. So copy this code and execute it on query window:

```
-- Enable Database Mail
sp_configure 'show advanced options', 1;
GO


RECONFIGURE;
GO


sp_configure 'Database Mail XPs', 1;
GO


RECONFIGURE
GO
-- Create a Database Mail profile
EXECUTE msdb.dbo.sysmail_add_profile_sp
@profile_name = 'SQL2008_DBMail_Profile',
@description = 'SQL Server 2008 Database Mail Profile';
-- Create a Database Mail account
EXECUTE msdb.dbo.sysmail_add_account_sp
@account_name = 'chibyke',
@description = 'Database Mail Account',
```

```
@email_address = 'miwuala@infotechconcerns.com',
@display_name = 'IWUALA M. C',
@replyto_address = 'miwuala@infotechconcerns.com',
@mailserver_name = 'smtpserver.domain_name.com' ;
-- Add the account to the profile
EXECUTE msdb.dbo.sysmail_add_profileaccount_sp
@profile_name ='SQL2008_DBMail_Profile',
@account_name = 'chibyke',
@sequence_number =1 ;
-- Grant permission for a user or a role to use the Database Mail profile
EXECUTE msdb.dbo.sysmail_add_principalprofile_sp
@profile_name = 'SQL2008_DBMail_Profile',
@principal_id = 0,
@is_default = 1 ;
```

With this, Database Mail is ready to send e-mails. To do so, use the sp_send_dbmail stored procedure. This stored procedure accepts a lot of parameters, most of which are optional. Here is an example of a simple text e-mail:

```
EXECUTE msdb.dbo.sp_send_dbmail @profile_name='SQL2008_DBMail_Profile',
@recipients='miwuala@infotechconcerns.com',
@subject='Database Mail Test',
@body='This is a test e-mail sent from Database Mail on SQL2008\INST1';
GO
```

To view the status of the e-mails, use the sysmail_allitems view as follows:
```
SELECT * FROM msdb.dbo.sysmail_allitems;
```

One of the important columns in this view is sent_status. It contains one of the following four values: sent, unsent, retrying, or failed. If your e-mails are not going out, check this view to verify that the e-mails are being queued up. If you notice messages with anything other than sent status, right-click the Database Mail folder in Management Studio and select View Database Mail Log from the context menu to view detailed error messages.

As you may guess, most of the arguments are optional. The explanation below is for those who choose to create configure database mail using the Mail Wizard:

a. The *profile_name* value must hold a valid for an existing profile. If you omit this argument, the database engine uses the current user or a default profile created in the **msdb** database. If there is no default profile, you must create one. To do this, copy and paste the codes given above.

b. The *recipients* value represents one or more email addresses that will receive the message. If you want to send the message to only one recipient, provide the address. To get the message to more than one recipient, separate their email addresses with commas

c. The *copy_recipient* value represents one or more email addresses that will receive a copy of the message. This is equivalent to cc. To send the message to one recipient, provide the address. To send the message to many recipients, provide the necessary email addresses separated by commas

d. The *blind_copy_recipient* value follows the same rules as the *copy_recipient* argument except that the recipients will not see each other's email address. This is equivalent to bcc

e. The *subject* value is the subject of the message

f. The *body* value is the actual message to send

g. The *body_format* value specifies the format to use

h. The *importance* value specifies the level of importance of the message

i. The *sensitivity* value specifies the type of sensitivity of the message

Here is an example of executing this stored procedure:

```
use gtBankLoan;
GO
EXEC msdb.dbo.sp_send_dbmail
        @profile_name = N'Central Administrator',
        @recipients = N'edna4Real@infotechconcerns.net',
        @body = N'The Persons table has received a new record.',
        @subject = N'New Record';
GO
```

9.4   FUNCTIONS

A function is a section of code that is used to perform an isolated assignment. Once it has performed its assignment, the function can be accessed in order to present its result(s). In Transact-SQL, a function is considered an object. After creating the function object, it becomes part of a database. You can then execute it when necessary.

9.4.1   Creating a Function

There are various ways you can start the creation of a function:
  i. In the Object Explorer, expand the desired database. Expand the programmatically node. Expand the Functions node. Right-click Scalar-Valued Function and click New Scalar-Valued Function. Sample code would be generated for   you:

```
-- ================================================
-- Template generated from Template Explorer using:
-- Create Scalar Function (New Menu).SQL
--
-- Use the Specify Values for Template Parameters
-- command (Ctrl-Shift-M) to fill in the parameter
-- values below.
--
-- This block of comments will not be included in
-- the definition of the function.
-- ================================================
SET ANSI_NULLS ON
GO
SET QUOTED_IDENTIFIER ON
GO
-- ================================================
```

```
-- Author:                    <Author,,Name>
-- Create date: <Create Date, ,>
-- Description:     <Description, ,>
-- =============================================
CREATE FUNCTION <Scalar_Function_Name, sysname, FunctionName>
(
        -- Add the parameters for the function here
        <@Param1, sysname, @p1> <Data_Type_For_Param1, , int>
)
RETURNS <Function_Data_Type, int>
AS
BEGIN
        -- Declare the return variable here
        DECLARE <@ResultVar, sysname, @Result> <Function_Data_Type, ,int>

        -- Add the T-SQL statements to compute the return value here
        SELECT <@ResultVar, sysname, @Result> = <@Param1, sysname, @p1>

        -- Return the result of the function
        RETURN <@ResultVar, sysname, @Result>

END
GO
```

   ii.   You can then modify to customize it

   iii.   You can open a new empty query window and start typing your code in it

In Transact-SQL, the primary formula of creating a function is:

CREATE FUNCTION *FunctionName*()

9.4.2 The Name of a Function

We mentioned already that, in SQL, a function is created as an object. As such, it must have a name. In this chapter I have discussed some naming rules during stored procedure section above. The same rules still apply for functions.

9.4.3 Returning a Value From a Function

For a function to be useful, it must produce a result. This is also said that the function returns a result or a value. When creating a function, you must specify the type of value the function would return. To provide this information, after the name of the function, type the **RETURNS** keyword followed by a definition for a data type. Here is a simple example:

```
CREATE FUNCTION Addition()
RETURNS Decimal(6,3)
```

After specifying the type of value that the function would return, you can create a body for the function. The body of a function starts with the **BEGIN** and ends with the **END** keywords. Here is an example:

```
CREATE FUNCTION Addition()
RETURNS Decimal(6,3)
BEGIN

END
```

Optionally, you can type the **AS** keyword before the **BEGIN** keyword:

```
CREATE FUNCTION Addition()
RETURNS Decimal(6,3)
AS
BEGIN

END
```

Between the **BEGIN** and **END** keywords, which is the section that represents the body of the function, you can define the assignment the function must perform. After performing this assignment, just before the **END** keyword, you must specify the value that the function returns. This is done by typing the **RETURN** keyword followed by an expression. Here is the syntax:

```
CREATE FUNCTION Addition()
RETURNS Decimal(6,3)
AS
BEGIN
    RETURN Expression
END
```

Here is an example

```
CREATE FUNCTION GetFullName()
RETURNS varchar(100)
AS
BEGIN
        RETURN 'Doe, John'
END
```

9.4.4   Creating Functions

1. In the Object Explorer, right-click RealEstate1 and click New Query...
2. To   create   a   function,   type   the   following   statement:

```
CREATE FUNCTION CalculateWeeklySalary()
RETURNS Decimal(8, 2)
AS
BEGIN
    RETURN 880.44
END;
GO
```

3. To execute the statement, on the SQL Editor toolbar, click the Execute button

Execute

4. To save the file that contains the code of the function, on the Standard toolbar, click the Save button

5. Type **Calculate** as the name of the file

6. Click Save

7. In the Object Explorer, expand the diograndeDB node, expand Programmability. Expand Functions. And expand Scalar-Valued Functions. Notice the presence of the CalculateWeeklySalary node

9.4.5 Calling a Function

After a function has been created, you can use the value it returns. Using a function is also referred to as calling it. To call a function, you must qualify its name. To do this, type the name of the database in which it was created, followed by the period operator, followed by **dbo**, followed by the period operator, followed by the name of the function, and its parentheses. The formula to use is:

DatabaseName.dbo.*FunctionName*()

Because a function returns a value, you can use that value as you see fit. For example, you can use either **PRINT** or **SELECT** to display the function's value in a query window. Here is an example that calls the above GetFullName() function:

PRINT Exercise.dbo.GetFullName();

As an alternative, to call a function, in the Object Explorer, right-click its name, position the mouse on Script Function As, SELECT To, and click New Query Editor Window.

1. In the Object Explorer, right-click diograndeDB and click New Query

2. To execute the function we just created, execute the following statement:

PRINT diograndeDB.dbo.CalculateWeeklySalary();
GO

3. To specify a column name for the returned value of a function, change the function as follows and execute it:

```
SELECT diograndeDB.dbo.CalculateWeeklySalary() AS [Weekly Salary];
GO
```

4. To save the current window, on the toolbar, click the Save button

9.4.6 Function Maintenance

Because a function in Transact-SQL is treated as an object, it may need maintenance. Some of the actions you would take include renaming, modifying, or deleting a function.

9.4.7 Renaming a Function

If you create a function and execute it, it is stored in the Scalar-Valued Functions node with the name you gave it. If you want, you can change that name but keep the functionality of the function. To rename a function, in the Object Explorer, right-click it and click Rename. Type the desired new name and press Enter.

9.4.8 Deleting a Function

If you create a function and decide that you don't need it any more, you can delete it. To delete a function in the Object Explorer, locate the function in the Functions section, right-click it and click Delete. The Delete Object dialog box would come up. If you still want to delete the function, click OK; otherwise, click Cancel.

To programmatically delete a function:

i. In a query window, type DROP FUNCTION followed by the name of the function and execute the statement

ii. In the Object Explorer, right-click the name of the function, position the mouse on Script Function As, DROP To, and click New Query Editor Window

Here is an example:

1. In the Object Explorer, under the Scalar-Valued Functions node, right-click dbo.CalculateWeeklySalary and click Delete
2. In the Delete Object dialog box, click OK
3. Type DROP FUNCTION followed by the function name in the Query window and execute

9.4.9 Modifying a Function

As mentioned already, in the body of the function, you define what the function is supposed to take care of. As a minimum, a function can return a simple number, typed on the right side of the **RETURN** keyword. Here is an example:

```
CREATE FUNCTION Addition()
RETURNS int
BEGIN
    RETURN 1
END
```

To modify a Function, use ALTER FUNCTION functionName as the syntax.

You can also declare new variables in the body of the function to help in carrying the assignment. A variable declared in the body of a function is referred to as a local variable. Once such a variable has been declared, it can be used like any other variable. Here is an example to modify the above function:

```
ALTER FUNCTION Addition()
RETURNS int
BEGIN
    DECLARE @Number1 int
    SET @Number1 = 588
```

```
      RETURN @Number1 + 1450
END
```

In the Calculate query window, change the code as follows (notice the addition of the schema):

```
ALTER FUNCTION diograndeDB.CalculateWeeklySalary()
RETURNS Decimal(8, 2)
AS
BEGIN
        DECLARE
                @HourlySalary Decimal(8, 2),
                @WeeklyHours Real,
                @FullName varchar(100);
                SET @HourlySalary = 24.15;
                SET @WeeklyHours = 42.50;
        RETURN @HourlySalary * @WeeklyHours
END;
GO
```

Press F5 to execute the statement

To call the function, select and delete the code. Replace it with the following:
```
SELECT diograndeDB.CalculateWeeklySalary()
AS [Weekly Salary];
GO
```

Execute the code by pressing F5

9.4.10 Function Arguments

In order to carry its assignment, a function can be provided with some values. Put it another way, when you create a function, instead of, or in addition to, local variables, you may want the code that will call the function to provide the values needed to perform the assignment. For example, imagine you want to create a function that would generate employees email addresses when a user has entered a first and last name. At the time you are creating the function, you cannot know or predict the names of employees, including those who have not even been employed yet. In this case, you can write the whole function but provide one or more placeholders for values that would be supplied when the function is called.

Thus, an external value that is provided to a function is called a parameter. A function can also take more than one parameter. Therefore, when you create a function, you also decide whether your function would take one or more parameters and what those parameters, if any, would be.

9.4.11 A Parameterized Function

We have already seen that a function's name is also followed by parentheses. If the function doesn't use an external value, its parentheses can be left empty. If a function will use an external value, when you create the function, you must specify a name and the type of value of the parameters. The name of the parameter is created with the @ sign, like a variable as we saw in the previous lesson. Here is an example:
CREATE FUNCTION Addition(@Number1 Decimal(6,2))

When a function takes a parameter, in the body of the function, you can use the parameter as if you knew its value, as long as you respect the type of that value. Here is an example:
CREATE FUNCTION Addition(@Number1 Decimal(6,2))
RETURNS Decimal(6,2)
BEGIN

```
    RETURN @Number1 + 1450
END
```

i. Calling a Parameterized Function

When you call a function that takes one parameter, you must supply a value for that argument. To do this, type the value of the parameter in the parentheses of the function. Here is an example:

```
USE [diograndeDB]
GO


SELECT [dbo].[CalculateWeeklySalary](452);
GO
```

ii. A Function With Many Arguments

Instead of only one parameter, you can also create a function that takes more than one parameter. In this case, separate the arguments in the parentheses of the function with a comma. Here is an example:

```
CREATE FUNCTION Addition(@Number1 Decimal(6,2), @Number2 Decimal(6,2))
```

Once again, in the body of the function, you can use the parameters as if you already knew their value. You can also declare local variables and involve them with parameters as you see fit. Here is an example:

```
CREATE FUNCTION Addition(@Number1 Decimal(6,2),
                     @Number2 Decimal(6,2))
RETURNS Decimal(6,2)
BEGIN
    DECLARE @Result Decimal(6,2)
    SET @Result = @Number1 + @Number2
    RETURN @Result
END;
GO
```

When calling a function that takes more than one parameter, in the parentheses of the function, provide a value for each parameter, in the exact order they appear in the parentheses of the function. Here is an example:

PRINT dbo.Addition(1450, 228);

You can also pass the names of already declared and initialized variables. Here is an example that calls the above function:

```
DECLARE @Nbr1 Decimal(6,2),
     @Nbr2 Decimal(6,2)
SET @Nbr1 = 4268.55
SET @Nbr2 =26.83
SELECT @Nbr1 As First,
    @Nbr2 As Second,
    dbo.Addition(@Nbr1, @Nbr2) AS Result
```

Here is another example of function with many arguments:

```
CREATE FUNCTION dbo.CalculateWeeklySalary(@WeeklyHours Decimal(6,2),
                    @HourlySalary SmallMoney)
RETURNS Decimal(8, 2)
AS
BEGIN
   DECLARE @Weekly SmallMoney
   SELECT  @Weekly = @WeeklyHours * @HourlySalary

   RETURN @Weekly
END;
GO
```

After that, clear the query window, type and execute the codes below:

```
DECLARE @Hours Decimal(5,2),
     @Hourly SmallMoney
SELECT  @Hours = 42.50
SELECT  @Hourly = 18.62
SELECT  'Hermine Singh' As [Employee Name],
```

```
        @Hours As [Weekly Hours],
        @Hourly As [Hourly Salary],
        dbo.CalculateWeeklySalary(@Hours, @Hourly)
            AS [Weekly Salary];
GO
```

iii.   Default Arguments

When a function with argument is called, a value must be passed for each argument. In some cases, if the function is usually called with the same value for an argument, you can specify a default value for that argument. When such a function is called, you (or the user) can omit the value of the argument. To specify a default value for an argument, in the parentheses of the function, after the name and data type of the argument, type =, followed by the desired value. Here is an example of such a function with default value:

```
USE diograndeDB;
GO


CREATE FUNCTION CalculateTaxAmount(@Price money, @Rate decimal(6, 2) = 5.75)
RETURNS decimal(6, 2)
AS
BEGIN
    DECLARE @ResultVar money

    SELECT @ResultVar = @Price * @Rate / 100
    RETURN @ResultVar
END
GO
```

When calling a function that has a default value for an argument, you don't have to pass a value for that argument, though you can if you want. When calling the function, in the placeholder of the argument, type the DEFAULT keyword. Here are examples of calling the latest version of our function:

```
USE diograndeDB;
```

GO

PRINT dbo.CalculateTaxAmount(140.00, DEFAULT);

PRINT dbo.CalculateTaxAmount(195.95, 5.75);

PRINT dbo.CalculateTaxAmount(250.00, 7.55);

PRINT dbo.CalculateTaxAmount(125.95, default);

GO

9.5. BUILT-IN FUNCTION

To help you identify the functions you can use, they are categorized by their types and probably their usefulness.

Because of their complexities, some values can be easily recognized or fixed. For example, a date such as January 6, 1995 is constant and can never change. This type of value is referred to as deterministic because it is always the same. In the same way, a time value such as 5PM is constant and cannot change. There are other values that cannot be known in advance because they change based on some circumstances. For example, the starting date of the school year changes from one year to another but it always occurs. This means that, you know it will happen but you don't know the exact date. Such a value is referred to as non-deterministic.

To support determinism and non-determinism, Transact-SQL provides two broad categories of functions. A function that always returns the same or known value is referred to as deterministic. A function whose returned value may depend on a condition is referred to as non-deterministic.

9.5.1 Application of Built-In Functions

i. Casting a Value

In most cases, a value the user submits to your database is primarily considered a string. This is convenient if that is what you are expecting. If the value the user provides must be treated as something other than a string, for example, if the user provides a number, before using such a value, you should first convert it to the appropriate type, that is, from a string to the expected number datatype. To assist with conversion, you can use either the **CAST()** or the **CONVERT()** function. The syntax of the **CAST()** function is:

CAST(*Expression* AS *DataType*)

The *Expression* is the value that needs to be cast. The *DataType* factor is the type of value you want to convert the *Expression* to.

Here is an example of converting a string value to decimal.
DECLARE @StrSalary Varchar(10),
         @StrHours Varchar(6),
         @WeeklySalary Decimal(6,2)
SET @StrSalary = N'22.18';
SET @StrHours = N'38.50';
SET @WeeklySalary = CAST(@StrSalary As Decimal(6,2)) * CAST(@StrHours As Decimal(6,2));
SELECT @WeeklySalary;
GO

ii.   Converting a Value

Like **CAST()**, the **CONVERT()** function is used to convert a value. Unlike **CAST()**, **CONVERT** can be used to convert a value its original type into a non-similar type. For example, you can use **CONVERT** to cast a number into a string and vice-versa.
The syntax of the **CONVERT()** function is:

CONVERT(*DataType* (length) , *Expression* , style)

The first argument must be a known data type. If you are converting the value into a string (**varchar**, **nvarchar**, **char**, **nchar**) or a binary type, you should specify the number of allowed characters the dataTypes own in parentheses. As reviewed for the CAST() function, the *Expression* is the value that needs to be converted.

Here is an example that will convert values from decimal to varchar

```
-- Square Calculation
DECLARE @Side As Decimal(10,3),
        @Perimeter As Decimal(10,3),
        @Area As Decimal(10,3);
SET    @Side = 48.126;
SET    @Perimeter = @Side * 4;
SET    @Area = @Side * @Side;
PRINT 'Square Characteristics';
PRINT '----------------------';
PRINT 'Side     = N' + CONVERT(varchar(10), @Side, 10);
PRINT 'Perimeter = N' + CONVERT(varchar(10), @Perimeter, 10);
PRINT 'Area     = N' + CONVERT(varchar(10), @Area, 10);
GO
```

iii.   Transact-SQL Macros

A macro is an action that can be performed on a database or certain parts of a database or of a database server. A macro resembles a function without being exactly one. Transact-SQL provides various macros to assist you with managing databases and their objects.

Checking the Existence of a Record

One of the simplest operations a user can perform on a table consists of looking for a record. To do this, the user would open the table that contains the records and visually check them, looking for a piece of information, such as a student's last name. As the database developer, you too can look for a record and there are various techniques you can use. To assist you with this, Transact-SQL provides a macro called **EXISTS**. Its syntax is:

BIT EXISTS(SELECT *Something*)

This macro takes one argument. The argument must be a **SELECT** statement that would be used to get the value whose existence would be checked. For instance, I have said a lot about a system database names databases that contains a record of all databases stored on your server. You can use the EXISTS() macro to check the existence of a certain database. The formula you would use is:

IF EXISTS (
    SELECT name
    FROM sys.databases
    WHERE name = N'*DatabaseName*'
)

The *DatabaseName*, is the name of the database you want to search for.

String-Based Functions

The string is the most basic, the primary value that is presented to a database. This is because, any value, before being treated particularly, is firstly considered a string. In an application, there are various ways you can use to get a string. You can get it or provide it to a function as a constant string, that is, a string whose value you know certainly and that you pass to a function. You can also get a string that a user provides. Other functions also can produce or return a string.

To assist you with managing strings or performing operations on them, Transact-SQL provides various functions. The functions can divide in categories that include character-based, conversions, addition, sub-strings, etc.

The Length of a String

Some operations performed on strings require that you know the number of characters of a string. This is because some operations require a minimum number of characters and some other functions require that the string have at least one character. The number of characters of a string is also called the length of the string. To get the length of a string, you can use the **LEN()** function. Its syntax is:

int LEN(*String*)

This function takes one argument as the string to be considered. It returns the number of characters in the string.

Here is an example:

```
DECLARE @myGod varchar(120)
SET @myGod = N'My God is able, abundantly able...'
SELECT @myGod AS 'MY GOD'
SELECT LEN(@myGod) AS [Number of Characters];
GO
```

String Conversions: Converting From Integer to ASCII

As you may know already, a string is primarily one or a group of characters. These characters are ASCII values. If you have a string, to get the ASCII code of its leftmost character, you can use the **ASCII()** function. Its syntax is:

int ASCII(*String*)

This function takes as argument as string and returns the ASCII code of the first (the left) character of the string.

Here is an example:
DECLARE @ES varchar(100)
SET @ES = N'Alba Father'
SELECT @ES AS MyFather
SELECT ASCII(@ES) AS [In ASCII Format]

String Conversions: Converting From ASCII to Integer

If you have the ASCII code of a character and want to find its actual character, you can use the **CHAR()** function. Here is the syntax:
char CHAR(int *value*)
Here is an example:
DECLARE @ES int
SET @ES = 255
SELECT @ES AS MyFather
SELECT CHAR(@ES) AS [In ASCII Format];
GO

This function takes as argument a numeric value as an integer, the numeric value should not be more than 255. Upon conversion, the function returns the ASCII equivalent of that number.

String Conversions: Lowercase

As you may know already, a string can be made of uppercase, lowercase, and symbols that don't have a particular case. When you receive a string, if you want to convert all of its characters to lowercase, you can use the **LOWER()** function. Its syntax is:
varchar LOWER(String)

This function takes as argument a string. Any lowercase letter that is part of the string would not change. Any letter that is part of the string would be converted to lowercase. Any other character or symbol would be kept "as is". After conversion, the **LOWER()** function returns a new string.

Here is an example:

```
USE diograndeDB ;
GO


CREATE FUNCTION GetUsername
        (@FirstName varchar(40),
         @LastName varchar(40))
RETURNS varchar(80)
AS
BEGIN
        DECLARE @Username AS varchar(80);
        SELECT @Username = LOWER(@FirstName) + LOWER(@LastName);
        RETURN @Username;
END
GO
```

Execute the function and supply the values with last name: N' Eze' and first name: N'Dr. Mrs Udoka F' as the arguments.

Sub-Strings: The Starting Characters of a String

A sub-string is a section gotten from a string. The idea is to isolate one or a group of characters for any necessary reason. You can isolate the initial from someone's middle name. A left sub-string is one or a group of characters retrieved from the left side of a known string. To get the left sub-string of a string, you can use the LEFT() function. Its syntax is:

varchar LEFT(*String, NumberOfCharacters*)

This function takes two arguments. The first argument specifies the original string. The second argument specifies the number of characters from the most-left that will constitute the sub-string. After the operation, the **LEFT()** function returns a new string made of the left character + the *NumberOfCharacters* on its right from the *String*.

Here is an example:

```
USE diograndeDB;
GO

CREATE FUNCTION GetUsername
        (@FirstName varchar(40),
         @LastName varchar(40))
RETURNS varchar(50)
AS
BEGIN
        DECLARE @Username AS varchar(50);
        SELECT @Username = LOWER(LEFT(@FirstName, 1)) +
                        LEFT(LOWER(@LastName), 4)
        RETURN @Username;
END
GO
```

To execute the function, type this code and execute it.

```
SELECT diograndeDB.dbo.GetUsername(N'Vigor', N'Eze');
GO
```

Sub-Strings: The Ending Characters of a String

Instead of the starting characters of a string, you may want to create a string using the most-right characters of an existing string. To support this operation, Transact-SQL provides the **RIGHT()** function. Its syntax is:

varchar RIGHT(*String*, *NumberOfCharacters*)

This function takes two arguments. The first argument specifies the original string. The second argument specifies the number of characters from the most-right that will constitute the sub-string.

Here is an example:

```
USE diograndeDB ;
GO


CREATE FUNCTION Last4DigitsOfVISA(@visaCard varchar(16))
RETURNS char(4)
AS
BEGIN
        RETURN RIGHT(@visaCard, 4);
END
GO
```

Sub-Strings: Replacing Occurrences in a String

One of the most annoying situations you may encounter with a string is to deal with one that contains unexpected characters. This could be due to its formatting or any other reason. For example, if you request a telephone number from a user, there are various ways the string could be presented to you. Examples are 0000-000-0000, or 00000000000, or (0000) 000-0000. Every one of these formats is an acceptable Nigerian mobile number but if you involve that string in an operation, you could get an unpredictable result. One way you can solve this type of problem is to remove any undesired characters from the string. This operation can also consist of replacing some character(s) with other(s). To replace one character or a sub-string from a string, you can use the **REPLACE()** function. Here is the syntax:

varchar REPLACE(*String, FindString, ReplaceWith*)

or

binary REPLACE(*String, FindString, ReplaceWith*)

This function takes three arguments. The first is the string that will be used as reference. The second argument, *FindString*, is a character or a sub-string to look for in the *String* argument. If the *FindString* character or sub-string is found in the *String*, then it is replaced with the value of the last argument, *ReplaceWith*.

Here is an example:

```
USE diograndeDB ;
GO


CREATE FUNCTION Last11Digits(@Num varchar(13))
RETURNS char(11)
AS
BEGIN
        DECLARE @realNum As varchar(12);
        -- First remove empty spaces
        SET @realNum = REPLACE(@Num, N' ', N'');
        -- Now remove the "234" if they exist
        SET @realNum = REPLACE(@realNum, N'234', N'0');
        RETURN RIGHT(@realNum, 11);
END
GO
```

Execute the function using the code below:

```
Select dbo.Last11Digits(234809578457) AS 'CELLPHONE NUMBER';
GO
```

Arithmetic Functions

i. The Sign of a Number

In arithmetic, a number is considered as being negative (less than 0), null (equal to 0), or positive (higher than 0). When a number is negative, it must have a - sign to its left. If it is positive, it may display a + sign to its left, though it's optional. A number without the - or + signs to its left is considered positive, also referred to as unsigned. The symbol that determines whether a number is positive or negative is referred to as its sign. The sign is easily verifiable if you know the number already. In some cases, when a number is submitted to your application, before taking any action, you may need to get this piece of information, though your application is capable of handling this if properly developed. To find out if a value is positive, null, or negative, Transact-SQL provides the SIGN() function. Its syntax is:

SIGN(*Expression*)

This function takes as argument a number or an expression that can be evaluated to a number. The interpreter would then examine the number:

Here is an example, if the number is positive the interpreter will return 1:

DECLARE @Number As int;
SET @Number = 24.75;
SELECT SIGN(@Number) AS [Sign of the Number];
GO

Here is an example, if the number is null the interpreter will return 0:

DECLARE @Number As int;
SET @Number = 0;
SELECT SIGN(@Number) AS [Sign of Number];
GO

Here is an example, if the number is negative the interpreter will return -1
DECLARE @Number As int;

```sql
SET @Number = -57.05;
SELECT SIGN(@Number) AS [Sign of -57.05];
GO
```

Based on this, you can use the SIGN() function to find out whether a value is negative, null, or positive: simply pass the value (or a variable) to SIGN() and use a logical operator to check its sign. Here is an example:

```sql
-- Square Calculation
DECLARE @Side As Decimal(10,3),
        @Perimeter As Decimal(10,3),
        @Area As Decimal(10,3);
SET    @Side = 48.126;
SET    @Perimeter = @Side * 4;
SET    @Area = @Side * @Side;
IF SIGN(@Side) > 0
   BEGIN
       PRINT 'Square Characteristics';
       PRINT '----------------------';
       PRINT 'Side     = ' + CONVERT(varchar(10), @Side, 10);
       PRINT 'Perimeter = ' + CONVERT(varchar(10), @Perimeter, 10);
       PRINT 'Area     = ' + CONVERT(varchar(10), @Area, 10);
   END;
ELSE
       PRINT 'You must provide a positive value';
GO
```

Execute the code and change the value of side to a negative number and notice that the interpreter acts differently in response to the result of the SIGN() function.

ii. The Absolute Value of a Number

The decimal numeric system counts from minus infinity to infinity. This means that numbers are usually negative or positive, depending on their position from 0, which is considered as neutral. In some operations, the number considered will need to be only positive even if it is provided in a negative format. The absolute value of a number x is x if the number is (already) positive. If the number is negative, its absolute value is its positive equivalent. For example, the absolute value of 12 is 12, while the absolute value of –12 is 12. To get the absolute value of a number, you can use the ABS() function. Its syntax is:

ABS(*Expression*)

This function takes an expression or a number as argument and returns its absolute value. Here is an example:

```
DECLARE @NumberOfStudents int;
SET @NumberOfStudents = -123;
SELECT ABS(@NumberOfStudents) AS [Number of Students];
GO
```

iii. The Ceiling of a Number

Consider a decimal value such as 12.155. This number is between the integer 12 and 13

In the same way, consider a number such as –24.06. As this number is negative, it is between –24 and –25, with –24 being greater. In algebra, the ceiling of a number is the closest integer that is greater than or higher than the number considered. In the first case, the ceiling of 12.155 is 13 because 13 is the closest integer greater than or equal to 12.155. The ceiling of –24.06 is –24. To get the ceiling of a number, Transact-SQL provides the **CEILING()** function. Its syntax is:

CEILING(*Expression*)

This function takes as argument a number or an expression that can evaluate to a number. After the conversion, if the function succeeds, it returns a double-precision number that is greater than or equal to *Expression*. Here is an example:

```
DECLARE @Num1 As Numeric(6, 2),
            @Num2 As Numeric(6, 2)
SET @Num1 = 12.523;
SET @Num2 = -24.96;

SELECT CEILING(@Num1) AS [Ceiling of 12.155],
    CEILING(@Num2) AS [Ceiling of –24.06];
GO
```

Here is another example, a way of displaying the above results:

```
DECLARE @Num1 As Numeric(6, 2),
            @Num2 As Numeric(6, 2)
SET @Num1 = 12.596;
SET @Num2 = -24.96;

PRINT 'The ceiling of 12.155 is ' +
        CONVERT(varchar(10), CEILING(@Num1));
PRINT 'The ceiling of –24.06 is ' +
    CONVERT(varchar(10), CEILING(@Num2));
GO
```

iv.   The Floor of a Number

Consider two decimal numbers such as 128.44 and -36.72. The number 128.44 is between 128 and 129 with 128 being the lower. The number –36.72 is between –37 and –36 with –37 being the lower. The lowest but closest integer value of a number is referred to as its floor, so simply put that *floor* is opposite of *ceiling*. Based on this, the floor of 128.44 is 128. The floor of –36.72 is –37. To support finding the floor of a number, Transact-SQL provides the FLOOR() function. Its syntax is:

FLOOR (*Expression*)

The FLOOR() function takes as argument a numeric value or an expression that can be evaluated to a number. If the function succeeds during its conversion, it produces the integer that is the floor of the argument. Here is an example:

```
DECLARE @Number1 As Numeric(6, 2),
       @Number2 As Numeric(6, 2);
SET @Number1 = 128.84;
SET @Number2 = -36.72;

SELECT FLOOR(@Number1) AS [Floor of 128.44],
    FLOOR(@Number2) AS [Floor of –36.72];
GO
```

v. The Exponent of a Number

To calculate the exponential value of a number, Transact-SQL provides the **EXP()** function. Its syntax is:

```
EXP(Expression)
```

This function takes one argument as a number or an expression that can be evaluated to a number. Here is an example:

```
DECLARE @Number As Numeric(6, 2);
SET @Number = 6.48;

SELECT EXP(@Number) AS [Exponent of 6.48];
GO
```

vi. The Power of a Number

The power of a number is the value of that number when raised to another number. This is done using the following formula:

$$\text{ReturnValue} = x^y$$

To support finding the power of a number, Transact-SQL provides the **POWER()** function. Its syntax is:

```
POWER(x, y)
```

This function takes two required arguments. The first argument, x, is used as the base number to be evaluated. The second argument, y, also called the exponent, will raise x to this value. Here is an example:

```
DECLARE @x As Decimal(6, 2),
        @y As Decimal(6, 2);
SET @x = 20.38;
SET @y = 2.12;
SELECT POWER(@x, @y) AS [Power of 20.38 raised to 4.12];
GO
```

vii.   The Natural Logarithm of a Number

To assist with finding the natural logarithm of a number, Transact-SQL provides the LOG() function. Its syntax is:

LOG(*Expression*)

This function takes one argument as a number or an expression that can evaluate to a number. After the calculation, it returns the natural logarithm of the argument. Here is an example:

```
DECLARE @Number As Decimal(6, 2);
SET @Number = 48.16;

SELECT LOG(@Number) AS [Natural Logarithm of 48.16];
GO
```

viii.   The Base-10 Logarithm of a Number

To calculate the base 10 logarithm of a number, Transact-SQL provides the LOG10() function. Its syntax is:

LOG10(*Expression*)

The number to be evaluated is passed as the argument X. The function returns the logarithm on base 10 using the formula:

y = log10x which is equivalent to x = 10^y

Here is an example:
```
DECLARE @Number As Decimal(6, 2);
SET @Number = 48.16;

SELECT LOG10(@Number) AS [Base-10 Logarithm of 48.16];
GO
```

ix.   The Square Root

To support the calculation of a square root, Transact-SQL provides the **SQRT()** function. Its syntax is:
```
SQRT(Expression)
```

This function takes one argument as a positive decimal number. If the number is positive then the statement will execute else you would receive an error; after the calculation the function returns the square root of x. Here is an example:
```
DECLARE @Number As Decimal(6, 2);
SET @Number = 48.16;

SELECT SQRT(@Number) AS [The square root of 48.16 is];
GO
```

In this case, you can use a control statement hence, *sign* function to find out whether the *Expression* is positive. Here is an example:
```
DECLARE @Num As Decimal(6, 2);
SET @Num = 258.4062;

IF SIGN(@Number) > 0
    PRINT 'The square root of 258.4062 is ' +
        CONVERT(varchar(12), SQRT(@Num));
ELSE
        PRINT 'You must provide a positive number';
GO
```

Measure-Based Functions

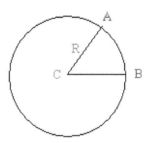

A circle is a series of distinct opposite points positioned each at an exact same distance from another point referred to as the center. The distance from the center C to one of these equidistant points is called the radius, R. The line that connects all of the points that are equidistant to the center is called the circumference of the circle. The diameter is the distance between two points of the circumference to the center. In other words, a diameter is double the radius. To manage the measurements and other related operations, the circumference is divided into 360 portions. Each of these portions is called a degree. The unit used to represent the degree is the degree, written as °. Therefore, a circle contains 360 degrees, that is 360°. The measurement of two points A and D of the circumference could have 15 portions of the circumference. In this case, this measurement would be represents as 15°. The distance between two equidistant points A and B is a round shape geometrically defined as an arc. An angle is the ratio of the distance between two points A and B of the circumference divided by the radius R. This can be written as:

$$\theta = \frac{AB}{R}$$

i.   **PI**

The letter π, also written as PI, is a number used in various mathematical calculations. Its approximate value is 3.1415926535897932. The calculator of Microsoft Windows represents it as 3.14159265358979323846264338332795. To get the value of PI, Transact-SQL provides the PI() function. Its syntax is simply:

PI()

ii.   Radians

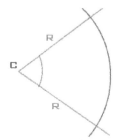

An angle is the ratio of an arc over the radius. Because an angle is a ratio and not a "physical" measurement, which means an angle is not a dimension, it is independent of the size of a circle. Obviously the angle represents the number of portions covered by three points. A better unit used to measure an angle is the radian or rad. If you know the value of an angle in degrees and you want to get the radians, Transact-SQL provides the RADIANS() function. Its syntax is:

RADIANS(*Expression*)

This function takes as argument a value in degrees. If it succeeds in its calculation, it returns the radians value. A cycle is a measurement of the rotation around the circle. Since the rotation is not necessarily complete, depending on the scenario, a measure is made based on the angle that was covered during the rotation. A cycle could cover part of the circle, in which case the rotation would not have been completed. A cycle could also cover the whole 360° of the circle and continue thereafter. A cycle is equivalent to the radian divided by 2 * PI.

iii.   Degrees

If you know the radians but want to get the degrees of an angle, you can use the DEGREES() function. Its syntax is:

DEGREES(*Expression*)

This function takes as argument a value in radians. If it succeeds, it returns the equivalent value in degrees.

Trigonometric Functions

i.   The Cosine of a Value

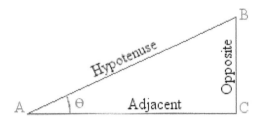

Consider AB the length of A to B, also referred to as the hypotenuse. Also consider AC the length of A to C which is the side adjacent to point A. The cosine of the angle at point A is the ratio AC/AB. That is, the ratio of the adjacent length, AC, over the length of the hypotenuse, AB:

$$\cos\theta = \frac{AC}{AB} = \frac{Adjacent}{Hypotenuse}$$

The returned value, the ratio, is a double-precision number between –1 and 1. To get the cosine of an angle, you can call the **COS()** function. Its syntax is:

COS(*Expression*)

The angle to be considered is passed as the argument to this function. The function then calculates and returns its cosine. Here is an example:

DECLARE @Angle As Decimal(6, 3);

SET @Angle = 270;

SELECT COS(@Angle) AS [Cosine of 270];

GO

ii.   The Sine of a Value

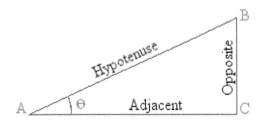

Consider AB the length of A to B, also called the hypotenuse to point A. Also consider CB the length of C to B, which is the opposite side to point A. The sine represents the ratio of CB/AB; that is, the ratio of the opposite side, CB over the hypotenuse AB. To get the sine of an angle, you can use the **SIN()** function whose syntax is:

SIN(*Expression*)

The angle to be considered is passed as the argument. After its calculation, the function returns the sine of the angle between −1 and 1. Here is an example:

DECLARE @Angle As Decimal(6, 3);

SET @Angle = 270;

SELECT SIN(@Angle) AS [Sine of 270];

GO

iii.   The Tangent of a Value

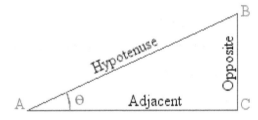

In geometry, consider AC the length of A to C. Also consider BC the length of B to C. The tangent is the result of BC/AC, that is, the ratio of BC over AC. To get the tangent of an angle, you can use the **TAN()** function of Transact-SQL. Its syntax is:

TAN(Expression)

Here is an example:

DECLARE @Angle As Decimal(6, 3);

SET @Angle = 270;

SELECT TAN(@Angle) AS [Tangent of 270];

GO

Date and Time Based Functions

Date and time values are highly used in database applications. They involve sales, time sheets, taxes, overtime work, etc. Based on this usefulness, their operations are supported by various libraries you will be using when developing your application. Without being the most elaborate on this issue, Transact-SQL provides its own level of support for date and time values. Before using a date or a time value in a calculation, remember that you must first get it one way or another. You can define a date or a time constant in your application. An example would be '1992/10/28'. You can declare a *datetime2* variable and initialize it as you see fit. You may get a date or a time from another function. As the last alternative, you may get a date or time from another application or from a user. Once you have an appropriate date, you can use it.

i.   The Current System Date and/or Time

One of the ways you can assist the user with date and time is to get the current date or the current time of the server or PC. For example, if you create a time sheet, when the user starts using it, it would be convenient to fill part of the time sheet with such predictable values. To get the current date and the current time of the computer that a user is using, you can use the **GETDATE()** function of Transact-SQL. Its syntax is:
GETDATE()

This function simply returns the current date and time of the operating system.

ii.   Date/Time Addition

One of the primary operations you may want to perform on a date or a time value would consist of adding a value to it. To support this operation, Transact-SQL provides the **DATEADD()** function. Its syntax is:
DATEADD(*TypeOfValue, ValueToAdd, DateOrTimeReferenced*)

The third argument to this function is the value of a date or a time on which the operation will be performed. It can be a constant value in the form of 'year/month/day' for a date or 'hour:minutes AM/PM' for a time. The second argument is the value that will be added. It should be a constant integer, such as 8, or a floating point value, such as 4.06.

When calling this function, you must first specify the type of value that you want to add. This type is passed as the first argument. It is used as follows:

- If you want to add a number of years to a date, specify the *TypeOfValue* as **Year** or **yy**, or **yyyy.** Here is an example:

```
DECLARE @Anniversary As datetime2;
SET @Anniversary = N'02/10/2002';
SELECT DATEADD(yy, 4, @Anniversary) AS Anniversary;
GO
```

- If you want to add a number of quarters of a year to a date, specify the *TypeOfValue* as **Quarter**, q or **qq**. Here is an example:

```
DECLARE @NextVacation As datetime2;
SET @NextVacation = N'02/10/2002';
SELECT DATEADD(Quarter, 2, @NextVacation) AS [Next Vacation];
GO
```

- If you want to add a number of months to a date, specify the *TypeOfValue* as **Month** or **m**, or **mm**. The following example adds 5 months to its date:

```
DECLARE @SchoolStart As datetime2;
SET @SchoolStart = N'12/05/2004';
SELECT DATEADD(m, 5, @SchoolStart) AS [School Start];
GO
```

In the same way, you can add values as follows:

Type of	Abbreviation	As a result

Value		
Year	yy	A number of years will be added to the date value
	yyyy	
quarter	q	A number of quarters of a year will be added to the date value
	qq	
Month	m	A number of months will be added to the date value
	mm	
dayofyear	y	A number of days of a year will be added to the date value
	dy	
Day	d	A number of days will be added to the date value
	dd	
Week	wk	A number of weeks will be added to the date value
	ww	
Hour	hh	A number of hours will be added to the time value
minute	n	A number of minutes will be added to the time value
	mi	
second	s	A number of seconds will be added to the time value
	ss	
millisecond	ms	A number of milliseconds will be added to the time value

iii.   Date/Time Subtraction

Another regular operation performed on a date or a time value consists of getting the number of units that has elapsed in the range of two dates or two time values. To support this operation, Transact-SQL provides the **DATEDIFF()** function. Its syntax is:

DATEDIFF(*TypeOfValue, StartDate, EndDate*)

The starting time of the range is to be considered. The third argument is the end or last date or time of the considered range. You use the first argument to specify the type of value you want the function to produce. This argument uses the same value as those of the **DATEADD()** function.

Here is an example that calculates the number of years that an employee has been with the company:

```
DECLARE @DateEmployed As datetime2,
     @CurrentDate As datetime2;
SET @DateEmployed = N'04/10/1996';
SET @CurrentDate = GETDATE();
SELECT DATEDIFF(YY, @DateEmployed, @CurrentDate)
     AS [Current Experience];
GO
```

9.6   VIEWS

A *view* is the saved text of a SQL SELECT statement that may be referenced as a data source within a query; similar to how a subquery can be used as a data source. Or simply put that view is a virtual table that represents the data in one or more tables in an alternative way. A view cannot be executed by itself; it must be used within a query. This is not an accurate description because views do not store any data. Like any other SQL query, views merely refer to the data stored in tables. With this in mind, it is important to fully understand how views work, the pros and cons of using views, and the best place to use views when designing your database.

Why Use Views?

Because *"information . . . must be . . . made readily available in a usable format for daily operations and analysis by individuals, groups, and processes . . ."*; presenting data in a more useable format is precisely what views can do best. Based on the premise that views are best used to increase data integrity and ease of writing ad hoc queries, and not as a central part of a production application, here are some ideas for building ad hoc query views:

i. Use views to denormalize or flatten complex joins and hide any surrogate keys used to link data within the database schema. Thus, a well-designed view invites the user to get right to the data of interest.

ii. Save complex aggregate queries as views. Even power users will appreciate a well-crafted aggregate query saved as a view. Use aliases to change cryptic column names to recognizable column names. Just as the SQL SELECT statement can use column or table aliases to modify the names of columns or tables, these features may be used within a view to present a more readable record set to the user.

iii. Include only the columns of interest to the user. When columns that do not concern users are left out of the view, the view is easier to query. The columns that are included in the view are called *projected columns*, meaning they project only the selected data from the entire underlying table(s).

iv. Plan generic, dynamic views that will have long, useful lives. Single-purpose views quickly become obsolete and clutter the database. Build the view with the intention that it will be used with a WHERE clause to select a subset of data. The view should return all the rows if the user does not supply a WHERE restriction. For example, considering a calendar that has a lot of events, the vEventList view returns all the events; the user should use a WHERE clause to select the local events, or the events in a certain month.

v. If a view is needed to return a restricted set of data, such as the next month's events, then the view should calculate the next month so that it will continue to function over time.

vi. If the view selects data from a range, then consider writing it as a user-defined function which can accept parameters.

vii. Consolidate data from across a complex environment. Queries that need to collect data from across multiple servers are simplified by encapsulating the union of data from multiple servers within a view. This is one case where basing several reports, and even stored procedures, on a view improves the stability, integrity, and maintainability of the system.

The goal when developing views is two types. They are to enable users to get to the data easily and to protect the data from the users. By building views that provide the correct data, you are preventing erroneous or inaccurate queries and misinterpretation.

9.6.1 The Basic View

Using SQL Server Management Studio, views may be created, modified, executed, and included within other queries, using either the Query Designer or the DDL code within the Query Editor.

Creating views using the Query Designer

Because a view is nothing more than a saved SQL SELECT statement, the creation of a view begins with a working SELECT statement. Any SQL SELECT statement, as long as it is a valid SQL SELECT statement (with a few minor exceptions), can be cut and pasted from nearly any other tool into a view. Within SQL Server Management Studio, views are listed in their own node under each database.

The New View command in the context menu launches the Query Designer in a mode that creates views, as shown in Figure 14-1.

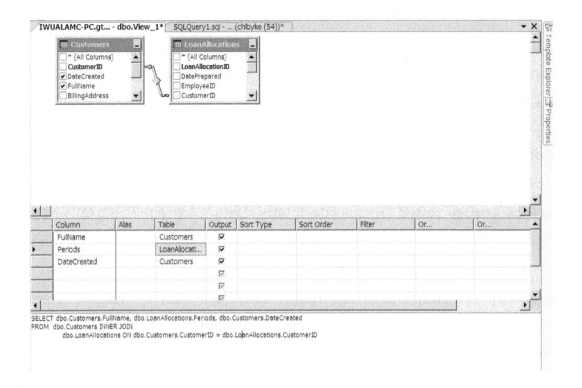

The View Designer mode functions within Management Studio's Query Designer, which is also used to query tables. The actual SQL code for the view is displayed or edited in the SQL pane at the bottom. Columns may be added to the view by using the Diagram pane, the Grid pane, or the SQL pane. The Add Table feature, available in the context menu or toolbar, can be used to add tables, other views, synonyms, and table-valued functions. Tables or other views can be added to the new view by dragging them to the Diagram pane from the Object Explorer or using the Add Table context menu option.

There is a toolbar button and a context menu item to add a derived table to the view, but all it does is slightly modify the *FROM* clause to create a placeholder for the subquery. The SQL code for the subquery is then manually entered in the SQL pane. The Verify SQL Syntax button in the toolbar verifies only the SQL syntax; it does not verify the names of tables, views, or columns in the SQL SELECT statement.

To test the view's SQL SELECT statement within Query Designer, use the Execute SQL button or press F5. This will run the SELECT statement by itself, without creating the view. The Save toolbar button actually runs the script to create the view in the database.

Note that the view must be a valid, error-free SQL SELECT statement in order to be saved. Once the view is created, several tasks may be performed on the view using Object Explorer's view context menu:

i. **Redesign the view:** Opens the Query Designer tool with the view's SELECT statement.

ii. **Select top n rows:** Opens the Query Editor with a SELECT statement referencing the view. The number of rows selected can be modified in Management Studio's options.

iii. **Edit top n rows:** Opens the Query Designer with a SELECT statement referencing the view, with only the results pane visible, and executes the view.

iv. **Script the view:** Management Studio can script the DDL statements to CREATE, ALTER, or DROP the view, as well as sample DML statements referencing the view.

v. **View dependencies:** This option can be very important because views, by definition, reference other data sources, and are often referenced themselves.

vi. **Full-text indexes:** A full-text index can be created and managed based on data selected by the view.

vii. **Policies:** Apply and manage policy-based management policies for the view.

viii. **Rename/Delete the view:** The view may also be renamed or dropped by selecting it and pressing Rename or Delete, respectively.

ix. **Properties:** Opens the properties dialog with pages for security permissions and extended properties.

x. **Double-clicking the view opens its subnodes**: columns, triggers (instead of tasks), indexes (indexed views), and statistics.

9.6.2 Managing Views

Views may be managed using the Query window by executing SQL scripts with the *data definition language (DDL)* commands; which includes: CREATE, ALTER, and DROP. The basic syntax for creating a view is as follows:

CREATE VIEW schemaname.ViewName [(Column aliases)]
AS
SQL Select Statement;
GO

For example, to create the view vEmployeeList in code, the following command would be executed in a query window:

USE gtBankLoan;
GO

CREATE VIEW dbo.vEmployeeList
AS
SELECT P.BusinessEntityID, P.Title, P.LastName,
P.FirstName, E.JobTitle
FROM AdventureWorks2008.Person.Person P
INNER JOIN AdventureWorks2008.HumanResources.Employee E
ON P.BusinessEntityID = E.BusinessEntityID;
GO

As with creating any object, the create command must be the only command in the batch. The view name must be unique in the database. Attempting to create a view with a name shared by any other object or reserved words of SQL Server interpreter will generate an error.

9.6.3 Executing views

Technically, a view by itself cannot be executed. A view can only patiently wait to be referenced by a SQL query.

A query (SELECT, INSERT, UPDATE, DELETE, or MERGE) can include the view as a data source, and that query can be executed. Thus, one can say that a view is useful only as a data source within a query. The following SELECT statement references the vEmployeeList view:

```
USE gtBankLoan;
GO


SELECT BusinessEntityID, LastName, FirstName, JobTitle
FROM dbo.vEmployeeList;
GO
```

When the query that references a view is submitted to SQL Server, the query parser picks the query apart and replaces the name of the view with the view's select statement. When views are referenced from ad hoc queries, a WHERE condition is typically added to filter the data from the view.

Here is an example:

```
SELECT BusinessEntityID, LastName, FirstName, JobTitle
FROM dbo.vEmployeeList
WHERE JobTitle = 'Production Technician - WC50';
GO
```

9.6.4 Altering and dropping a view

It's likely that the view's SELECT statement will need to be changed at some point in time. Once a view has been created, the SQL SELECT statement may be easily edited by using the ALTER command. Altering the view changes the saved SELECT statement while keeping any properties and security settings in place. This is preferable to dropping the view, losing all the security settings and properties, and then recreating the view. The ALTER command supplies a new SQL SELECT statement for the view. This is the syntax:

ALTER SchemaName.ViewName

AS

SQL Select Statement;

GO

Management Studio can automatically generate an ALTER statement from an existing view. In Object Explorer, select the view and then choose Script View as, Alter to, New Query Editor Window from the pop-out menu. If the view is no longer needed, it can be completely erased from the database using the DROP command. The syntax is:

DROP VIEW SchemaName.ViewName;

GO

Within a script that is intended to be executed several times, the following code can drop and recreate the view:

USE databaseName;

GO

IF OBJECT_ID('vEmployeeList') IS NOT NULL

DROP VIEW dbo.vEmployeeList

GO

CREATE VIEW *SchemaName.ViewName*

AS

SQL Select Statement;

GO

Just to reiterate, views do not contain any data, so there is no danger that dropping a view will cause any data loss. However, applications, reports, and other objects might depend on the view, and dropping the view might break links which can do some harm to the users using the aforementioned. For more about viewing dependencies within SQL Server, see the section "Nesting Views" later in this chapter. Below is diagram showing how views work.

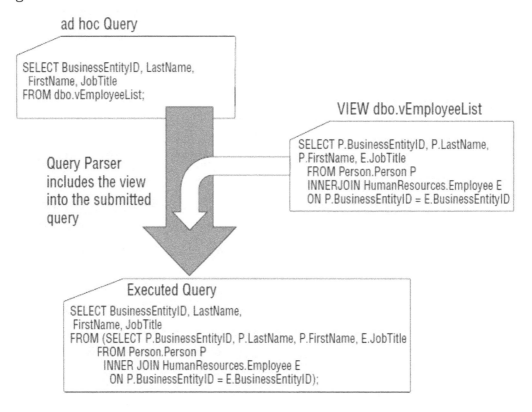

9.6.5   More on Views

The basic mechanics of creating a view and selecting data from the view are pretty straightforward, but views have their own particular nuances — topics such as sorting data, updating data through a view, and nesting views several levels deep. This section examines views from a broader point of view.

i. Column aliases

The column aliases option is rarely used. With syntax similar to the column list for a common table expression, the view's column list renames every output column just as if every column had those alias names in the SELECT statement. The view's column list names override any column names or column aliases in the view's SELECT statement.

The following query alters the vEmployeeList view so that the result columns become ID, Last, First, and Job.

```
USE gtBankLoan;
GO

ALTER VIEW dbo.vEmployeeList (ID, Last, First, Job)
AS
SELECT P.BusinessEntityID,
P.LastName, P.FirstName, E.JobTitle
FROM AdventureWorks2008.Person.Person P
INNER JOIN AdventureWorks2008.HumanResources.Employee E
ON P.BusinessEntityID = E.BusinessEntityID;
GO

SELECT *
FROM dbo.vEmployeeList;
GO
```

ii. Order by and views

Views serve as data sources for other queries and do not support sorting the data within the view. To sort data from a view, include the ORDER BY clause in the query referencing the view. For example, the following code selects data from the vEmployeeList view and orders it by LastName, FirstName. The ORDER BY clause is not a part of vEmployeeList , but it is applied to the view by the executing SQL statement.

Here is what I mean:

```
USE gtBankLoan;
GO


SELECT *
FROM dbo.vEmployeeList
ORDER BY [Last], [First];
GO
```

iii. View restrictions

Although a view can contain nearly any valid SELECT statement, a few basic restrictions still apples. They are:

a. Views may not include the SELECT INTO option that creates a new table from the selected columns. SELECT INTO fails if the table already exists and it does not return any data, so it is not a valid view:

b. SELECT * INTO *Table*

c. Views may not refer to a temporary table (one with a # in the name) or a table variable (preceded with an @), because these types of tables are very transient.

d. The OPTION clause, which gives table or query hints for the entire query, is not allowed.

e. The tablesample table option, which can randomly select pages, is not allowed within a view.

f. Views may not contain compute or compute by columns. Instead, use standard aggregate functions and groupings. (Compute and compute by are obsolete and are included for backward compatibility only, so beware.)

iv. Nesting views

Because a view is nothing more than a SQL SELECT statement, and a SQL SELECT statement may reference any data source, views may reference other views. Views referred to by other views are sometimes called *nested views*.

The following view uses vEmployeeList and adds a WHERE clause to restrict the results to the smartest and best-looking employees.

Here is what I mean:

USE gtBankLoan;

GO

CREATE VIEW dbo.vEmployeeListDBA

AS

SELECT BusinessEntityID, LastName, FirstName, JobTitle

FROM dbo.vEmployeeList AS vE

WHERE JobTitle = 'Database Administrator';

GO

In this example, the view vEmployeeList is nested within vEmployeeListDBA. Another way to express the relationship is to say that vEmployeeListDBA depends on vEmployeeList. Dependencies from other objects in SQL Server can be easily viewed using Object Explorer's view context menu, View Dependencies. The dependency chain for nested views is easily seen in the Object Dependencies dialog. Here, the vEmployeeListDBA includes the nested view vEmployeeList, which in turn is based on the Employee table, and so on.

From code dependencies may be seen using the sys.dm_sql_referencing_entities()function. For example, the following query would indicate whether any other SQL Server object references vEmployeeList.

SELECT *

FROM sys.dm_sql_referencing_entities

('dbo.vEmployeeList', 'Object');

GO

v. Updating through views

One of the main complaints concerning views is that unless the view is a simple single table view, it is difficult to update the underlying data through the view. While the SQL Server Query Optimizer can update through some complex views, there are some hard-and-fast limitations. Any of the following factors may cause a view to be un-updatable:

a. Only one table may be updated. If the view includes joins, then the UPDATE statement that references the view must change columns in only one table.

b. Aggregate functions or GROUP BYs in the view will cause the view to be un-updatable. SQL Server could not possibly determine which of the summarized rows should be updated.

c. If the view includes a subquery as a derived table, and any column(s) from the subquery are exposed as output from the view, then the view is not updateable. However, aggregates are permitted in a subquery that is being used as a derived table, so long as any columns from the aggregate subquery are not in the output columns of the view.

d. If the view includes the WITH CHECK OPTION, the INSERT or UPDATE operation must meet the view's WHERE-clause conditions.

vi. Views and performance

Views have an undeserved reputation for poor performance. I think the reason for this belief is based on several factors. They are:

a. Views are often used by power users who submit ad hoc SQL code. In earlier versions of SQL Server, ad hoc SQL did not perform as well as stored procedures.

b. Views are often used by power users who use front-end UI applications to select and browse data. Some of these applications opened the connections and held locks, causing all sorts of performance problems.

c. Views are often used by power users who find useful data in a view and then build new views on top of views. These nested views might contain a horribly complex view several layers deep that kills performance, while the top-level view appears to be a simple, easy view. Let me put the myth to rest: Well-written views will perform well. The reason to limit views to ad hoc queries and reports is not for performance, but for extensibility and control.

vii. **Locking Down the View**

Views are designed to control access to data. There are several options that protect the data or the view. The WITH CHECK OPTION causes the WHERE clause of the view to check the data being inserted or updated through the view in addition to the data being retrieved. In the sense that, it makes the WHERE clause a two-way restriction.

The WITH CHECK OPTION is useful when the view should limit inserts and updates with the same restrictions applied to the WHERE clause.

Unchecked data

To understand the need for the WITH CHECK OPTION, it is important to first understand how views work without the CHECK OPTION. The following view will generate a list of pilgrims to the Holy Land.

```
USE pilgrimsDB;
GO
CREATE VIEW dbo.vPilgrimsTour
AS
```

```
SELECT TourName, tourID
FROM dbo.Tour
WHERE tourID = 2;
GO
```

```
SELECT TourName, tourID FROM dbo.vCapeHatterasTour;
GO
```

If a record about a tour is inserts it through the view without the CHECK OPTION, the INSERT is permitted. Here is an example:

```
INSERT dbo. vPilgrimsTour (TourName, tourID)
VALUES (N'Iwuala Chibueze', 1);
GO
```

The INSERT worked, and the new row is in the database, but the row is not visible through the view because the WHERE clause of the view filters out the inserted row. This phenomenon is called *disappearing rows*, because when you select records from the view it will not appear.

Here is what I mean:

```
SELECT TourName, tourID FROM dbo.vPilgrimsTour;
GO
```

If the purpose of the view were to give users who travelled to Israel access to their tours alone, then the view failed. The WITH CHECK OPTION would have prevented this fault.

Protecting the data

A view with a WHERE clause and the WITH CHECK OPTION can protect the data from undesired inserts and updates. The following code will back out the previous INSERT and redo the same scenario, but this time the view will include the WITH CHECK OPTION.

Here is an example:

```
DELETE dbo.vPilgrimsTour
WHERE TourName = 'Iwuala Chibueze';
GO
```

```
ALTER VIEW dbo. vPilgrimsTour
AS
SELECT TourName, tourID
FROM dbo.Tour
WHERE tourID = 2
WITH CHECK OPTION;
GO

INSERT dbo.vPilgrimsTour (TourName, tourID)
VALUES ('IWUALA M. C', 1);
GO
```

The attempted insert or update failed because the target view either specifies WITH CHECK OPTION or spans a view that specifies WITH CHECK OPTION and one or more rows resulting from the operation did not qualify under the CHECK OPTION constraint. The statement has been terminated. This time the INSERT failed and the error message attributed the cause to the WITH CHECK OPTION in the view, which is exactly the effect desired. Some developers employ views and the WITH CHECK OPTION as a way of providing row-level security — a technique called *horizontally positioned views*. As in the Pilgrim's view example, they create a view for each department, or each sales branch, and then give users security permission to the view that pertains to them. While this method does achieve row-level security, it also has a high maintenance cost.

viii. Protecting the view

Three options protect views from data schema changes and prying eyes. These options are simply added to the CREATE command and applied to the view, in much the same way that the WITH CHECK OPTION is applied. Database code is fragile and tends to break when the underlying data structure changes. Because views are nothing more than stored SQL SELECT queries, changes to the referenced tables may break the view. Creating a view with schema binding locks the underlying tables to the view and prevents changes. Here is an example:

```
CREATE TABLE dbo.Test (
[Name] NVARCHAR(50));
GO


CREATE VIEW dbo.vTest
WITH SCHEMABINDING
AS
SELECT [Name] FROM dbo.Test;
GO


ALTER TABLE Test
ALTER COLUMN [Name] NVARCHAR(100);
GO
```

Some restrictions apply to the creation of schema-bound views. The SELECT statement must include the schema name for any referenced objects.

ix.   Encrypting the view' s select statement

The WITH ENCRYPTION option is another security feature. When views or stored procedures are created, the text can be retrieved through the sys.sql_modules and sys.syscomments system views. The code is therefore available for viewing. The view may contain a WHERE condition that should be kept confidential, or there may be some other reason for encrypting the code. The WITH ENCRYPTION option encrypts the code in the system tables, hides them from sys.sql_modules and sys.syscomments, and prevents anyone from viewing the original code.

In the following code example, the text of the view is inspected within sys.sql_modules, the view is encrypted, and sys.sql_modules is again inspected (as expected, the SELECT statement for the view is then no longer readable).

```
SELECT definition
FROM sys.sql_modules
WHERE object_id = OBJECT_ID(N'dbo.vTest');
GO
```

The following ALTER command rebuilds the view WITH ENCRYPTION.

```
ALTER VIEW vTest
WITH ENCRYPTION
AS
SELECT [Name] FROM dbo.Test;
GO
```

Be careful with this option. Once the code is encrypted, Management Studio can no longer produce a script to alter the view, and will instead generate this message:

```
/****** Encrypted object is not transferable, and script cannot be generated. ******/
```

In addition, be aware that the encryption affects replication. An encrypted view will not be published. More so, type and execute this code:

```
SELECT definition
FROM sys.sql_modules
WHERE object_id = OBJECT_ID(N'dbo.vTest');
GO
```

x.   Using Synonyms

Views are sometimes employed to hide cryptic database schema names. Synonyms are similar to views, but they are more limited. Whereas views can project columns, assign column aliases, and build data using joins and subqueries, synonyms can only assign alternative names to tables, views, and stored procedures. Synonyms are primarily used to simplify complex object names, particularly with lengthy schema names.

A synonym can change HumanResources.EmployeeDepartmentHistory into EmpHist. Which would you rather type 100 times? Synonyms are part of the SQL standard and are used frequently by Oracle DBAs. Note that Oracle includes both private and public synonyms. SQL Server synonyms are only public. Even though they were introduced to SQL Server with version 2005, I have seen very little acceptance or use of synonyms in the SQL community.

Schemas enhance security and help prevent SQL injection attacks. The hacker needs to guess the schema name as well as the table name. Synonyms can be managed using Object Explorer, or CREATE and DROP DDL commands. Here is an example of synonym:

```
USE gtBankLoan;
GO

CREATE SYNONYM vEmp
FOR dbo.vEmployeeList;
GO
```

9.7 TRIGGERS

When an action has been performed on a table, such as adding a new record, modifying (editing/updating) an existing record, or deleting a (or some) records, the table produces a notification. We say that the table fires an event. You can use this occurring event to take some action. Triggers are special stored procedures attached to table events. They cannot be directly executed; they fire only in response to an INSERT, UPDATE, or DELETE events on a table. In the same way that attaching code to a form or control event in Visual Basic or Access causes that code to execute on the form or control event, triggers fire on table events. Users cannot bypass a trigger; and unless the trigger sends a message to the client, the end-user is unaware of the trigger. Developing triggers involves several SQL Server topics. Understanding transaction flow and locking, T-SQL, and stored procedures is a prerequisite for developing smooth triggers. Triggers contain a few unique elements and require careful planning, but they provide rock-solid execution of complex business rules and data validation.

9.7.1 Trigger Basics

SQL Server triggers fire once per data-modification operation, not once per affected row. This is different from Oracle, which can fire a trigger once per operation, or once per row. While this may seem at first glance to be a limitation on the other hand is still an advantage, because being forced to develop set-based triggers actually helps ensure clean logic and fast performance. Triggers may be created for the three table events that correspond to the three data-modification commands, which are INSERT, UPDATE, and DELETE. SQL Server has two kinds of transaction triggers; they are *instead of* triggers and *after* triggers. They differ in their purpose, timing, and effect, as shown in the Table below:

	Instead of Trigger	**After Trigger**
DML Statement	Simulated but no executed	Executed, but can be rolled back in the trigger
Timing	Before PK and FK constraints	After the transaction is complete, but before it is committed
Number possible per table event	One	Multiple
May be applied to views	Yes	No
Nested	Depends on server option	Depends on server option
Recursive	No	Depends on database option

9.7.2 Transaction flow

Developing triggers requires understanding the overall flow of the transaction; otherwise, conflicts between constraints and triggers can cause designing and debugging nightmares, because you may spend a decade trying to debug errors. Every transaction moves through the various checks and code in the following order.

i.   IDENTITY INSERT check

ii. Nullability constraint

iii. Data-type check

iv. INSTEAD OF trigger execution. If an INSTEAD OF trigger exists, then execution of the DML stops here. INSTEAD OF triggers are not recursive. Therefore, if the INSERT trigger executes another DML command, then the INSTEAD OF trigger will be ignored the second time around (recursive triggers are covered later in this chapter).

v.   Primary-key constraint

vi. Check constraints

vii. Foreign-key constraint

viii. DML execution and update to the transaction log

ix. AFTER trigger execution

x.   Commit

Based on SQL Server's transaction flow, the few key points about developing triggers are:

i.   An AFTER trigger occurs after all constraints. Because of this, it cannot correct data, so the data must pass any constraint checks, including foreign-key constraint checks.

ii. An INSTEAD OF trigger can circumvent foreign-key problems, but not nullability, datatype, or identity column problems.

iii. An AFTER trigger can assume that the data has passed all the other built-in data integrity checks.

iv. The AFTER trigger occurs before the DML transaction is committed, so it can roll back the transaction if the data is unacceptable.

9.7.3 Creating triggers

Triggers are created and modified with the standard DDL commands, CREATE, ALTER, and DROP. The syntax is:

CREATE TRIGGER Schema.TriggerName ON Schema.TableName

AFTER | INSTEAD OF [Insert, Update, (and or) Delete]

AS

Trigger Code;

GO

The trigger can be fired for any combination of insert, update, or delete events. Prior to SQL Server 2000, SQL Server had AFTER triggers only. Because no distinction between AFTER and INSTEAD OF was necessary, the old syntax created the trigger FOR INSERT, UPDATE, or DELETE. To ensure that the old FOR triggers will still work, AFTER triggers can be created by using the keyword FOR in place of AFTER. Although I strongly recommend that triggers be created and altered using scripts and version control; nevertheless, you can still view and modify triggers using MS SQL Server Management Studio's Object Explorer.

9.7.4 After triggers

A table may have several AFTER triggers for each of the three table events. AFTER triggers may be applied to tables only, not to views. The traditional trigger is an AFTER trigger that fires after the modification implied by the statement is complete, but before the statement ends and before the transaction is committed. AFTER triggers are useful based on the following reasons:

i. Complex data validation

ii. Enforcing complex business rules

iii. Writing data-audit trails

iv. Maintaining modified date columns

v. Enforcing custom referential-integrity checks and cascading deletes

The following AFTER trigger simply prints 'In the After Trigger' when the trigger is executed:

```
USE idealSuits;
GO


CREATE TABLE dbOperations (
    ObjectType nchar(50),
    ObjectName nvarchar(40),
    EmpName nvarchar(70),
    ActionPerformed nvarchar(70),
    TimePerformed datetime2
);
GO


CREATE TRIGGER RecordInsertion
ON dbo.Room
AFTER INSERT
AS
BEGIN
    INSERT INTO dbOperations
    VALUES(N'Table', N'Rooms', SUSER_SNAME(),
        N'New record is created', GETDATE())
END
GO
```

With the AFTER trigger enforced, when you insert a record into the room table a record will be on dbOperations table.

9.7.5 Instead of triggers

INSTEAD OF triggers execute "instead of" (as a substitute for) the submitted transaction, so that the submitted transaction does not occur. It is as if the presence of an INSTEAD OF trigger signals the submitted transaction to be ignored by SQL Server. As a substitution procedure, each table is limited to only one INSTEAD OF trigger per table event. In addition, INSTEAD OF triggers may be applied to views as well as tables. Do not confuse INSTEAD OF triggers with BEFORE triggers or before update events because are not the same. A BEFORE trigger, if such a thing existed in SQL Server, would not interfere with the submitted DML statement execution unless the code in the trigger executed a transaction rollback. INSTEAD OF triggers are useful when it is known that the DML statement firing the trigger will always be rolled back and some other logic will be executed *instead of* the DML statement. For example:

i.   When the DML statement attempts to update a non-updatable view, the INSTEAD OF trigger updates the underlying tables instead.

ii. When the DML statement attempts to directly update an inventory table, an INSTEAD OF trigger updates the inventory transaction table instead.

iii. When the DML statement attempts to delete a row, an INSTEAD OF trigger moves the row to an archive table instead.

Here is an example of INSTEAD OF trigger; it will attempt to INSERT a row into Person table of idealSuits database:

```
USE idealSuits;
GO


CREATE TRIGGER dbo.insteadOfTrigger ON dbo.Room
INSTEAD OF INSERT
AS
PRINT 'A record has been inserted via the Instead of Trigger';
GO
```

```
INSERT dbo.Room(RoomNumber,RoomType,Rate,Available)
VALUES (51, 'Single', 5900,1);
GO
```

The INSERT statement worked as if one row were affected, although the effect of the INSERT statement was blocked by the INSTEAD OF trigger. The PRINT command was executed instead of the rows being inserted. In addition, the AFTER trigger is still in effect, but its PRINT will message failed to print.

9.7.6   Trigger limitations

Given their nature (i.e. code attached to tables), triggers have a few limitations. The following SQL commands are not permitted within a trigger.

i.   CREATE, ALTER, or DROP database

ii.   RECONFIGURE

iii. RESTORE database or log

iv.   DISK RESIZE

v.   DISK INIT

9.7.7   Disabling triggers

A user's DML statement can never bypass a trigger, but a system administrator can temporarily disable it, which is better than dropping it and then recreating it if the trigger gets in the way of a data-modification task. To temporarily turn off a trigger, use the ALTER TABLE DDL command with the ENABLE TRIGGER or DISABLE TRIGGER option. Here is the syntax:

```
ALTER TABLE schema.TableName ENABLE or DISABLE TRIGGER
schema.TriggerName;
GO
```

For example, the following code disables the INSTEAD OF trigger created on Room table of the idealSuits database.

```
USE idealSuits;
GO


ALTER TABLE dbo.Room
DISABLE TRIGGER insteadOfTrigger;
GO
```

More exameples:

Use DISABLE TRIGGER to disable triggers that can harm the integrity of the database or server if the triggers execute under escalated privileges.

Here is an example of T-SQL statement that disables all database-level DDL triggers in the current database:

```
USE idealSuits;
GO


DISABLE TRIGGER ALL ON DATABASE;
GO
```

Here is another example of T-SQL statement that disables all server-level DDL triggers on the server instance:

```
DISABLE TRIGGER ALL ON ALL SERVER;
GO
```

To view the enabled status of a trigger, use the OBJECTPROPERTY() function, passing to it the objectID of the trigger and the ExecIsTriggerDisabled option:

```
USE idealSuits;
GO


SELECT    OBJECTPROPERTY(OBJECT_ID('insteadOfTrigger'),'ExecIsTriggerDisabled')
AS 'Trigger Status';
GO
```

By default, both DML and DDL triggers execute under the context of the user that calls the trigger. The caller of a trigger is the user that executes the statement that causes the trigger to run. For example, if user Edna executes a DELETE statement that causes DML trigger DML_trigEdna to run, the code inside DML_trigEdna executes in the context of the user privileges for Edna. This default behavior can be exploited by users who want to introduce malicious code in the database or server instance. For example, the following DDL trigger is created by user Chikodi:

```
CREATE TRIGGER DDL_trigChikodi
ON DATABASE
FOR ALTER_TABLE
AS
GRANT CONTROL SERVER TO Chikodi;
GO
```

What this trigger means is that as soon as a user that has permission to execute a GRANT CONTROL SERVER statement, such as a member of the sysadmin fixed server role, executes an ALTER TABLE statement, Chikodi is granted CONTROL SERVER permission. In other words, although Chikodi cannot grant CONTROL SERVER permission to himself, he enabled the trigger code that grants him this permission to execute under escalated privileges. Both DML and DDL triggers are open to this kind of security threat.

9.7.8 Listing triggers

Triggers tend to hide in the table structure, so some querying need to be done to list the triggers in the database sys.triggers. Here is an example:

```
USE idealSuits;
GO

SELECT Sc.name + '.' + Ob.name as [table],
Tr.Name as [trigger],
CASE (Tr.is_instead_of_trigger )
```

```
WHEN 0 THEN 'after'
WHEN 1 THEN 'instead of'
END AS type,
CASE (Tr.is_disabled)
WHEN 0 THEN 'enabled'
WHEN 1 THEN 'disabled'
END AS status
FROM sys.triggers Tr
JOIN sys.objects Ob
ON Tr.parent_id = Ob.object_id
JOIN sys.schemas Sc
ON Ob.schema_id = Sc.schema_id
WHERE Tr.Type = 'TR' and Tr.parent_class = 1
ORDER BY Sc.name + '.' + Ob.name, Tr.Name;
GO
```

9.7.9 Triggers and Security

Only users who are members of the sysadmin fixed server role, or are in the dbowner
or ddldmin fixed database roles, or are the tables' owners, have permission to create,
alter, drop, enable, or disable triggers. Code within the trigger is executed with the
security permissions of the owner of the trigger's table. So, is will be ideal to know the
triggers that run on your database or server and then know how to control them. Here
is how to do that:

```
SELECT type, name, parent_class_desc FROM sys.triggers
UNION
SELECT type, name, parent_class_desc FROM sys.server_triggers;
GO
```

Here is an example for disabling all DML triggers in the current database:

```
DECLARE   @schema_name   sysname,   @trigger_name   sysname,   @object_name
sysname;
DECLARE @sql nvarchar(max) ;
```

```sql
DECLARE trig_cur CURSOR FORWARD_ONLY READ_ONLY FOR
    SELECT SCHEMA_NAME(schema_id) AS schema_name,
        name AS trigger_name,
        OBJECT_NAME(parent_object_id) as object_name
    FROM sys.objects WHERE type in ('TR', 'TA');

OPEN trig_cur;
FETCH NEXT FROM trig_cur INTO @schema_name, @trigger_name, @object_name ;

WHILE @@FETCH_STATUS = 0
BEGIN
    SELECT @sql = 'DISABLE TRIGGER ' + QUOTENAME(@schema_name) + '.'
        + QUOTENAME(@trigger_name) +
        ' ON ' + QUOTENAME(@schema_name) + '.'
        + QUOTENAME(@object_name) + ' ; ' ;
    EXEC (@sql);
    FETCH NEXT FROM trig_cur INTO @schema_name, @trigger_name, @object_name;
END
GO


-- Verify triggers are disabled. Should return an empty result set.
SELECT * FROM sys.triggers WHERE is_disabled = 0;
GO

CLOSE trig_cur;
DEALLOCATE trig_cur;
GO
```

9.7.10 Working with the Transaction

A DML INSERT, UPDATE, or DELETE statement causes a trigger to fire. It is important that the trigger has access to the changes being caused by the DML statement so that it can test the changes or handle the transaction. SQL Server provides four ways through which you code within the trigger to determine the effects of the DML statement. The first two methods are the update() and columns_updated() functions, which may be used to determine which columns were potentially affected by the DML statement. The other two methods use deleted and inserted images, which contain the before and after data sets.

9.7.11 Determining the Updated Columns

SQL Server provides two methods for detecting which columns are being updated. The first is the UPDATE() function, which returns true for a single column if that column is affected by the DML transaction. This is the syntax: IF UPDATE(*ColumnName*)

An INSERT affects all columns, and an UPDATE reports the column as affected if the DML statement addresses the column. The following example demonstrates the UPDATE() function:

```
ALTER TRIGGER dbo.insteadOfTrigger ON dbo.Room
AFTER INSERT, UPDATE
AS
IF Update(RoomNumber)
BEGIN;
PRINT 'You might have modified the RoomNumber column';
END;
ELSE
BEGIN;
PRINT 'The didn''t touch the RoomNumber column.';
END;
```

GO

With the trigger looking for changes to the RoomNumber column, the following DML statement will test the trigger:

```
UPDATE dbo.Room
SET RoomNumber = 105
WHERE RoomID = 1000;
```

This function is generally used to execute data checks only when needed. There is no reason to test the validity of column A's data if column A is not updated by the DML statement. However, the UPDATE() function will report the column as updated according to the DML statement alone, not the actual data. Therefore, if the DML statement modifies the data from 'abcd' to 'abcd', then the UPDATE() will still report it as updated. The columns_updated() function returns a bitmapped varbinary data type representation of the columns updated (again, according to the DML statement). If the bit is true, then the column is updated. The result of columns_updated() can be compared with integer or binary data by means of any of the bitwise operators to determine whether a given column is updated or not. The columns are represented by right-to-left bits within left-to-right bytes. A further complication is that the size of the varbinary data returned by columns_updated() depends on the number of columns in the table. The following function simulates the actual behavior of the columns_updated() function. Passing the column to be tested and the total number of columns in the table will return the column bitmask for that column. Here is the example:

```
CREATE FUNCTION dbo.AllUpdatedCol
(@Col INT, @ColTotal INT)
RETURNS INT
AS
BEGIN;
-- Copyright 2001 Paul Nielsen
-- This function simulates the Columns_Updated() behavior
DECLARE
@ColByte INT,
```

```
@ColTotalByte INT,
@ColBit INT;
-- Calculate Byte Positions
SET @ColTotalByte = 1 + ((@ColTotal-1) /8);
SET @ColByte = 1 + ((@Col-1)/8);
SET @ColBit = @Col - ((@ColByte-1) * 8);
RETURN Power(2, @ColBit + ((@ColTotalByte-@ColByte) * 8)-1);
END;
GO
```

To use this function, perform a bitwise AND (&) between columns_updated() and GenColUpdated(). If the bitwise AND is equal to GenColUpdated(), then the column in question is indeed updated. Here is what I mean:

If COLUMNS_UPDATED() & dbo.GenColUpdated(@ColCounter,@ColTotal) = @ColUpdatedTemp

9.7.12 Inserted and deleted logical tables

SQL Server enables code within the trigger to access the effects of the transaction that caused the trigger to fire. The inserted and deleted logical tables are read-only images of the data. Think of them as views to the transaction log. The deleted table contains the rows before the effects of the DML statement, and the inserted table contains the rows after the effects of the DML statement as shown in the table below.

DML Statement	Inserted Table	Deleted Table
Insert	Rows being inserted	Empty
Update	Rows in the database after the update	Rows in the database before the update
Delete	Empty	Rows being deleted

The inserted and deleted tables have a limited scope. Stored procedures called by the trigger will not see the inserted or deleted tables. The SQL DML statement that originated the trigger can see the inserted and deleted triggers using the OUTPUT clause.

The following example uses the inserted table to report any new values for the RoomType column:

```
USE idealSuits;
GO

ALTER TRIGGER InsteadOfTrigger ON dbo.room
AFTER UPDATE
AS
SET NOCOUNT ON;
IF Update(RoomType)
SELECT 'You modified the RoomType column to "N    ' + Inserted.RoomType
FROM Inserted;

--With InsteadOfTrigger implemented on the room table, the following update will modify a --RoomType value

UPDATE room
SET RoomType = 'Large'
WHERE RoomID = 1002;
GO
```

9.7.13 Developing multi-row-enabled triggers

Many triggers I see in production are not written to handle the possibility of multiple-row INSERT, UPDATE, or DELETE operations. They take a value from the inserted or deleted table and store it in a local variable for data validation or processing. This technique checks only one of the rows affected by the DML statement which is a serious data integrity flaw. I have also seen databases that use cursors to step through each affected row. This is the type of slow code that gives triggers a bad name. A join between the inserted table and the deleted or underlying table will return a complete set of the rows affected by the DML statement. The table below lists the correct join combinations for creating multi-row-enabled triggers; from my perspective.

DML Type	FROM Clause
Insert	FROM Inserted
Update	FROM Insert INNER JOIN Deleted ON Inserted.PK = Deleted.PK
Insert, Update	FROM Inserted LEFT OUTER JOIN Deleted ON Inserted.PK = Deleted.PK
Deleted	FROM Deleted

Here is an example which alters InsteadOfTrigger to look at the inserted and deleted tables:

```
USE idealSuits;
GO

ALTER TRIGGER InsteadOfTrigger ON room
AFTER UPDATE
AS
SELECT D.RoomType  + N' changed to ' + I.RoomType AS N'Column Name'
FROM Inserted AS I
```

```
INNER JOIN Deleted AS D
ON I.RoomID = D.RoomID;
GO


UPDATE room
SET RoomType = 'Conference'
WHERE RoomType = 'Large';
GO
```

The following AFTER trigger, extracted from the Family sample database, enforces a rule that not only must the FatherID point to a valid person (that's covered by the foreign key), the person must be male:

```
USE gtBankLoan ;
GO


CREATE TRIGGER DMLTrStaffMeb
ON staffMebs
AFTER INSERT, UPDATE
AS
IF UPDATE(EmployeeID)
BEGIN
-- Incorrect Father Gender
      IF EXISTS(SELECT * FROM staffMebs
      INNER JOIN Inserted
      ON Inserted.EmployeeID = staffMebs.EmployeeID
      WHERE staffMebs.Title = 'Mrs')
            BEGIN
                  ROLLBACK
                  RAISERROR('Incorrect Title for Male',14,1);
                  RETURN
            END
END;
GO
```

Note: Without a clear plan, a database that employs multiple triggers can quickly become disorganized and extremely difficult to troubleshoot.

9.7.14 Trigger organization

In early version of SQL Server, each trigger event could have only one trigger, and a trigger could apply only to one trigger event. However, from MS SQL Server 2005, SQL Server allows multiple AFTER triggers per table event, and a trigger can apply to more than one event. This enables more flexible development styles. Having developed databases that include several hundred triggers, I recommend organizing triggers not by table event, but by the trigger's task, as follows:

i.   Data validation

ii. Complex business rules

iii. Audit trail

iv. Modified date

v.   Complex security

9.7.15 Nested triggers

Trigger nesting refers to whether a trigger that executes a DML statement will cause another trigger to fire. For example, if the Nested Triggers server option is enabled, and a trigger updates TableA, and TableA also has a trigger, then any triggers on TableA will also fire, as demonstrated in Figure 9.22. The Nested Triggers configuration option enables a DML statement within a trigger to fire additional triggers.

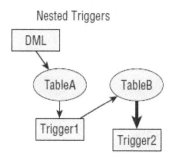

Nested Triggers

By default, the Nested Triggers option is enabled; but this configuration command is used to disable trigger nesting:

EXEC sp_configure 'Nested Triggers', 1;
GO

RECONFIGURE;
GO

If the database is developed with extensive server-side code, then it is likely that a DML will fire a trigger, which will call a stored procedure, which will fire another trigger, and so on. This is called *recursion;* SQL Server triggers have a limit of 32 levels of recursion. Do not blindly assume that nested triggers are safe. Test the trigger's nesting level by printing the Trigger_NestLevel() value, so you know how deep the triggers are nested. When the limit is reached, SQL Server generates a fatal error, those the error message can be customized using a little line of codes.
Here is an example:
IF ((SELECT TRIGGER_NESTLEVEL(OBJECT_ID('DMLTrStaffMeb') , 'AFTER' , 'DML')) > 5)
   RAISERROR('Trigger DMLTrStaffMeb nested more than 5 levels.',16,-1)
GO

9.7.16 Recursive triggers

A recursive trigger is a unique type of nested AFTER trigger. If a trigger executes a DML statement that causes itself to fire, then it is a recursive trigger (see Figure 9-3). If the database recursive triggers option is off, then the recursive iteration of the trigger will not fire. (Note that nested triggers is a server option, whereas recursive triggers is a database option.) A trigger is considered recursive only if it directly fires itself. If the trigger executes a stored procedure that then updates the trigger's table, then that is an indirect recursive call, which is not covered by the recursive-trigger database option. Recursive triggers are enabled with the ALTER DATABASE command:

```
ALTER DATABASE DatabaseName SET RECURSIVE_TRIGGERS ON | OFF ;
GO
```

Practically speaking, recursive triggers are very rare. I have needed to write a recursive trigger only for production. One example that involves recursion is a ModifiedDate trigger. This trigger writes the current date and time to the modified column for any row that is updated. Using the IwuEstateMgt, this script first adds a Created and Modified column to the PropertyInfo table:

```
USE IwuEstateMgt;
GO

ALTER TABLE estateMgt.PropertyInfo
ADD
Created SmallDateTime NOT NULL DEFAULT CURRENT_TIMESTAMP,
Modified SmallDateTime NOT NULL DEFAULT CURRENT_TIMESTAMP;
GO
```

A recursive trigger is a self-referencing trigger. One that executes a DML statement that causes itself to be fired again, if you are conversant with programming in VB.NET you would know about looping; recursive trigger is like looping.

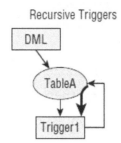

The issue is that if recursive triggers are enabled, then this trigger might become a runaway trigger. Then, after 32 levels of recursion, it will error out. The trigger in the example below prints the Trigger_NestLevel() level. This is very helpful for debugging nested or recursive triggers, but it should be removed when testing has finished. The second if statement prevents the Created and Modified date from being directly updated by the user. If the trigger is fired by a user, then the nest level is 1. The first time the trigger is executed, the UPDATE is executed. Any subsequent executions of the trigger RETURN because the trigger nest level will be greater than 1, this will prevent runaway recursion. Here is an example of the trigger DDL code:

```
USE IwuEstateMgt;
GO


ALTER TRIGGER propertyInfoModifiedDate ON estateMgt.PropertyInfo
AFTER UPDATE
AS
IF @@ROWCOUNT = 0
RETURN;
If Trigger_NestLevel() > 1
Return;
SET NOCOUNT ON;
PRINT TRIGGER_NESTLEVEL();
If (UPDATE(Created) or UPDATE(Modified))
Begin
Raiserror('Update failed.', 16, 1);
ROLLBACK;
Return;
```

```
End;
-- Update the Modified date
UPDATE PropertyInfo
SET Modified = CURRENT_TIMESTAMP
WHERE EXISTS
(SELECT * FROM Inserted AS i
WHERE i.PropertyID = PropertyInfo.PropertyID);
GO
```

To test the trigger, the next UPDATE command will cause the trigger to update the Modified column. The SELECT command returns the Created and Modified date and time:

```
USE IwuEstateMgt;
GO

UPDATE estateMgt.PropertyInfo
SET [Address] = 'Modified Trigger'
WHERE PropertyID = 10003;

SELECT PropertyID, Created, Modified
FROM estateMgt.PropertyInfo
WHERE PropertyID = 10003;
GO
```

9.7.17 Instead of and after triggers

If a table has both an INSTEAD OF trigger and an AFTER trigger for the same event, then it will assume following sequence in its operation:

i. The DML statement initiates a transaction.

ii. The INSTEAD OF trigger fires in place of the DML.

iii. If the INSTEAD OF trigger executes DML against the same table event, then the process continues.

iv. The AFTER trigger fires.

9.7.18 Multiple after triggers

If the same table event has multiple AFTER triggers, then they will all execute. The order of the triggers is less important than it may seem at first time. Every trigger has the opportunity to ROLLBACK the transaction, if well coded. If the transaction is rolled back, then all the work done by the initial transaction and all the triggers are rolled back. Any triggers that had not yet fired will not fire because the original DML is aborted by the ROLLBACK. Nevertheless, it is possible to designate an AFTER trigger to fire first or last in the list of triggers. I recommend doing this only if one trigger is likely to roll back the transaction and for performance reasons, you want that trigger to execute before other demanding triggers. Logically, however, the order of the triggers has no effect. The sp_settriggerorder system stored procedure is used to assign the trigger order using the following syntax:

sp_settriggerorder
@triggername = 'TriggerName',
@order = 'first' or 'last' or 'none',
@stmttype = 'INSERT' or 'UPDATE' or 'DELETE'

The effect of setting the trigger order is not cumulative. For example, setting TriggerOne to first and then setting TriggerTwo to first does not place TriggerOne in second place. In this case, TriggerOne returns to being unordered.

Here is an example of trigger settings:
EXEC sp_settriggerorder 'estateMgt.propertyInfoModifiedDate','first','UPDATE';
GO

9.7.19 Trigger Management

A trigger is a database object and as such has a name. Thus, it can be modified and can also be deleted.

i.   Modifying a Trigger

If the behaviour of a trigger is not appropriate, you can change it. In previous headings, I have demonstrated in so many ways, how to modify a *Trigger* using *ALTER* clause. The formula to modify a trigger is:

ALTER TRIGGER *schema_name.trigger_name*
ON *schema_name.table_name*
AFTER , UPDATE>
AS
   Statement
Here is an example of trigger modification:
ALTER TRIGGER InsteadOfTrigger ON room
AFTER UPDATE
AS
SELECT D.RoomType + N' changed to ' + I.RoomType AS N'Column Name'
FROM Inserted AS I
INNER JOIN Deleted AS D
ON I.RoomID = D.RoomID;
GO

ii.   Deleting a Trigger

If you do not need a trigger anymore, you can get rid of it at will, from the table. The formula to do this is:
DROP TRIGGER *TriggerName*

After the DROP TRIGGER expression, enter the name of the trigger.

Here is an example of deleting a trigger with the name InsteadOfTrigger:

DROP TRIGGER InsteadOfTrigger;

GO

9.8 T-SQL EXCEPTION HANDLING

In reality, when it comes to a Microsoft SQL Server database application, you can take care of problems on either the Microsoft SQL Server side or on a programming environment you are using to create a graphical application. Of course, all robust programming languages provide some method for trapping, logging, and handling errors. In this area, T-SQL has a sad history (almost as sad as that joke), but it is made significant progress with SQL Server 2005.

There are two distinctly different ways to code error handling with SQL Server, they are:

i. Legacy error handling is how it is been done since the beginning of SQL Server, using @@error to see the error status of the previous SQL statement.

ii. Try/catch was introduced in SQL Server 2008, bringing SQL Server into the 21st century.

9.8.1 Types of Errors

There are various categories of errors you can deal with, but the two major types are:

a. Syntax error

b. Run-time error

a.   Syntax Errors

A syntax error occurs if you try writing code that Transact-SQL does not understand or allow. Examples are:

i.   If you try typing an operator or a keyword where it should not be, an error will occur. Here is an example:

This error is because the **SET** operator, although part of the Transact-SQL, was used or placed wrongly.

ii.   If you wrongly type a keyword or an operator probably because you don't remember it, the Code Editor would signal it. Here is an example:

iii. If you forget to type something necessary or required, when you try executing the code, it would produce an error.

Syntax errors are usually easy to detect because the Code Editor points them out right away. Consequently, these errors are easy to fix. If you use a command-based application such as SQLCMD or PowerShell, it would not show the error right way. It would show it when you execute the code or at run-time.

b.   Run-Time Errors

A run-time error is the type that occurs if your application tries to perform an operation that either or both Microsoft SQL Server and/or the operating system do not allow. These errors can be difficult to fix because sometimes they are not clear, or what happens as the error is not clearly identified or is external to the database. The problem could be that, when testing the database in Microsoft SQL Server, it may work just fine, but after the application has been distributed and is used, problems start occurring.

Examples of run-time errors are:

i.   Trying to execute code that is not available or is not clearly defined
ii. Performing a bad calculation such as trying to divid by 0

```
SQLQuery1.sql ...strateur (53))*    Object Explorer Details
    USE Exercise;
    Go


□ DECLARE @Number1 tinyint;
└ SET @Number1 = 228 / 0;
    GO

◄

Messages

Msg 8134, Level 16, State 1, Line 3
Divide by zero error encountered.
```

Notice that the Code Editor does not signal any problem, because this is not a syntax error

iii. Trying to use a function, a stored procedure, or a trigger that does not exist.
iv.   Using or accessing computer memory that is not available or enough
v.   Trying to perform an operation that either a variable or an object cannot handle. An example is trying to store in a variable that is not capable of accommodating the value. Here is an example:

```
SQLQuery1.sql ...strateur (53))*    Object Explorer Details
    USE Exercise;
    Go


□ DECLARE @Number1 tinyint;
└ SET @Number1 = 2258;
    GO

◄

Messages

Msg 220, Level 16, State 2, Line 3
Arithmetic overflow error for data type tinyint, value = 2258.
```

Notice that the Code Editor does not signal any problem, because this is not a syntax error

vi.   Performing an operation on incompatible datatypes.
vii. Wrongly using a conditional statement, or using a mis-constructed conditional statement.

Run-time errors can be difficult to locate and fix.

9.9 Handling an Exception

i. Trying an Exception

Exception handling is the ability to deal with errors that occur or can occur on a database. The error is called an exception. To assist you with handling exceptions, Transact-SQL provides a general formula. You start with a section as shown below:
BEGIN TRY
Normal code
END TRY

Between the BEGIN TRY and the END TRY lines, write the normal code you want to execute. The section of code that starts from BEGIN TRY to END TRY is called a try block or a try clause.

ii. Catching an Exception

After the try block, you must create another section that starts with BEGIN CATCH and ends with END CATCH:
BEGIN TRY
Normal code
END TRY
BEGIN CATCH

END CATCH
The section of code that goes from BEGIN CATCH to END CATCH is called a catch block or a catch clause.
This following rules must be observe:
  a. If you create a try block, you must also create a catch block
  b. There must not be any Transact-SQL code (except a comment, that is not SQL code anyway) between the END TRY and the BEGIN CATCH lines

If no error happens in the try block, you can leave the catch block empty. Here is an example:

```
USE diograndeDB ;
Go

BEGIN TRY
   DECLARE @Side decimal(6, 3),
        @Perimeter decimal(6, 3);

   SET @Side = 124.36;
   SET @Perimeter = @Side * 4;

   SELECT @Side AS Side, @Perimeter AS Perimeter;
END TRY
BEGIN CATCH

END CATCH;
GO
```

You can imagine what will happen when you write code that could produce an error. Here is an example:

```
USE Exercise;
GO

DECLARE @Number tinyint,
    @Result tinyint;

SET @Number = 252;
SET @Result = @Number + 20;

SELECT @Number AS Number, @Result AS Result;
GO
```

This would produce:

```
SQLQuery1.sql -... (chibyke (53))*

    USE diograndeDB ;
    GO

  DECLARE @Number tinyint,
       @Result tinyint;

    SET @Number = 252;
    SET @Result = @Number + 20;

    SELECT @Number AS Number, @Result AS Result;
    GO
```

```
Results   Messages
Msg 220, Level 16, State 2, Line 6
Arithmetic overflow error for data type tinyint, value = 272.

(1 row(s) affected)
```

To address this type of problem, you can use exception handling and include the normal code in a try block. Then, if an error occurs in the try block, you can use the catch block to display a message. Here is an example:

```
USE diograndeDB ;
GO

BEGIN TRY
    DECLARE @Number tinyint,
         @Result tinyint;

    SET @Number = 252;
    SET @Result = @Number + 20;

    SELECT @Number AS Number, @Result AS Result;
END TRY
BEGIN CATCH
    PRINT N'There is a problem with the program';
END CATCH
```

```
GO
```

On the other hand, if no error occurs in the try block, that try block executes but when it ends, the execution skips the catch block and continues execution with code below the END CATCH line, if any.

Identifying an Error

To assist you with identifying an error that has occurred, Transact-SQL provides various functions.

i.   The Error Line

When an error occurs in your code, probably the first thing you want to know is where the error occurred. To assist you with this, Transact-SQL provides a function named ERROR_LINE. The syntax is:

```
int ERROR_LINE();
```

This function does not take an argument. It returns a number that represents the line number where the error occurred. Using a conditional statement, you can question the database engine to know the line where the error occurred. With this information, you can take the necessary action.

Here is an example:

```
USE diograndeDB ;
GO

BEGIN TRY
    DECLARE @Number tinyint,
        @Result tinyint;

    SET @Number = 252;
    SET @Result = @Number + 20;
```

```
    SELECT @Number AS Number, @Result AS Result;
END TRY
BEGIN CATCH
    PRINT N'The Error Line is: '+ CAST(ERROR_LINE() AS nvarchar(100));
END CATCH
GO
```

ii.   The Error Number

Every type of error is recognized with a specific number, which is just a type of identity (we will see how you can use that number; but, as a numeric value, it does not indicate anything). To know the number of an error, you can call the **ERROR_NUMBER()** function. This is the syntax:

```
int ERROR_NUMBER();
```

You can then get the error number to take action. Here is an example of finding out the number:

```
USE diograndeDB ;
GO


BEGIN TRY
    DECLARE @Number tinyint,
        @Result tinyint;


    SET @Number = 252;
    SET @Result = @Number + 20;


    SELECT @Number AS Number, @Result AS Result;
END TRY
BEGIN CATCH
 select N'The Error Number is: '+ CAST (ERROR_NUMBER() as char(4));
END CATCH
GO
```

To find out what error number was produced by your code, though this is for the people who has been working with MS SQL Server for a long time; you can inquire about the value produced by the ERROR_NUMBER() function. To do that, you can write an **IF** conditional statement. If you know the error number; you can take an appropriate action by at least replacing the number with a message, though there is a function that can display the message type of error. Here is an example:

```
SQLQuery1.sql -... (chibyke (53))*

    USE diograndeDB ;
    GO

BEGIN TRY
    DECLARE @Number tinyint,
        @Result tinyint;

    SET @Number = 252;
    SET @Result = @Number + 20;

    SELECT @Number AS Number, @Result AS Result;
END TRY
BEGIN CATCH
    IF ERROR_NUMBER () = 220
    select N'Error occured, because the number is too big for the variable.' AS N'ERROR';
END CATCH
    GO
```

Results | Messages

	ERROR
1	Error occured, because the number is too big for the variable.

On the other hand, you can take better action than that. In previous versions of Microsoft SQL Server, the means of getting an error number was to call a function named @@**ERROR**. You can still use this function to find out what the error number is in order to take an appropriate action. Its syntax is:

int @@ERROR();

This function can be called to get the error number produced by an exception. Here is an example;

USE diograndeDB ;

GO

BEGIN TRY

```
    DECLARE @Number tinyint,
        @Result tinyint;

    SET @Number = 252;
    SET @Result = @Number + 20;

    SELECT @Number AS Number, @Result AS Result;
END TRY
BEGIN CATCH
    PRINT N'The Error number is : ' + CAST(@@ERROR AS NVARCHAR(50));
END CATCH
```

iii.   The Error Message

An error number is just a number built-in the function code and known by the database engine. That number does not give any meaningful indication about the error. To give you a message related to the error, Transact-SQL provides the ERROR_MESSAGE() function. Its syntax is:

nvarchar ERROR_MESSAGE();

This function takes no argument and it returns a string. Here is an example of error_message function:

```
~vsF3A1.sql - I... (chibyke (51))*

    USE diograndeDB ;
    GO

  BEGIN TRY
      DECLARE @Number tinyint,
          @Result tinyint;

      SET @Number = 252;
      SET @Result = @Number + 20;

      SELECT @Number AS Number, @Result AS Result;
  END TRY
  BEGIN CATCH
      select ERROR_MESSAGE() as N'ERROR MESSAGE';
  END CATCH
  GO
```

```
◄

  Results   Messages
      ERROR MESSAGE
  1   Arithmetic overflow error for data type tinyint, value = 272.
```

Because you are a programmer, you should understand the meaning of the words overflow error, and tinyint. Unfortunately, this message may not be very clear to a regular user. For this reason, you should provide an easy way to read the message. You can even combine your customized error message to the value of the ERROR_MESSAGE() function.

```
USE diograndeDB ;
GO

BEGIN TRY
     DECLARE @Number tinyint,
         @Result tinyint;

     SET @Number = 252;
     SET @Result = @Number + 20;

     SELECT @Number AS Number, @Result AS Result;
END TRY
BEGIN CATCH
```

Select N'Error Message: ' + ERROR_MESSAGE() as N'ERROR MESSAGE';
END CATCH
GO

iv.   The Severity of an Error

Errors have different levels of consideration. Some must be dealt with as soon as possible while others can wait. To help you identify the severity of an error, Transact-SQL provides the **ERROR_SEVERITY()** function. This is the syntax:

int ERROR_SEVERITY();

This function takes no argument and returns an integer. Here is an example of how to identify the severity of an error:

```
USE diograndeDB ;
GO


BEGIN TRY
        DECLARE @Number tinyint,
            @Result tinyint;


        SET @Number = 252;
        SET @Result = @Number + 20;


        SELECT @Number AS Number, @Result AS Result;
END TRY
BEGIN CATCH
        select N'The Error Severity Level is : ' + CAST(error_severity() as nvarchar(100))
as N'ERROR MESSAGE';
END CATCH
GO
```

The value of this number is not a level of severity. It is just an indication of the severity. You as the database developer must find out what this number is and take appropriate action. You can write an IF conditional statement to find out the value produced by this function and do what you judge necessary.

Here is an example:

```
USE diograndeDB ;
GO

BEGIN TRY
        DECLARE @Number tinyint,
            @Result tinyint;

        SET @Number = 252;
        SET @Result = @Number + 20;

        SELECT @Number AS Number, @Result AS Result;
END TRY
BEGIN CATCH
        IF ERROR_SEVERITY() = 16
        PRINT N'An error has occurred on the database.';
        PRINT N'---------------------------------------------';
        PRINT N'The error severity number is 16.';
        PRINT N'Don''t worry, all is well. Contact the database administrator and state
this number.';
END CATCH
GO
```

v.   The State of an Error

The state of an error is a number that specifies the section of code where an error occurred. This is because the same code can produce different errors at different sections of the code. To help you identify the state of an error, Transact-SQL provides the **ERROR_STATE()** function. The syntax is:

```
int ERROR_STATE();
```

This function takes no argument. It returns an integer that specifies the state of the error. Here is an example:

```
USE diograndeDB ;
GO


BEGIN TRY
    DECLARE @Number tinyint,
            @Result tinyint;


    SET @Number = 252;
    SET @Result = @Number + 20;


    SELECT @Number AS Number, @Result AS Result;
END TRY
BEGIN CATCH
        IF ERROR_STATE () = 2
 select N'Error occured, because the number is too big for the variable.' AS N'ERROR';
END CATCH
GO
```

Characteristics of Exception Handling

Just as you can write various statements in your code, you can also create various exception sections. Here are examples:

```
USE diograndeDB ;
GO


BEGIN TRY
    DECLARE @Number tinyint,
            @Result tinyint;


    SET @Number = 252;
    SET @Result = @Number + 2;
```

```
      PRINT N'Number = ' + CAST(@Number AS nvarchar(20));
      PRINT N'Result = ' + CAST(@Result AS nvarchar(20));
END TRY
BEGIN CATCH
   PRINT N'Error: ' + ERROR_MESSAGE();
END CATCH


PRINT N'-------------------------------------';

BEGIN TRY
   DECLARE @Value decimal(6,2),
         @Division decimal;

   SET @Value = 15.50;
   SET @Division = @Value / 0;

   PRINT N'Number = ' + CAST(@Value AS nvarchar(20));
   PRINT N'Result = ' + CAST(@Division AS nvarchar(20));
END TRY
BEGIN CATCH
   PRINT N'Error Message: ' + ERROR_MESSAGE();
END CATCH
GO
```

The first expression will execute successfully while the second expression will not, the error message will be displayed. In the above example, each section will handle its own exception.

i.   Nesting an Exception

You can create an exception handling code inside of another. This is referred to as nesting. The basic formula is:

```
BEGIN TRY
   BEGIN TRY
         -- Nested try block
```

```
        END TRY
        BEGIN CATCH
            -- Nested catch block
        END CATCH
END TRY
BEGIN CATCH

END CATCH
```

Here is an example:

```
USE diograndeDB;
GO

BEGIN TRY
    BEGIN TRY
        DECLARE @Number tinyint,
                @Result tinyint;

            SET @Number = 252;
                SET @Result = @Number + 42;

            PRINT N'Number = ' + CAST(@Number AS nvarchar(20));
                PRINT N'Result = ' + CAST(@Result AS nvarchar(20));
    END TRY
    BEGIN CATCH
                PRINT N'Error: ' + ERROR_MESSAGE();
    END CATCH
        PRINT N' '
PRINT N'----- Another Section inside a Try...End Try Block ------';
        PRINT N' '
    BEGIN TRY
            DECLARE @Value decimal(6,2),
                        @Division decimal;

            SET @Value = 15.50;
```

```
        SET @Division = @Value / 0;


        PRINT N'Number = ' + CAST(@Value AS nvarchar(20));
            PRINT N'Result = ' + CAST(@Division AS nvarchar(20));
    END TRY
    BEGIN CATCH
            PRINT N'Error: ' + ERROR_MESSAGE();
    END CATCH
END TRY
BEGIN CATCH
    PRINT N'There was a problem with your code';
END CATCH
GO
```

ii.   Raising an Error

If an error occurs in your code, you can take initiative for it, as we have done so far. To better customize how an exception is handled when it occurs, you can raise an error. To support this, Transact-SQL provides the **RAISERROR()** function. The syntax is:

RAISERROR ({ *msg_id* | *msg_str* | *@local_variable* }

   { ,*severity* ,*state* }

   [,argument [,...n]])

   [WITH option [,...n]]

This function takes three required arguments:

1. The first argument can be one of three things:

    i.   The argument can be represented as a constant integer. To start, create a message, assign it a number higher than 50000, and pass that message to Transact-SQL by storing it in the **sys.messages** library. If you do this, to access the message, you would use the number you specified

    ii.   The argument can be represented as a *msg_str* object. In this case, the argument is the message you want to produce (or display) if an error occurs. The argument is created and formatted like the **printf()** function of the C language

   iii. The first argument can be a string-based locally declared variable. It is then initialized and formatted as done for the *msg_str* option

2. The second argument is a number that represents the severity level of the error. You specify this number as you see fit, knowing that you will manage it later as you so desire. The number specified for this argument should be between 0 and 18. If you are a member of the sysadmin group, you can specify a number higher than that. If you use a number between 20 and 25, this is considered very high (or a dangerous error) and can close the connection to the database

3. The third argument is a number that represents the error state. For this argument, you can specify any number between 1 and 127. If you are creating different exceptions sections, you should provide a unique *state* number for each.

Here is an example:

```
BEGIN TRY
    -- RAISERROR with severity 11-19 will cause execution to
    -- jump to the CATCH block.
    RAISERROR ('Error raised in TRY block.', -- Message text.
            16, -- Severity.
            1 -- State.
            );
END TRY
BEGIN CATCH
    DECLARE @ErrorMessage NVARCHAR(4000);
    DECLARE @ErrorSeverity INT;
    DECLARE @ErrorState INT;

    SELECT
        @ErrorMessage = ERROR_MESSAGE(),
        @ErrorSeverity = ERROR_SEVERITY(),
        @ErrorState = ERROR_STATE();

    -- Use RAISERROR inside the CATCH block to return error
    -- information about the original error that caused
    -- execution to jump to the CATCH block.
```

```
    RAISERROR (@ErrorMessage, -- Message text.
            @ErrorSeverity, -- Severity.
            @ErrorState -- State.
            );
END CATCH;
GO


Here is another example:
sp_addmessage @msgnum = 50005,
            @severity = 10,
            @msgtext = N'<<%7.3s>>';
GO
RAISERROR (50005, -- Message id.
            10, -- Severity,
            1, -- State,
            N'abcde'); -- First argument supplies the string.
-- The message text returned is: <<  abc>>.
GO


sp_dropmessage @msgnum = 50005;
GO
```

CHAPTER TEN

IMPROVING DATA RETRIEVAL AND QUERY PERFORMANCE TECHNIQUES

At this point I am not forced to believe that you can now do a lot with MS SQL Server in terms of database development.

This chapter will tell you more about data retrieval from the database with ease and to ensure that your query does not hut the performance of your Server. A major cause of query performance degradation is that a query involving very large tables can require that all of the data from one or more tables be downloaded to the client. So when you write well structured query for all select statement, then be sure that the data will be retrieved with ease. I will repeat some of the topics discussed in chapter eight (METHODS OF DATA RETRIEVAL), though not exactly, but in different ways because it will explain more on data retrieval and performance improvement. On the other hand the images of pictures of the codes and results will minimal in this chapter, because the user of this book is believed to be conversant with the MS SQL Server Management Studio by now.

10.1 Data Selection and Expressions

i. Using an Alias Name for a Column

In your **SELECT** statement, after specifying the column(s), when you execute the SQL statement, the name of each column would appear as the column header. Fortunately, you can display any string of your choice for a column header. To specify a column header other than the default column name; you can use either the Query Designer or the Query Window: if you are using the Query Designer, type the desired string in the Alias column corresponding to the column. Here is an example:

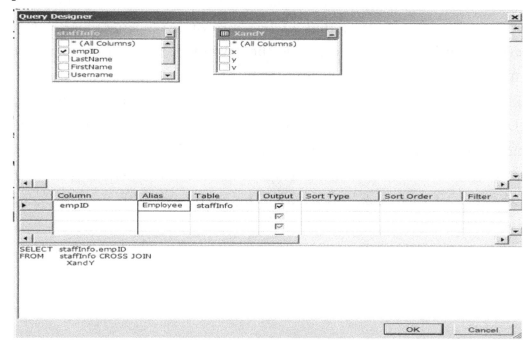

If you are using a query window or if you are writing your **SELECT** statement, on the right side of the column name, type **AS** followed by the desired name of the column header and enclose them with square-bracket or single-quote, the AS word is not necessary but I recommend you add it. If the desired column header is in one word, you can simply type it. Here is an example of a single Alias Column:

    SELECT FirstName,
           LastName,
           HomePhone AS PhoneNumber,

```
        ParentsNames AS NamesOfParents
FROM    Students;
GO
```

Here is an example of single-quotes or square brackets:
```
SELECT FirstName AS [First Name],
        LastName AS [Last Name],
        HomePhone AS [Phone Number],
        ParentsNames AS [Names of Parents]
FROM    Students;
GO
```

By qualifying each column, the above statement can also be written as follows, I explained this in chapter eight of this book:
```
SELECT Students.FirstName AS [First Name],
        Students.LastName AS [Last Name],
        Students.HomePhone AS [Phone Number],
        Students.ParentsNames AS [Names of Parents]
FROM    Students;
GO
```

It can also be written as follows:
```
SELECT dbo.Students.FirstName AS [First Name],
        dbo.Students.LastName AS [Last Name],
        dbo.Students.HomePhone AS [Phone Number],
        dbo.Students.ParentsNames AS [Names of Parents]
FROM    Students;
GO
```

It can also be written as follows:
```
SELECT std.FirstName AS [First Name],
        std.LastName AS [Last Name],
        std.HomePhone AS [Phone Number],
        std.ParentsNames AS [Names of Parents]
FROM    Students std;
```

GO

ii. A Combination or Expression of Columns

Using the **SELECT** keyword, we have learned to create a list of isolated columns. These columns were rendered separate of each other. Instead of having separate columns, you can combine them to create a string or a value that is in fact an expression. For example, you can combine a first name and a last name to produce a full name as an expression. Another expression can use a date on the table, add a number to it to get a date on another day. An expression can also be used to perform a calculation on two or more columns such as employees weekly hours multiplied by their hourly salary to get their weekly salary.

The most common operator used is the addition. It can be used to combine two or more strings to get a new one. Here is an example:

    SELECT FirstName + ' ' + LastName
    FROM Students;
    GO

The addition can also be used on numeric values. All other arithmetic operators can be used. For example, you can multiply a weekly hours value to an hourly salary to get a weekly salary. The statement of such an expression can be written as follows:

    SELECT WeeklyHours * HourlySalary
    FROM Payroll
    GO

You can also create an alias for an expression to give it the desired name. To do this, on the right side of the expression, type AS followed by the name. Here is an example:

    SELECT FirstName + ' ' + LastName AS 'Full Name',
        EmrgName + ' ' + EmrgPhone AS [Emergency Contact]
    FROM   Students;
    GO

Here is another example:

```sql
SELECT PropertyType + N' in ' + City + N', ' + State + N', in ' + Condition +
       N' condition. Equipped with ' + CAST(Bedrooms AS nvarchar(20)) +
       N' bedrooms, ' + CAST(Bathrooms AS nvarchar(20)) +
       N' bathrooms. Built in ' + CAST(YearOld AS nvarchar(20)) +
       N' and selling for ' + CAST(MarketValue AS nvarchar(20))
       AS [Property Description]
FROM   estateMgt.PropertyInfo
GO
```

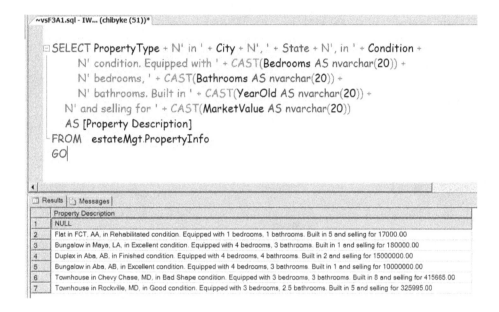

iii. The Assignment Operator

If you just create a regular expression using arithmetic operators, the new column would not have a name. The SQL allows you to specify a different name for any column during data analysis or a name for an expression. This is done using the assignment operator "=". To change the name of a column during data analysis, on the right side of **SELECT**, type the desired name, followed by the assignment operator, followed by the actual name of the column. Here is an example:

```sql
SELECT EmergencyName = EmrgName
FROM Students;
GO
```

If you want to use more than one column, type each and assign it the desired name, separate them with commas. Here is an example:

```
SELECT LastName,
     EmergencyName = EmrgName,
     EmergencyPhone = EmrgPhone
FROM   Students;
GO
```

You can also include the name between single-quotes or the square brackets, as explained above. Here are examples:

```
SELECT LastName + ', N' + FirstName AS [Full Name],
     [Emergency Name] = EmrgName,
     'Emergency Phone' = EmrgPhone
FROM   Students;
GO
```

10.2   Sorting the Records

10.2.1 Query Window or Query Designer Records Sorting

The list of records we get with a SELECT statement is presented in the order the records appear in the table. The SQL allows you to arrange records in alphabetical order, in chronological order or in numeric incremental order. After selecting a series of columns, you may want to list the records following an alphabetical order from one specific field. To get an alphabetical or an incremental order of records, you must let the database engine know what field would be used as reference point. Here is an example:

   i.   In the Diagram section, you can right-click a field and select either Sort Ascending or Sort Descending
   ii. In the Criteria section of the window, under the Sort Type column, click the corresponding box of the desired column. This would reveal that it is a combo box. Then click the arrow of that combo box and make your selection between Ascending and Descending, exactly as shown below:

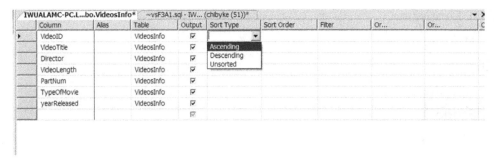

If you select Ascending or Sort Ascending, the list of records would be re-arranged based on the datatype of the selected column, below are examples:

- If the column is text-based (**char**, **varchar**, and their variants), the records would be arranged in alphabetical order.

- If the column is date or time-based (**date**, **time**, or **datetime2**), the records would be arranged in chronological order.

- If the column is number-based, the records would be arranged in incremental numerical order.

- If the column is Boolean-based (bit), the FALSE records would appear first

If you select Descending or Sort Descending, the list of records would be re-arranged based on the type of the selected column, below are examples:

- If the column is text-based (**char**, **varchar**, and their variants), the records would be arranged in reverse alphabetical order

- If the column is date or time-based (**date**, **time**, or **datetime2**), the records would be arranged in reverse chronological order

- If the column is number-based, the records would be arranged in decremental numerical order

- If the column is Boolean-based (bit), the TRUE records would appear first

After selecting the desired Sort Type, you can execute the SQL statement.

Here are some examples of record sorting using SQL Code:

In SQL, to specify the sorting order, use the **ORDER BY** expression. The syntax used would be:

SELECT *What* FROM *WhatObject* ORDER BY *WhatField*;

The column used as the basis must be recognized as part of the selected columns. For example, to get a list of students in alphabetical order based on the LastName column, you can use the following statement. This is what I mean:

```
SELECT FirstName,
    LastName,
    Gender,
    ParentsNames
FROM Students
ORDER BY LastName;
GO
```

In the same way, you can get the list of girls followed by the list of boys by ordering the list in alphabetical order based on the Gender.
Here is an example:

```
SELECT FirstName, LastName, Gender, EmailAddress
FROM Students
ORDER BY Gender;
GO
```

As another example, to list all students arranged in alphabetical order by their last name, you can change the statement as follows:

```
SELECT * FROM Students
ORDER BY LastName;
GO
```

By default, records are ordered in ascending order. Nevertheless, the ascending order is controlled using the **ASC** keyword specified after the based field. For example, to sort the last names in ascending order, type and execute the statement below:

```
SELECT * FROM Students
ORDER BY LastName ASC;
GO
```

On the other hand, if you want to sort records in reverse order, you can use the **DESC** keyword. It produces the opposite result to the **ASC** effect. Here is an example:

```
SELECT FirstName,
    LastName,
```

```
      Gender,
      ParentsNames
   FROM Students
ORDER BY LastName DESC;
GO
```

Here are other examples:

```
SELECT YearOld AS [Year Built],
      PropertyType AS [Type],
      Bedrooms AS [Beds],
      Bathrooms AS [Baths],
      MarketValue AS [Value]
FROM estateMgt.PropertyInfo
ORDER BY MarketValue DESC;
GO
```

Here is another example, that will show newest houses or apartments:

```
SELECT YearOld AS [Year Built],
      PropertyType AS [Type],
      Bedrooms AS [Beds],
      Bathrooms AS [Baths],
      MarketValue AS [Value]
FROM estateMgt.PropertyInfo
ORDER BY YearOld ASC;
GO
```

10.3 Restrictions on Data Selection

We know that we can analyze data from the table or using a Query window. Instead of selecting all data as we have done so far using the **SELECT** keyword, you can present a condition that the database would follow to isolate specific records that are not required.

Here is an example:

1. From the Object Explorer, expand Databases
2. Expand the Table
3. Right-click PropertyInfo and click Edit Top 200 Rows
4. Right click PropertyInfo and Select TOP 1000 Rows

If you have a long group of records, you can specify that you want to see only a certain number of records. To do this, after the SELECT operator, type TOP followed by an integral number. Continue the SELECT statement as you see fit. Here is an example:

```
SELECT TOP 5 * FROM Employees;
GO
```

You can also include the number in parentheses. Here is an example:

```
SELECT TOP(5) * FROM Employees;
GO
```

This statement asks the SQL interpreter to select the first 5 records from the Employees table.

i. Application of WHEN Clause

You can use a **WHEN** conditional statement to refine data selection. Imagine you want to select records and assign gender to each record via the GenderID column.

If a column has values that are difficult to identify, you can use a **CASE** conditional statement to customize the result(s). Here is an example:

```
USE [LOLOITFDB.MDF];
GO
SELECT FName, LName, Gender =
   CASE GenderID
    WHEN 1 THEN N'Male'
    WHEN 2 THEN N'Female'
    ELSE N'Unknown'
    END
```

```
FROM studTable;
GO
```

ii.   WHERE is the Condition

When analysing data or if you are creating a query using the Table window, you can type an expression that uses one or more logical operators. Here is an example of an expression: > '12/31/1993'

This means that the dates that occur after 1993 would be selected. If you are writing your **SELECT** statement, to formulate a condition, you use the **WHERE** keyword with this basic formula:

SELECT *What* FROM *WhatObject* WHERE *Expression*;

The expressions used in conditions are built using algebraic, logical, and string operators. The *Expression* factor is called a criterion. Although a group of expressions, making it plural is called criteria, the word criteria is sometimes used for a singular expression also. The expression is written using the formula:

ColumnName=Value

The *ColumnName* factor must be an existing column of a table. It is followed by the assignment operator. The *Value* factor is the value that would set the condition. If the value is a word or a group of words (also called a string), you must include it in single-quotes. If it is a number, you can type its numeric value. Here is an example from a database of students, from a table named Students, to get a list of female students:

```
SELECT DateOfBirth, LastName, FirstName,
    Gender, State, ParentsNames
FROM Students
WHERE Gender = N'Female';
GO
```

In a WHERE statement, you can also use the ORDER BY expression to sort a list of records based on a column of your choice. Here is an example:

```
SELECT DateOfBirth, LastName, FirstName,
```

```
      Gender, State, ParentsNames
FROM Students
WHERE State = N'AB'
ORDER BY LastName;
GO
```

Here is another example on the use of *WHERE* clause.

```
SELECT PropertyNumber AS [Prop #],
     Address,
     City,
     State,
     ZIPCode AS [Location],
     YearBuilt AS [Year Built],
     PropertyType AS [Type],
     MarketValue AS [Value]
FROM Properties
WHERE ZIPCode < 20500;
GO
```

To get a list of only the newest properties built in or after 2000, in the SQL section, change the statement as follows:

```
SELECT Address,
     City,
     State,
     YearBuilt AS [Year Built],
     PropertyType AS [Type],
     MarketValue AS [Value]
FROM Properties
WHERE YearBuilt >= 2000
```

iii. Negating a Condition

Without negating the statement below, when the statement is executed, a list of female students would display. Instead of girls, to get a list of male students, you can negate this condition. To do this, type **NOT** before the condition. Here is what I mean:

> SELECT DateOfBirth, LastName, FirstName,
>
> > Gender, State, ParentsNames
>
> FROM Students
>
> WHERE NOT Gender = N'Female';
>
> GO

To make this condition easier to read, you should include the positive expression in parentheses. This would be done in this way:

> SELECT DateOfBirth, LastName, FirstName,
>
> > Gender, State, ParentsNames
>
> FROM Students
>
> WHERE NOT (Gender = N'Female');
>
> GO

This clearly indicates that it is the expression in the parentheses that is being negated. In the same way, you can use the IS NOT NULL to find the records that are not null. For example, you can create a list of only records that do not have a null value on a certain column. Here is an example:

> SELECT DateOfBirth, LastName, FirstName,
>
> > State, ParentsNames
>
> FROM Students
>
> WHERE State IS NOT NULL;
>
> GO

When this statement is executed, the table would display only the records that include a state for each student.

10.4   CREATING A TABLE VIA AN EXISTING TABLE USING *SELECT*

You can use all or some records from an existing table to create a new table that contains those records. To do this, you use the following formula:

SELECT *Columns* INTO *NewTableName* FROM *ExistingTable* [WHERE *Condition*]

To use all columns and all records, start with the SELECT operator, followed by *, followed by INTO, followed by a name for the table you want to create, followed by FROM, and the name of the original table that contains the records. Here is an example:

```
USE diograndeDB;
GO
SELECT * INTO CompanyRecipients FROM Employees;
GO
```

Instead of using all columns, you can specify only the desired columns after the SELECT keyword. Here is an example:

```
USE diograndeDB;
GO


SELECT EmployeeNumber, LastName, FirstName, EmploymentStatus
INTO Salaried FROM Employees;
GO
```

Instead of using all records, you can use a condition by which the records would be selected and added to the new table you are creating. To set the condition, you can create a WHERE statement as the last in the whole expression. Here is an example:

```
USE diograndeDB;
GO
SELECT *
INTO FullTimeEmployees
FROM Employees
WHERE EmploymentStatus = N'Full Time';
GO
```

10.5.1 Selecting from Different Tables

In a Query window or the Query Designer, you can show the records of as many tables as you want and those tables do not need to have anything in common. They don't even have to belong to the same database. To show the records of more than one table, in a query window, write a SELECT statement for each table and execute it. If the tables belong to different databases, make sure you indicate this. Here is an example:

```
USE [LOLOITFDB.MDF];
GO
SELECT FName, LName, Gender
FROM studTable;
GO

USE diograndeDB;
GO
SELECT *
INTO FullTimeEmployees
FROM Employees;
GO
```

When executed, the lower part of the window displays the records of the tables.

Here are more examples:

I will create a database and some tables, because it will make the explanation of selecting from different tables easy.

```
USE master;
GO

IF EXISTS(SELECT name
        FROM sys.databases
```

```
            WHERE name = N'MusicCollection'
)
DROP DATABASE MusicCollection
GO


CREATE DATABASE MusicCollection
GO


USE MusicCollection;
GO


CREATE TABLE AfricanPop (
        Artist nchar(50),
        AlbumName nvarchar(50),
        Releaser nvarchar(50),
        CopyrightYear int);
GO


CREATE TABLE Rock (
        Musician nvarchar(50),
        Title nvarchar(50) not null,
        RecordLabel nvarchar(50),
        YearReleased smallint);
GO


INSERT INTO AfricanPop
VALUES(N'Salif Keita', N'Folon... The Past', N'Mango', 1995),
      (N'Vincent Nguini', N'Symphony-Bantu', N'Mesa Records', 1994),
      (N'Tshala Muana', N'Mutuashi', N'Stern''s Music', 1996);
GO


INSERT INTO Rock
VALUES(N'Taylor Dayne', N'Can''t Fight Fate', N'Arista Records', 1989),
      (N'Cyndi Lauper', N'She''s So Unusual', N'CBS', 1983),
      (N'Beverly Hills Cop', N'Soundtrack', N'MCA Records', 1984),
```

(N'Michael Jackson', N'Dangerous', N'MJJ Productions', 1991),

(N'Bruce Hornsby and the Range', N'The Way It Is',

 N'Arista/Ariola International', 1986);

GO

USE MusicCollection

GO

SELECT * FROM AfricanPop;

GO

SELECT ALL * FROM Rock;

GO

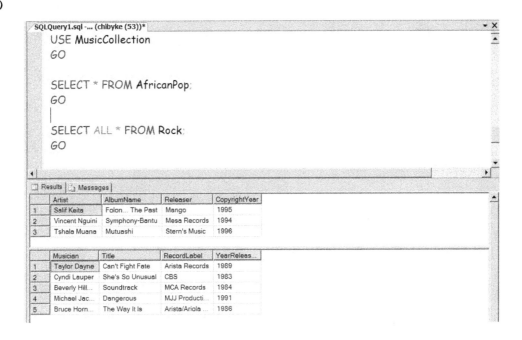

10.5.2 Uniting the Records

Sometimes, either for the sake of comparing records or for preparing to merge them, you may want to display, in one view, the records of more than one table. To support the ability to select records of various tables and show them together, you use the UNION operator. The basic formula is:

SELECT *What* FROM *OneTable*

UNION

SELECT *What* FROM *AnotherTable*;

There are rules you must follow:
- Both tables must have the same number of columns
- The sequence of data types of the columns in each table must be the same. For example, if the column in one table is string-based, the corresponding column in the other table must also be string-based
- The data types in the order of the columns of both tables must be compatible. For example, if the first column of one table has an integer based datatype, the first column of the other table must also have an integer-based data type that can be reconciled with the corresponding column of the other table
- The columns must not have have the same name

Here is an example:

SELECT * FROM AfricanPop
UNION
SELECT * FROM Rock;
GO

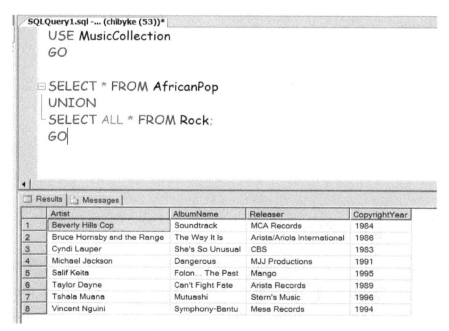

Notice that, by default, the studio uses the column names of the first table as headers. Of course, if you want, you can specify the captions you want, using the AS operator as we did in our previous examples above.

10.6 Copying Records

Imagine you have two tables that are supposed to hold the same values. Maybe the tables were created by different people for the same goal. Maybe there is an old table that holds the records from previous business transactions and there is a new table with the new records. At one time, you may want to merge these records. You have various options.

10.6.1 Copying a Table

Copying the records consists of transferring them from one table, the source, to another table, the target. You can copy all records from the source to the target. You can select what columns to copy. Or you can specify under what conditions some records would be copied. To copy all records from one table to another, the source and the target must have the same number of columns and the same sequence of columns with regards to their datatypes. To copy the records, Start an INSERT or INSERT INTO statement. Instead of the VALUES keyword, create a SELECT statement that involves the source table. Here is an example:

```
USE Exercise;
GO


INSERT INTO Employees SELECT * FROM Seasonals;
GO
```

Once this statement has been executed, all records from the source table are copied to the target table.

If you use the above formula, the records of a column from the source table would be copied to the corresponding column of the target table. Sometimes, you will want to merge tables that neither share the same sequence of columns nor have the same number of columns. In such a case, before copying the records, you must analyze the table to figure out a way to converge the records. Here is an example:

```
INSERT INTO MusicCollection.dbo.AfricanPop SELECT
L.Director,L.VideoTitle,L.Director,L.yearReleased FROM
LoloVideoClub.dbo.VideosInfo L;
GO
```

In the same way, you can set a condition to follow when copying the records.

10.6.2 Merging Records

Imagine you have two tables created at different times, or by different people, or for different reasons. You may have two tables that have duplicate records (the same record in more than one table, for example the same employee number and same name in two tables). You may have records in different tables but some of those records share a field's value (you may have an employee A in one table and another employee B in another table but both have the same employee number with different names, perhaps when two companies merge). As an assignment, you may be asked to combine the records of those tables into one. A database called CarDealer already exist in the SQL Server, the tables below is selected from the database:

```
USE CarDealer;
GO


SELECT CarCode AS [Car Code], CarYear AS [Year],
     Make, Model, Price AS [Market Value] FROM NewCars;
GO


SELECT VehicleNumber AS [Vehicle #], YearManufactured AS [Year],
```

Make, Model, Mileage, OriginalPrice AS [Original Value],

CurrentValue AS [Market Value] FROM UsedVehicles;

GO

Record merging consists of inserting the records of one table, referred to as the source, into another table, referred to as the target. When performing this operation, you will have the option of:

    i.   Inserting all records from the source to the target

   ii.   Updating the records that meet a criterion

  iii.   Deleting some records based on a condition

The basic formula to merge two tables is:

    MERGE *Table1* AS Target

    USING *Table2* AS Source

    ON *Table1.CommonField* = *Table2.CommonField*

    WHEN MATCHED *Matched Options*

       THEN *Match Operation(s)*

    WHEN NOT MATCHED BY TARGET *Not Matched By Target Options*

       THEN *Not Matched By Target Operation(s)*

    WHEN NOT MATCHED BY SOURCE *Not Matched By Source Options*

       THEN *Not Matched By Source Operation(s)*

You start with the MERGE operator followed by the table to which the records will be added. You continue with the USING operator followed by the table from which the records will be retrieved. You must specify the condition by which the records must correspond. To merge the records, each of the tables must have a common column. The columns must not have to have the same name but they should be of the same type (and size). To provide this information, type ON followed by the condition. After specifying the tables and the records corresponding conditions, you must indicate what to do if/when a record from the source condition meets a record from the target table.

Here is an example:

    USE CarDealer;

    GO

```
MERGE UsedVehicles AS Target
USING NewCars AS Source
ON (Target.VehicleNumber = Source.CarCode)
WHEN NOT MATCHED BY Target
    THEN INSERT(VehicleNumber, YearManufactured,
            Make, Model, OriginalPrice)
        VALUES(CarCode, CarYear, Make, Model, Price)
WHEN MATCHED
    THEN UPDATE SET Target.YearManufactured = Source.CarYear,
                Target.Make = Source.Make,
                Target.Model = Source.Model,
                Target.OriginalPrice = Source.Price;
```

10.6.3 Outputting the Results of a Merge

If you do a merge using the above formula, after the merge has been performed, you would see result (but will assume that the execution is successful) unless you run a new query on the target table. Fortunately, you can ask the database engine to immediately display a summary of what happened. To do this, after the last THEN statement, create an OUTPUT expression. The formula to is as follows:

MERGE *Table1* AS Target
USING *Table2* AS Source
ON *Table1.CommonField = Table2.CommonField*
WHEN MATCHED *Matched Options*
    THEN *Match Operation(s)*
WHEN NOT MATCHED BY TARGET *Not Matched By Target Options*
        THEN *Not Matched By Target Operation(s)*
WHEN NOT MATCHED BY SOURCE *Not Matched By Source Options*
        THEN *Not Matched By Source Operation(s)*
OUTPUT $action, DELETED | INSERTED | *from_table_name.**

To get a summary of the merging operation(s), if you are performing only one type of operation, type OUTPUT, followed by either inserted.* or deleted.*. If you are performing different types of operations, type OUTPUT, followed by $action, followed by either inserted.* or deleted.* or both.

Here is an example of outputting the result of merged records:

```
USE CarDealer;
GO


MERGE UsedVehicles AS Target
USING NewCars AS Source
ON (Target.VehicleNumber = Source.CarCode)
WHEN NOT MATCHED BY Target
     THEN INSERT(VehicleNumber, YearManufactured,
               Make, Model, OriginalPrice)
          VALUES(CarCode, CarYear, Make, Model, Price)
WHEN MATCHED
     THEN UPDATE SET Target.YearManufactured = Source.CarYear,
                    Target.Make = Source.Make,
                    Target.Model = Source.Model,
                    Target.OriginalPrice = Source.Price
OUTPUT $action, inserted.*, deleted.*;
GO
```

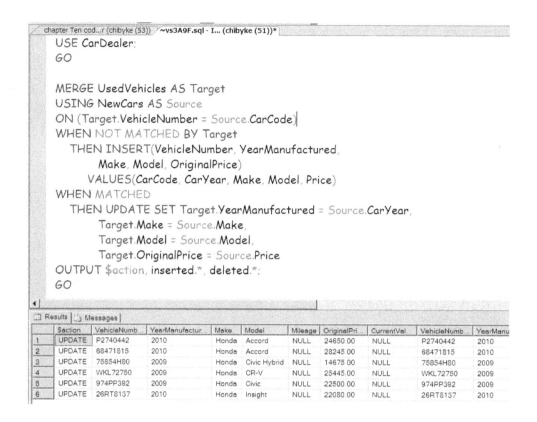

```
chapter Ten cod...r (chibyke (53))    ~vs3A9F.sql - I... (chibyke (51))*
    USE CarDealer;
    GO


    MERGE UsedVehicles AS Target
    USING NewCars AS Source
    ON (Target.VehicleNumber = Source.CarCode)
    WHEN NOT MATCHED BY Target
       THEN INSERT(VehicleNumber, YearManufactured,
           Make, Model, OriginalPrice)
           VALUES(CarCode, CarYear, Make, Model, Price)
    WHEN MATCHED
       THEN UPDATE SET Target.YearManufactured = Source.CarYear,
           Target.Make = Source.Make,
           Target.Model = Source.Model,
           Target.OriginalPrice = Source.Price
    OUTPUT $action, inserted.*, deleted.*;
    GO
```

Results | Messages

	Section	VehicleNumb...	YearManufactur...	Make	Model	Mileage	OriginalPri...	CurrentVal...	VehicleNumb...	YearManu
1	UPDATE	P2740442	2010	Honda	Accord	NULL	24650.00	NULL	P2740442	2010
2	UPDATE	68471815	2010	Honda	Accord	NULL	28245.00	NULL	68471815	2010
3	UPDATE	75854H80	2009	Honda	Civic Hybrid	NULL	14675.00	NULL	75854H80	2009
4	UPDATE	WKL72750	2009	Honda	CR-V	NULL	25445.00	NULL	WKL72750	2009
5	UPDATE	974PP392	2009	Honda	Civic	NULL	22500.00	NULL	974PP392	2009
6	UPDATE	26RT8137	2010	Honda	Insight	NULL	22080.00	NULL	26RT8137	2010

10.7   Common Table Expressions (CTE)

A common table expression, or CTE, is a temporary selection or other query operation of records from one or more tables; simply put that CTE is a demo table. You use it to get an idea of what the query operation would produce if performed on a table. You can create a CTE to create, select, merge, or delete records. There are two types of common table expressions: recursive and non-recursive.

10.7.1 Application of Common Table Expressions

i.   Creating a Common Table Expression

The formula to create a common table expression (CTE) is:

[WITH <*common_table_expression*> [,...n]]

<common_table_expression>::=

    expression_name [(column_name [,...n])]

  AS

    (*CTE_query_definition*)

You start with the WITH keyword followed by a name for the temporary set. The name must be different from any table that will be used in the CTE's expression. Later we will see the parameters you can add after the name. After the name, type AS followed by parentheses. In the parentheses, create a simple or composite SELECT expression. After the code that defines the CTE, that is, after the AS(*CTE_query_definition*) expression, create a SELECT statement that will produce the results.

Here is an example of CTE:

```
USE guestInn;
GO

WITH BedRooms AS
(
    SELECT * FROM SleepingRooms
)

SELECT * FROM BedRooms;
GO
SELECT * FROM SleepingRooms;
GO
```

```
USE guestInn;
GO

WITH BedRooms AS
(
    SELECT * FROM SleepingRooms
)

SELECT * FROM BedRooms;
GO
SELECT * FROM SleepingRooms;
GO
```

Results | Messages

	RoomNumber	RoomType	BedType	Rate	Available
1	104	Bedroom	Single	80.25	0
2	105	Bedroom	Double	95.50	1
3	106	Bedroom	Single	65.95	1
4	107	Bedroom	Single	65.95	1
5	108	Bedroom	Double	92.50	1
6	109	Bedroom	Single	68.95	0
7	110	Bedroom	Single	74.95	1
8	116	Family	Double	112.95	0
9	202	Family	Double	105.95	1
10	203	Family	Single	102.50	1
11	204	Bedroom	Double	115.95	1

	RoomNumber	RoomType	BedType	Rate	Available
1	104	Bedroom	Single	80.25	0
2	105	Bedroom	Double	95.50	1
3	106	Bedroom	Single	65.95	1
4	107	Bedroom	Single	65.95	1
5	108	Bedroom	Double	92.50	1
6	109	Bedroom	Single	68.95	0

Query executed successfully.   IWUALAMC-PC (10.0 RTM) | chibyke (

Here is another example:

```
USE guestInn;
GO

WITH BedRooms AS
(
    SELECT * FROM SleepingRooms WHERE Available = 1
)
SELECT * FROM BedRooms
GO
```

ii.   A CTE With Parameters

To make sure you can externally control the results of a CTE, you can pass a type of parameter to it. To do this, after the name of the CTE and before the AS operator, add the parentheses and pass one or more parameters, each represented by a name. The names of parameters must be the exact same names of columns of the table(s) from which the CTE's statement will be based. The number of columns must be the same as the number of columns that will be involved in the final SELECT statement. In the body of the CTE, use the parameter(s) as you wish. For example, you can involve the parameter(s) in a condition in the CTE.

Here is an example:

```
USE guestInn;
GO

WITH BedRooms(RoomNumber, RoomType, BedType, Rate, Available)
AS
(
    SELECT RoomNumber, RoomType, BedType, Rate, Available
    FROM SleepingRooms
    WHERE BedType = N'Single'
)
SELECT RoomNumber, RoomType, Rate, Available FROM BedRooms;
GO
```

Here is another example:

```
USE guestInn;
GO

WITH BedRooms(RoomNumber, RoomType, BedType, Rate, Available)
AS
(
    SELECT RoomNumber, RoomType, BedType, Rate, Available
    FROM SleepingRooms
    WHERE BedType = N'Single'
```

```
)
SELECT RoomNumber, RoomType, Rate, Available
FROM BedRooms
WHERE Available = 1;
GO
```

10.7.2 Recursive Common Table Expressions

The most direct solution to the subtree problem is the recursive common table expression, introduced in SQL Server 2005. A recursive common table expression is a CTE that can contain more than one SELECT statement. In the body of the CTE, you can create as many SELECT statements as you want but those statements must be joined. To join them, you can use a UNION, UNION ALL, or MERGER operator.

The first SELECT statement defines the anchor node from which the recursion will start, i.e., the top of the subtree. When the recursion starts, the row(s) returned by this query are added to the CTE. The second SELECT defines how rows are recursively added to the result set. Therefore, using a CTE offers the advantages of improved readability and ease in maintenance of complex queries. The query can be divided into separate, simple, logical building blocks. These simple blocks can then be used to build more complex, interim CTEs until the final result set is generated.

Here is an example:
```
USE guestInn;
GO

WITH HotelRooms
AS
(
    SELECT * FROM SleepingRooms
    UNION
    SELECT * FROM ConferenceRooms
```

```
)
SELECT * FROM HotelRooms;
GO
```

This is an example that will list all the available rooms:

```
USE guestInn;
GO

WITH HotelRooms
AS
(
    SELECT * FROM SleepingRooms
    UNION
    SELECT * FROM ConferenceRooms
)
SELECT * FROM HotelRooms
WHERE Available = 1;
GO
```

10.7.3 Data Joins

When studying relationships, we reviewed techniques of making data from one table available to the records of another table. This is demonstrated to reduce data duplication and mistakes. Another issue that involves the combination of tables consists of creating records from more than one table and making the result into a single list; this is the basis of data joins.

A data join is a technique of creating a list of records from more than one table, using all columns from all tables involved, or selecting only the desired columns from one or all of the tables involved. This means that a data join is essentially created in three steps:

    1. Selecting the tables that will be involved in the join

    2. Selecting a column that will create the link in each table

3. Writing a SQL statement that will create the records

i. The Tables of a Join

Before creating a join, you must have the tables that would be involved. The tables are created using the techniques we have seen in previous lessons. It is also important to create a primary key for each table. The parent table would usually need only this primary key that would be used to "link" it to a child table. If needed, you can then create the necessary records for the table. Here is an example:

```
CREATE TABLE Genders
(
    GenderID int identity(1, 1) not null,
    Gender nchar(15),
    CONSTRAINT PK_Genders PRIMARY KEY(GenderID)
);
GO


INSERT INTO Genders(Gender)
VALUES(N'Male'),(N'Female'),(N'Unknown');
GO
```

When creating the child table, remember to create a column that would serve as the link with the parent table. By a (good) habit as we saw when studying relationships, the name of the foreign key and the datatype of this column are the same as the primary key of the parent table. Here is an example:

ii. Join Creation

Equipped with the necessary tables and their columns, you can create the join. To do this in the SQL Server Management Studio, in the Object Explorer, right-click the database and click open a Query window. Then do any of the following:

- On the main menu, click Query, Design Query in Editor... Or
- Right-click somewhere in the Query window and click Query Design in Editor

    Any of these actions would display the Table window as shown below.

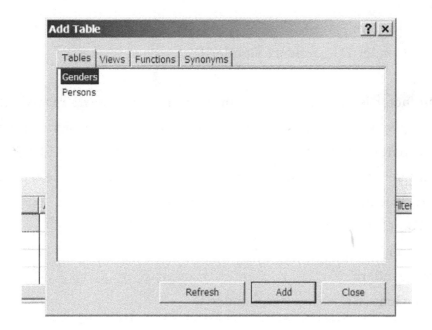

Because the foundation of a join lies on at least two tables, you should add them. If a relationship was already established between the tables, a joining line would show it.

In the SQL Server, the basic formula to create a join is:

SELECT *WhatColumn(s)*
FROM *ChildTable*
TypeOfJoin ParentTable
ON *Condition*

The *ChildTable* factor specifies the table that holds the records that will be retrieved. It can be represented as follows:

SELECT *WhatColumn(s)*
FROM Persons
TypeOfJoin ParentTable
ON *Condition*

The *ParentTable* factor specifies the table that holds the column with the primary key that will control the record that is related to the child table, which will be displayed. This factor would be represented as follows:

SELECT *WhatColumn(s)*

FROM Persons

TypeOfJoin Genders

ON Persons.GenderID = Genders.GenderID

The *Condition* factor is a logical expression used to validate the records that will be returned or displayed. To create the condition, you should assign the primary key column of the parent table to the foreign key column of the child table. Because both columns likely have the same name, to distinguish them, their names should be qualified. Here is an example of what I mean:

SELECT *WhatColumn(s)*

FROM Persons

TypeOfJoin Genders

ON Persons.GenderID = Genders.GenderID

The *WhatColumn(s)* factor of our formula allows you to make a list of the columns you want to select from the table(s). As you are aware, you can include all columns by using the * operator. Here is an example:

SELECT *

FROM Persons

TypeOfJoin Genders

ON Persons.GenderID = Genders.GenderID

In this case, all columns from all tables would be included in the result. Instead of all columns, you may want a restricted list. In this case, create the list after the SELECT keyword separating them with commas. You can use the name of a column normally if that name is not duplicated in more than one column. Here is an example:

SELECT LastName, FirstName, Gender

FROM Persons

TypeOfJoin Genders

ON Persons.GenderID = Genders.GenderID

If the same name of a column is found in more than one table, as is the case for a primary-foreign key combination, you should qualify the name(s) with the corresponding table names. Here is an example:

```
SELECT LastName, FirstName, Persons.GenderID,
     Genders.GenderID, Gender
FROM Persons
TypeOfJoin Genders
ON Persons.GenderID = Genders.GenderID
```

If you have a schema, you can use it to qualify each table. Here is an example:

```
SELECT dbo.Persons.LastName, dbo.Persons.FirstName, dbo.Persons.GenderID,
     dbo.Genders.GenderID, dbo.Genders.Gender
FROM dbo.Persons
TypeOfJoin dbo.Genders
ON dbo.Persons.GenderID = dbo.Genders.GenderID
```

You can also use an alias name for each table. Here is an example:

```
SELECT pers.LastName, pers.FirstName, pers.GenderID,
     Genders.GenderID, Genders.Gender
FROM Persons pers
TypeOfJoin Genders
ON pers.GenderID = Genders.GenderID
```

iii. Cross and Inner Joins

When studying data relationships, we saw the role of the primary and foreign keys in maintaining the exchange of information between the two tables. This technique of linking tables plays a major part when creating a join. It allows you to decide whether you want to include all records or isolate some of them. To respect the direction of a relationship between two tables as it is applied to a query, Transact-SQL supports three types of joins. They are:

a. Cross Joins

A cross join creates a list of all records from both tables. The first record from the parent table is associated to each record from the child table, then the second record from the parent table is associated to each record from the child table, and so on. In this case, there is no need of a common column between both tables. In other words, you will not use the ON clause.

To create a cross join, you can replace the *TypeOfJoin* factor of our formula with CROSS JOIN or CROSS OUTER JOIN. Here is an example:

```
SELECT Persons.PersonID, Persons.FirstName, Persons.LastName,
        Genders.GenderID, Genders.Gender
FROM Persons
CROSS JOIN Genders
GO
```

By default, in the SQL Server Management Studio, after you have just added a table to another one (if no relationship was already established between both tables), the query will automatically make a cross join. All you have to do is to select the needed columns. See below for diagram explanation:

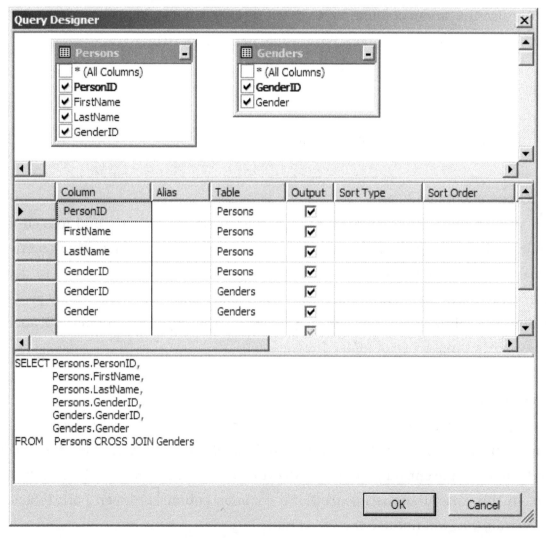

After selecting the columns, you can click OK and execute the query.

b. Inner Joins

Imagine you have two tables that can be linked through a table's primary key and another table's foreign key.

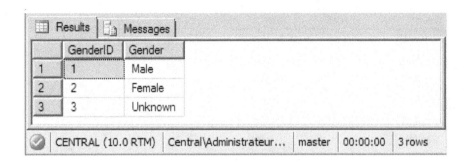

Later you will notice that some records in the Persons table do not have an entry for the GenderID column and were marked with *NULL* by the database engine. When creating a query of records of the Persons table, if you want your list to include only records that have an entry, you can create it as inner join.

By default, from the SQL Server Management Studio, when creating a new query, if a relationship was already established between both tables, the query is made an inner join. If there was no relationship explicitly established between both tables, you would have to create it or edit the SQL statement. Here is an example:

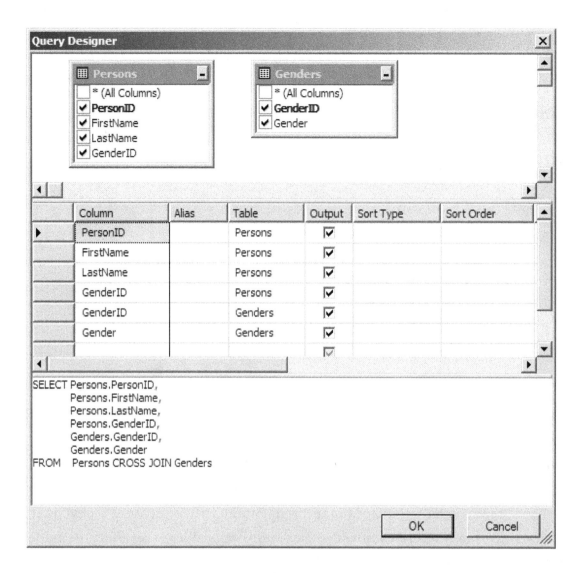

Notice that, because no relationship is established between both tables, the join is crossed. To create an inner join, you have two options. You can drag the primary key from the parent table and drop it on the foreign key in the child table. Here is an example:

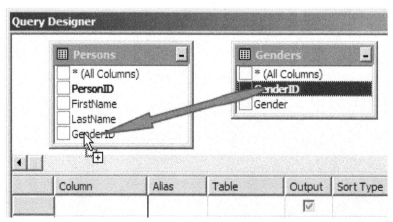

Alternatively, you can edit the SQL statement manually to make it an inner join. To do this, you would specify the *TypeOfJoin* factor of our formula with the expression INNER JOIN. Here we go:

```
SELECT Persons.PersonID, Persons.FirstName, Persons.LastName,
Persons.GenderID,
    Genders.GenderID AS [Gender ID], Genders.Gender
FROM Persons INNER JOIN Genders ON Persons.GenderID =
Genders.GenderID;
GO
```

After creating the join, in the Diagram section, a line would be created to join the tables as show below.

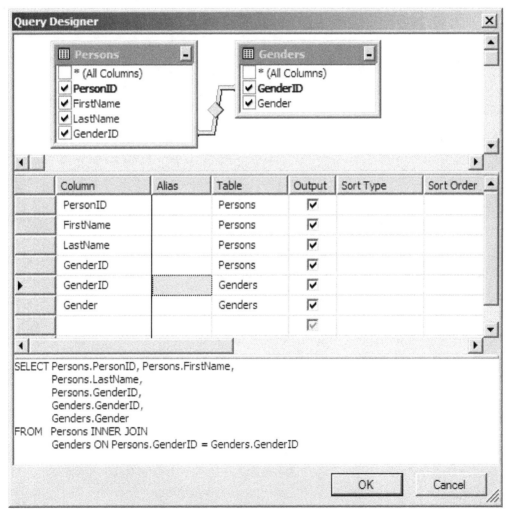

You can then execute the query to see the result.

	PersonID	FirstName	LastName	Gender	Gender	Gender
1	1	John	Iwuji	1	1	Male
2	2	Peter	Nwafor	1	1	Male
3	4	Mary	Iwuala	2	2	Female
4	5	Onyinye	Ubochi	2	2	Female
5	6	Helen	Okey	3	3	Unknown
6	7	Joy	John	2	2	Female
7	8	Robert	Nwaogu	2	2	Female
8	10	NULL	Millam	1	1	Male
9	11	NULL	Goodluck	2	2	Female
10	12	Stanley	Chidi	2	2	Female
11	13	Nneoma	Goodluck	3	3	Unknown
12	14	Mike	Okeogu	1	1	Male
13	16	Edna	Uja	2	2	Female
14	17	Lawrence	Iwuala	2	2	Female
15	19	Obinna	NULL	1	1	Male
16	20	Obinna	Iwuala	1	1	Male
17	21	Onyeka...	Goodluck	1	1	Male
18	22	Esther	Okunwa	2	2	Female

Query executed successfully. IWU/

We mentioned earlier that you can include all columns in the query. In our result, since we are more interested in the gender of each Persons record, we would not need the GenderID column from the Genders table. Here is an example:

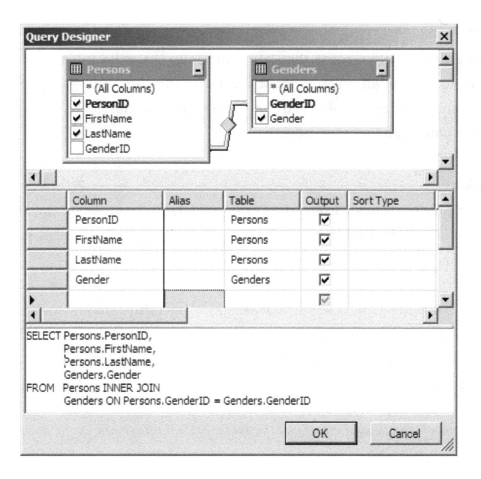

As mentioned earlier, notice that the result includes only records that have an entry (a non-NULL entry) in the GenderID foreign key column of the Persons table. An alternative to the **INNER JOIN** expression is to simply type **JOIN**. Here is an example:

    SELECT Persons.PersonID, Persons.FirstName, Persons.LastName,
        Genders.Gender
    FROM Persons
    JOIN Genders
    ON Persons.GenderID = Genders.GenderID
    GO

To destroy a join between two tables, if you are working in the Table window, you can right-click the line that joins the tables and click Remove. In SQL code, you must modify the expressions that make up the join (the JOIN and the ON expressions).

c. Outer Joins

Instead of showing only records that have entries in the child table, you may want your query to include all records, including those that are null. To get this result, you would create an outer join. You have three options, namely: Left Outer Joins, Right Outer Joins and Full Outer Joins

Left Outer Joins

A left outer join produces all records of the child table, also called the right table. The records of the child table that do not have an entry in the foreign key column are marked as *NULL*.

To create a left outer join, if you are working in the Table window, in the Diagram section, right-click the line that joins the tables and click the option that would select all records from the child table (in this case, that would be Select All Rows From Genders):

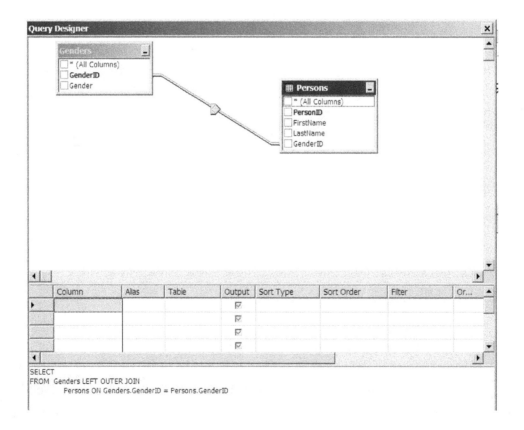

Alternatively, you can replace the *TypeOfJoin* factor of our formula with either LEFT JOIN or LEFT OUTER JOIN. Here is an example:

```
SELECT  Persons.PersonID, Persons.FirstName, Persons.LastName,
        Genders.GenderID, Genders.Gender
FROM Persons
LEFT OUTER JOIN Genders
ON Persons.GenderID = Genders.GenderID
GO
```

In both cases, the button in the middle of the line would be added an arrow that points to the parent table. You can then execute the query to see the result. Notice that the result includes all records of the Persons (also called the Left) table and the records that do not have an entry in the GenderID column of the Genders (the right) table are marked with *NULL*.

Right Outer Joins

A right outer join considers all records from the parent table and finds a matching record in the child table. To do this, it starts with the first record of the parent table (in this case the Genders table) and shows each record of the child table (in this case the Persons table) that has a corresponding entry. This means that, in our example, a right outer join would first create a list of the Persons records that have a 1 (male) value for the GenderID column. After the first record, the right outer join moves to the second record, and so on, each time, listing the records of the child table that have a corresponding entry for the primary key of the parent table.

To visually create a right outer join in the Table window, after establishing a join between both tables, if you had previously created a left outer join, you should remove it by right-clicking the line between the tables and selecting the second option under Remove. Then, you can right-click the line that joins them and click the option that would select all records from the parent table. In our example, you would click Select All Rows From Genders.

To create a right outer join in SQL code, you can replace the *TypeOfJoin* factor of our formula with RIGHT JOIN or RIGHT OUTER JOIN. Here is an example:

```
SELECT Persons.PersonID, Persons.FirstName, Persons.LastName,
```

```
        Genders.GenderID, Genders.Gender
FROM Persons
RIGHT OUTER JOIN Genders
ON Persons.GenderID = Genders.GenderID
GO
```

In both cases, the button on the joining line between the tables would have an arrow that points to the child table. You can then run the query. Here is an example:

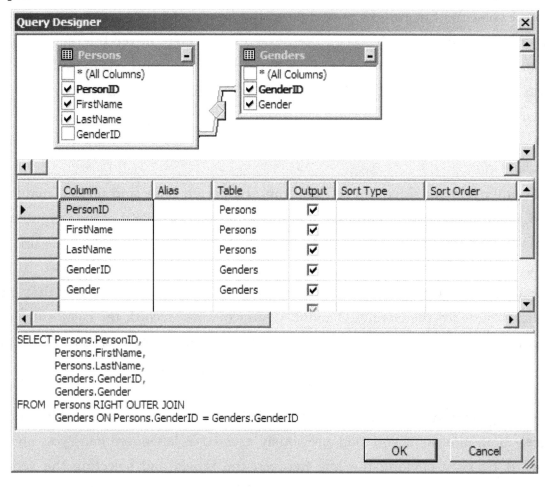

	PersonID	FirstName	LastName	Gender..	Gender
1	1	John	Iwuji	1	Male
2	2	Peter	Nwafor	1	Male
3	8	Robert	Nwaogu	1	Male
4	11	NULL	Goodluck	1	Male
5	12	Stanley	Chidi	1	Male
6	14	Mike	Okeogu	1	Male
7	17	Lawrence	Iwuala	1	Male
8	19	Obinna	NULL	1	Male
9	20	Obinna	Iwuala	1	Male
10	21	Onyekachi	Goodluck	1	Male
11	4	Mary	Iwuala	2	Female
12	5	Onyinye	Ubochi	2	Female
13	7	Joy	John	2	Female
14	10	NULL	Millam	2	Female
15	13	Nneoma	Goodluck	2	Female
16	16	Edna	Uja	2	Female
17	22	Esther	Okunwa	2	Female
18	6	Helen	Okey	3	Unknown

Notice that the query result starts with the first record of the parent table, also called the left table (in this case the Genders table), and lists the records of the child table, also called the right table (in this case the Persons table), that have the entry corresponding to that first record. Then it moves to the next GenderID value. Also, notice that there are no *NULL* records in the Gender.

Full Outer Joins

A full outer join produces all records from both the parent and the child tables. If a record from one table does not have a value in the other value, the value of that record is marked as *NULL*.

To visually create a full outer join, in the Table window, right-click the line between the tables and select each option under Remove so that both would be checked. To create a full outer join in SQL code, replace the *TypeOfJoin* factor of our formula with FULL JOIN or FULL OUTER JOIN. Here is an example:

    SELECT Persons.PersonID, Persons.FirstName, Persons.LastName,
        Genders.GenderID, Genders.Gender
    FROM Persons
    FULL OUTER JOIN Genders
    ON Persons.GenderID = Genders.GenderID
    GO

The button on the line between the tables would now appear as a square. You can then execute the query. Here is an example:

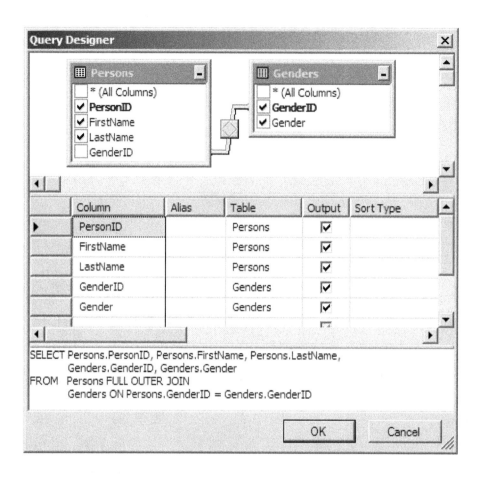

	PersonID	FirstName	LastName	Gender...	Gender
1	1	John	Iwuji	1	Male
2	2	Peter	Nwafor	1	Male
3	3	Peter	Iwuala	NULL	NULL
4	4	Mary	Iwuala	2	Female
5	5	Onyinye	Ubochi	2	Female
6	6	Helen	Okey	3	Unknown
7	7	Joy	John	2	Female
8	8	Robert	Nwaogu	1	Male
9	9	Helène	Chibueze	NULL	NULL
10	10	NULL	Millam	2	Female
11	11	NULL	Goodluck	1	Male
12	12	Stanley	Chidi	1	Male
13	13	Nneoma	Goodluck	2	Female
14	14	Mike	Okeogu	1	Male
15	15	Chinwendu	NULL	NULL	NULL
16	16	Edna	Uja	2	Female
17	17	Lawrence	Iwuala	1	Male
18	18	NULL	Nwabe...	NULL	NULL
19	19	Obinna	NULL	1	Male
20	20	Obinna	Iwuala	1	Male
21	21	Onyekachi	Goodluck	1	Male
22	22	Esther	Okunwa	2	Female

Just as we have involved only two tables in our joins so far, you can create a join that includes as many tables as possible.

iv.   Joins and Data Analysis

As demonstrated so far and in previous lessons, the main reason for creating queries is to isolate unwanted records during data retrieval. This is done using conditions and criteria. Joins enhance this capability because they allow you to consider records from different tables and include them in a common SQL statement. In the joins we have created so far, we considered all records and let the database engine list them using only the rules of joins built-in the T-SQL. To make such a list more useful or restrictive, you can pose your own conditions that should be respected to isolate records like a funnel. As done in previous lessons, to include a criterion in a SELECT statement, you can create a WHERE clause.

Here is an example:

```
SELECT Persons.PersonID, Persons.FirstName, Persons.LastName,
    Genders.GenderID, Genders.Gender
FROM   Persons LEFT OUTER JOIN
    Genders ON Persons.GenderID = Genders.GenderID
```

```
WHERE  Genders.Gender = N'female';
GO
```

10.8   Logical Conjunctions and Disjunctions

So far, we have stated the conditions one at a time. This made their interpretation easier. Sometimes, you will need to test a condition that depends on another. Boolean algebra allows you to combine two conditions and use the result, or to test two conditions but consider if either is true.

10.8.1 Logical Conjunctions

For an IwuEstateMgt estate company, suppose you have a customer who is considering purchasing a bungalow at Aba, Abia state, you have to check the Property Details table to know if you have such request. To respond to this request, you must examine two conditions for each property:

i.   The property must be a Bungalow
ii.   The property must be located in Aba

When preparing your listing prior to seeing the customer, you will have to build a query that will retrieve the required information. Here is an example:

```
select P.PropertyType, P.City, P.Bedrooms, P.MarketValue
from estateMgt.PropertyInfo  P
where (P.PropertyType = N'Bungalow') and (P.City = N'Aba');
GO
```

From these two results, notice that there is no relationship between the fact that a property is a Bungalow and that it is located in Aba. But our customer would purchase the property only if BOTH conditions are met. This type of condition is referred to as logical conjunction. To create a logical conjunction in SQL Server, you use the AND operator. To write the statement, you use the following formula:

```
SELECT WhatColumn(s)
```

FROM *WhatObject*

WHERE *Condition1* AND *Condition2*

The *WhatColumn(s)* and the *WhatObject* factors are the same thing we have been using. The AND keyword is the operator that joins the conditions. Each condition is written as a SQL operation using the formula:

Column operator Value

In this case, the WHERE operator resembles the IF conditional statement. The *Condition1* is the first that would be examined. If the first condition is false, the whole statement is false and there is no reason to examine the second condition. If the first condition is true, then the second condition would be examined. Based on this, suppose we want to get a list of female students who live in Abia. The SQL statement used to get this list can be written as follows:

SELECT FirstName, LastName, Gender, City, State

FROM   Students

WHERE Gender = N'female' AND State = N'AB';

GO

We stated that each condition was separately evaluated. For this reason, to make the conjunction statement easier to read, each condition should be included in parentheses. Therefore, the above SQL statement can be written as follows:

SELECT FirstName, LastName, Gender, City, State

FROM   Students

WHERE (Gender = N'female') AND (State = N'md')

You can also negate a condition by preceding it with the NOT operator.

Here are more examples on Logical Conjunction

Suppose a prospective customer is considering renting a Flat but cannot spend more than 400,000 naira.

SELECT p.PropertyID AS [Property Number],

        p.PropertyType AS Type,

        p.YearOld AS [Year Built],

```
        p.City,
        p.State,
        p.status AS [Status],
        p.Bedrooms AS Beds,
        p.Bathrooms AS Baths,
        p.MarketValue AS Value
FROM estateMgt.PropertyInfo  P
WHERE (p.PropertyType = N'Flat') AND (p.MarketValue < 400000);
GO
```

Suppose the above customer would prefer that the house be in Owerri Imo State. Then to get a list of buildings with Flats in Owerri Imo State that cost less than 400,000 naira; type and execute this code:

```
SELECT D.PropertyID  AS [Prop. Number],
        D.PropertyType AS Type,
        D.YearOld  AS [Year Built],
        D.City,
        D.status  AS [Status],
        D.Bedrooms AS Beds,
        D.Bathrooms AS Baths,
        D.MarketValue AS Value
FROM estateMgt.PropertyInfo D
WHERE (D.PropertyType = N'Flat') AND
    (D.MarketValue < 400000) AND
    (D.City = N'Owerri');
GO
```

10.8.2 Logical Disjunction

Suppose a customer is considering purchasing either a bungalow or a Land. To prepare the list of properties, you must create a query that considers only these two options.

When creating the list, you would want to include a property only if it is either a bungalow or a Land:

1. If the property is a bungalow , our statement is true and we don't need to check the second condition
2. If the property is not a Land, then we consider the second condition. If the property is a Land, our statement becomes true

This type of statement is referred to as logical disjunction. The logical disjunction is expressed in SQL with the **OR** operator.

Here is an example:

```
SELECT D.PropertyID AS [Prop Number],
       D.PropertyType AS Type,
       D.Yearold AS [Year Built],
       D.City,
       D.status  AS [Status],
       D.Bedrooms AS Beds,
       D.Bathrooms AS Baths,
       D.MarketValue AS Value
FROM estateMgt.PropertyInfo D
WHERE (D.PropertyType = N'bungalow ') OR
    (D.PropertyType = N'Land');
GO
```

10.8.3 Logical Operations on Queries

i. BETWEEN

If you have a logical range of values and you want to know if a certain value is contained in that range, you can add a BETWEEN operator to a WHERE statement. The BETWEEN operator is combined with AND to get a list of records between a range values. The basic formula of this operator is:

WHERE *Expression* BETWEEN *Start* AND *End*

The *Expression* placeholder is usually the name of the column whose values you want to examine. The *Start* factor is the starting value of the range to consider. The *End* factor is the highest value to consider in the range. After this condition is executed, it produces the list of values between *Start* and *End.* To create a BETWEEN expression in the Table window, select the desired columns. Under the Filter column that corresponds to the field on which you want to set the condition, type the BETWEEN expression. Here is an example that produces a list of students' whose Registration Number are from 20070000001 to 20102569999:

```
SELECT FirstName, LastName, Gender, City, State
FROM   Students
WHERE RegNo BETWEEN 20070000001 AND 20102569999;
GO
```

It is a good habit to include the whole BETWEEN statement in parentheses. Here is another example that will retrieve the records of students who are in 500 Level who has no reference and made the final CGPA of between 3.5 to 5.0:

```
SELECT FirstName, LastName, Gender, City, [State]
FROM   Students
WHERE ([level] = 500 and ref <> N'F') and (grades= (SELECT grades WHERE grades
between 3.5 AND 5.0));
GO
```

ii. IN a Selected Series

If you have a series of records and you want to find a record or a group of records among them, you can use the **IN** operator by adding it to a **WHERE** statement. The **IN** operator is a type of various **OR** operators. It follows this formula:

IN(*Expression1*, *Expression2*, *Expression_n*)

Each *Expression* factor can be one of the values of a column. This is equivalent to *Expression1* OR *Expression2* OR *Expression_n*, etc. To create an IN expression in the Table window, select the desired columns. Under the Filter column that corresponds to the field on which you want to set the condition, type the IN expression.

From our list of students, imagine that you want to get a list of students who are from Abia, Imo, Anambra, Ebonyi and Enugu and the DB developer did not add zone when developing the database. IN expression can be used to retrieve such records. Here is an example:

```
SELECT FirstName, LastName, Gender, City, [State]
FROM   Students
WHERE  [State] IN (N'AB', N'IM', N'AN', N'EB', N'EN');
GO
```

Here is another example:

```
SELECT D.PropertyID AS [Prop Number],
       D.PropertyType AS Type,
       D.Yearold AS [Year Built],
       D.City,
       D.status  AS [Status],
       D.Bedrooms AS Beds,
       D.Bathrooms AS Baths,
       D.MarketValue AS Value
FROM estateMgt.PropertyInfo D
WHERE D.PropertyType IN (N'bungalow', N'Land');
GO
```

This example will retrieve list of bungalow(s) and Duplexes located in Aba.

```
SELECT D.PropertyID AS [Prop Number],
     D.PropertyType AS Type,
     D.Yearold AS [Year Built],
     D.City,
     D.status  AS [Status],
     D.Bedrooms AS Beds,
     D.Bathrooms AS Baths,
     D.MarketValue AS Value
FROM estateMgt.PropertyInfo D
WHERE (D.PropertyType IN (N'Bungalow ', N'Duplex')) AND
     (D.City = N'Aba');
GO
```

10.9 Data Selection using Functions

10.9.1 Data Selection and Built-In Functions

During your data analysis, you can use functions, whether functions you created yourself or the Transact-SQL built-in functions. To use a built-in function, in the placeholder of the column, type the name of the function, followed by its parentheses. If the function takes some parameters, remember to follow the laydown rules of calling a parameterized function. Here is an example that uses some date-based built-in functions to display the ages of the students:

```
SELECT FirstName, LastName, Gender,
     DATEDIFF(year, '1986-04-27', GETDATE()) AS Age
FROM   Students;
GO
```

You can also include a function in any of the operators we have reviewed so far. Here is an example of the age difference of my wife and I:

```
SELECT DATEDIFF(yy, CONVERT(datetime2, N'1967-12-26', 102),
CONVERT(datetime2, N'1974-04-27', 102)) AS Age
GO
```

Here is another example:
```
SELECT FirstName, LastName, Gender, City, [State]
FROM   Students
WHERE  (DateOfBirth BETWEEN CONVERT(datetime2, N'1990-01-01', 102)
AND
                     CONVERT(datetime2, N'2013-01-01', 102));
GO
```

You can also involve a built-in function in an expression.

10.9.2 User-Defined Functions and Data Selection

If none of the built-in functions satisfies your needs, you can create your own and use it during data analysis. Obviously, you should first create the function. Here is an example of a function that will retrieve students' fullname:

```
CREATE FUNCTION GetFullName
(
    @FName varchar(30),
    @LName varchar(30)
)
RETURNS varchar(61)
AS
BEGIN
    RETURN @LName + ', N' + @FName;
END;
GO
```

Once a function is ready, in the placeholder of your SQL statement, type dbo., if you created it using dbo schema followed by the name of the function, its parentheses, and its parameter(s) if any, inside of the parentheses. Here is an example:

```
SELECT StudentID,
    dbo.GetFullName(FirstName, LastName) AS [Student's Name],
    Gender,
    ParentsNames AS [Parents' Names]
FROM Students;
GO
```

10.10 Transactions

Transactions and locking in SQL Server can be complicated, so this chapter explains the foundation of ACID transactions and SQL Server's default behaviour first, followed by potential problems and variations.

10.10.1   The ACID Properties

Transactions are defined by the ACID properties. ACID is an acronym for four interdependent properties, namely: *atomicity, consistency, isolation,* and *durability.*

Understanding the ACID properties of a transaction is a prerequisite for understanding SQL Server.

i.   Atomicity

A transaction must be *atomic*, meaning all or nothing. At the end of the transaction, either all of the transaction is successful, or all of the transaction fails. If a partial transaction is written to disk, the atomic property is violated. The ability to commit or roll back transactions is required for atomicity.

ii.   Consistency

A transaction must preserve database *consistency*, which means that the database must begin the transaction in a state of consistency and return to a state of consistency once the transaction is complete. For the purposes of ACID, consistency means that every row and value must agree with the reality being modeling, and every constraint must be enforced. For example, if the order rows were written to disk but the order detail rows are not written, the consistency between the Order and OrderDetail tables, or more specifically, the OrderDetail table's OrderID foreign key constraint, would have been violated, and the database would be in an inconsistent state. This is not allowed. Consistency allows the database to be in an inconsistent state during the transaction. The key is that the database is consistent at the completion of the transaction. Like atomicity, the database must be able to commit the whole transaction or roll back the whole transaction if modifications resulted in the database being inconsistent.

iii.   Isolation

Each transaction must be *isolated*, or separated, from the effects of other transactions. Regardless of what any other transaction is doing, a transaction must be able to continue with the exact same data sets it started with. Isolation is the fence between two transactions. A proof of isolation is the ability to replay a serialized set of transactions on the original set of data and always receive the same result.

For example, assume Edna is updating 100 rows. While Edna's transaction is under way, Chibyke tries to read one of the rows Edna is working on. If Chibyke's read takes place, then Edna's transaction is affecting Chibyke's transaction, and their two transactions are not fully isolated from each other. This property is less critical in a read-only database or a database with only a few users. SQL Server enforces isolation with locks and row versioning.

iv.   Durability

The *durability* of a transaction refers to its permanence regardless of system failure. Once a transaction is committed, it stays committed in the state it was committed. Another transaction that does not modify the data from the first transaction should not affect the data from the first transaction. In addition, the Database Engine must be designed so that even if the data drive crashes, the database can be restored up to the last transaction that was committed a split second before the hard drive died. SQL Server ensures durability with the write-ahead transaction log.

10.10.2   The Myths of Transaction Abortion

The biggest mistake that some developers make is the assumption that if an exception occurs during a transaction, that transaction will be aborted. By default, that is almost *never* the case. Most transactions will live on even in the face of exceptions, as running the following SQL code will show:

```
BEGIN TRANSACTION;
GO
SELECT 1/0 AS DivideByZero;
GO
SELECT @@TRANCOUNT AS ActiveTransactionCount;
GO
```

10.10.3   Programming Transactions

A *transaction* is a sequence of tasks that together constitute a logical unit (batch) of work. All the tasks must complete or fail as a single unit. For example, in the case of a customer withdrawing money from an ATM, the update to the balance account must be written to the disk after he has been paid, else his account should not be updated and be written to the disk. If this did not happen, then the customer will raise alarm of been defrauded by the financial Institution. In SQL Server, every DML operation (SELECT, INSERT, UPDATE, DELETE, MERGE) is a transaction, whether or not it has been executed within a BEGIN TRANSACTION. For example, an INSERT command that inserts 25 rows is a logical unit of work. Each and every one of the 25 rows must be inserted. An UPDATE to even a single row operates within a transaction so that the row in the clustered index (or heap) and the row's data in every non-clustered index are all updated. Even SELECT commands are transactions; a SELECT that should return 1,000 rows must return all 1,000 rows. Any partially completed transaction would violate transactional integrity

i.   **Logical transactions**

If the logical unit of work involves multiple operations, some code is needed to define the perimeter of a transaction; such code is the *beginning* of the transaction, and the other at its completion, at which time the transaction is *committed* to disk. If the code detects an error, then the entire transaction can be *rolled back*, or undone. The following three commands appear simple, but a volume of sophistication lies behind them because they decide if transaction is successful or not:

    a. **BEGIN** TRANSACTION

    b. **COMMIT** TRANSACTION

    c. **ROLLBACK** TRANSACTION

A transaction, once begun, should be either committed to disk or rolled back. A transaction left hanging will eventually cause an error; either a real error or a logical data error, as data is never committed.

Putting T-SQL code to the inventory movement example, if Michael Ray, Production Supervisor at Adventure Works, moves 100 bicycle wheel spokes from miscellaneous storage to the subassembly area, the next code example records the move in the database. The two updates that constitute the logical unit of work (the update to LocationID = 6 and the update to LocationID = 50) are contained inside a BEGIN TRANSACTION and a COMMIT TRANSACTION. The transaction is then wrapped in a TRY block for error handling.

Here is an example:

```
USE AdventureWorks;
GO

BEGIN TRY
BEGIN TRANSACTION
UPDATE Production.ProductInventory
SET Quantity -= 100
WHERE ProductID = 527
AND LocationID = 6 -- misc storage
AND Shelf = 'B'
AND Bin = 4;
UPDATE Production.ProductInventory
SET Quantity += 100
WHERE ProductID = 527
AND LocationID = 50 -- subassembly area
AND Shelf = 'F'
AND Bin = 11;
COMMIT TRANSACTION;
END TRY
BEGIN CATCH
ROLLBACK TRANSACTION
RAISERROR('Inventory Transaction Error', 16, 1)
RETURN;
END CATCH;
GO
```

If all goes as expected, both updates are executed, the transaction is committed, and the TRY block completes execution. However, if either UPDATE operation fails, execution immediately transfers down to the CATCH block, the COMMIT is never executed, and the CATCH block's ROLLBACK TRANSACTION will undo any work that was done within the transaction.

When coding transactions, the minimum required syntax is only BEGIN TRAN, COMMIT, ROLLBACK, so you will often see these commands abbreviated as such in production code.

ii.   **Xact_State()**

Every user connection is in one of three possible transaction states, which may be queried using the Xact_State() function, introduced in SQL Server 2005.

   a. 1: Active, healthy transaction

   b. 0: No transaction

   c. -1: Uncommittable transaction.

It is possible to begin a transaction, experience an error, and not be able to commit that transaction (consider the consistency part of ACID). In prior versions of SQL server these were called *doomed transactions*. Typically, the error-handling catch block will test the Xact_State() function to determine whether the transaction can be committed or must be rolled back. The next CATCH block checks Xact_State() and determines whether it can COMMIT or ROLLBACK the transaction:. Here is an example to justify all the grammar:

```
BEGIN CATCH
IF Xact_State() = 1 -- there is an active committable transaction
COMMIT TRAN;
IF Xact_State() = -1 -- there is an uncommittable transaction
BEGIN
ROLLBACK TRANSACTION
RAISERROR('Inventory Transaction Error', 16, 1);
END
END CATCH;
```

Although the XactState() function is normally used within the error-handling catch block, it is not restricted to the catch block and may be called at any time to determine whether the code is in a transaction.

iii.   Xact_Abort

A common SQL Server myth is that an error condition will roll back the transaction. In fact, unless there is try-catch error handling in place, many error conditions only abort the statement. The batch continues, and the transaction is completed even though an error occurred. Turning on Xact_Abort solves some of these problems by doing two things to the error. First, it promotes statement-level errors into batch-level errors, solving the single-statement error issue. Second, Xact_Abort automatically rolls back any pending transaction. Therefore, Xact_Abort is a very good thing and should often be set in code. Xact_Abort also triggers the try-catch code and sends execution into the catch block. The syntax is: SET XACT_ABORT { ON | OFF }

Here is an example:
SET XACT_ABORT ON;
GO

10.10.4   Nested transactions

Multiple transactions can be nested, although they are rarely nested within a single stored procedure. Typically, nested transactions occur because a stored procedure with a logical transaction calls another stored procedure that also has a logical transaction. These nested transactions behave as one large transaction meaning that changes made in one transaction can be read in a nested transaction — they do not behave as isolated transactions, where actions of the nested transaction can be committed independently of a parent transaction.

When transactions are nested, a COMMIT only marks the current nested transaction level as complete. It does not commit anything to disk, but a rollback undoes all pending transactions. At first this sounds inconsistent, but it actually makes sense, because an error within a nested transaction is also an error in the outer transaction. The @@TranCount indicates the current nesting level. A commit when the trancount > 1 has no effect except to reduce trancount by 1. Only when trancount is 1, will the actions within all levels of the nested transaction be committed to disk. Here is an example returns the current transaction nesting level via the @@TranCount global variable:

```
SELECT @@TRANCOUNT; -- 0
BEGIN TRAN;
SELECT @@TRANCOUNT; -- 1
BEGIN TRAN;
SELECT @@TRANCOUNT; -- 2
BEGIN TRAN;
SELECT @@TRANCOUNT; -- 3
ROLLBACK; – undoes all nested transactions
SELECT @@TRANCOUNT; -- 0
```

If the code might have nested transactions, then it is a good idea to examine @@TranCount (or XactState()) because attempting to COMMIT or ROLLBACK a transaction if no pending transactions exist will raise a 3902 or 3903 error with a 16 severity code to the client.

10.10.5   Implicit transactions

While SQL Server requires an explicit BEGIN TRANSACTION to initiate a logical transaction, this behaviour can be modified so that every DML statement starts a logical transaction if one is not already started (so you do not end up with numerous nested transactions). It is as if there were a hidden BEGIN TRANSACTION before every DML statement. This means that once a SQL DML command is issued, a COMMIT or ROLLBACK is required. To demonstrate implicit transactions, the following code alone will not commit the UPDATE:

```
SELECT @@TRANCOUNT; -- 0
BEGIN TRAN;
SELECT @@TRANCOUNT; -- 1
BEGIN TRAN;
SELECT @@TRANCOUNT; -- 2
BEGIN TRAN;
SELECT @@TRANCOUNT; -- 3
ROLLBACK; -- undoes all nested transactions
SELECT @@TRANCOUNT; -- 0


USE AdventureWorks2008;
GO


SET Implicit_Transactions ON;
UPDATE HumanResources.Department
SET Name = 'Department of Redundant Departments'
WHERE DepartmentID = 2;


--Viewing the @@TranCount global variable does indeed show that there is one
pending transaction level awaiting a COMMIT or rollback
SELECT @@TRANCOUNT;


--Adding a COMMIT TRANSACTION to the end of the batch commits the
transaction, and the update is finalized
COMMIT TRANSACTION;
```

GO

Multiple DML commands or batches will occur within a single logical transaction, so it does not create a bunch of nested transactions.

Note: Turning off implicit transactions, as shown here, only affects future batches. It does not commit any pending transactions.

```
SET Implicit_Transactions OFF;
GO
```

10.10.6   Save points

It is also possible to declare a *save point* within the sequence of tasks and then roll back to that save point only. However, I believe that this mixes programmatic flow of control (IF, ELSE, WHILE) with transaction handling. If an error makes it necessary to redo a task within the transaction, it is cleaner to handle the error with standard error handling than to jury-rig the transaction handling.

10.10.7   Default Locking and Blocking Behaviour of Transaction

When two transactions both need the same resource, SQL Server uses locks to provide transactional integrity between the two transactions. Locking and blocking is not necessarily a bad thing; in fact, I think it is the best thing. It ensures transactional integrity.

There are different types of locks, including *shared* (reading), *update* (getting ready to write), *exclusive* (writing) and more. Some of these locks work well together (e.g., two people can have shared locks on a resource); however, once someone has an exclusive lock on a resource, no one can get a shared lock on that resource, this is referred to as blocking. SQL Server's default transaction isolation is *read committed*, meaning that SQL Server ensures that only committed data is read. While a writer is updating a row, and the data is still yet uncommitted, SQL Server makes other transactions that want to read that data wait until the data is committed. To demonstrate SQL Server's default locking and blocking behaviour, the following code walks through two transactions accessing the same row. Transaction 1 will update the row, while transaction 2 will attempt to select the row. The best way to see these two transactions is with two Query Editor Windows, as shown in the picture below

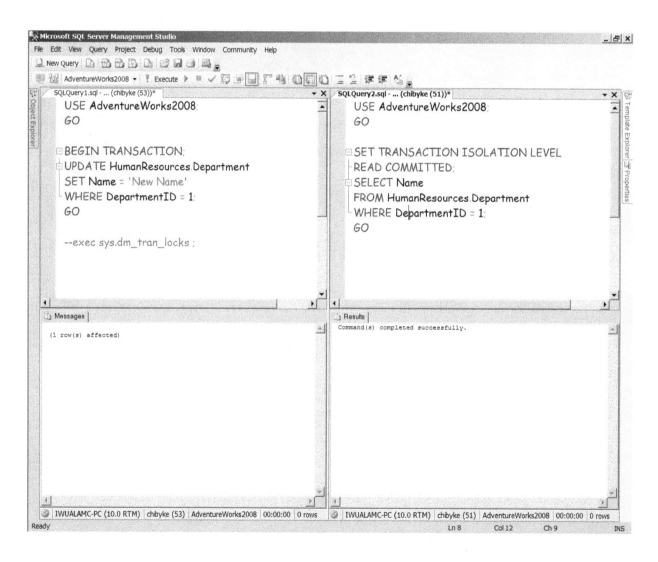

Transaction 1 opens a logical transaction and updates the Department table:

```
-- Transaction 1
USE AdventureWorks2008;
BEGIN TRANSACTION;
UPDATE HumanResources.Department
SET Name = 'New Name'
WHERE DepartmentID = 1;
```

Transaction 1 (on my PC it is on connection, or server process identifier (SPID) , 54) now has an exclusive (X) write lock on the row being updated by locking the key of the record I am updating. The locks can be viewed using the DMV sys.dm_tran_locks (the full query and more details about locks appear later in this chapter).

Transaction 2 ensures that the transaction isolation level is set to the default and then attempts to read the same row transaction 1 is updating. Here is an example:

```
-- Transaction 2
USE AdventureWorks2008;
GO

SET TRANSACTION ISOLATION LEVEL
READ COMMITTED;
SELECT Name
FROM HumanResources.Department
WHERE DepartmentID = 1;
GO
```

There is no result yet for transaction 2. It is waiting for transaction 1 to complete the transaction blocked by transaction 1's exclusive lock. Requerying sys.dm_tran_locks reveals that the second transaction (SPID 51) has *intent to share (IS)* read lock and is waiting for a *share (S)* read lock. While transaction 1 is holding its exclusive lock, transaction 2 has to wait. In other words, transaction 1 is blocking transaction 2. Now, transaction 1 commits the transaction and releases the exclusive lock.

COMMIT TRANSACTION

Immediately, transaction 1 completes and releases its locks. Transaction 2 springs to life and performs the select, reading the committed change. The point of transaction isolation level read committed is to avoid reading uncommitted data. What if the update does not change the data? If transaction 1 updates the data from "John" to "John," what is the harm of reading "John"?

SQL Server handles this situation by not respecting an exclusive lock if the page has not been changed, i.e., if the page is not flagged as dirty. This means that sometimes SQL Server can avoid locking and blocking if the data is not actually being changed. Cool, no? You can prove this behaviour by reexecuting the previous locking and blocking sample code with the same update value.

10.10.8   Deadlocks

A deadlock is a special situation that occurs only when transactions with multiple tasks compete for the same data resource out of order. For example:

1. Transaction 1 has a lock on data A and needs to lock data B to complete its transaction. and

2. Transaction 2 has a lock on data B and needs to lock data A to complete its transaction. Each transaction is stuck waiting for the other to release its lock, and neither can complete until the other does. Unless an outside force intercedes, or one of the transactions gives up and quits, this situation could be infinity.

While a deadlock typically involves two transactions, it can be a cyclic locking and blocking problem involving several transactions — for example, A is waiting on B, which is waiting on C, which is waiting on A. Deadlocks used to be a serious problem. Fortunately, SQL Server handles deadlocks refreshingly well.

i.   Creating a deadlock

It is easy to create a deadlock situation in MS SQL Server using two connections in Management Studio's Query Editor, as illustrated in the picture below. Transaction 1 and transaction 2 will simply try to update the same rows but in the opposite order. Use a third window to watch the locks using Activity Monitor or one of the DMV queries.

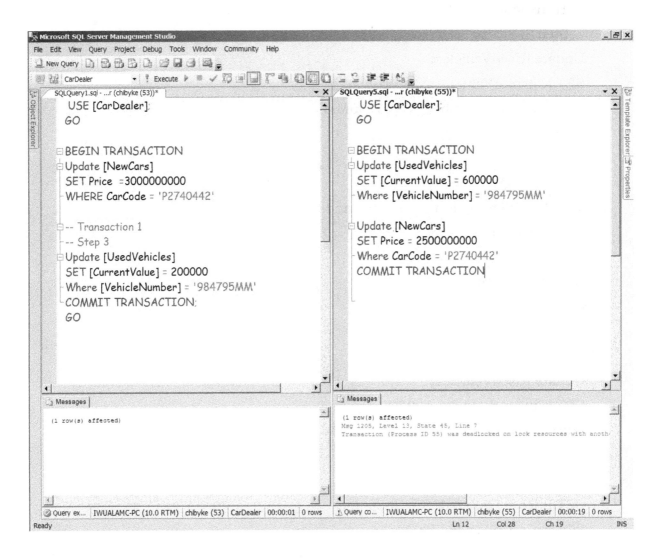

To execute the code, you will need to do the following:

1. Create two query windows. In one paste the following:

```
USE [CarDealer];
GO
-- Transaction 1
-- Step 1

BEGIN TRANSACTION
Update [NewCars]
SET Price  =3000000000
WHERE CarCode = 'P2740442'

-- Transaction 1
-- Step 3
Update [UsedVehicles]
SET [CurrentValue] = 200000
Where [VehicleNumber] = '984795MM'
COMMIT TRANSACTION;
GO
```

2. Paste the following in the second window:

```
-- Transaction 2
-- Step 2
USE [CarDealer];
GO

BEGIN TRANSACTION
Update [UsedVehicles]
SET [CurrentValue] = 600000
Where [VehicleNumber] = '984795MM'

Update [NewCars]
SET Price = 2500000000
Where CarCode = 'P2740442'
COMMIT TRANSACTION
```

Transaction 1 now has an exclusive lock on CarCode P2740442.

Execute in the code in the first query window

-- Transaction 1

-- Step 1

BEGIN TRANSACTION

Update [NewCars]

SET Price =3000000000

WHERE CarCode = 'P2740442'

Transaction 1 now has an exclusive lock on CarCode P2740442.

Execute step 2 in the second window:

-- Transaction 2

-- Step 2

USE [CarDealer];

GO

BEGIN TRANSACTION

Update [UsedVehicles]

SET [CurrentValue] = 600000

Where [VehicleNumber] = '984795MM'

Update [NewCars]

SET Price = 2500000000

Where CarCode = 'P2740442'

COMMIT TRANSACTION

Transaction 2 will gain an exclusive lock on CarCode P2740442 and then try to grab an exclusive lock on VehicleNumber 984795MM but transaction 1 already has it locked. It is not a deadlock yet because although transaction 2 is waiting for transaction 1, transaction 1 is not waiting for transaction 2. At this point, if transaction 1 finished its work and issued a COMMIT TRANSACTION, the data resource would be freed; transaction 2 could get its lock on the NewCars row and be on its way as well.

The trouble begins when transaction 1 tries to update VehicleNumber 984795MM. It cannot get an exclusive lock because transaction 2 already has an exclusive lock. So when the following code is executed:

```
-- Transaction 1
-- Step 3
Update [UsedVehicles]
SET [CurrentValue] = 200000
Where [VehicleNumber] = '984795MM'
COMMIT TRANSACTION;
GO
```

Transaction one will return an error.

10.10.9   Transaction Isolation Levels

Any study of how transactions affect performance must include *transactional integrity*, which refers to the quality, or fidelity, of the transaction. Three types of problems violate transactional integrity: dirty reads, nonrepeatable reads, and phantom rows.

The level of isolation, or the height of the fence between transactions, can be adjusted to control which transactional faults are permitted. The ANSI SQL-92 committee specifies four isolation levels: read uncommitted, read committed, repeatable read, and serializable. SQL Server 2005 introduced two additional row-versioning levels, which enables two levels of optimistic transaction isolation, they are: *snapshot* and *read committed snapshot*. All six transaction isolation levels are listed in Table 10-3 and detailed in this section.

ANSI-92 Isolation Levels

Isolation Level (Transaction isolation level is set for the connection)	Table Hint (override the connection's transaction isolation level)	Dirty Read (Seeing another transaction's noncommitted changes)	Non-Repeatable Read (Seeing another transaction's committed changes)	Phantom Row (Seeing additional rows selected by where clause as a result of another transaction)	Reader/Writer Blocking (A write transaction blocks a read transaction)
Read Uncommitted (least restrictive)	NoLock, Read-Uncommitted	Possible	Possible	Possible	Yes
Read Committed (Sql Server default; moderately restrictive)	ReadCommitted	Prevented	Possible	Possible	Yes
Repeatable Read	RepeatableRead	Prevented	Prevented	Possible	Yes
Serializable (most restrictive)	Serializable	Prevented	Prevented	Prevented	Yes
Snapshot		Prevented	Prevented	Possible	No
Read Committed Snapshot		Prevented	Possible	Possible	No

i.   Setting the transaction isolation level

The transaction isolation level can be set at the connection level using the SET command. Setting the transaction isolation level affects all statements for the duration of the connection, or until the transaction isolation level is changed again. Here is an example:

```
SET TRANSACTION ISOLATION LEVEL
READ COMMITTED;
GO
```

To view the current connection transaction isolation level, use Database Console Commands (DBCC) UserOptions, or query sys.dm_exec_sessions. Here is an example:

```
SELECT TIL.Description
FROM sys.dm_exec_sessions dmv
JOIN (VALUES(1, 'Read Uncommitted'),
(2, 'Read Committed'),
(3, 'Repeatable Read'),
(4, 'Serializable'))
```

```
AS TIL(ID, Description)
ON dmv.transaction_isolation_level = TIL.ID
WHERE session_id = @@spid;
GO
```

Alternately, the transaction isolation level for a single DML statement can be set by using table-lock hints in the FROM clause (WITH is optional). These will override the current connection transaction isolation level and apply the hint on a per-table basis. For example, in the next code, the Department table is actually accessed using a read uncommitted transaction isolation level, not the connection's read committed transaction isolation level:

```
SET TRANSACTION ISOLATION LEVEL
REPEATABLE READ;


SELECT Price
FROM  [NewCars] WITH (NOLOCK)
Where CarCode = 'P2740442';
GO
```

10.11   Committing a Transaction

I have demonstrated ways of committing and rolling back transactions in this chapter, but it will be ideal to explain what committing and rolling back transactions entails. After defining the operations that are part of the transaction, the database engine would execute them in the sequence they are written. You must indicate where this series of transactions ends. To do this, type the COMMIT TRAN or COMMIT TRANSACTION expression as shown below:

```
BEGIN TRAN Name or BEGIN TRANSACTION Name
    Operations
COMMIT TRAN Name or COMMIT TRANSACTION Name
Here is an example:


USE diograndeDB;
```

```sql
GO

CREATE TABLE Employees
(
    EmpID nchar(10),
    EmpName nvarchar(50),
    DateEmployed date,
    HourlySalary money
);
GO

INSERT INTO Employees
VALUES(N'593705', N'Frank Somah', N'20061004', 26.15),
    (N'720947', N'Paul Handsome', N'20000802', 36.05);
GO

INSERT INTO Employees(EmpName , EmpID , DateEmployed)
VALUES(N'Clarice Simms', N'971403', N'20011112');
GO

BEGIN TRANSACTION AddEmployees

INSERT INTO Employees
VALUES(N'595002', N'John Meah', N'20000212', 32.25),
    (N'928375', N'Chuck Stansil', N'20080628'),
    (N'792764', N'Orlando Perez', N'20000616', 12.95);

COMMIT TRANSACTION AddEmployees;
GO

INSERT INTO Employees(EmpName, EmpID ,
        HourlySalary, DateEmployed )
VALUES(N'Gina Palau', N'247903', 18.85, N'20080612');
GO
```

This code asks the database engine to create a table named Employees in the diograndeDB database. After creating the table, it must first one, followed by two records. Then it must process a transaction that consists of creating three records. After that transaction, data entry continues with the addition of a record. For illustration purposes, we included an error in the code for the transaction. Here is an example:

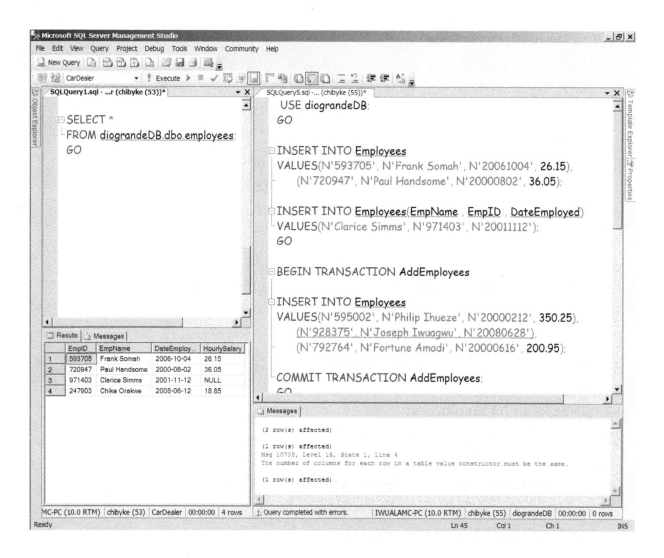

The result of the anticipated four rows are on the left window. Notice that the code where the transaction was held did not complete and its records were not created.

10.12   Rolling Back a Transaction

Rolls back an explicit or implicit transaction to the beginning of the transaction, or to a savepoint inside the transaction. Here is a purported correct code example:

```
USE diograndeDB;
GO


INSERT INTO Employees
VALUES(N'593705', N'Late Chibuisi Iwuala', N'20061004', 500.15),
     (N'720947', N'Elder Timothy Iwuala', N'20000802', 800.05),
     (N'595002', N'John Ani', N'20000212', 350.25);


INSERT INTO Employees(EmpName, EmpID, DateEmployed)
VALUES(N'Dr. Mrs. Eze U. F', N'971403', N'20011112');


INSERT INTO Employees
VALUES(N'928375', N'Edna C. Uja', N'20080628');


INSERT INTO Employees
VALUES(N'792764', N'Ifeanyi Ochije S.', N'20000616', 12.95);


INSERT INTO Employees(EmpName, EmpID,HourlySalary, DateEmployed)
VALUES(N'Engr. Kenny Uchie-Okoro ', N'247903', 18.85, N'20080612');


COMMIT TRANSACTION AddEmployees;
GO
```

When executed, the Query window will look this:

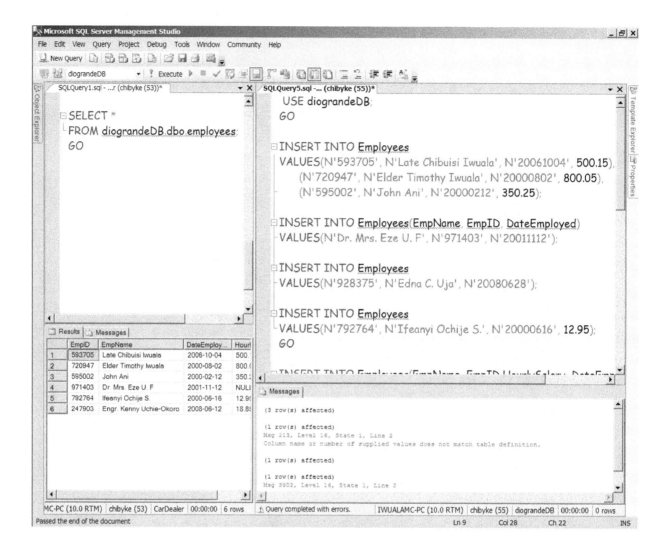

You noticed that errors occurred, despite the error, the transaction was performed and the section with error was ignored. In some cases, to apply the rules or atomicity, you may want to dismiss the whole transaction if a section in it fails. In other words, you would want either the whole transaction to be successful or fail. To ask the database engine to either validate the whole transaction or to dismiss it, you would ask it to roll back the whole transaction. To support this, instead of committing, you would use the ROLLBACK TRANSACTION expression. Its syntax is:

```
ROLLBACK { TRAN | TRANSACTION }
    [ transaction_name | @tran_name_variable
    | savepoint_name | @savepoint_variable ]
[ ; ]
```

You start with a ROLLBACK TRAN or ROLLBACK TRANSACTION. If the transaction has a name, type it or the variable that holds its name. If you plan to save this operation, use the *savepoint_name* or the *@savepoint_variable* factor.

Here is an example of indicating that the transaction should be rolled back if any section of it fails:

```
USE diograndeDB;
GO

BEGIN TRANSACTION AddEmployees

INSERT INTO Employees
VALUES(N'593705', N'Nwanyi-Sunday Madubuike', N'20061004', 100.15),
    (N'720947', N'Chinasa Ibekwe', N'20000802', 150.05),
    (N'595002', N'Jame Ochiagha', N'20000212', 120.25);
GO
INSERT INTO Employees(EmpName, EmpID, DateEmployed)
VALUES(N'Ngbeke Okoroji', N'971403', N'20011112');
GO
INSERT INTO Employees
VALUES(N'928375', N'Mashi Madubuike', N'20080628');
GO
INSERT INTO Employees
VALUES(N'792764', N'Chidinma Iwuji', N'20000616', 450.95);
GO
INSERT INTO Employees(EmpName, EmpID,
        HourlySalary, DateEmployed)
VALUES(N'Eze Vigor', N'247903', 500.85, N'20080612');
GO

ROLLBACK TRANSACTION AddEmployees;
GO
```

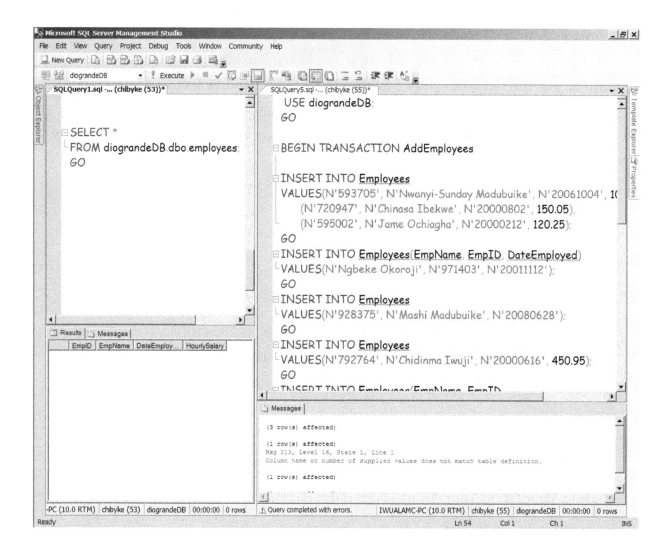

The database engine is asked to add some records to it. The creation of records is included in a transaction with the roll back option. You noticed that error occurred during execution of the code. When the code on the left window is executed, the resulting table is empty:

The code that caused the (one) error is inside the transaction; so, the whole transaction was dismissed, that is why the table remained empty after the execution.

CHAPTER ELEVEN

DATABASE AUTHENTICATION AND AUTHORIZATION

Security, like every other aspect of the database project, must be carefully designed, implemented, and tested. Because security may affect the execution of some procedures, it must be taken into account when the project code is being developed. A simple security plan with a few roles and the IT users as *sysadmins* may suffice for a small organization. Larger organizations — such as the military, banks, or international organizations — require a more complex security plan that's designed as carefully as the logical database schema.

SQL Server security is a broad subject area, with enough potential avenues of exploration that entire books have been written on the topic. This chapter's goal is not to cover the whole spectrum of security knowledge necessary to create a product that is secured from end to end, but to focus on those areas that are most important during the software design and development process as a database developer.
Broadly speaking, data security can be broken into two areas:

i. **Authentication**: The act of verifying the identity of a user of a system
ii. **Authorization**: The act of giving a user access to the resources that a system controls

These two realms of database security can be delegated separately in many cases; so long as the authentication piece works properly, the user can be handed off to authorization mechanisms for the remainder of a session. SQL Server authentication on its own is a big topic, with a diverse range of subtopics including network security, operating system security, and so-called surface area control over the server. While production DBAs should be very concerned with these sorts of issues, authentication is an area that developers can mostly ignore. Developers need to be much more concerned with what happens *after* authentication: that is, how the user is authorized for data access and how data is protected from unauthorized users.

This chapter introduces some of the key issues of data privilege and authorization in MS SQL Server from a development point of view. Included here is an initial discussion on privileges and general guidelines and practices for securing data using MS SQL Server permissions. A related security topic is that of data encryption, which is not covered in this piece.

11.1 DIFFERENCE BETWEEN USER AND LOGINS

The topics covered in this chapter relate to various privilege and authorization scenarios handled within MS SQL Server itself. However, in many database application designs, authorization is handled in the application layer rather than at the database layer. In such applications, users typically connect and log into the application using their own personal credentials, but the application then connects to the database using a single shared application login. This login is given permission to execute all of the stored procedures in the database related to that application, and it is up to authorization routines in the application itself to determine those actions that can be performed by any given user.

There are some benefits to using this approach, such as being able to take advantage of connection pooling between different sessions. However, it means that features provided by MS SQL Server to handle per-user security do not apply. If a bug were to exist in the application, or if the credentials associated with the application login were to become known, it would be possible for users to execute any queries against the database that the application had permission to perform and you know what that means to SQL injection by hackers. For the examples in this chapter, I assume a scenario in which users are connecting to the database using their own personal credentials.

The SQL Server security model is large and complex. In some cases it's more complex than the Windows security model. Because the security concepts are tightly intertwined, the best way to begin is to walk through an overview of the model. SQL Server security is based on the concept of securables "Authorizing Securables", objects that can be secured, and principals, objects that can be granted access to a securable. Principals are logins, users, and roles. Granting CONTROL SERVER to a login gives it equivalent rights to being a member of the sysadmin fixed server role. Logins can also be assigned to server roles. Users are assigned to roles, both of which may be granted permission to objects, as illustrated below. Each object has an owner, and ownership also affects the permissions.

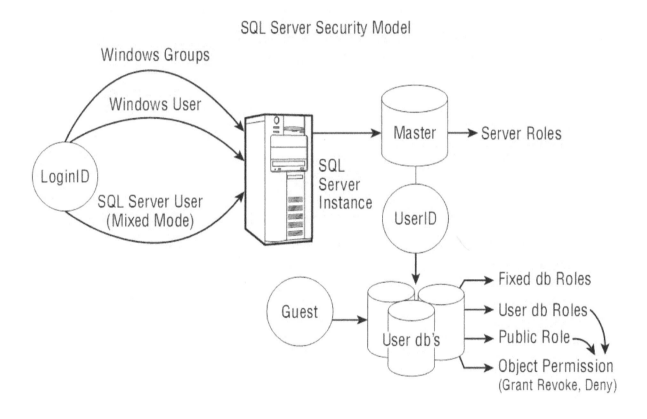

11.1.1 Server-Level Security

A user may be initially identified to SQL Server via one of three methods:

i. **Windows user login**

ii. **Membership in a Windows user group**

iii. **SQL Server-specific login (if the server uses mixed-mode security)**

At the server level, users are known by their login name, which is either a SQL Server login, or a Windows domain and username. Once the user is known to the server and identified, the user has whatever server-level administrative rights have been granted via fixed server roles. If the user belongs to the sysadmin role, he or she has full access to every server function, database, and object in the server. Users also have permissions granted against server securables. A user can be granted access to a database, and his or her network login ID can be mapped to a database-specific user ID in the process. If the user doesn't have access to a database, he or she can gain access as the guest user with some configuration changes within the database server.

11.1.2 Database-Level Security

At the database level, a user may be granted certain administrative-level permissions by belonging to fixed database roles, but the user still can't access the data. He or she must be granted permission to the database objects (e.g., tables, stored procedures, views, functions). User-defined roles are custom roles that serve as groups. The role may be granted permission to a database object, and users may be assigned to a database user-defined role. All users are automatically members of the public standard database role. Certain database fixed roles also affect object access, such as the right to read from or write to the database.

Object permissions are assigned by means of *grant, revoke,* and *deny.* A deny permission trumps a grant permission. Revoke removes the permission assigned, regardless of whether it's deny or grant, which overrides a revoke permission. A user may have multiple permission paths to an object (individually, through a standard database role, and through the public role). If any of these paths are denied, the user is blocked from accessing the object. Otherwise, if any of the paths are granted permission, then the user can access the object. Object permission is very detailed and a specific permission exists for every action that can be performed (select, insert, update, run, and so on) for every object. It's entirely possible for a user to be recognized by SQL Server and not have access to any database other than master, msdb, and tempdb. It's also possible for a user to be defined within a database but not recognized by the server. Moving a database and its permissions to another server, but not moving the logins, causes such orphaned users.

11.1.3 Windows Security

Because SQL Server exists within a Windows environment, one aspect of the security strategy must be securing the Windows server.

Using Windows Security

SQL Server databases frequently support websites, so Internet Information Server (IIS) security and firewalls must be considered within the security plan. Windows security is an entire topic in itself, and therefore outside the scope of this book. If, as a DBA, you are not well supported by qualified network staff, then you should make the effort to become proficient in Windows Server technologies, especially security.

11.1.4 SQL Server login

Donot confuse user access to SQL Server with SQL Server's Windows accounts. The two logins are completely different. SQL Server users don't need access to the database directories or data files on a Windows level because the SQL Server process, not the user, performs the actual file access. However, the SQL Server process needs permission to access the files, so it needs a Windows account. Three types are available:

i.   **Local user account: If network access is not required, this is a viable option. Local user accounts cannot be used outside the server.**

ii. **Local system account: SQL Server can use the local system account of the operating system for permission to the machine. This option is adequate for single-server installations, but fails to provide the network security required for distributed processing. The local system account has more rights than even a member of the Administrators account because the local system account has implicit privileges in the operating system and Active Directory that go beyond membership in the Administrators group.**

iii. **Domain user account (recommended): SQL Server can use a Windows user account created specifically for it. The SQL Server domain user account can be granted administrator rights for the server and can access the network through the server to talk to other servers.**

11.2   Server Security

SQL Server uses a two-phase security-authentication scheme. The user is first authenticated to the server. Once the user is "in" the server, access can be granted to the individual databases. SQL Server stores all login information within the master database that is why I warned you to stay away from the master database if you don't know much about it.

From code, the authentication mode can be checked by using the xp_loginconfig system stored procedure, copy the code below and execute on the Query window:

EXEC xp_loginconfig 'login mode'

For the system stored procedure to report the authentication mode is an extended stored procedure.
That's because the authentication mode is stored in the registry in the following entry:

HKEY_LOCAL_MACHINE\SOFTWARE\Microsoft\MicrosoftSQLServer\<instance_name>\MSSQLServer\LoginMode

A LoginMode value of 1 is for Windows authentication; 0 is for mixed mode. The only ways to set the authentication mode are to use either Management Studio or RegEdit.

11.3 Windows Authentication

Windows Authentication mode is superior to mixed mode because users don't need to learn another password and because it uses the security design of the network. Using Windows Authentication means that users must exist as Windows users in order to be recognized by MS SQL Server. The Windows SID (security identifier) is passed from Windows to MS SQL Server. Windows Authentication is very robust in that it will authenticate not only Windows users, but also users within Windows user groups.
When a Windows user group is accepted as a SQL Server login, any Windows user who is a member of the group can be authenticated by SQL Server. Access, roles, and permissions can be assigned for the Windows user group, and they will apply to any Windows user in the group; isn't that great?

SQL Server also knows the actual Windows username, so the application can gather audit information at both the user level and the group level.

11.3.1 Adding a new Windows login

To use T-SQL code to add a Windows user or group, run the CREATE LOGIN command. Be sure to use the full Windows username, including the domain name. The syntax below suggests what the code should look like:

```
CREATE LOGIN domainName\windowsUserName FROM WINDOWS;
GO
```

Here is an example of creating Windows login:

```
CREATE LOGIN [User-PC\Dr Mrs Eze] FROM WINDOWS;
GO
```

Here is another example:

```
IF EXISTS (SELECT * FROM sys.server_principals WHERE name = N'GODISGOOD-PC\Software N DB')
DROP LOGIN [GODISGOOD-PC\Software N DB]
GO
```

```
CREATE LOGIN [GODISGOOD-PC\Software N DB] FROM WINDOWS WITH DEFAULT_DATABASE=[master], DEFAULT_LANGUAGE=[us_english]
GO
```

11.3.2 Removing a Windows login

Removing a windows login from SQL Server is very simple with MS SQL Management Studio. Select the login in Object Browser and use the context menu to delete the user. To remove a Windows user or group from MS SQL Server, use the DROP LOGIN command. The Windows user or group will exist in Windows; it just won't be recognized by MS SQL Server. The syntax is as follows:

```
DROP LOGIN domainName\windowsUserName;
GO
```

Here is an example of deleting a login from MS SQL Server:

DROP LOGIN [GODISGOOD-PC\Software N DB]

11.3.3 Denying a Windows login

Using the paradigm of grant, revoke, and deny, a user may be blocked for access using ALTER LOGIN for Windows users and DENY CONNECT for Windows groups. This can prevent users or groups from accessing MS SQL Server even if they could otherwise gain entry from another method. For example, suppose the Lecturers' group is granted normal login access, while the Students' group is denied access. If Dr Mrs Eze is a member of both the Lecturers' group and the group; the Students' group's denied access blocks Dr Mrs Eze from the MS SQL Server even though he is granted access as a member of the Lecturers' group, because deny overrides grant.

To deny a Windows user or group, use the DENY CONNECT command. If the user or group being denied access doesn't exist in SQL Server it will report, else DENY CONNECT adds and then denies him, her, or it.

Here is an example:
DENY CONNECT SQL TO [GODISGOOD-PC\Software N DB];
GO

To restore the login after denying access, you must first grant access with the *sp_grantlogin* system stored procedure.

You can deny the ability to log in using T-SQL.

11.4 Setting the default database

The default database is set in the Login Properties form in the General page, if you didn't use the SQL code during the design. The default database can be set from SQL code by means of the ALTER LOGIN command after creating the login. You can recall that in my examples above, I created two login – one with the default database. Here is an example:

```
USE [master]
GO


ALTER LOGIN [User-PC\Dr Mrs Eze] WITH DEFAULT_DATABASE=[smatDB];
GO
```

11.4.1 SQL Server logins

The optional SQL Server logins are useful when Windows authentication is inappropriate or unavailable. It's provided for backward compatibility and for legacy applications that are hard-coded to a SQL Server login. To manage SQL Server users in Management Studio, use the same Login-New dialog used when adding Windows users, but select SQL Server Authentication. In T-SQL code, use the CREATE LOGIN command. Because this requires setting up a user, rather than just selecting one that already exists, it's more complex than adding a sp_grantlogin. So sp_grantlogin creates a new SQL Server login that allows a user to connect to an instance of SQL Server by using SQL Server authentication. Below is the syntax:

sp_addlogin @loginame = '*login*'

, @passwd = '*password*'

, @defdb = '*database*'

, @deflanguage = '*language*'

, @sid = *sid*

, @encryptopt= '*encryption_option*'

[**@loginame** =] '*login*'

Is the name of the login. *login* is **sysname**, with no default.

[**@passwd** =] '*password*'

Is the login password. *password* is **sysname**, with a default of NULL.

For example, the following code adds Edna as a SQL Server user and sets her default database to the FedMinOfHealthDB sample database:

```
EXEC sp_addlogin 'Edna', 'edna4real', 'FedMinOfHealthDB';
GO
```

The server user ID, or SID, is an 85-bit binary value that SQL Server uses to identify the user. If the user is being set up on two servers as the same user, then the SIDs need to be specified for the second server. Query the sys.server_principals catalog view to find the user's SID:

```
SELECT Name, SID
FROM sys.server_principals
WHERE Name = 'Edna';
GO
```

11.4.2 Updating a password

The password can be modified by means of the ALTER LOGIN command:
ALTER LOGIN 'edna4real', 'edna4love', 'Edna'
If the password is empty, use the keyword NULL instead of empty quotes (' ').
Before I talk about authorization, it will be ideal for me to tell you the ingredients of MS SQL Server roles and privileges that can be given to a user.

11.5   Server roles

SQL Server includes only fixed, predefined server roles. Primarily, these roles grant permission to perform certain server-related administrative tasks. A user may belong to multiple roles. The following roles are best used to delegate certain server administrative tasks:

i. *Bulkadmin:* **Can perform bulk insert operations**

ii. *Dbcreator:* **Can create, alter, drop, and restore databases**

iii. *Diskadmin:* **Can create, alter, and drop disk files**

iv. *Processadmin:* **Can kill a running SQL Server process**

v. *Securityadmin:* **Can manage the logins for the server**

vi. *Serveradmin:* **Can configure the serverwide settings, including setting up full-text searches and shutting down the server**

vii. *Setupadmin:* **Can configure linked servers, extended stored procedures, and the startup stored procedure**

viii. *Sysadmin:* **Can perform any activity in the SQL Server installation, regardless of any other permission setting. The sysadmin role even overrides denied permissions on an object.**

SQL Server automatically creates a user, BUILTINS/Administrators, that includes all Windows users in the Windows Admins group and allows a choice of what groups or users are added during setup. The BUILTINS/Administrators user can be deleted or modified if desired. If the SQL Server is configured for mixed-mode security, it also configures the sa account to be disabled.

The sa user is there for backward compatibility.

In code, a user is assigned to a server role by means of a system stored procedure. The syntax:

sp_addsrvrolemember 'login', 'role'

For example, the following code adds the login "XPS\Lauren" to the sysadmin role:

EXECUTE sp_addsrvrolemember 'Edna', 'sysadmin';
GO

The counterpart of sp_addsrvrolemember, sp_dropsrvrolemember, removes a login from a server fixed role:

EXECUTE sp_dropsrvrolemember 'Edna', 'sysadmin';
GO

11.6 Database Security

Once a user has gained access to the server, access may be granted to the individual user on databases basis. Database security is potentially complex. Users are initially granted access to databases by adding them to the database.

11.6.1 Guest logins

Any user who wishes to access a database but has not been declared a user within the database will automatically be granted the user privileges of the guest database user if the guest user account exists (refer to Figure 49-1). The guest user is not automatically created when a database is created. It must be specifically added in code or as a database user. The guest login does not need to be predefined as a server login:

```
USE transdb;
GO

EXEC sp_adduser 'Guest';
GO
```

The guest user must be removed from a database when guests are no longer welcome, because it poses a major treat to the database.

11.6.2 Granting access to a database

Users must be explicitly granted access to any database. Because this is a many-to-many relationship between logins and database, you can manage database access from either the login side or the database side. When a login is granted access to the database, the login is also assigned a database username, which may be the same as the login name or some other name by which the login will be known within the database.

Granting access using Object Explorer

To grant access to a database from the login side using Object Explorer, use the User Mapping page of the Login Properties form

To grant access from the database point of view, use the New User Context Menu command under the Database, Security, and Users node; to open the Database User-New form. Enter the login to be added in the Login Name field. To search for a login, use the ellipses (. . .) button. You must enter a name by which the user will be known within the database in the User Name field.

Granting access using T-SQL code

Of course, a stored procedure is available to grant database access to a user: *CREATE USER*. The stored procedure must be issued from within the database to which the user is to be granted access. The first parameter is the MS SQL Server login, and the second is the optional database username, its optional because you can use the MS SQL Server login name as the user name. The syntax is:

CREATE USER 'LoginName', 'UserName';
GO

Here is an example of creating a user to that will have access to the database:
USE transdb;
GO

```
CREATE USER [chibyke] FOR LOGIN [Main Security];
GO
```

Main Security now appears in the list of database users as "chibyke"

To remove 'Main Security' database access, the system stored procedure *DROP USER* requires her database username, not her server login name.

Here is an example of how to drop the database:

```
USE transdb;
GO
```

```
DROP USER 'chibyke';
GO
```

11.7 Fixed database roles

MS SQL Server includes a few standard, or fixed, database roles. Like the server fixed roles, these are primarily organize administrative tasks. A user may belong to multiple roles, meaning the user can issue commands for many task based on these roles. The fixed database roles include the following:

i.   **db_accessadmin:** Can authorize a user to access the database, but not manage database-level security

ii. **db_backupoperator:** Can perform backups, checkpoints, and DBCC commands, but not restores (only server sysadmins can perform restores)

iii. **db_datareader:** Can read all the data in the database. This role is the equivalent of a grant on all objects, and it can be overridden by a deny permission.

iv. **db_datawriter:** Can write to all the data in the database. This role is the equivalent of a grant on all objects, and it can be overridden by a deny permission.

v.   **db_ddladmin:** Can issue DDL commands (create, alter, drop)

vi. **db_denydatareader:** Can read from any table in the database. This deny will override any object-level grant.

vii. **db_denydatawriter:** Blocks modifying data in any table in the database. This deny will override any object-level grant.

viii. **db_owner:** A special role that has all permissions in the database. This role includes all the capabilities of the other roles. It is different from the dbo user role. This is not the databaselevel equivalent of the server sysadmin role; an object-level deny will override membership in this role.

ix. **db_securityadmin:** Can manage database-level security — roles and permissions

Assigning fixed database roles with Management Studio

The fixed database roles can be assigned with Management Studio with either of the following two procedures:

i. *Adding the role to the user in the user's Database User Properties form, either as the user is being created or after the user exists.*

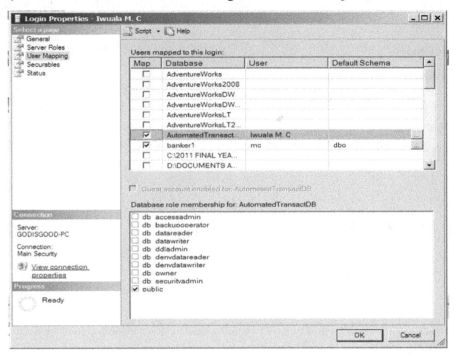

ii. *Adding the user to the role in the Database Role Properties dialog. Select Roles under the database's Security node, and use the context menu to open the Properties form*

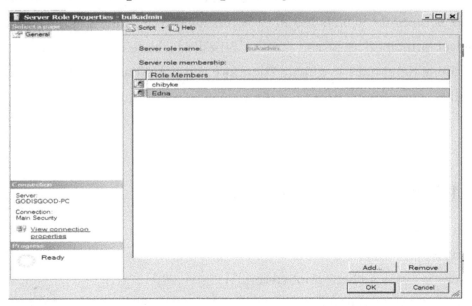

Assigning fixed database roles with T-SQL

From code, you can add a user to a fixed database role with the *sp_addrole* system stored procedure.

Here is the syntax:

sp_addrole rolename, ownername

Here is an example:

USE [AutomatedTransactDB]

GO

exec sp_addrole N'sysadmin', N'chibyke';

GO

11.8   Application roles

An application role is a database principal that enables an application to run with its own, user-like permissions. You can use application roles to enable access to specific data to only those users who connect through a particular application. Unlike database roles, application roles contain no members and are inactive by default. Application roles work with both authentication modes. Application roles are enabled by using sp_setapprole, which requires a password. Because application roles are a database-level principal, they can access other databases only through permissions granted in those databases to guest. Therefore, any database in which guest has been disabled will be inaccessible to application roles in other databases.

11.8.1 Connecting with an Application Role

The following steps make up the process by which an application role switches security contexts:

1. A user executes a client application.
2. The client application connects to an instance of SQL Server as the user.

3. The application then executes the sp_setapprole stored procedure with a password known only to the application.
4. If the application role name and password are valid, the application role is enabled.
5. At this point the connection loses the permissions of the user and assumes the permissions of the application role.

The permissions acquired through the application role remain in effect for the duration of the connection.

Therefore, an application role is a database-specific role intended to allow an application to gain access regardless of the user. For example, if a specific Visual Basic program is used to search the *students* table and it doesn't handle user identification, the VB program can access SQL Server using a hard-coded application role. Anyone using the application gains access to the database.

Here is an example of application roles:
The following example creates an application role called studAppRole that has the password Dr.Mrs.Eze@Uf and studSchma as its default schema.

```
create application role studAppRole
            with password = 'Dr.Mrs.Eze@Uf',
            default_schema=studSchma;
GO
```

The following example activates an application role named studAppRole, with the plain-text password Dr.Mrs.Eze@Uf, created with permissions specifically designed for the application used by the current user.

11.9   Objects

11.9.1 Object Ownership

A very important aspect of SQL Server's security model involves object ownership. Every object is contained by a schema, simply put that every object now belongs to a schema unlike in the old versions of MS SQL Server. The default schema is dbo — not to be confused with the dbo role. Ownership becomes critical when permission is being granted to a user to run a stored procedure when the user doesn't have permission to the underlying tables. If the ownership chain from the tables to the stored procedure is consistent, then the user can access the stored procedure, and the stored procedure can access the tables as its owner. However, if the ownership chain is broken, meaning there's a different owner somewhere between the stored procedure and the table, then the user must have rights to the stored procedure, the underlying tables, and every other object in between. There is a fine point in the details. A schema is owned; and because a schema is owned, anything that is contained by it has the same owner. Most security management can be performed in Management Studio. In SQL Server code, security is managed by means of the GRANT, REVOKE, and DENY via Data Control Language (DCL) commands and several system stored procedures.

11.9.2 Object Security

If a user has access to the database, then permission to the individual database objects may be granted. Permission may be granted either directly to the user or to a standard role and the user assigned to the role. Users may be assigned to multiple roles, so multiple security paths from a user to an object may exist.

Standard Database Roles

Standard database roles, sometimes called user-defined roles, can be created by any user in the server sysadmin, database db_owner, or database security admin role. These roles are similar to those in user groups in Windows. Permissions, and other role memberships, can be assigned to a standard database role, and users can then be assigned to the role.

Object Permissions

Several specific types of permissions exist, hence:

i.   **Select:** The right to select data. Select permission can be applied to specific columns, depending on what you want to do.

ii. **Insert:** The right to insert data

iii. **Update:** The right to modify existing data. Update rights for which a WHERE clause is used require select rights as well. Update permission can be set on specific columns.

iv. **Delete:** The right to delete existing data

v.   **DRI (References):** The right to create foreign keys with DRI (declared referential integrity).

vi. **Execute:** The right to execute stored procedures or user-defined functions.

Object permissions are assigned with the SQL DCL commands which are: GRANT, REVOKE, and DENY. The permissions in SQL Server work like they do in the operating system because all of them are product of *Microsoft Systems*. SQL Server aggregates all the permissions a given user might have, whether directly assigned against the user or through the roles. Then SQL Server gives the MAXIMUM of what has been granted. DENY is an exception and functions as a trump or outmaneuver. If anywhere a DENY has been issued, then just like in Windows, the user is blocked. For instance, if a user can SELECT against a table directly assigned, but a role the user is a member of has a DENY for SELECT, then the user is blocked from issuing a SELECT against the table. Whether security is being managed from Management Studio or from code, it's important to understand these three commands.

Granting object permission interacts with the server and database roles. Here's the overall hierarchy of roles and grants, with 1 overriding 2, and so on:

1. The sysadmin server role. A Windows login that owns a database will be mapped to dbo, and because it maps to dbo, it ignores all security on the database.
2. Deny object permission or the db_denydatareader database role or the db_denydatawriter database role.
3. Grant object permission or object ownership or the db_datareader database role or the db_datawriter database role.

Granting object permissions with code

Setting an object's permission is the only security command that can be executed without a system stored procedure being called.
Here is the syntax:

```
GRANT Permission, Permission
ON Object
TO User/role, User/role
WITH GRANT OPTION
```

The permissions may be ALL, SELECT, INSERT, DELETE, REFERENCES, UPDATE, or EXECUTE. The role or username refers to the database username, any user-defined public role, or the public role. For example, the following code grants select permission to chibyke for the finalAssTable table:
Here is an example:

```
GRANT Select ON dbo.finalAssTable TO [chibyke];
GO
```

This is another example that grants all permissions to the public role for the itfTable table:

```
GRANT ALL ON dbo.itfTable TO dbcreator;
GO
```

Multiple users or roles, and multiple permissions, may be listed in the command. The following code grants select and update permission to the guest user and to udokaf.

```
GRANT Select, Update ON AddminInfotable to guest, [udokaf];
GO
```

The WITH GRANT option provides the ability to grant permission for the object. For example, the following command grants udokaf the permission to select from the AddminInfotable table and grant select permission to others:

```
GRANT Select ON OBJECT::AddminInfotable TO udokaf WITH GRANT OPTION
GO
```

Revoking and denying object permission with code

Revoking and denying object permissions uses essentially the same syntax as granting permission. The following statement revokes select permissions from Joe on the Marriage table.
Here is an example:

```
REVOKE All ON dbo.itfTable TO dbcreator;
GO
```

If the permission included the WITH GRANT OPTION, then the permission must be revoked or denied with the CASCADE option so that the WITH GRANT OPTION will be removed.

Here is an example to deny select permissions to AddminInfotable on the AddminInfotable table:

```
DENY Select ON AddminInfotable TO udokaf CASCADE
```

Because using CASCADE will revoke the WITH GRANT OPTION permission, the DBA can get rid of the ability to GRANT but must first get rid of the permission which includes WITH GRANT OPTION, and then re-GRANT the original permission, but this time without specifying WITH GRANT OPTION.

Managing roles with SQL Server code

Creating standard roles with code involves using the sp_addrole system stored procedure. The name can be up to 128 characters and cannot include a backslash, be null, or be an empty string. By default, the roles will be owned by the dbo user. However, you can assign the role an owner by adding a second parameter.

Here is the syntax:

```
CREATE ROLE role_name [ AUTHORIZATION owner_name ];
GO
```

Here is an example to create the OGA role:

```
USE smatDB;
GO
```

```
CREATE ROLE OGA AUTHORIZATION chibyke;
GO
```

Once a role has been created, users may be assigned to the role by means of the sp_addrolemember system stored procedure. The following code sample assigns chibyke to the 'OGA' role

```
USE smatDB;
GO
```

```
EXEC sp_addrolemember 'OGA', chibyke;
GO
```

The opposite of creating a role is removing it. A role may not be dropped if any users are currently assigned to it. The sp_droprole system stored procedure will remove the role from the database.

Here is an example:

```
USE smatDB;
GO


DROP ROLE OGA;
GO
```

Not surprisingly, the system stored procedure sp_droprolemember removes a user from an assigned role.

Here is an example that removes OGA from the drudgery or labour of management:

```
USE smatDB;
GO


EXEC sp_droprolemember 'OGA', chibyke;
GO
```

Hierarchical role structures

If the security structure is complex, then a powerful permission-organization technique is to design a hierarchical structure of standard database roles. In other words, you can nest user-defined database roles.

   i.   The worker role may have limited access.

   ii.   The manager role may have all worker rights plus additional rights to look up tables.

  iii.   The administrator role may have all manager rights plus the right to perform all other database administration tasks.

To accomplish this type of design, follow these steps:

i. Create the worker role and set its permissions.

ii. Create the manager role and set its permissions. Add the manager role as a user to the worker role.

iii. Create the admin role. Add the admin role as a user to the manager role.

The advantage of this type of security organization is that a change in the lower level affects all upper levels. As a result, administration is required in only one location, rather than dozens of locations.

11.10 Stored procedure Execute As

When developing stored procedures, the effective security access of the code within the stored procedures can be explicitly determined. This is far better than just guessing that the security, or the ownership chain, will be correct. The Execute As stored procedure option defines how the ownership is determined. Although execute as is typically associated with stored procedures, it also applies to scalar user-defined functions, multi-line table-valued user-defined functions, and DML and DDL triggers.

Here is an example that creates a stored procedure that will execute with the permissions of the user which created the stored procedures:

```
USE loloitf;
GO

IF OBJECT_ID ( 'dbo.studReport', 'P' ) IS NOT NULL
    DROP PROCEDURE dbo.studReport;
GO

CREATE PROCEDURE dbo.studReport
WITH EXECUTE AS SELF
AS
SELECT * FROM dbo.siwesOfficialsTable;
GO
```

The options for execute as are:

i. **Caller** — execute with the owner permissions of the user executing or calling the stored procedure.

ii. **Self** — execute with the permission of the user who created or altered the stored procedure.

iii. **Owner** — execute with the permissions of the owner of the stored procedure.

iv. **'hard-coded user name'** — execute with the permission of the specific named user.

Model For Database Security

For a few examples of permissions using the smartDB database, DATABASE FIXED ROLES Table lists the permission settings of the standard database roles. DATABASE USERS Table lists a few of the users and their roles.

DATABASE FIXED ROLES

Standard Role	Hierarchical Role Structures	Primary Filegroup Tables	Static Filegroup Tables	Other Permissions
IT	Sysadmin server role	-	-	-
Staff	-	-	-	Execute permissions for several stored procedures that read from and update required day-to-day tables
Admin	db_owner database fixed role	-	-	-
Students	-	Select permissions	-	-

DATABASE USERS

USER	DATABASE STANDARD ROLES
Udoka	Admin
Lolo	Public
Chibueze	IT DBA
Staff Windows group (Oluchi, Vivian, Chidiebere, and Ikechukwu)	Staff

Using this security model, the following users can perform the following tasks:

i. Vigor, as a member of the Staff role, can execute the application that executes stored procedures to retrieve and update data. Vigor can run select queries as a member of the Public role.

ii. Chibueze, as the IT DBA, can perform any task in the database as a member of the sysadmin server role.

iii. Lolo can run select queries as a member of the public role.

iv. As a member of the admin role, Udoka can execute all stored procedures. She can also manually modify any table using queries. As a member of the admin role that includes the db_owner role, Udoka can perform any database administrative task and select or modify data in any table.

v. Only Chibueze can restore from the backups.

11.11 Data Organization Using Schemas

SQL Server 2008 supports ANSI standard schemas, which provide a method by which tables and other objects can be segmented into logical groups. Schemas are essentially containers into which any database object can be placed, and certain actions or rules applied en masse to every item in the schema. This makes tasks such as managing authorization considerably easier since, by dividing your database into schemas, you can easily group related objects and control permissions without having to worry about what objects might be added or removed from that collection in the future. As new objects are added to a schema, existing permissions propagate, thereby allowing you to set up access rights for a given schema once, and will not have to manipulate them again as the database changes; I guess that makes some sense to you?

To create a schema, use the CREATE SCHEMA command, though I discussed about Schema. The following T-SQL creates a schema called Sales:

```
CREATE SCHEMA Sales;
GO
```

Optionally you can specify a schema owner by using the AUTHORIZATION clause. If an owner is not explicitly specified, SQL Server will assign ownership to the user that creates the schema.

Once a schema is created, you can begin creating database objects within the schema, using two-part naming.

Here is an example of creating a table on Sales schema:

```
CREATE TABLE Sales.SalesData
(SaleNumber int,
SaleDate datetime
);
GO
```

If an object belongs to a schema, then it must be referenced with its associated schema name; so to select from the SalesData table, the following SQL Code is used:

```
SELECT *
```

FROM Sales.SalesData;
GO

Caution: In previous versions of SQL Server, references to tables were prefixed with the name of their owner (e.g., Owner.SalesData). This syntax is deprecated and two-part naming in SQL Server 2008 references a schema rather than an object owner. The reason is because all objects are now associated with schemas and not object owners.

The beauty of schemas becomes obvious when it is time to apply permissions to the objects in the schema, whence I decided to repeat schema as topic in this book. Assuming that each object should be treated identically from a permissions point of view, only a single grant is necessary to give a user access to every object within a schema. For instance, after the following T-SQL is run, the chibyke user will have access to select rows from every table in the Sales schema, even if new tables are added later:

```
USE [loloitf]
GO
IF EXISTS (SELECT * FROM sys.database_principals WHERE name = N'chibyke')
DROP USER [chibyke]
GO


CREATE USER Chibyke
WITHOUT LOGIN;
GO


GRANT SELECT ON SCHEMA::Sales
TO Chibyke;
GO
```

It is important to note that, when initially created, the owner of any object in a schema will be the same as the owner of the schema itself. The individual object owners can be changed later, but in most cases I recommend that you keep everything in any given schema owned by the same user. This is especially important for ownership chaining. To explicitly set the owner of an object requires the ALTER AUTHORIZATION command, as shown in the following T-SQL:

```
--Create a user
CREATE USER Udoka
WITHOUT LOGIN;
GO


--Create a table
CREATE TABLE UdokaTbl
(SomeColumn int
);
GO


--Set Udoka as the owner of the table
ALTER AUTHORIZATION ON UdokaTbl
TO Udoka;
GO
```

As a final note on schemas, there is also a command that can be used to move objects between schemas. By using ALTER SCHEMA with the TRANSFER option, you can specify that a table should be moved to another schema.

Here is an example:

```
--Create a new schema
CREATE SCHEMA Purchases;
GO


--Move the SalesData table into the new schema
ALTER SCHEMA Purchases
TRANSFER Sales.SalesData;
GO
```

```
--Reference the table by its new schema name
SELECT *
FROM Purchases.SalesData;
GO
```

Schemas are powerful feature, and I recommend that you consider using them any time you are dealing with sets of tables that are tightly related to one another. Legacy database applications that use multiple databases in order to create logical boundaries between objects might also benefit from schemas. The multiple databases can be consolidated to a single database that uses schemas. The benefit is that the same logical boundaries will exist, but because the objects are in the same database, they can participate in declarative referential integrity and can be backed up together.

11.12 Basic Impersonation Using EXECUTE AS

Though, I have discussed about *execute as* in previous lessons in this chapter; but wish to throw more light on impersonation using it. Switching to a different user's execution context has long been possible in SQL Server, using the SETUSER command, as shown in the following code listing:

```
SETUSER 'Chibyke';
GO
```

To revert back to the previous context, call SETUSER again without specifying a username:

```
SETUSER;
GO
```

The SETUSER command is only available to members of the sysadmin or db_owner roles (at the server and database levels, respectively). Furthermore, although still implemented by SQL Server 2008, the Microsoft Books Online documentation states that SETUSER may not be supported in future versions of SQL Server, and recommends usage of the EXECUTE AS command instead.

The EXECUTE AS command can be used by any user, and access to impersonate a given user or server login is controlled by a permissions setting rather than a fixed role. The other benefit over SETUSER is that EXECUTE AS automatically reverts to the original context at the end of a module. SETUSER, on the other hand, leaves the impersonated context active when control is returned to the caller. This means that it is impossible to encapsulate impersonation within a stored procedure using SETUSER and guarantee that the caller will not be able to take control of the impersonated credentials.

To show the effects of EXECUTE AS, start by creating a new user and a table owned by the user:

```
CREATE USER Ogoo
WITHOUT LOGIN;
GO
CREATE TABLE OgoosTbl
(AColumn int
);
GO

ALTER AUTHORIZATION ON OgoosTbl TO Ogoo;
GO
```

Once the user is created, it can be impersonated using EXECUTE AS, and the impersonation context can be verified using the USER_NAME() function.
Here is an example:

```
EXECUTE AS USER = 'Ogoo';
GO

SELECT USER_NAME();
```

GO

Note In order to use the EXECUTE AS statement to impersonate another user or login, a user must have been granted IMPERSONATE permissions on the specified target. The *SELECT* statement returns the value Ogoo, indicating that this is the currently impersonated user. Any action performed after running EXECUTE AS will use Ogoo's credentials. For example, the user can alter the OgoosTbl table, since Ogoo owns the table. However, an attempt to create a new table will fail, since Ogoo does not have permission to do so.

Here is an example:

```
--This statement will succeed
ALTER TABLE OgoosTbl
ADD AnotherColumn datetime;
GO


--This statement will fail with CREATE TABLE PERMISSION DENIED
CREATE TABLE MoreData
(YetAnotherColumn int
);
GO
```

Once you have completed working with the database in the context of Ogoo's permissions, you can return to the outer context by using the REVERT command. If you have impersonated another user inside of that context (i.e., called EXECUTE AS more than once), REVERT will have to be called multiple times in order to return context to your login. The USER_NAME() function can be checked at any time to find out whose context you are executing under.

To see the effects of nested impersonation, first be sure to revert back out of Ogoo's context, and then create a second user as shown following. The user will be given the right to impersonate Ogoo, using GRANT IMPERSONATE:

```
CREATE USER Ugonna
WITHOUT LOGIN;
GO
```

```
GRANT IMPERSONATE ON USER:: Ogoo TO Ugonna;
GO
```

If Ugonna is impersonated, the session will have no privileges to select rows from the OgoosTbl table. In order to get those permissions, Ogoo must be impersonated from within Ugonna's context.

Here is what I mean:

```
EXECUTE AS USER='Ugonna';
GO

--This statement fails
SELECT *
FROM OgoosTbl;
GO

EXECUTE AS USER='Ogoo';
GO

--This statement succeeds
SELECT *
FROM OgoosTbl;
GO
REVERT;
GO

--Returns 'Ugonna' -- REVERT must be called again to fully revert
SELECT USER_NAME();
GO
REVERT;
GO
```

The most important thing to understand is that when EXECUTE AS is called, all operations will run as if you are logged in as the impersonated user. You will lose any permissions that the outer user has that the impersonated user does not have, in addition to gaining any permissions that the impersonated user has that the outer user lacks.

For logging purposes, it is sometimes important to record the actual logged-in principal. Since both the USER_NAME() function and the SUSER_NAME() function will return the names associated with the impersonated user, the ORIGINAL_LOGIN() function must be used to return the name of the outermost server login. Use of ORIGINAL_LOGIN() will allow you to get the name of the logged-in server principal, no matter how nested their impersonation scope is.

REFERENCES

Expert SQL Server 2008 Encryption

By Michael Coles and Rodney Landrum 2009

Database Fundamentals

By Robert J. Robbins of Johns Hopkins University 1995

Expert SQL Server 2008 Development

By Alastair Aitchison and Adam Machanic 2009

A Hands-On Guide to Relational Database Design

By Michael J. Hernandez

Microsoft SQL Server 2008 Bible 2009

By Paul Nielsen with Mike White and Uttam Parui

SQL Developer User Manual

By Jan Borchers 2006

Designing and Managing Data

By J.G. Zheng of Georgia State University 2010

Microsoft SQL Server TechNet Forum Support Team

http://msdn.microsoft.com/en-us/library

http://www.learn-sql-tutorial.com

http://www.functionx.com/sqlserver

http://www.sqlserverclub.com

http://technet.microsoft.com

A

access, 5, 7, 18, 32, 34, 76, 110, 111, 120, 123, 188, 261, 286, 340, 380, 440, 441, 457, 460, 489, 586, 587, 588, 589, 590, 591, 594, 598, 599, 600, 603, 604, 605, 611, 614, 616, 619

account, 4, 21, 22, 23, 31, 32, 89, 91, 94, 256, 371, 384, 385, 386, 558, 585, 590, 591, 597, 598

Accounts, 22, 354

ACID, 556, 561

application, 4, 6, 18, 48, 49, 51, 54, 55, 56, 57, 66, 67, 68, 70, 71, 75, 76, 78, 81, 82, 85, 86, 100, 125, 126, 248, 259, 260, 261, 264, 282, 352, 369, 404, 411, 423, 427, 471, 472, 473, 586, 592, 603, 604, 614

architecture, 17, 51

attach, 384

Audit, 464

Authentication, 592, 595

AUTHORIZATION, 121, 585, 609, 615, 617, 619

B

backup, 94, 126

backups, 601, 614

batches, 79, 565

bitwise operators, 459

Boolean, 128, 161, 178, 194, 372, 499, 546

bulk, 597

business, 3, 193, 242, 244, 359, 446, 449, 464, 514

C

Calculated columns, 190

cascading, 243, 449

CASE, 503

catalog, 94, 126, 596

character, 63, 87, 126, 129, 133, 134, 137, 138, 139, 164, 168, 264, 282, 362, 372, 404, 405, 406, 408, 409, 410

CHECK, 439

CHECK OPTION, 439, 440, 441, 442, 443

checkpoint, 601

client, 2, 312, 383, 446, 492, 563, 603, 604

clustered, 85, 197, 202, 203, 204, 205, 206, 208, 209, 242, 245, 249, 558

collaboration, 82

columns, 2, 3, 7, 59, 66, 85, 124, 165, 166, 167, 168, 171, 172, 173, 174, 176, 177, 179, 180, 181, 182, 184, 189, 190, 191, 192, 194, 197, 198, 199, 202, 203, 208, 218, 237, 241, 243, 244, 247, 248, 260, 261, 263, 266, 269, 272, 273, 278, 282, 303, 309, 310, 317, 319, 323, 325, 327, 340, 341, 346, 348, 365, 380,

386, 427, 428, 430, 431, 436, 437, 439, 445, 449, 457, 458, 460, 495, 498, 500, 507, 508, 512, 513, 514, 516, 522, 525, 527, 528, 529, 531, 532, 537, 551, 552, 606

comments, 77, 78, 79, 112, 389

Comments, 77

COMMIT TRANSACTION, 559, 560, 565, 569, 571, 572, 573, 576, 578, 580

Common Table Expressions, 519, 520, 524

compatibility, 73, 156, 437, 595, 597

complex, 6, 52, 64, 82, 164, 255, 313, 352, 427, 428, 439, 440, 445, 446, 449, 524, 585, 587, 595, 598, 611

Composite, 202

conceptual, 1

conditions, 48, 50, 55, 61, 66, 67, 310, 439, 504, 514, 516, 545, 546, 547, 562

configuration, 6, 16, 31, 37, 46, 61, 95, 194, 198, 384, 464, 465, 589

connections, 95, 166, 440, 570

constraints, 165, 176, 193, 194, 218, 242, 250, 251, 252, 253, 256, 447, 448

containers, 117, 614

context, 198, 251, 252, 387, 429, 430, 438, 454, 593, 602, 618, 619, 620, 621

conversion, 402, 406, 414, 415

CREATE command, 90, 443

CREATE DATABASE, 90, 96, 101, 102, 103, 104, 106, 108, 111, 112, 200, 209, 213, 219, 261, 291, 296, 328, 353, 510

cross join, 531

cursors, 95, 461

D

Data

 The Length of Data, 172

Data Auditing, 6, 7

Data Encryption, 6, 7

data integrity, 70, 172, 190, 427, 448, 461

data modification, 7, 95, 312

Data security, 2

data sources, 310, 431, 436

data type, 7, 124, 127, 130, 131, 132, 133, 134, 135, 137, 139, 141, 144, 147, 153, 157, 159, 160, 162, 165, 172, 173, 176, 177, 180, 181, 191, 193, 198, 215, 247, 248, 249, 261, 263, 264, 279, 369, 379, 390, 400, 402, 459, 513

Data Types, 124, 128, 156, 157

Database Design, 623

Database Diagram, 361

Database Engine, 16, 29, 32, 95, 111, 557

database mail, 75, 384, 387

database mirroring, 94, 96, 97, 98

database snapshot, 96

database system, 3

Database-Level Security, 589

databases, 1

Databases

Refreshing the List of Databases, 117

date

keyword, 126

Date

Application of Date/Time Variables, 151

Date and Time Based Functions, 423

Date and Time Types, 143

Date Values, 145

Date/Time Addition, 423

Date/Time Subtraction, 426

The Current System Date and/or Time, 423

DBA, 98, 590, 609, 614

DBCC, 96, 575, 601

DBMS, 2

DCL, 605, 606

DDL, 90, 99, 101, 202, 233, 246, 247, 253, 263, 290, 295, 305, 429, 431, 445, 448, 452, 453, 454, 467, 601, 611

DATABASE CREATION SYNTAX, 101

Removing Records, 305

Deadlocks

Creating a deadlock, 569

debugging, 49, 51, 447, 467

decision, 64, 316, 364

Declarative

Declarative referential integrity, 251

Default Databases, 93

DELETE

Deleting a Column, 187

Deleting a Database Using SQL, 115

Deleting a Function, 394

Deleting a Trigger, 471

Deleting an Index, 235

Outputting the Deleting Results, 306

Removing all Records, 304

Developers

Defensive Programming, 48

WHAT SQL QUERY FLOW IS ALL ABOUT, 309

DIFFERENCE

DIFFERENCE BETWEEN USER AND LOGINS, 586

Distinct

Distinct Field Selection, 347

DML, 258, 295, 311, 431, 447, 448, 451, 452, 454, 456, 457, 458, 460, 461, 462, 464, 465, 466, 467, 469, 558, 563, 565, 575, 611

DMV, 74, 568, 570

Domain

Domain integrity, 244

Windows login, 592

DROP. *See* DELETE

durability. See ACID

dynamic, 1, 71, 74, 428

E

editions, 12, 14

ENCRYPTION

Encrypting the view's select statement, 444

Enforce

Enforce Foreign Key Constraint, 252

error handling

T-SQL EXCEPTION HANDLING, 471

Types of Errors, 471

Xact_Abort, 562

errors

Handling an Exception, 474

Run-Time Errors, 473

Syntax Errors, 472

The Severity of an Error, 483

The State of an Error, 485

ETL, 6

events

After triggers, 449

execute

BUILT-IN STORED PROCEDURES, 382

Creating a Schema, 121

Executing a Procedure, 366

Executing views, 432

Managing Procedures, 363

EXECUTE

Basic Impersonation Using EXECUTE AS, 618

Stored procedure Execute As, 611

expression

Tables Columns and Expressions, 274

Expression

Application of Expression During Data Entry, 276

Expressions and Functions in Stored Procedures, 366

The Assignment Operator, 497

F

failover clustering, 13, 17

filegroups, 94, 96, 97, 107

files

multiple files, 105

parent files, 255

Filestream, 6, 7

foreign keys

Cascading deletes and updates, 255

Creating foreign keys, 250

Creating Keys, 241

Natural keys, 243

optional foreign keys, 255

Fragmentation, 199

FROM clause, 180

   Table aliases, 315

Full Outer Joins, 539, 543

full-text index, 94

Full-text indexes, 431

Full-Text Search, 16

G

GROUP BY, 309, 310

GUIDs, 243, 244, 248

H

HAVING, 310

headers, 513

historical, 1

I

identity columns. *See* columns

if statement, 467

implicit CAST, 65

Implicit transactions, 563

Import, 283

indexes

   Checking the Existence of an Indexes, 235

   Clustered Indexes, 203

   composite indexes, 202

   Data Entry and Analysis with Indexes, 208

   Disabling an index, 233

   Full-text indexes. *See* Full-text indexes

   Index Uniqueness, 208

   Table Creation and Indexes, 206

   Types of Indexes, 203

Indexes

   Creating Indexes, 197

Inner Joins, 530, 532

INSERT

   Column Default, 194

   Creating Multiple Records, 268

   INSERT INTO, 270

   MERGE, 7

Installing SQL Server, 25

instead of trigger, 447

Instead of trigger, 451

INSTEAD OF trigger

   execution, 448

Integration Services, 6, 17

Isolation Levels, 574

J

jobs, 97, 172

joins

   complex. *See* complex

   cross, 68

Cross Joins. *See* cross join

Data, 525

Data Analysis, 545

Full Outer. *See* Full Outer Joins

inner. *See* Inner Joins

Left Outer, 539

multiple, 310

Outer, 539

Right Outer, 541

K

key columns. *See* columns

keys

foreign. *See* Creating foreign keys

Natural, 243

Primary, 241

surrogate, 243

L

language

Collation, 350

Data Control. *See* DCL

Data Definition. *See* DDL

Data Manipulation. *See* DML

declarative, 258

DEFAULT_LANGUAGE, 593

User-Defined Types, 157

Legacy error. *See* Types of Errors

linked, 532, 597

local

system account. *See* account

table, 248

temporary tables, 95

user account. *See* account

lock

Deadlocks. *See* COMMIT
TRANSACTION

exclusive lock. *See* COMMIT
TRANSACTION

log

file, 88

function, 417

installation, 40

Mail, 387

transaction, 105

logical

blocks, 79

boundaries, 618

database schema, 585

file_name, 88

Inserted and deleted logical tables, 460

Logical Conjunctions and Disjunctions,
546

Logical flow of the query statement, 311

Logical Operations on Queries, 550

Logical transactions, 558

name, 88

operator, 412

WHAT SQL QUERY FLOW IS ALL ABOUT, 309

lookup, 244, 245

M

maintenance, 17

Maintenance

   Columns, 180

   Data, 282

   Database, 112

   Function, 393

   Index, 234

   Record, 290

   Tables, 237

malicious, 71, 454

management policies, 431

Management Studio

   Designing Columns, 169

   Designing tables, 164

   SQL Server Management Studio, 88

many-to-many relationship, 2, 599

MAPI, 383

MARS, 95

master database

   Restrictions, 94

Master database, 93

MAX, 7

MDAC, 11

Measure

   Based Functions, 418

memory

   Declaring a Variable, 124

merge

   Uniting the Records, 512

Merge

   Outputting the Results of a Merge, 517

MERGE, 7

metadata, 234

Microsoft Access, 260, 283, 285

models, 1

Modifying a Procedure, 363

msdb

   database, 97

   restrictions, 97

multiple AFTER, 469

multiple queries, 313

Multiple transactions, 562

multiple triggers, 464

N

Namespaces, 118

Natural keys. *See* Foreign Keys

nested

   transactions, 562

   triggers, 464

views, 438

network access. *See* access

Network configuration. *See* configuration

NIC, 250

nodes, 187, 198, 260, 364

non-clustered indexes, 197, 205

NOT, 277

　Negating a Condition, 506

numeric data types, 134

O

Object Explorer

　Calling a Function, 393

　Column Review, 180

　Creating a Function, 388

　Creating a Table, 174

　Creating triggers, 449

　Data Entry, 260

　Databases node, 113

　Deleting a Function, 394

　Granting access to database. *See* access

　Join Creation, 527

　Opening a Table, 237

　Renaming a Column, 186

　Schemas, 121

　Tables Review, 237

　Updating Records, 295

Object Security, 605

object-level, 601

Objects Names, 125

one-to-many, 2

one-to-one. *See* one-to-many

operating systems, 4, 6, 12, 13

Operators

　Assignment, 497

　bitwise. *See* bitwise operators

　Compound Assignment, 8

　IN, 552

　OR, 552

ORDER BY, 500

orphaned users, 590

OS

　Introduction to security, 18

Outer Joins. *See* joins

OUTPUT, 270

　Deleting Result, 306

　Inserted Result, 270

　Parameters, 378

　Results of Merge. *See* Outputting the
　　Results of a Merge

　Update Result, 303

ownership chain, 605, 611

P

packages. *See* ETL

page split problem, 244, 249

parameters

    columns. *See* columns

    CTE, 522

    default, 90

    file growth, 98

    function, 397

    stored procedure, 372

parent-child, 1

PARTITION

    FUNCTION, 215

    SCHEME, 217

partitioning

    column, 215

    Table, 215

password

    Application role, 604

    Authentication. *See* Authentication

    Database Engine. *See* Database Engine

    Introduction to Security. *See* OS

    Updating, 596

performance

    filestream. *See* Filestream

    index. *See* clustered

    multiple files. *See* files

    testing, 67

    transactions, 574

performance improvement, 492

permissions

    Application roles, 603

    Database Level Security. *See* Database
        Level Security

    db_owner, 601

    db_securityadmin, 601

    granting permissions with code, 607

    impersonate, 620

    model for database security, 612

    moving a database, 590

    Object, 589, 606

    revoking and denying object permissions,
        608

phantom rows, 574

physical flow, 311

physical layer, 255

policies, 6, 83

post-installation, 41

PowerShell, 14, 141, 350, 472

primary keys. *See* keys

    Creating primary keys, 245

    identity column surrogate, 247

    uniqueidentifier surrogate, 247

processors, 12

programming

    defensive. *See* Developers

    environments, 47

    validate all input, 70

protocols, 12

public role, 589, 607, 608, 614

Q

Query Designer, 311

Creating views, 429

Records Sorting, 498

Query Editor. *See* Query Designer

query execution, 258, 309, 313

query flow, 309

Query Optimizer, 258, 313, 439

R

RAISERROR

Severity, 490

Transaction, 489

ranking, 312

read committed. *See* COMMIT
TRANSACTION

read uncommitted, 574, 576

recursive triggers, 448, 466, 467

referential integrity, 243, 251, 255, 606, 618

relational database, 1, 3, 163, 242

REPLACE(), 409

replication, 248, 249, 445

Report Manager, 16

Reporting Services, 13, 16

reports, 428, 434, 458

restore, 96, 594, 614

RI, 250

roles

application. *See* application

Fixed Database, 600

managing, 609

multiple users, 608

standard database, 605

ROLLBACK, 559

Rolling, 579

row-level, 442

rows

disappearing, 441

Edit, 431

Select, 431

S

Save points, 565

Scalar-Valued Function, 388

scheduling, 97

schema, 117

Schema, 119, 121

scripts, 240, 431, 449

Security. *See* Authorization

Database, 598

Database Level. *See* Database-Level Security

Main, 600

Object. *See* Object Security

Object Ownership, 605

Server, 591

Server Level, 588

Windows, 590

SELECT

Altering and dropping a view, 433

Arithmetic Functions, 411

Data Manipulation, 258

Distinct, 348

Encrypting views, 443

exists(), 404

Expression of columns, 495

Field Selection, 342

Flow of the query statement, 309

Index, 198

Nesting views, 437

query, 60

Stored Procedures, 365

variable, 128

Views, 427

Virtual Selecting of records, 294

SELECT statements, 524

self-referencing, 467

serializable, 574

Server Agent, 31, 97

Server Configuration Manager, 45

servers, 4, 7, 46, 248, 428, 591, 596, 597

Service Broker

Server Agent, 97

service packs, 9, 17

Services. *See* Integration Services

MS SQL Server, 31

Starting MS SQL Server, 11

SET command, 575

shared locks, 566

Shared memory, 12

Simple Mail Transfer Protocol, 383

SMO, 87

snapshot isolation, 95

SORT_IN_TEMPDB, 233

sorting data, 435

sp_help, 238

Sparse columns, 192

SQL injection, 71, 445, 587

SQL QUERY FLOW. *See* query flow

SQL Script, 186, 306, *See* scripts

SQL Server 2008

Data Organization, 614

Installation, 16, 17

User's Account. *See* account

SQL SERVER 2008, 4

Features, 6

SQL Server Agent. *See* Server Agent

SSIS. *See* Integration Services

SSMS, 87

startup

stored procedure, 597

STATISTICS_NORECOMPUTE, 234

Stored procedures

Arguments and Parameters, 368

Built-In, 382

Stored Procedures, 365

Expressions and Functions, 366

subqueries, 445

SUM, 64

Supporting, 245

surrogate keys. *See* keys

system database, 33, 95, 404

system stored procedures, 605

T

Table Designer, 165, 252

tables

clustered, 207

columns. *See* expression

copying records, 514

create database tables, 163

Data Analysis, 545

Data Navigation, 259

design, 165

Hierarchy of database tables, 85

Join, 526

logical, 460

Maintenance. *See* Maintenance

merging records, 515

naming, 163

naming of tables, 87

nodes. *See* nodes

Opening, 237

referring, 241

Review, 237

Selecting Differently, 508

table-valued, 430, 611

Tasks, 283

TCP/IP, 12, 45, 46

tempdb, 95

Templates, 159

time

table and index partitioning, 212

values, 143

TOP, 310, 502, 503

tracing, 51

transactional integrity, 558, 565, 574

transactions. *See* Logical

Transact-SQL, 157, 404

　Data Selection, 327

transparent data encryption, 7

U

UNION, 456

　ALL, 524

　Merger, 524

　operator, 512

unions

　Multiple queries. *See* multiple queries

unique

　constraint, 194, 245, 250

　elements, 446

　field. *See* Primary Key

　global identifiers, 243

　identifier, 247

　index, 242, 249, 250, *See* clustered

　name. *See* Namespaces

　uniqueness of an index, 210

　values, 208

unique indexes, 250

uniqueidentifier, 250, *See* data type

UPDATE. *See* Compound Assignment, *See* MERGE

　ALTER INDEX, 234

　Cascading, 255

　Data Manipulation. *See* DML

Logical Flow of query. *See* data

　modification

multi-row-enabled triggers, 461

Permission, 606

Protecting the data, 441

Records, 295

Rule, 252

Stored procedure, 364

Transaction, 457

Views. *See* Executing views

Where Operator, 300

With SQL Script, 295

UPDATE() function, 457

usability, 241

user interface, 313

User-Data Columns, 165

user-defined functions, 606, 611

User-Defined Functions, 554

users. *See* client

　access. *See* access

　authentication. *See* access

　database application, 56

　Granting access to database. *See* access

　Main Security. *See* Security

　objects, 117

　public standard database role, 589

　roles, 587

　SQL Server login. *See* access

Triggers and Security, 455

T-SQL Programming, 352

Windows Authentication. *See*

Authentication

USERS

DATABASE, 613

V

validation, 70, 172, 193, 446, 449, 461, 464

Variables

Assignment, 8

Declaration. *See* Data Types

Default Initialization, 125

Incremental, 125

Initialization, 6, 8

multiple comma-variables, 124

naming, 125

Table, 95

views

basic, 429

dependencies, 431

query design, 429

Views. *See* Nesting Views

Execution. *See* Executing Views

Locking Down, 440

Management, 431

Nesting, 435

Order By Clause, 436

Protection, 443

Synonyms, 445

VIEWS, 426

virtual tables, 312

W

WHERE clause

Examples, 505

Option for Index, 199

WHILE, 565

Windowing, 312

Windows authentication, 595, *See*
Authentication

Windows Authentication

Users, 592

Windows authentication mode, 32

windows OS. *See* OS

Windows security, 590

model, 587

WITH CHECK OPTION, 442

WITH ENCRYPTION option, 444

write-ahead transaction, 557

X

Xact_Abort, 562

Xact_State(), 561